Civil Wars in Africa

Civil Wars in Africa

Edited by
Kelechi A. Kalu and George Klay Kieh Jr.

LEXINGTON BOOKS
Lanham • Boulder • New York • London

Published by Lexington Books
An imprint of The Rowman & Littlefield Publishing Group, Inc.
4501 Forbes Boulevard, Suite 200, Lanham, Maryland 20706
www.rowman.com

86-90 Paul Street, London EC2A 4NE

All research participants are anonymized to protect their identities in Chapter 4.

British Library Cataloguing in Publication Information Available

Library of Congress Cataloging-in-Publication Data

Names: Kalu, Kelechi Amihe, editor. | Kieh, George Klay, 1956- editor.
Title: Civil wars in Africa / edited by Kelechi A. Kalu and George Klay Kieh Jr.
Description: Lanham, Maryland : Lexington Books, [2022] | Includes bibliographical references and index.
Identifiers: LCCN 2022017593 (print) | LCCN 2022017594 (ebook) | ISBN 9781793649331 (cloth) | ISBN 9781793649355 (paperback) | ISBN 9781793649348 (epub)
Subjects: LCSH: Civil war—Africa—Case studies. | Decolonization—Africa—Case studies. | Imperialism. | Africa—History—1960—Case studies. | Africa—Politics and government—1960—Case studies.
Classification: LCC DT30.5 .C58 2022 (print) | LCC DT30.5 (ebook) | DDC 303.64096—dc23
LC record available at https://lccn.loc.gov/2022017593
LC ebook record available at https://lccn.loc.gov/2022017594

Contents

List of Figures and Tables

FIGURE

TABLES

Preface

The end of colonialism was greeted with joy and excitement by Africans from divergent ethnic, regional, class, gender, and other backgrounds. The reason was twofold. A major one was that Africans were disgusted by the vagaries of colonialism, including ethnic manipulation, political oppression, repression, and suppression and socioeconomic malaise. The other was that Africans entertained the hope that with independence they could build new democratic and prosperous societies that were human-centered. Unfortunately, the celebration that greeted the demise of colonialism quickly turned into sadness, as the "first generation" of African leaders (with few exceptions) unveiled their plans to retain the colonial state and its vagaries, although in the postcolonial garbs. This was followed by the implementation of the colonial script that included ethnic manipulation and marginalization, the violation of political human rights, corruption, and the failure to invest in human material wellbeing, among others. The resultant effect was the germination, nurturing, and subsequent manifestation of civil conflicts. And some of these civil conflicts degenerated into civil wars in countries like Sudan, Nigeria, and Senegal, thereby commencing the first cycle of civil wars on the African Continent. Similarly, the subsequent generations of African leaders (with few exceptions) failed to democratically reconstruct the state. Thus, the second and subsequent cycles of civil wars incepted. Currently, for examples, Democratic Republic of the Congo and Somalia are plagued by seemingly unending civil wars that have experienced various iterations. In sum, civil wars have had, and continue to have, profound ramifications for war-affected African states, including deaths, injuries, internal displacement, the refugee crises, the collapse of state authority, and socioeconomic deprivation.

Against this background, the African Studies and Research Forum (ASRF) commissioned a Research Project on "Civil Wars in Africa" in collaboration with the Office of International Affairs at the University of California at Riverside. The research project focused on civil wars in Burundi, Cameroon, Ghana, Liberia, Nigeria, Rwanda, Sierra Leone, South Sudan, and Uganda. We would like to thank the African Studies and Research Forum (ASRF) and the Office of International Affairs at the University of California at Riverside for sponsoring the research project that has produced this volume. At the African Studies and Research Forum (ASRF), we would like to thank Samuel Zalanga, director of research and publications, and the members of the committee for their encouragement and support. At the Office of International Affairs at the University of California at Riverside, we would like to thank Mely Fitzgerald, Carmen Rivera, and Reyna Alarcon, for their help with coordinating the logistics for the research project with scholars from different parts of the world.

Furthermore, we extend our gratitude to the researchers, who participated in the research project, including writing the chapters that constitute this volume. We appreciate their patience in waiting for comments on their draft chapters and for their diligence in addressing the issues raised. Clearly, they have made major contributions to the understanding of the civil wars that have afflicted several African states, including the ones discussed in this volume, since the postindependence era.

Last, but not the least, we would like to thank Lexington Books for publishing this volume. Specifically, we are grateful to Shelby Russell and Sydney Wedbush of the African Studies Program for their patience, encouragement, and support, which contributed to the publication of this volume. In addition, we would like to thank the Production Department for preparing the book for publication.

Kelechi Kalu and George Klay Kieh Jr.

Part I

BACKGROUND

Introduction

Mapping the Civil War Landscape in Africa

Kelechi A. Kalu and George Klay Kieh Jr.

INTRODUCTION

Civil wars in Africa remain an interesting research area because of their persistence and impacts on the economic and political development and human security in various states in the continent. Some of the civil wars, like the ones in Angola, Burundi, the Democratic Republic of the Congo, Ethiopia, Liberia, Nigeria, Rwanda, and Sierra Leone, are globally well known, while others, like the civil wars in Cameroon, Casamance region of Senegal, and the chieftaincy conflicts in Ghana, rarely attract international attention or serious research. Often, explanations of civil wars in Africa range from ethnic, religious, and language differences to corruption, economic and political exclusions, and external resources extractions. In many instances, the lines between external and internal explanations are blurred and do not provide adequate insights on what triggers civil wars in many states in Africa. Also, for ease of measurement, formal studies about civil war are often quantitatively defined and operationalized to enable explanations about the onset of wars, recurrences, and terminations.

However, why civil wars occur in the first place and their impacts on the people in a given society are rarely the focus of quantitative research. For example, Collier and Hoeffler operationalize the study of civil war by defining it as an internal conflict with at least 1,000 battle-related deaths in any given year. From their perspective, government forces have to be one of the combatants against an identifiable rebel organization that suffers at least 5 percent of the fatalities. Collier and Hoeffler examine 161 countries and 78 civil wars over the period 1960–1999. Thus, based on the Correlates of War projects,[1] and civil war literature, Sambanis (2000: 444) provides an empirical definition of civil wars "as an armed conflict that has (1) caused more than one thousand deaths; (2) challenged the sovereignty of an internationally recognized state; (3) occurred within the recognized boundaries of that state; (4) involved the state as one of the principal combatants; (5) included rebels with the ability to mount an organized opposition; and (6) involved parties concerned with the prospect of living together in the same political unit after the end of the war."[2] These research efforts sanitize the gory details of the decimation of communities, ecological environments, rape, and genocide as strategies that have been deployed in many civil wars in states in Africa, including, but not limited to, Angola, Ethiopia, Nigeria, Rwanda, and the DRC. And, as Laurie Nathan argues, "Collier & Hoeffler use the terms 'civil war' and 'rebellion' interchangeably,"[3] thereby failing to differentiate between marginalized groups' agitators who fought for political inclusions in their country, for example, Angola and Uganda and those like Eritrea and South Sudan that fought for a separate homeland.

Indeed, part of the challenge with making sense of civil wars in Africa has been the tendency for ahistorical attention paid to the nature of colonial politics and the bifurcation of the internal and external triggers of particular civil wars. For example, Matthews's conceptualization of interstate conflict as one that involves two independent countries within the continent of Africa, or involving countries outside of the continent,[4] is problematic because it excludes wars of national liberations fought by many colonized states in Africa against their former colonizers. Instead, for neat empirical convenience, such conflicts are not coded as either interstate wars or as intrastate wars. Yet, as Kalu argues (see chapter 1 in this volume), many civil wars in Africa like those in the DRC and Somalia are rooted in the colonial adventures of European states whose control of many geographical territories in Africa from the seventeenth to the twentieth century introduced new weapons of war that exacerbated conflicts over scarce resources in the continent.

COLONIALISM AND INTRASTATE WARS IN AFRICA

As Strachan (2004: 1) documents, the jostling over resources in Africa by colonial powers, like Germany and Britain, did not spare Africans from World War I. Strachan states that:

> On 12 August 1914, in Togoland, Regimental Sergeant-Major Alhaji Grunshi of the West African Frontier Force became the first soldier in British service to fire a round in the Great War. On 25 November 1918, two weeks after the signature of the armistice in Europe, at Abercorn in Northern Rhodesia Colonel Paul von Lettow-Vorbeck surrendered, the last German commander of the war to do so.

European colonialists' wars within the continent of Africa (see Kalu, chapter 1 in this volume) did not end with political independence for states in Africa. Indeed, after independence, European governments have continued to influence the internal and external affairs of their former colonies, supporting governments, political parties, or ethnic groups whose interests or policies they agree with.

Thus, the line between interstate and intrastate conflicts in Africa is not always clear; indeed some interstate wars are civil wars in their own right. For example, some wars involve former colonizers supporting an incumbent or opposition leader, for example, the Portuguese's attempt to maintain control of Guinea Bissau, Cabo Verde, Mozambique, and Angola in the 1970s; the continuing involvement of France in Senegal, Mali, Chad, Central Africa Republic, and Niger; or the white-dominated Apartheid South Africa regime fighting African independent movements in Southern Africa in the 1980s. However, interstate conflict can also entail territorial disputes; for example, the oil-rich Bakassi Peninsula dispute between Nigeria and Cameroon—a conflict that dates back to British, German, and French resolution of their quarrels over the same territory—or Eritrea and Ethiopia over Badme. Some of these wars can be about migrants entering a country illegally or fleeing a conflict zone in search of asylum as the cases of the DRC and Liberia demonstrate.

Thus, considering the external and internal triggers of civil wars in Africa can provide a more complete picture for better empirical research on the challenges of civil wars in many states in the continent. The various reasons for conflicts in many African states range from citizens in a particular state challenging the existing government's authority because of marginalization, for example, Cameroon; perceived incompetence, corruption, and/or nepotism that excludes one or more ethnic groups by the ruling party, for example, Nigeria, Chad, Mali, and South Sudan; or the conflict can simply be about control of a country's rich natural resources, for example, the DRC. It can also be the result of one or more ethnic groups attempting to secede from the country via internal warfare (civil war) or the ballot box—for example, Somalia, Sudan, and Ethiopia.

For this volume, to help us better understand and explain the nature of intrastate conflicts in several states in Africa, we commissioned scholars from different parts of the continent to analyze intrastate conflicts in Burundi, Cameroon, Ghana, Liberia, Nigeria, Rwanda, Sierra Leone, Sudan, and Uganda. As editors, it is our view that under colonial rule, Africa was front and center in the Great European war of 1914. And, colonized Africans were not only conscripted to fight and die for quarrels among Europeans, the experiences from World War I (1914–1918) and World War II (1939–1945), informed wars of national liberations that Africans fought for self-determination within the structures of the colonial states that did not accord them equal liberty with the colonizers in their homelands.

With political independence secured, no sustained efforts have been made to reform and restructure the postcolonial state apparatus to be inclusive of all within formerly colonized territories. This is important because since colonial states and their institutional structures in Africa were products of autocracy, economic exploitation, and primitive accumulation with outward-facing functions, and political exclusions, the postcolonial state is primed to face civil wars, especially in the post–Cold War era. Thus, non-state actors' challenge to state authority in Africa reflects the unfinished business of state reconstitution and reform.

Unreformed state institutions and structures under autocratic leaderships attract constant challenges from secessionists, rebels, terrorists, and criminally organized groups. For example, in addition to Belgian atrocities in the Congo, postcolonial wars, especially in 1996–1997 and 1998–2003, that have claimed over 4 million lives in the Democratic Republic of the Congo reflect the nature of the unfinished business of state reform, which is usually characterized by accountable institutions, participatory leadership selections, and policies that advance the peoples' sense of security so they can be free to pursue survival strategies within an enabling environment. And in the absence of state reconstitutions and accountable leadership that places human security and inclusive governance on the policy agenda as its primary functions, strategies for peace and security (e.g., in the DRC, Cameroon, Central African Republic, and Nigeria) will continue to be undermined by territorial challenges to state authorities by groups that seek to build their own states, those with grievances against their governments but have no exit options, as well as others whose greed undergird their pursuit of unrestrained access to natural/economic resources across rich but poorly governed territories in countries like the Central Africa Republic, DRC, Nigeria, Liberia, and Sierra Leone.

TERRITORIAL IMPERATIVES OF STATES AND CIVIL WARS IN AFRICA

In their highly cited publication on the onset of civil wars, Collier and Hoeffler (2004: 570)[5] tested the robustness of ethnic, religious, and political repression, political exclusion, and economic inequality, as explanations for rebellion against a state. Based on a regression analysis, Collier and Hoeffler conclude that rebellions and civil conflicts are explained by the following: (1) availability of finance which is associated with "primary commodity exports"; (2) cost of rebellion operationalized as "male secondary education enrollment, *per capita income*, and the growth rate," interpreted as, "low foregone earnings [that] facilitate conflict"; (3) military advantage—captured by the notion "that a dispersed population increases the risk of conflict"; and (4) that "conflict is proportional to a country's population," understood as opportunities and grievances that lead to rebellion increases with a population of a country, especially in a heterogeneous population (588). These are important empirical findings on the outbreak of rebellion and civil wars in Africa, and elsewhere. However, contextually, the nature of states as an important dimension of the sources of civil conflicts in Africa did not factor into Collier and Hoeffler's analysis. This is a significant omission because ethnic, religious, and political repression, exclusion, and economic inequality—finance, costs, military advantage, and population—are significant opportunities for the onset of rebellion—that are reflected in the conclusion that occurs within the context of territoriality in which a state finds itself. This is significant because, in the case of many African states, territoriality remains a contested environment. Thus, especially in Africa, while certain economic and political variables are measurable for purposes of empirical research, the reality of colonial and postcolonial politics and the contestations between groups and individuals within a territorially bounded space that often lead to violent conflicts do not lend themselves to easy counting and measurement; they must be carefully and contextually researched and explained. The messy nature of rebellions and civil conflicts in countries like the DRC, Nigeria, Central Africa Republic, Burundi, Rwanda, Ethiopia, South Sudan, and elsewhere in Africa are connected to states as a social organizing framework for governance, which its European architects, perhaps, assumed would organize the various nations and their territories to coexist within externally imposed state boundaries. Such unity, if it was expected, is yet to materialize as the postcolonial states in Africa still wear its unwieldy autocratic cloak that neither helps the people to feel safe nor provides them with enabling environments for economic and social survival. Thus, the failure of the colonial and postcolonial states to unify indigenous Africa's various nations and serve as an organizing framework for governance explains why state legitimacy remains contested. That problem continues because the geographic territories and histories of the people are not present in contemporary Africa's state institutions, but in the people's memories of space and land, which have insufficient funds in the check that both departing colonialists and their nationalists' co-conspirators for state power presented Africans at independence.

In examining the role territory plays in the formation of nationalist thought, Jan Penrose argues that part of our understanding of the connection between territory and nationalism should be based on how the concept of *space* is defined and territorially contextualized in the real world.[6] He conceptualizes *space* as "structures of the real world . . . [that result from] . . . slow processes of long duration" (Penrose 2002: 278) as perceived, experienced, and inter-preted by human beings. According to Penrose (2002: 278–279),

> . . . space holds two sources of latent power for human beings. First, it com-prises the substance that is fundamental to human life on this planet. Through its constitution of land, water, and atmosphere, space encompasses the basic prerequisites of human survival: the food that we eat, the water that we drink, the air that we breathe, and the resources for protecting ourselves. The exis-tence of these things reflects the material dimension of space, but the deploy-ment of these qualities (for example, the identification of what constitutes food and its procurement) is relational. This relationship between space and human life in any form means that space is a source of latent material power: the power to sustain human life. Second, space is a source of latent emotional power. When the substantive qualities of space (for example, its physical features) are filtered through human experiences of time and process (the relational dimension of space) they . . . [can] invoke or release an emotional response. For example, where space is perceived as beautiful it moves us; where it is perceived as threatening it frightens us; where it is perceived as powerful we respect it.

Penrose (2002: 279) also argues that "space is present whether anyone knows about it or not, but space only becomes a place when it acquires a 'perceptual unity' . . . and . . . becomes a territory when it is delimited in some way." Thus, "territories are the product of human agency and this agency is usu-ally referred to as 'territoriality'" (Ibid). As a product of human agency, the territory is the issue that nations, communities, and families go to war for because of the inherent value of physical security, wealth, prestige, and independence it provides.[7] In this context, "territoriality . . . [is] the attempt by an individual or group to affect, influence or control people, phenomena and relationships by delimiting and asserting control over a geographic area . . . called a territory" (quoted in Penrose 2002: 279). And, ultimately, "the *control* of space is an extremely potent component of power relations . . . [as] there is power in the actual *creation* of territories because the application of territoriality reflects the needs and values of those who design and maintain them" (Penrose 2002: 279–280).

EFFECTS OF EXTERNALLY IMPOSED TERRITORIAL BOUNDARIES

Analytically, Great Britain, Austria-Hungary, Belgium, Denmark, France, Germany, Italy, the Netherlands, Portugal, Russia, Spain, Sweden, Norway, and Turkey (the Ottoman Empire) met in Berlin, Germany, in 1884 to discuss, map out, and impose European will on Africa's peoples and its geography. The Berlin Conference had no African representative, and therefore the notion of territory and territoriality that emerged from that conference primarily reflects European states and their peoples' latent power and disregard for the people, communities, and historical memories of space across the continent of Africa. In the so-called *General Act of the Berlin Conference on West Africa*, which is the formal title of the treaty, the signatories vowed: "in the name of God almighty," to "obviate the misunderstanding and disputes which might in future arise from new acts of occupation (prises de possession) on the coast of Africa" (*The Berlin Act*). In their efforts to maintain political stability in Europe after the devastating impacts of the Napoleonic wars, European leaders collaborated to emasculate the masses' ability to revolt against them in their homelands in various European states. One strategy in the leaders' arsenals was to create opportunities for potential trouble makers among them to let off steam in an unaccountable violent far away "territories" in search of diamond, gold, and glory—in Africa. That action—dividing territories that Lord Salisbury said European leaders "knew nothing about,"[8]— sowed the seeds of violence that have remained at the heart of states as a social organization of governance in the continent of Africa. Therefore, *The Berlin Act* was nothing but European leaders' continued efforts to maintain peace between the different kingdoms in Europe with acceptable occasional wars/skirmishes between European countries in Africa over African territories and between European colonizing armies against resistant Africans in Africa (Kalu, chapter 1).

With potential conflicts between European leaders over Africa averted, France, Britain, Belgium, Germany, and other European states took, occupied, and exploited African territories as if they belonged to Europeans. While that action temporarily buried and subjugated the latent power of relevant indigenous ethnic nationalities, it did not and could not bury or subjugate the memories and emotional powers of peoples in territories and communities they know all too well. In the interim, with their "sovereignty" declared over African spaces and territories, European colonizers imposed their values on Africa. And one of the legacies of those values is the violent repression of "others," especially in the context of agitations for control of territorially based scarce resources.[9] Indeed, while European states' sovereign control allowed them to act with impunity in their various African territories, other parties and signatories to the Berlin Conference simply exercised "neutrality" per Article X of the Act, inter alia:

> . . . to give a new guarantee of security to trade and industry, and to encourage the maintenance of peace, . . . the High Signatory Parties to the present Act, and

those who shall hereafter adopt it, bind themselves to respect the neutrality of
the territories, or portions of territories, belonging to the said countries, . . . so
long as the Powers which exercise or shall exercise the rights of sovereignty or
Protectorate over those territories . . . shall fulfil [sic] the duties which neutrality
requires. (*The Berlin Act*)

Thus, while the *Concert of Europe* helped maintain relative stability among
European monarchies, which was partly secured by their partition of Africa,
issues of economic resources, ideology, identity, and territory later triggered
two major wars in European homelands that consequently led to political
independence for Africans within the territorial boundaries of European-
created states in Africa. Indeed, the external remapping of territories in the
continent continued well into the early 1900s. As Matthews (1970: 339–
340)[10] notes, while France and Spain reached a new territorial agreement on
Morocco in 1912, the defeat of Germany in World War I provided Britain and
France opportunities to remap former German territories in Cameroon and
Togo; and by 1944, France tinkered some more with the territories between
Mali and Mauritania. Thus, the external interference in the form of arbitrary
boundary divisions of the continent of Africa and continued intervention to
remake the nature of foisted states on communities in Africa did not end with
the Berlin Conference. European efforts to secure their economic access and
interests are reflected in the continuous efforts to map and remap several
states—even as the colonial powers were losing their capacity to hold on to
African territories in the 1940s. And while African states became independent from European colonialists, the ties that bound them to their European
leaders and states stretch from imperial to colonial and postcolonial periods
and remain strong in the current international system in which custodians
of state power and authority in Africa remain moored to their contemporary
principals in Europe.

This means that political independence did not lead to policy autonomy
because the new leaders[11] of the various independent states in Africa made
no efforts to restructure or reform the colonial state and its inherent repressive
institutions. And leaders like Nkrumah and Lumumba that sought economic
and political development autonomy for reclaiming sovereign and territorial
space for their people became victims of the violent European states in Africa.
The unreformed state boundaries, spaces, and territoriality remain the sources
of suffocating violent challenges to state authority and legitimacy in the form
of civil wars and rebellions in countries like the Democratic Republic of the
Congo, Nigeria, Cameroon, the Central African Republic, and Sudan where
space and land remain contested as sources of physical security, access to
water, food, and homeland.

POPULATION CONCENTRATION
AND CIVIL CONFLICTS

To paraphrase the UNESCO Constitution, since memories of the loss of community cohesion in the form of political exclusion remain in the minds of people, civil wars in the continent of Africa will continue to be fueled by memories of "our land" in the minds of ethnic nationalities forced into unrestructured and unreformed multiethnic and religious states. And, like megacities whose residents come from all walks of life, nationalities, regions, religions, and other forms of identifications without productive considerations for their immediate communities, the postcolonial state in Africa remains a space where different groups are in search of an ever-elusive community. According to Ofeimum (2001: 12), community memories of space in African states,

> . . . is a poetics linked to origins, size, and geography, defined by its parts rather than by a fraction of it . . . . The citiness of a city lies in the absorption of its many parts into a common whirlpool. Its core experience intimates a civis: a place of civilization where people who may not have the same occupation, or accept the same ancestors, and people who may not bow to the same deity, can live within a common frame of politics, thus entrenching the possibility of shared decision-making as a permanent way of life. The city is, in this sense, an ever-ready challenge.

Thus, contrary to the argument that "countries with a highly concentrated population have a very low risk of conflict, whereas those with a highly dispersed population have a very high risk" (Collier and Hoeffler 2004: 581; Herbst 1989: 679) of conflicts may provide analysts with a basis for statistical analysis, but it is based on poor historical and political insights on communal land-based (territoriality) practices in many communities across Africa. If a highly concentrated population, for example, in the United States, Britain, France, Germany, and other industrialized Western states, whose social formations were internally driven to establish states, governments, and institutionalization of norms of governance, and civic nationalism, then the high concentration of populations in countries like Nigeria and the Democratic Republic of the Congo should have a low risk of conflict.

Instead, as Williams (2007: 1026) aptly states:

> In 1890 approximately 5 percent of Africans resided in urban areas; by 1900 the figure was 34 percent. The number of mega-cities on the continent . . . mushroomed: in 1900 there was just one (Cairo); by 2000 there were 36 cities with populations of between 1 million and 10 million people, and two (Cairo

and Lagos) with populations of over 10 million. In effect, these cities have giant metabolisms: they have massive appetites for energy, water, and food, and they spew out huge quantities of pollutants, garbage, and solid wastes. And around the urban cores, shanty towns and slums have quickly arisen. In many respects, Africa's slums are the very epitome of urbanized insecurity, with their residents generally lacking law enforcement, regular sources of employment, sanitation, water, electricity, and health-care facilities.[12]

Thus, if the argument that "high concentration of populations" portends less risk for intrastate conflicts, one would expect a geometric decline in intrastate wars and other forms of violent civil conflicts with increasing populations and urbanization in many African cities and states. However, the reality is one of increasing insecurity and state-sponsored violence against groups outside of the central governing elites, leading to challenges to postcolonial state authority and legitimacy.

For example, Nigeria, Sudan, DRC, and several other African states that were externally created and remain unreformed have a high probability of violent conflicts, intrastate wars, and high levels of casualties in the densely populated cities and urban communities. Thus, it is possible that a highly dispersed population in the European landmass may be more likely to have a high risk of conflict than the densely populated communities of the contemporary African states. What this suggests is that the high risk of conflict is simply rooted in the unresolved territorial issues—a legacy of colonialists' concatenated state boundaries created without regard to ethnonational realities and existing communal arrangements of power and governance in the continent. Except for Eritrea and South Sudan, Europeans' drawing of lines that have mostly remained sacrosanct across the continent holds the bone of contention that maintains the threats to the state's political stability, crippling its capacity to protect its territory and citizens and provide an enabling environment for citizens to pursue their economic, social, and political interests.

Thus, across several states in Africa, the concatenation of geographic boundaries produces disturbing experiences of intrastate conflicts largely associated with ideational issues such as religion and ethnicity that are instrumentalized for the creation of conflicts in densely populated towns and cities across the continent. The indirect effect of these ideational issues contributes to state fragility across the continent. The *Fragile State Index* 2021[13] indicates that Guinea is unstable and teetering on the brink of failure because of poor economic performance, human rights abuses, political instability, and corruption—factors associated with state fragility. For Chad, the factors that indicate state fragility include poverty, the influx of refugees, radicalized youth population, ethnic and religious conflicts; in the Congo, it is manifested by the presence of civil wars, human rights abuses, disease, mass rape, and torture.

Corruption, poverty, food shortages, armed conflict, and human rights abuses are dominant factors in South Sudan, while jihadist terrorism, piracy, poverty, and food insecurity characterize state fragility in Somalia. In Sudan, the challenge is an authoritarian government, civil war, terrorism, monocultural economy, and associated poverty that continue to threaten political stability. Globally, and in terms of the ranking in the Fragile State Index, the overwhelming majority of the states in the top 50 are states in Africa.[14] Of the nine case studies in this volume, only Ghana has a low state legitimacy challenge. Each of the remaining states is faced with state legitimacy, external intervention in one form or another, human rights violations, refugees and internally displaced persons, and security challenges. And all are characterized by low and high levels of intrastate conflicts. Each of these cases has problems rooted in central government political exclusion of a specific ethnic-nationality or region whose unresolved grievances are all connected to issues of territory and political and economic justice. Although dispersed populations are not the cause of intrastate conflicts across these states, the problems evoke the persistent effects of unresolved issues with externally imposed colonial and unreformed postcolonial state institutions and autocracy.

Thus, the unusual concatenation of geographic boundaries out of the Berlin Conference continues to undermine peace and unity in Africa. For example, it remains a bone of contention between the government and several politically excluded communities in Nigeria, DRC, Sudan, and other African states. Overcoming such challenges requires transforming a geographic space whose recent memory is of state violence fused by imposing new and uplifting narratives into community spaces of political inclusion, expanded political and economic opportunities for all, and where civic nationalism[15]—unity based on common citizenship without regard to language, religion, region, and ethnicity, and other identities—and the rule of law are preferred over Kalashnikov AK-47s.

THE FOCUS OF THE BOOK AND METHODOLOGY

This book is the third in a four-part research project with several major interrelated objectives. In this project, we examine the causes of conflicts in Africa, including the forces and factors that shape those conflicts. As a corollary to conflict, we interrogate the efforts to build durable peace in several conflict-affected African states and proffer policy-relevant suggestions for tackling the root causes of conflicts in the continent. This volume, *Civil Wars in Africa*, examines the causes of civil conflicts, and wars, including the forces and factors that shaped them. The case studies focus on Burundi, Cameroon, Liberia, Nigeria, Rwanda, Sierra Leone, Sudan, and Uganda.

The theoretical chapter (Kalu) responds to the question, what are the causes of civil wars in Africa? It examines the intersections between external and domestic factors and contradictions and their roles in the persistence of contemporary civil wars in Africa. Using mixed methods such as the cross-tracing approach, the case studies explain the onset of intrastate wars.

THE ORGANIZATION OF THE BOOK

The book comprises ten chapters, an introduction, and conclusion. In chapter 1, Kelechi A. Kalu and George Klay Kieh Jr. framed the foci of the volume. First, they examined the epistemological issues regarding the concepts of conflict, intrastate war, and interstate war from selected studies from the extant literature on conflicts and war. Kalu and Kieh contend that one of the major weaknesses of quantitative studies on conflicts and wars is the failure to analyze the root causes of these conflicts and their ramifications. Second, they interrogate some of the major causes of civil wars in general, and Africa in particular. They identified and discussed the role of colonialism, especially its legacy of ethnic and primordial manipulation, economic exploitation, and authoritarianism, among others, as well as the colonially induced territorial conflicts as major causes of civil conflicts and war in Africa. In addition, Kalu and Kieh probed the continued roles of external powers such as France in fueling and sustaining civil wars on the African Continent. Second, they mapped out the focus of the volume, including its central research questions. Third, they discussed the volume's methodological approach to addressing the research questions. Finally, Kalu and Kieh summarized the various chapters that constitute the volume.

In chapter 1, Kelechi A. Kalu provides the theoretical crucible and its constituent paradigms that provide the various trajectories for examining the major causes of civil conflicts and wars in Africa. He begins by examining the contending conceptualizations of civil wars in the extant literature. Thereafter, he provides the conceptual framework of civil conflicts and wars that provides the foundation for the book. Furthermore, he surveys some of the major paradigms about civil conflicts and wars, including the ethnic, grievance, greed, secessionist, territorial, realist, and structural realist theories. He observes that each of the theories explains some dimensions of the root causes of civil wars in Africa. In other words, none of the theories provides comprehensive explanations for the causes of civil wars in Africa.

In chapter 2, Dawn Nager interrogates the causes of the three major civil wars that have plagued Burundi, and the domestic and external factors that have shaped these wars. She contends that the overarching cause of the civil wars was the ethnicization and instrumentalization of the social structures that existed under the Burudian Monarchy during the precolonial era by German and Belgian colonizers. For example, under the monarchical social order, the Tutsi class consisted of cattle owners, and the Hutus were farmers. In the case of the Twas, they were the offsprings of the intermarriage between the Tutsis and the Hutus. Importantly, the members of all three tiers of the precolonial social structure spoke Bantu as a common language. However, the German and Belgian colonizers transformed the social structure into an ethnically based one: the Hutus, Tutsis, and Twas were reconstructed as ethnic groups. In addition, the colonizers sowed and nurtured the seeds of antagonisms, hatred, and conflict between and among the three groups, especially by privileging the Tutsi minority. Since the postcolonoial era, these antagonisms have been reproduced and have served as the driving force for the civil conflict and resulting wars in the country.

Avitus Agbor examines the major causes of the civil conflict and war in Cameron in chapter 3. A key one is the Ahidjo and Biya regimes' policies of discrimination against the English-speaking linguistic minority. Another is the exploitation of natural resources in the English-speaking section of Cameroon without the concomitant socioeconomic development. Further, there were, and still are, flawed legal and political arrangements that serve as the foundational pillars of the Cameroonian polity. In addition, English-speaking Cameroonians are discriminated against in terms of employment opportunities, political appointments in the public bureaucracy, and access to public services. Moreover, the culture of the English-speaking section is suffocated by the state. Against this background, the antigovernment forces that are involved in the civil war are demanding various reforms, including the restructuring of the state system and the preferred establishment of a federal structure with the ten constituent states. At the extreme is the demand for secession by the English-speaking section of the country.

In chapter 4, Sabina Appiah-Boateng, Stephen Kendie, and Kenneth Aikins probe the nature and dynamics of the chieftaincy conflict in Tuobodom Chieftaincy in Ghana and the resulting posttraumatic stress disorder that inflicted the citizens of the area. They contend that two rival traditional chiefs—Barima Obeng Ameya I and Nana Baffour Asare II—are the two major actors that serve as the driving forces of the conflict and recurrent wars. Significantly, the rivalry between the two chiefs is mediated by power struggle between them, competing loyalties, contestations over land, and interethnic conflict between the Bono lineage from the Brong-Ahafo region—the Abromenu group—and the Asanties—Krotia people. The most recent cycle of the civil war was triggered by the kidnapping and subsequent arrest of Chief Nana Baffour Asare II by some youth on the orders of the rival chief, Barima Obeng Ameya I. One of the major consequences of the conflict and wars is that people in the area are suffering from posttraumatic stress disorder. This is because the people have experienced sundry violent acts, including the killing of relatives and friends by forces of the rival power blocs.

In chapter 5, George Klay Kieh Jr. interrogates the root causes and examines the internal and external actors that shaped the two Liberian civil wars (1989–1997 and 1999–2003). In the case of the first Liberian civil war, the overarching cause was anchored in the state in both its settler and peripheral capitalist phases. That is, the Liberian state-generated multidimensional crises of development—cultural, economic, political, and social—that sowed, nurtured, and germinated the seeds of civil conflict and war. The major internal actors in the war were the regime of Samuel Kanyon Doe, Taylor-led National Patriotic Front of Liberia (NPFL), which started the insurgency that led to the outbreak of the war, and various rival warlordist militias, including the Independent National Patriotic Front of Liberia (INPFL), Liberia Peace Council (LPC), ULIMO-J, and ULIMO-K. As for the external actors, they included Cote d'Ivoire, Nigeria, the United States, the Economic Community of West African States(ECOWAS), the Organization of African Unity(OAU) (now the African Union), and the United Nations(UN). In terms of the second civil war, it was caused by the failure of the Taylor regime to democratically reconstitute the Liberian state as the centerpiece of the postconflict peacebuilding project, coupled with the horrendous performance of the Taylor regime. The major internal actors during the second civil war were the Taylor regime, Liberians United for Reconciliation and Democracy (LURD), and the Movement for Democracy in Liberia (MODEL). In the case of the major external actors, they included Guinea, Ghana, the United States, ECOWAS, and the UN.

In chapter 6, Michael Ediabonya examines the role of personality conflicts as contributors to the Nigerian civil war (1967–1970). He contends that personality conflicts between and among various politicians have been an enduring feature of Nigerian politics since the colonial era. For example, he analyzes the various personality conflicts between and among the leaders of the Nigerian independence movement that underpinned the writing of the constitutions. Subsequently, during the postindependence era, various personality conflicts shaped the political economy during the "First Republic." One notable case was the conflict between Chief Akintola, the premier of the western region, and Chief Awolowo, the leader of the Action Group, the ruling party in the Western Union. Similarly, after the July 1966 coup, General Yakubu Gowon, the military head of state, and Col. Ojukwu, the military governor of the eastern region, developed a personality conflict that served as the proximate contributor to the outbreak of the Nigerian civil war.

In chapter 7, Fiacre Bievenu interrogates the determinants of the Rwandan civil war, especially the external dimension. The rationale is that the Rwandan civil war was caused by a confluence of domestic and external factors and forces. The foundation for the war was laid by Belgian colonialism, especially its "zero sum" framework as the core of the political arrangements. During the postcolonial era, France became the dominant neocolonial patron that supported the various authoritarian regimes that ruled the country. The regimes, among others, violated human rights, manipulated the social structure, and visited socioeconomic malaise on the majority of the people. Significantly, the civil war was shaped by various international actors. France supported the authoritarian Habyarimana regime; Uganda backed the Rwandan Patriotic Front (RPF) with the support of the United Kingdom; Egypt served as a conduit through which France funneled arms to the Habyarimana regime; and South Africa served as arms merchants by selling arms to both sides in the war.

In chapter 8, Earl Conteh-Morgan examines the internal, regional, and global factors that caused and shaped the Sierra Leonean civil war. At the internal level, the major causes were internal fragmentation and the resulting ethnic and linguistic cleavages that have their roots in British colonialism; authoritarianism, especially during the Stevens and Momoh regimes; and human insecurity as evidenced by food shortage and inadequate state provision for health care and other basic human needs. In sum, the domestic roots of the war were anchored in the structural violence-relative deprivation nexus. For the regional dimension, the first Liberian civil war, especially the alliance between Charles Taylor's National Patriotic Front of Liberia (NPFL) and the Foday Sankoh-headed Revolutionary United Front (RUF), the main rebel group, as well as the role of Burkina Faso as a patron of the alliance partly explain the onset of the civil war in Sierra Leone. Globally, British colonialism laid the foundation for the civil conflict and the resulting war. In addition, the neoliberal development model, including its Structural Adjustment Programs (SAPS) through the International Monetary Fund (IMF) and the World Bank, contributed to both structural violence and relative deprivation.

Francis Onditi interrogates the major causes of the South Sudanese civil war in chapter 9. He posits that the sine qua non for understanding the war is based on the examination of Sudanese history, including the civil war that eventually led to the breakup of Sudan into two independent states—Sudan and South Sudan. In addition, the war was caused by the hegemony of the Sudan People's Liberation Movement (SPLM), the ruling party of South Sudan. Within the context of a one-party state, political elites lack flexibility in terms of the vehicles they can use to compete for state power. Furthermore, authoritarianism became the governance system for the independent South Sudan; and within this structure, there have been vitriolic human rights abuses by the Salva regime. In addition, ethnicity has been instrumentalized, thereby pitting one ethnic group against the other as an integral part of the old colonial strategy of "divide, rule, and conquer." Furthermore, there is massive corruption, and human insecurity, amid the generation of oil revenues by the state.

In chapter 10, Sabatiano Rwengabo and Julius Niringiyimana examine the roots of the Lord Resistance Army's (LRA) war against the Ugandan state. They argue that the key factors revolve around British colonial security policies. At the core of the policies was the overrepresentation of the Acholi ethnic group in the colonial, military, and security establishments. In turn, this led to the development of the threat perception—counter-threat dynamic between the Acholi and other ethnic groups. Essentially, other ethnic groups perceived the Acholi as a threat to their well-being and survival. During the postindependence era, the Obote regime (the first government) sought to counterbalance Acholi dominance in the military and security establishments by increasing the Langis' representation. Under the Amin regime, the Acholis faced political persecution and the further diminution of their role in the military and security establishments. Interestingly, when Obote returned to power (Obote II), he relied on the Acholis for their military skills in battling the insurgent National Resistance Movement (NRA) led by Yoweri Museveni (the current Ugandan president). When the NRA overthrew the Ugandan regime and assumed power on January 26, 1986, the Acholi influence in the country's military and security establishments ended. Exasperated by the orientation of the Museveni regime toward them, several Acholi soldiers joined the rebel LRA and even took various leadership positions. This gave the LRA trained and skilled military personnel.

Kelechi A. Kalu and George Klay Kieh Jr. draw lessons from the various chapters in the volume and provide some insights about ways in which civil wars can be minimized and possibly avoided in the African states that have not experienced it and prevented from reoccurring in those African states that have experienced it. Kalu and Kieh proposed major issues that need to be addressed: the postcolonial state, governance, nation-building, and human well-being. In terms of the postcolonial state, they assert that it must be democratically reconstituted, because it cannot shepherd the process of human-centered democracy and development. In addition, they argue that democratic governance is the best model for conducting and managing the affairs of African states. In the area of nation-building, Klau and Kieh argue that a democratically reconstituted state will provide an enabling environment in which inclusive nation-building can occur. As for human material well-being, they assert that the state must address issues such as poverty, inequalities in wealth and income, mass unemployment, food insecurity, and inadequate physical infrastructure.

CONCLUSION

The chapter has attempted to lay the foundation for the book by addressing several major issues. First, it deciphered some of the major factors such as colonialism that served as the general root causes of civil conflicts and wars in Africa. In addition, the chapter argues that with few exceptions, the first and subsequent generations of African leaders failed to jettison the colonial model governance and its associated authoritarianism, ethnic polarization, human rights violations, and socioeconomic malaise. Instead, they kept and built upon the colonial model of governance, thereby sowing, nurturing, and germinating the seeds of conflict and war.

Second, the chapter articulated the thrust of the book: the examination of the root causes of civil wars and the forces that shaped them. In order to address these two research problems, the book used an interdisciplinary approach. The rationale is that multiple disciplinary perspectives and approaches are quite useful in examining the complexities, including the multidimensionality of conflict and wars in Africa. In addition, the book employed the mixed method research tradition as its methodological compass. This entailed the use of both qualitative (case studies) and quantitative research methods.

Finally, the chapter summarized the various case studies, as well as the theoretical and concluding chapters. The rationale is to provide insights about the various chapters, including their approaches to the research problems and their findings. In addition, the summaries provide a framework for teasing out the similarities and differences between and among the various chapters, especially the case studies.

NOTES

1. The Correlates of War project and data is available here: www.correlatesofwar .org. For empirical studies on civil war, see Paul Collier, "Doing Well Out of War," Paper Prepared for the Conference on Economic Agendas in Civil Wars, London, April 26–27, 1999. Available at www.worldbank.org/research/conflict/papers/econa-gendas.pdf; Paul Collier, "Economic Causes of Civil Conflict and Their Implications for Policy," 2000a. Available at www.worldbank.org/research/conflict/papers/civil-conflict.pdf; Paul Collier, "Rebellion as a Quasi-Criminal Activity," *Journal of Conflict Resolution*, 44, no. 6 (2000b): 839–853; and Paul Collier and Anke Hoeffler, "On the Incidence of Civil War in Africa," *Journal of Conflict Resolution*, 46, no. 1 (2000a): 13–28.

2. Nicholas Sambanis, "Partition as a Solution to Ethnic War: An Empirical Critique of the Theoretical Literature," *World Politics*, 52, no. 4 (2000): 437–483.

3. L. Nathan, "The Causes of Civil War: The False Logic of Collier and Hoeffler," *South Africa Review of Sociology*, 39, no. 2 (2012): 262–275,.

4. Robert O. Matthews, "Interstate Conflicts in Africa: A Review," *International Organization*, 34, no. 2 (1970): 335–360.

5. Paul Collier and Anke Hoeffler, "Greed and Grievance in Civil War," *Oxford Economic Papers*, 56 (2004): 563–595.

6. For a full treatment and contextualization of the issues of territoriality, space, and nation, see Kelechi A. Kalu, Laura Joseph, and David Kraybill, "Territorial Origins of African Civil Conflicts: Space, Territoriality and Institutions," in *Territoriality, Citizenship and Peacebuilding: Perspectives on Challenges to Peace in Africa*, edited by Kelechi Kalu, Ufo Okeke Uzodike, David Kraybill, and John Moolakkattu (London: Adonis & Abbey, 2012), 15–45.

7. Territoriality as an issue-based approach to understanding and explaining world politics, see Paul R. Hensel, Sara McLaughlin Mitchell, Thomas E. Sowers II, and Clayton L. Thyne, "Bones of Contention: Comparing Territorial, Maritime, and River Issues," *Journal of Conflict Resolution*, 52, no. 1 (2008): 117–143.

8. See Kalu, chapter 1 in this volume.

9. This section benefits from Kalu's earlier work on this subject. See note no. 6.

10. See Robert O. Matthews, "Interstate Conflicts in Africa: A Review," *International Organization*, 24, no. 2 (1970): 335–360.

11. The exceptions here could be the likes of Kwame Nkrumah in Ghana, Patrice Lumumba in Zaire, and Thomas Sankara in Burkina Faso—whose attempts to unmoor their states from their former colonial masters were met with their untimely deaths.

12. Paul D. Williams, "Thinking About Security in Africa," *International Affairs*, 83, no. 6 (2007): 1021–1038.

13. For the Fragile States Index global data, see: https://fragilestatesindex.org/global-data/. The indicators of state fragility are in four broad categories: 1. Cohesion (security, apparatus, factionalized elites, and group grievance); 2. Economic (economic decline, uneven development, and human flights and brain drain); 3. Political factors (operationalized as state legitimacy, public services, and human rights & the rule of law); and 4. Social, which are denoted as demographic pressure, refugees and internally displaced persons, and external interventions). For how the database measures the indicators, see https://fragilestatesindex.org/indicators/.

14. Ibid. In the 2021 Fragile State Index, Yemen is ranked 1st and Finland is ranked last at 179th. The lower a state is ranked, the more vulnerable a state is to collapse. And, except for Yemen (1st), Syria (3rd), and Afghanistan (9th), states in Africa occupy the majority of the spots in the top 10 and majority of the top 50 states that are facing capacity, security, political, and social challenges.

15. See Steven L. Lamy, et al., *Introduction to Global Politics*, 6th ed. (New York: Oxford University Press, 2021), 127.

REFERENCES

Collier, Paul. 1999. "Doing Well Out of War." Paper Prepared for the Conference on Economic Agendas in Civil Wars. London. April 26–27. Available at www.world-bank.org/research/conflict/papers/econagendas.pdf;

Collierc, Paul. 2000a. "Economic Causes of Civil Conflict and Their Implications for Policy." Available at www.worldbank.org/research/conflict/papers/civilconflict.pdf.

Collier, Paul. 2000b. "Rebellion as a Quasi-Criminal Activity." *Journal of Conflict Resolution*, 44(6): 839–853.

Collier, Paul and Anke Hoeffler. 2000. "On the Incidence of Civil War in Africa." *Journal of Conflict Resolution*, 46(1): 13–28.

Collier, Paul and Anke Hoeffler. 2004. "Greed and Grievance in Civil War." *Oxford Economic Papers*, 56: 563–595.

Fragile States Index Global Data. Available at https://fragilestatesindex.org/global-data/. Accessed July 4, 2021.

Hensel, Paul R., Sara McLaughlin Mitchell, Thomas E. Sowers II, and Clayton L. Thyne. 2008. "Bones of Contention: Comparing Territorial, Maritime, and River Issues." *Journal of Conflict Resolution*, 52(1): 117–143.

Kalu, Kelechi A., Laura Joseph, and David Kraybill. 2013. "Territorial Origins of African Civil Conflicts: Space, Territoriality and Institutions." In *Territoriality, Citizenship and Peacebuilding: Perspectives on Challenges to Peace in Africa*, edited by Kelechi Kalu, Ufo Okeke Uzodike, David Kraybill, and John Moolakkattu, 15–45. London: Adonis & Abbey.

Lamy, Steven L. et. al. 2021. *Introduction to Global Politics*. 6th ed. New York: Oxford University Press.

Matthews, Robert O. 1970. "Interstate Conflicts in Africa: A Review." *International Organization*, 34(2): 335–360.

Nathan, L.2012. "The Causes of Civil War: The False Logic of Collier and Hoeffler." *South Africa Review of Sociolog*, 39(2): 262–275.

Ofeimun, Odia. 2001. "Imagination and the City." *Glendora: A Quarterly Review on the Arts*, 3(2): 11–15 and 137–41.

Penrose, Jan. 2002. "Nations, States and Homelands: Territory and Territoriality in Nationalist Thought." *Nations and Nationalism*, 8(3): 277–97.

Sambanis, Nicholas. 2000. "Partition as a Solution to Ethnic War: An Empirical Critique of the Theoretical Literature." *World Politics*, 52(4): 437–483.

Sithole, Mpilo Pearl. 2010. "'Modernity and 'Traditionality' in African Governance: Conceptual and Pragmatic Issues." *Africa Insight*, 39(4): 53–62.

Williams, Paul D. 2007. "Thinking About Security in Africa." *International Affairs*, 83(6): 1021–1038.

Chapter 1

Theories and Explanations of Civil Conflicts and Wars in Africa

Kelechi A. Kalu

This chapter responds to the question, what are the causes of civil wars in Africa? Quantitatively defining civil war, Collier and Hoeffler state that a civil war is an internal conflict with at least 1,000 battle-related deaths per annum, and when government forces and an identifiable rebel organization suffer at least 5 percent of the fatalities. They examine 161 countries and 78 civil wars over the period 1960–1999. The dataset for their study of civil wars and the definition of civil war are drawn from the Correlates of War project.[1] And, as Nathan (2012: 263) argues, "Collier & Hoeffler use the terms 'civil war' and 'rebellion' interchangeably." With a specific focus on Africa, Matthews (1970: 335–360) argues that interstate conflict is a conflict involving two independent countries within the continent of Africa, or involving countries outside of the continent. According to him, intrastate conflicts in Africa tend to take the form of an aggrieved group directly challenging the power and authority of national leaders. Examples include the civil war in Angola or secessionist efforts by one of the nations that would like to territorially separate from a particular state boundary of a postcolonial state, for example, South Sudanese in former Sudan, or Igbos in Nigeria.

Civil wars or intrastate conflicts in Africa have been persistent in one form or the other since colonizing European states combined different African nations—many with dissimilar cultures, religions, and civilizations—into states within boundaries that were illiberally governed. The resulting traumatic governance crises and challenges to the legitimacy of the power and authority of national leaders, amid ethnic and religious fragmentations, have made it difficult to achieve genuine nation-building results in Africa's postcolonial states. In this chapter, I argue that the persistence of intrastate wars in Africa is caused by external and internal factors and that those violent conflicts in many African states are linked to the externally determined territorial boundaries of states in Africa. Using a modified realist perspective, this chapter argues that continuing external pressures and impacts on African states by their former colonizers, business interests, in collaboration with many African leaders, significantly impact the outbreaks of intrastate conflicts in the continent. The intersections between those external and domestic factors and contradictions will be fully examined to determine their roles in the persistence of contemporary civil wars in Africa.

ORIGINS OF CIVIL WARS IN AFRICA

In a speech, published in *The Times* (UK) on August 7, 1890, British prime minister Lord Salisbury stated that "We have been engaged . . . in drawing lines upon maps where no white man's feet have ever trod; we have been giving away mountains and rivers and lakes to each other, but we have only been hindered by the small impediment that we never knew exactly where those mountains and rivers and lakes were."[2] Not evident in Lord Salisbury's speech is the fact that outright war was also used, as necessary, for ensuring continuing Europeans' extraction of gold and diamonds across Africa. It was clear that Europeans knew the benefits of natural resources that their representatives were evacuating from various parts of Africa, and when necessary, they used both external and internal violence, for example, in Belgian Congo to extract resources from African territories.

According to one report on the beneficial relationship between Africa's rich resources and war, the British fought against the Ashanti (in the present day) Ghana. For example, one report states, "Thirty four thousand ounces of gold dust are said to have arrived at that place alone during the last six months, and if peace can be kept with the Ashantees, a great increase may be expected" (African Expeditions 1828). And, as McCorquodale and Pangalangan (2001: 867–869) argue, it was the European "tea and macaroons approach to drawing boundaries [that] has led to long-term causes of conflicts" in Africa. To be sure, there are contributing internal causes to civil wars in Africa. But at the root of interstate and intrastate conflicts in many contemporary African states is the post-conflict "peace" between the European states over the continent of Africa; especially the peace that ended World War II, which was also part of the foundation for political independence in Africa. For example, the postindependence civil war in Angola that erupted in 1975 is rooted in European colonial wars in the Central Africa region involving the Germans, the British, the Belgians, and the Portuguese in the latter part of the 1890s.

Colonial European skirmishes over territory and resources across Sub-Saharan Africa— sometimes fighting against each other, and other times, collaborating against Africans—continued well into the early 1900s and with some internal European "peace" established in the early days of agitation for African independence in the 1960s. A few examples will suffice. In a report in *Aberdeen Journal* (1909: 5), a diplomatic dispatch stated that "according to an official report from the Governor of the Cameroons, the Anglo-German Boundary Commission engaged in the demarcation of the frontier between the Cameroons and British Southern Nigeria has been *fiercely attacked on British territory* by a native tribe, who were driven back and dispersed in several engagements by the German and British troops . . . . After a severe engagement and several skirmishes the natives fled to the mountains"[3] (my italics). Two interesting items in the report are that (1), the introduction of British arms and soldiers who forcefully occupied the region known today as southern Nigeria and northeastern regions of Cameroon translated into Britain claiming ownership of the region and (consequently?), that made the indigenous people from the region "foreign invaders" of British territory. Interestingly, that same militarized region, which includes the oil-rich Niger Delta region of Nigeria and the Bakassi part of Cameroon, remains the hotbed of insurgencies and Boko Haram terrorist activities that continue to challenge the authorities of the Nigerian and Cameroonian governments. Second, the epistemological frame of reference for many Western, especially North American scholars continue to privilege the lives of European descended people when they fail, similar to the British and the German colonial officers that only counted European lives lost during those intracolonial wars that were fought in Africa. For example, the report on the "Fighting in Nigeria" stated that "The total losses on the side of the British and Germans are given as five killed and nineteen wounded." In a different report on "Anglo-German Commission Attacked,"[4] the dispatch document that British commissioner, Lt.-Col. Whitlock, who was in an unmapped "Hinterland of Calabar," announced "heavy fighting between tribes and the Commission." The telegram dated December 29, 1909, came from Lagos "where it was sent by runner." In the report, "Col. Whitlock states that he, and all his available troops, together with the German Commissioner, Lieut. Von Stephani, and 42 German soldiers, with a Maxim . . . , was attacked. Heavy fighting ensued in which the German Commissioner was dangerously wounded, and two German non-commissioned officers wounded. The total casualties were three."[5] In that report, there is no mention of casualties among the indigenous people that were killed by the British soldiers or the German wielding Maxims.

However, "In the Cameroons,"[6] the report from the field acknowledged the loss of non-European lives lost, which mainly included the lives of "native soldiers" fighting in the British or German armies. For example, the December report, updated as November 25, 1909 report, stated that an encounter between British soldiers and the natives resulted in the killing of "Lieut. H. H. Schneider, R. E. Special Reserve, Nigeria Survey Dept. Three native soldiers. Wounded: Lieut. C. Luxford, East Surrey Regiment, and Nigerian Regiment, West African Frontier Force. Eight native soldiers. Temporary Lieut. L. C. Patter, Regiment, West African Frontier Force, was severely wounded on December 9. The number of the enemy's casualties has not been reported, but about 60 European prisoners were taken" (ibid.) As documented, these historical narratives are both an example of the disregard colonial Europeans had for African lives, as well as indicators of the arbitrary nature of the mapping of colonized African states/territories. According to Stone (2020: 142), "Counting heightens our awareness of the things we've decided to count and makes us ignore things we (or someone else) decided doesn't matter." Thus, the decision to count anything is a decision that indicates what we value; therefore, what we do not count also indicates what is not important to us. Second, a deep understanding of the causes of civil wars in Africa has to look to the legacies of how states were created in Africa by European colonizers and the violent methods used to pacify, govern, and transfer those states to Africans as dependencies rather than a legitimate sovereign and independent states.

The geographic lines that were drawn without regard to ethnic, cultural, linguistic, and internal processes of state formation in Africa continue to exert significant tolls on sociopolitical and security challenges on many African states. Collusion and collaboration between European and other internal nation-building destroyers in African states used an authoritarian governing approach to force African peoples into compliance with unpaid labor demands and payment of taxes. For example, although there were many agitations against European authoritarianism, like the Mau Mau Movement in Kenya, the Railway Strikes in Senegal, and the Aba Women's War in Nigeria, external-internal collaborators used force to maintain a semblance of internal stability.

With the end of World War II and the onset of the ideological Cold War between the West and the East, agitations for political independence in Africa were mostly peaceful. Thus, the transitions from colonialism to independence within the ambit of the East-West collaborations provided the new African leaders a security advantage from the ideologically structured bipolar Cold War (1947 and 1990) system, which helped to forestall internal challenges to the authority of states in Africa. Consequently, the "peace" that the Cold War period provided newly independent states became a missed opportunity on the part of postindependence African leaders. And, since former colonizers of African territories did not completely leave after independence, they were able to collaborate with many African leaders from Zaire to Ghana. Consequently, many African leaders did not seize the advantage of the Cold War "security umbrella" to build sovereign nations out of the many ethnicities and religions that Europeans cobbled together as states. With the end of the Cold War, old problems that had been ignored during the colonization schemes resurfaced (Musah and Fayemi 2000: 15), "where boundaries of a state rarely match boundaries of a 'nation' and borders bear little congruence with the ethnic distribution of their component units." The result was that having failed to build sovereign nations along the lines of European states' formations, African leaders had to rely on their former colonizers and an international network of arms dealers for military and security support, and in some cases, for mercenaries to maintain security to quell established internal challenges to (illiberal) state authority. As Musah and Fayemi (ibid.) notes, "In effect, any challenge to the state's supreme authority can only elicit a perpetual condition of anarchy, the solution of which resides in one size, fit-all conflict management service package and all you have to do is 'Dial an army.'" And, when those armies were not up to the task, African leaders followed the old colonial European model of contracting mercenaries, for example, in the civil wars in the Democratic Republic of the Congo, Nigeria, Angola, and Chad, to fight off challengers to state power.

And, as the Europeans engaged each other in externally orchestrated internal wars within Africa, they also introduced some non-African populations and co-opted indigenous Africans in their war efforts. The result can only be said to be part of the use of mercenaries in these "external" European internal wars fought inside the African continent. For example, in earlier encounters between the British and the Germans in East Africa, a British emissary stated that "we find the Punjabis in action west of the Tsavo River [in Kenya] displaying great gallantry, but suffering very severe losses from machine guns which they bravely but vainly endeavoured [*sic*] to charge down at the point of the bayonet. . . . [And in] Rhodesia [Zimbabwe], as far back as August 1914, for example, . . . The Germans are now enrolling the Rugaruga, that old fighting, and raiding people. The soldiers are as great a pack of scoundrels as one can meet, and now to these are added the Rugaruga."[7]

Thus, contemporary civil wars in Africa have their roots in the "civil wars" Europeans fought with each other during the colonial period within Africa. The use of regular European soldiers, co-opted indigenous fighters, and mercenaries did not end with colonialism in Africa. For example, as the civil war erupted in postindependent Angola in 1975, the United States, covertly and in collaboration with Apartheid South Africa and companies like De Beers were involved, directly and indirectly, in the war against the Popular Movement for the Liberation of Angola, MPLA that had fought the Portuguese for the independence of Angola. The MPLA government also received external support from Cuba's Fidel Castro government, which did not sit well with the United States that backed the apartheid South African forces and the National

Union for the Total Independence of Angola (UNITA) that fought against the MPLA. The Angolan war of independence against the Portuguese dates back to 1961 and metamorphosed into a civil war between the MPLA and UNITA in 1975, which ended in 2002. The human dimensions of that war and its atrocities led the United Nations Children's Fund (UNCF) to declare that Angola was the worst place to be a child in 2002. During that period in Angola and despite abundant natural resources like diamonds, oil, and so on that made external interests like Chevron and De Beers wealthy, almost 30 percent of Angola's children died before they reached the age of six. As Renner (2002: 149) states, nearly half of all Angolan children were underweight, two-thirds of Angolans scraped by on less than a dollar a day, and 42 percent of adults were illiterate. The international dimensions of the Angolan civil war were not only reflected in the connections to Portuguese colonialism stemming from the "tea and macaroons" partition of the continent, but the conflict also endured because various Western and African states provided arms and support for the warring factions over the control of natural resources without regard for the children and future of Angola. And, while the death of Jonas Savimbi in April 2002 forced UNITA to bring an end to the civil war, the legacies of external collaborators in Angola continued as both private firms and the government resorted to hiring mercenaries to maintain basic security functions of the government.

Further north, the civil war in Sudan in the 1980s was a battle over resources control that dates back to the British expeditions scouting for strategic resources in the region. As Michael Renner notes, the discovery of oil in 1980 in the rebel-controlled region was sufficient for the government to restart the war in 1983, "leading to more than 2 million deaths, 1 million refugees, and 4.5 million people displaced" (ibid.). With the export of oil in 1999, government revenues increased and tripled military expenditure, mostly in arms acquisition. Also, with the complicity of oil companies, the army was able to use the oil industry, roads, and airstrips to escalate the conflict with a scorched-earth strategy to "depopulate oil-producing and potentially oil-rich areas in southern Sudan . . . bombing villages, destroying harvests, and looting livestock, and . . . encouraging intertribal warfare by supplying arms to some factions" (ibid. 150). It is significant to note that the international dimensions of the conflicts in Sudan and Angola are not isolated cases in Africa. Preferring to focus on their profits from oil and other minerals exploration and arms shipments to both governments and rebels, multinational corporations, and in many instances, with the knowledge of their home governments, continue to ignore the human misery generated by African conflicts.

In the Doba region of Chad where oil production started in 2003, the suppression of a revolt sent hundreds of innocent citizens to their death.

The Chadian government bought weapons with part of its $25 million in "bonuses" paid by ExxonMobil, Chevron, and Petronas in 2000. Just as the multinational corporations do not concern themselves with the connection between their operations and conflicts/resource leakage in Africa, they also seem unperturbed about the impact of their activities on the environment and the inhabitants of the regions. For example, and as Michael Renner states, the "construction of a pipeline to Cameroon's coast threatens the land of the Baka Pygmies and may bring poaching and unregulated logging to Atlantic rainforest areas" (ibid.). However, oil drilling and the pipeline that was built to transport crude petroleum from landlocked Chad through Cameroon, to the Gulf of Guinea and the South Atlantic Coasts for export, brought resources to the autocratic government of Chad's Idriss Deby to fight challengers to state power. And, with the support of France and the United States, Deby's staying in power was more important than the potential conflict such pipeline projects were predicted to have on local communities. And with Deby's death in battle in 2021, Chad remains politically unstable as terrorists and insurgents continue their challenge to state power.

Thus, conflicts that were previously funded by the ideologically structured Cold War system in the Democratic Republic of the Congo, Angola, Ethiopia, and other states in Africa are now funded by illegal external resource extractions. The readily available profit-hungry global market for illegal resource extractions and arms trafficking has become an inducement for many disaffected and disgruntled elements within various African states to "initiate violence not to overthrow a government, but to gain and maintain control over lucrative resources . . . in [their] societies" (ibid.). And if the state government and legitimate authority have collapsed or are compromised by external resource extraction interests as is the case in Sierra Leone, Liberia, and the Democratic Republic of Congo, the challenges to the state's power intensifies into outright civil wars.

However, ideologically based rebel movements that dominated during the civil wars in Guinea Bissau and the early part of the war in Angola and Mozambique are now rare in Africa. Instead, many of the contemporary challenges to state power and authority in Africa, for example, the DRC, Chad, Nigeria, and Central Africa Republic are individuals who do not compete for the "hearts and minds" of the local people but rather employ boy-soldiers, young girls as sex slaves and fighters for their cause (Renner 2002: 151–153). Consequently, deliberate (e.g., the Chinese) external, "non-interference in domestic affairs" in Africa, and global businesses directly or indirectly sanction violence across the continent. In addition, regional "non-interference" practices, for example, in the DRC and Angola, create a "vicious cycle in which the spoils of resource exploitation fund war and violence; and war provides continued access to these resources"[8] without accountability or remorse on the part of the political elites, rebels, or international business entities that benefit from such violence.

An interesting example of the intersection of external and internal dynamics, as a primary cause of civil wars, is the Democratic Republic of the Congo, where the longest peacekeeping operations of the United Nations were first deployed in 1999. That operation remains in operation in the country as various efforts to curb national and regional conflicts in the DRC remain unabated. In a sense, the civil war in the DRC dates back to the massacres of Africans in the late 1880s on the orders of King Leopold and the subsequent inhumane exploitation of the Congolese and their resources by the Belgian state between 1908 and 1960. Indeed, as de Waal (2002: 117) notes:

> European mercenaries came to prominence in the Congolese civil wars of the 1960s. The Katangan secessionist leader Moise Tshombe employed the services of about 650 Belgian mercenaries to fight against the government of Patrice Lumumba. The Belgian company Union Miniere du Haut Katanga was the paymaster, also employing soldiers of fortune from Britain, France, Germany and South Africa. . . . [And, one of the chief mercenaries,] "Mad Mike" Hoare who commanded a contingent of 64 British mercenaries later went on to serve Tshombe in fighting against Laurent Kabila's forces in eastern Congo, supporting Ian Smith's Rhodesia against the nationalist struggle, and attempting a coup d'état in the Seychelles.

These incessant external involvements, sometimes in collaboration with domestic actors have forestalled political and economic progress in African states, sustained intrastate wars over minerals like diamonds and cobalt, and led to the elimination of potential good leaders like Patrice Lumumba in the DRC.

The purchase of "hot" commodities, like conflict diamonds from Angola and Liberia by De Beers and affiliated entities, and exploration of various minerals by Chinese government-owned or sponsored businesses across Africa, help to sustain civil wars in Sub-Saharan Africa. The latter is similar to the overt support of the government of South Africa during the apartheid era by De Beers. The provision of revenues to the government by oil companies like Chevron and Elf in Angola and ExxonMobil in Chad often ignore the fact that such revenues are often used for arms purchases that help sustain and, in many cases, escalate existing local conflicts. For example, companies like Shell have been complicit in the Nigerian government's brutal and repressive tactics against its citizens like the 1995 hanging of Ken Saro Wiwa in the oil-rich delta region. Other companies like Sabena Airlines fly Coltan (the raw materials used in cell-phone chips) from conflict zones like the Democratic Republic of Congo to Europe without regard to internationally agreed-upon principles of good business practice. For example, based on their conservative figures, De Beers estimated that in 1999, blood diamonds accounted for about 40 percent of the world's rough diamond production of $6.8 billion. When other illegally mined diamonds in nonconflict areas that attract the attention of global businesses are added, the estimates are as high as 10–20 percent more (Renner 2002: 156). As Ibrahim Kamara, former Sierra Leone's UN Ambassador, said in July 2000: "We have always maintained that the conflict is not about ideology, tribal or regional difference. . . . The root of the conflict is and remains diamonds, diamonds, and diamonds" (Cited in Renner 2002: 157). Indeed, in the case of Sierra Leone, it was not just the local rebels that depended on the diamonds, but rogue states like Liberia under Charles Taylor, as well as the Guinean and Gambian governments, participated in the illicit introduction of the RUF diamonds into the world market (Renner 2002: 159).

Therefore, because of the weak nature of the states in the continent, civil wars in Africa are not merely internal; rather, they are the convergence of external and internal forces in illicit and illegal plundering of resources in conflict zones in Africa that continue to fuel violence, especially against civilians. In the case of the Democratic Republic of the Congo, lawlessness and a weak central authority that can be traced back to the 1960s enabled the recent invasion of the country by several regional countries including Rwanda, Angola, Zimbabwe, and Uganda. That situation enabled Rwanda and Uganda to become major exporters and foreign exchange-earners in raw materials, which are yet to be proven to exist in significant quantities in those countries. "Uganda, for instance, is re-exporting gold, diamonds, cassiterite, coltan, coffee, tea, timber, elephant tusks, and medicinal barks" (ibid. 160–161) and the Congolese government continues to use "its natural resources as payments in kind to buy weapons" (ibid.). And, as part of a package for obtaining Chinese military equipment, the Congolese signed on to a joint venture with a Chinese company. In addition, "the Congolese government has granted several concessions, including offshore oil wells to Angola, diamond, and cobalt to Zimbabwe, and a share of a diamond mine to Namibia" (ibid.). The question is: Why are successive governments in various states in Africa continuing to choose violence and civil wars against their citizens and by extension, themselves since political independence? Why are governments in Africa seemingly unable to maintain sustainable security and socioeconomic stability in their respective states? A plausible explanation is that after several decades of political independence, the onset of indigenous civil wars in Africa requires that we examine the nature of the state and the intersection between the external and internal dynamics as primary and determinant causes of civil wars in Africa. For the rest of this chapter, I will: (1) examine contending explanations of civil wars and violence in Africa; (2) offer a structural explanation for civil wars in Africa; and (3) based on the assumption that if we know why civil wars occur, we have a better chance of ending them. I will conclude with suggestions for future research on war and peace in Africa.

CONTENDING EXPLANATIONS OF CIVIL WARS IN AFRICA

Much of the literature on civil wars in Africa read more like the Indian parable of the elephant and six blind men. Neither the nature nor the causes of civil wars are well understood and explained. Like the six blind men touching and describing different parts of the elephant, each blind man can only render his decision about the elephant based on how the part he touches/feels to him. To a community of blind persons, the conclusion that the part reflects the whole is similar to the literature on civil wars, especially civil wars on the African continent. The onset of civil wars and violent conflicts in Africa have been attributed to external military interventions in support of rebel movements, religious extremism, ethnic and regional rivalries, terrorism, internal power struggles overpopulation, internal repression and oppression of minority groups, demands for democratic participation, human rights violations, poverty, economic mismanagement, and corruption in many states in Africa.[9] Referencing World Bank economic data, Furley (1995: 4) argues that "A more basic and long-term cause of conflict [in Africa] has been the catastrophic economic performance of many African countries." One of the situations where economic dimensions, especially control of tropical timber, gold, and diamond mining, politicized ethnic differences, regional and external interventions in the civil wars converged in Liberia and the Sierra Leonean civil wars.

Richards (1995: 137) documents that, "a small group of about 100 and 150 commandos (mainly Liberians, but assisted by Burkinabes and Sierra Leoneans, trained . . . in guerrilla camps in Benghazi and Burkina Faso . . . and infiltrated Nimba County in north-east Liberia from Cote d'Ivoire on December 24, 1989, to launch a military campaign against the government of Samuel Doe." The organizational platform for the war in Liberia was the National Patriotic Front of Liberia (NPFL) whose twin organization was the Revolutionary United Front (RUF) of Sierra Leone. According to Richards (1995: 137), as RUF had earlier fought alongside the NPFL in the early stages of the Liberian civil war with assistance from Burkinabe mercenaries and NPFL military personnel, the RUF "crossed the eastern border of Sierra Leone from territory controlled by the NPFL on March 23, 1991" to start the campaign that was to last 10 years—costing tens of thousands of lives and leaving many survivors without limbs.

Contextually, a small group of individuals from Liberia and Sierra Leone, both countries with support from regional actors to overthrow "corrupt governments" resulted in massive human rights violations, economic desta-bilization, inhumane use of child soldiers in war fronts, terrorism against civilian populations, illegal minerals mining, and a legacy of massive loss of hundreds of thousands of lives between 1989 and 2003. Scholars, like Sikod (2008: 200), see location as an incubator and an explanation of civil wars in Sub-Saharan Africa. Linking economic issues like greed to poverty as a framework for explaining food insecurity in the region, Sikod(2000: 200) argues that "sub-Saharan Africa is a breeding place for rebel groups . . . [and that] this apparent propensity for violence is a root cause of the poverty and stagnation or retrogression the economies of the sub-region face. Nearly half the population of sub-Saharan Africa lives below the international poverty line, a higher percentage than in any other region."

Also, ethnic and ideological reasons are often seen by some scholars as causes of civil wars in Africa. For example, while the late Mazrui (1986: 291)[10] argued that most, if not all, civil wars in Africa are caused by ethnic-ity, Mason, McLaughlin Mitchell, and Prorok (2016: 2–3) argue that civil wars can be categorized based on what motivates rebel groups to fight and the nature of the population that is mobilized in support of the cause. In that respect, Mason, Mitchell, and Prorok identify three types of inter-related categories—ideological, secessionist, and ethnic revolutions. They argue that while these categories seek to replace existing regimes, ethnic seces-sion is different because its fight with the government is over *territory* for an independent homeland. For example, Biafrans during the Nigerian civil war, 1967–1970, Eritreans in the Ethiopian civil war, 1974–1991, and South Sudanese in Sudan's second civil war, (1983–2011), during which, and fol-lowing a referendum in 2011, the South Sudanese opted for independence from Northern Sudan. Mason, Mitchell, and Prorok argue that "The distinc-tion between ideological and ethnic civil wars revolves around the issues that motivated the rebellion and the identity basis of the rebel movement. In an *ideological civil war*, the issues that divide rebels from government usually concern matters of governance and extreme inequality in the distribution of land, wealth, income, and political power" (ibid. 4). Other examples, based on the foregoing characterization of ideologically based civil wars, include Nicaragua, Cambodia, Vietnam, and El Salvador. The antiapartheid struggle in South Africa, the revolutionary movements against the Portuguese in Mozambique, Cape Verde, and Guinea Bissau are other cases that qualify but are not often seen as civil wars by Western scholars.

Lastly, ethnic revolutions are similar to ideological revolutions that aim to overthrow an existing regime. The core difference of ethnic from ideologi-cal revolutions is the emphasis on "ethnicity as a source of identity for the rebels," which sometimes embeds class dynamics in the composition of the ruling elite. For example, "one ethnic group dominates the government and monopolizes high-status positions in the economy while other ethnic groups are relegated to subordinate status in the economy and the political arena" (ibid.) And, in their examination of "Patterns of Armed Conflict since 1945," Gleditsch, Melander, and Urdal, (2016: 28) state that:

> A majority of civil conflicts in the post-World War II period have been fought along ethnic lines. This is true for almost all conflicts over territory but even for almost half of the conflicts over the government. That does not, however, imply that ethnicity itself is the primary issue in civil wars. On the contrary, such conflicts appear to be driven by the same grievances that account for other conflicts as well (e.g., weak state, low income), but ethnicity provides a stable pattern of identification that facilitates the organization of an insurgency.

However, while these different categories of ethnic and ideological causes of civil wars are helpful, they do not adequately explain the robustness of ethnicity and ideological causes of war. If anything, the notion that ethnic or ideological differences are causes of particular civil wars or violent conflicts in Africa needs further research and explanation. Similarly, Young's idea (2016: 37) that grievances may be, "an intuitively plausible explanation for civil war as they are constantly expressed by the rebels and are often what media report as the underlying cause of conflict," is not convincing. While the correlational studies may point to those conclusions, they do not answer the question of why every state, including the United States and the United Kingdom, characterized by ethnic and ideological/political differences, and economic or social grievances, do not engage in civil wars, especially since the twentieth century! The question is: Why are most civil wars occurring in economically developing postcolonial states, especially in Africa?

In addition to the issue of ethnicity as a cause of civil wars, some scholars (Gleditsch 2011; Hendrix et al. 2016; Roble 2011; Uvin 1996) argue that civil wars in Africa are explained by some aspect of environmental variables like renewal and nonrenewal of natural resources, like diamonds and gold, access to freshwater, drought, arable land, temperatures, climate change, desertification, deforestation, and even decreasing level of rainfalls.[11] Compared with the foregoing studies about the nature of sociopolitical characteristics of societies and group grievances, and also environmental factors, I agree with Gurr (1970) that the structure of governance in a given society and the peaceful or violent institutional processes that a government uses to respond to demands by its citizens will determine if an aggrieved group follows a legal process in resolving its grievances or launches civil war against the government. And, while many statistical studies that find a relationship between environmental factors and civil wars are intellectually exciting; I contend that how droughts, access to freshwater, natural resources, deforestation, and changing temperatures result in the onset of civil wars in Africa reflect more the nature of states in Africa and how leadership capacities to translate ideas into enforceable policies that determine issues of war and peace. Given the histories of disruption to political structures and governance in most African states, it seems more plausible that environmental factors are symptoms of deep-rooted challenges to governance processes rather than direct causes of civil wars in Africa. We will return to this issue in the paragraphs below.

Structural Explanations of Civil Wars in Africa

In his study of the causes of crisis and violence in Africa, Nathan (2001: 22), argues that it is the responsibility of government and its associated institutions to carry out their core functions of "conflict management" and the "business of governance." Crises and violence are more likely in situations where a state cannot carry out its security functions. And, "Where a state lacks the resources and expertise to resolve disputes and grievances, manage competition and protect the rights of citizens, individuals and groups may resort to violence. If the state is too weak to maintain law and order, then criminal activity and private security arrangements may flourish" (ibid. 4) as evident in the cases of the DRC, Nigeria, Somalia, Libya, and Liberia. Nathan concludes that a "large-scale violence in the national sphere should be viewed as a manifestation of intra-state crises that arise from four structural conditions: authoritarian rule; the marginalization of minorities; relative socio-economic deprivation; and weak states" (ibid. 22).

While Nathan's assessment of the causes of crises and violence across Africa is important, it is necessary to pay attention to issues of the legitimacy of the state in Africa, government's marginalization of specific minorities, impacts of relative socioeconomic deprivation to enable a better understanding of how well those states manage conflict resolution within their territories. It is the nature of the state and the larger external contexts in which contemporary African states were created and have learned to exist within the structure of the international system that partly explain the incessant intrastate conflicts in the continent. The impacts of external interests within existing international political and economic structures that continue to be sources of support for, and legitimacy crises for, African *governments* deserve closer evaluation on how they exert influence on the perpetrators—both states and non-state actors—of civil wars in Africa. A more objective and thorough examination of the external, regional, and domestic causes of the weakness of *states* in Africa that leave the state and its people vulnerable to violence from civil wars would be helpful for any attempt to reduce the impacts of intrastate wars in the continent.

Although modern realism is not monolithic, many scholars agree that the idea of *power* is often measured by the strength of a state's military force, and how that power is distributed in the international system determines the relevance of a state. From Hans Morgenthau, E. H. Carr, Kenneth Waltz, John Mearsheimer to Stephen Krasner, the world is a dangerous place and is, structurally, without a government to make and enforce rules against states' behavior in the international system. Given the anarchic condition, the need for survival and security compels states to protect themselves against external threats. And given the distribution of powers in the anarchic structure of the international system, effective states are those with the capability to protect their sovereignty against external domination and interference. Therefore, weak states are confined to the periphery of global politics and are vulnerable to external interference by more powerful states,[12] even as such external interference does not always lead to the resolution of internal grievances among domestic actors jockeying for power within the state; for example, in Libya and Somalia.

Thus, for many structural realists like Kenneth Waltz , Robert Gilpin , J. D. Singer, John Mearsheimer, and Krasner, the anarchy of the system forms the central analytical premise for explaining international behavior and outcomes. Underlying that framework are some common assumptions which are based on the claims that the anarchic international system structure is (a) comprised of sovereign states whose foreign policies are shaped primarily by security concerns;[13] (b) that states are rational in their policies, and as unitary actors with stable power-maximizing preferences, states rely on the threat or use of military force to achieve their international objectives relative to other states; and (c) that states will consistently prefer security over welfare in an international system whose ordering mechanism is based on balances of power.[14]

Therefore, realists generally agree that given anarchy, war retains its utility in the current international system, just as it did in the classical Greek city-states. And, as Krasner (1992: 39) points out, "the basic explanation for the behavior of states is the distribution of power in the international system and the place of a given state within that distribution."

Although the basic analytical premise of both classical and contemporary realists is largely similar, the goals of foreign policy tend to differ. For example, classical realists argue that *power* is the most important objective of a state's foreign policy in the international political system. For neorealists, *power* is a means that states employ for the attainment of their core policy objective; security. Strongly opposing the classical realists' focus on individual human nature, Waltz insists that this view fails to consider the international *political structure* and its mechanisms that constrain states' behavior. As a result, Waltz (1979) defines political structure according to the principles by which a particular system is ordered. For him, the first principle is anarchy. This view leads to a definition of political structures that is based on the specification of functions of differentiated units. However, he argues that in the resulting anarchic system of international politics, there are no specifications of functions since consequent sovereign units are all alike. Also, since states are the central units, they are similar in their functions. Finally, the similarity of functions will exist despite unit differences in the power of states. Indeed, states are truly equal solely and in terms of the legal concept of sovereignty.

According to Waltz, the distribution of capabilities across units (Waltz 1979: 97) becomes the defining factor for political structure. This means that changes in the system will only result from (a) changes in capabilities or (b) changes in the ordering principles within the system itself. But, given the overall fact of inequality among nations, major states will tend to exercise their powers while the small states will either bandwagon or form alliances as a strategy for economic and political survival. This suggests that structural constraints (which give rise to self-help) may explain why these methods are repeatedly used despite differences in the persons and the states that use them. For Waltz (1979: 118), a self-help system is "one in which those who do not help themselves, or who do so less effectively than others, will fail to prosper, will lay themselves open to dangers, will suffer." He insists that "Fear of such unwanted consequences stimulates states to behave in ways that tend toward the creation of balances of power" (Ibid.) Given that states are seen as the main actors in the international system, realists assert that those who control the affairs of each state will work to increase the power of their states relative to other states for whatever reason, but largely for state security and power.

According to Waltz (1979: 91–92), constructing a sensible theory that richly describes the motivations and actions of states within the constraining structure of the international system characterized by anarchy, one has to assume that "survival is a prerequisite to achieving any goals that states may have." Analytically, therefore, for realism, war is inevitable; especially war in the international system. As a theory for explaining why war is likely in the international system, realism's explanation of the structure of the international system holds insights for understanding both interstate and *intrastate conflicts*; and, with some qualification, explains intrastate wars in Africa. The architecture or structure of the international political system is not only constituted by anarchy, states, and non-state actors but also by the interactions between states. And, contrary to realists like Kenneth Waltz and John Mearsheimer, interactions between government leaders and non-state domestic actors inside a state have a direct impact on a state's behavior beyond its borders. This means that irrespective of a state's international capabilities, the motive of a leader at the domestic level, especially the desire to hold on to power, has a direct impact on that state's internal and external decisions for war or peace. As members of the international political structure, the lessons leaders of less powerful states learn about how to resolve thorny issues like war and, about access to mercenaries and arms shipments, impact their internal and regional decisions on matters of peace and security, which realism ignores. Compared to major state leaders like those of the United States, Britain, and Germany, one of the lessons leaders of less powerful states like Nigeria, Angola, and the Democratic Republic of the Congo learn from their interactions within the international system is that survival and security for major states are the same as survival and security for the leaders of less powerful states. This suggests that, to the world community, the narrative of state sovereignty is presented for purposes of seeking and securing power and security. However, power and security are necessary tools that support major states to "maintain state security." This means that internally, less powerful state leaders can, and do use the "non-interference in the domestic affairs of sovereign states" to deploy externally generated tools like military training, weapons, and mercenaries to suppress domestic challengers to state security, power, and authority. Thus, leaders acting within domestic political structures, especially on security issue areas, mimic the observed policy behavior of major states' intervention actions in Iraq, Afghanistan, Kuwait, Nicaragua, Libya, and Somalia, albeit on a lower scale, to protect individual leaders' authority and security. The difference is that while major states' actions are mostly interstate, African leaders' actions are mainly intrastate. Thus, as Gourevitch (1978: 911) argues, sometimes "the international system is not only a consequence of domestic politics and structures but a cause of them." Consequently, to the extent that contemporary African states were created by major states and brought into the international system, the major states' agencies, mercenaries, arms dealers, and corporate economic entities interactions with African states, leaders, and non-state entities, act as external actors with significant impact on civil wars in Africa. How external and internal political and economic factors complement each other and their connections to the onset of civil wars in Africa are of important theoretical interest and can be explained within a *modified* realist paradigm.

Modified Structural Realism

Analytically, the concept of *modified structural realism* (see Krasner 1985) is a useful theoretical approach to bridge the gap between the domestic and the international system structures to explain how learning and interactions between states in these structures impact state behavior and actions at the domestic and international levels. Thus, in their interactions with states in Africa, major states like Britain, the United States, Belgium, and France, exert material influence on states engaged in civil wars in Africa; a basic fact that realists ignore.[15] Stephen Krasner uses structural realism to move beyond conventional realists' view of regimes as an inconsequential cause of state behavior. He acknowledges that political power is important for creating international regimes but argues that once created, regimes not only can assume a life of their own but could indeed be altered by new members. Significant here is that new actors within a given structure are in a relationship in which their interactions yield new knowledge and ideas that are useful for maintaining or changing their behavior.[16] In their interactions within the structure of the international system, African leaders have learned that to the extent they represent an entity abstractly referred to as a *sovereign state*, and to the extent that their territories contain one or two important natural resources that are desired by other states in the international system, they can be as illiberal as they choose in their governance of their people. Such determinations include having access to weapons and finances to set up domestic institutions of violence to eliminate domestic threats. Furthermore, with the end of the Cold War, African leaders have also learned that the massive availability of experienced military personnel and weapons, especially from Eastern Europe following the fall of the former Soviet Union, can also be a source of certain nuisances as those mercenaries and weapons find their ways into the hands of organized terrorists and legitimately organized regional groups seeking to challenge the legitimacy of their governments. For example, Boko Haram in the northeast region of Nigeria and Al-Shabab across East Africa dominate and control ungoverned spaces and use the power of such groups to also shield them from government forces. Making sense of these lessons requires that we understand how the national/domestic level (second-image) interacts with the international level to produce political insecurity in the form of civil wars in Africa.

Consistent with Peter Gourevitch's "second image reversed," *modified* structural realism bridges the gap between international and internal sources of state behavior. The second image, which is the domestic arena of politics, provides robust data for understanding states' decision to wage war against other states and to wage war against perceived domestic enemies of the state, that is,, an organized civil or intrastate war. In this respect, constructivists' insights about structures that are permissive of interactive learning, ideas, and knowledge are helpful complements to understanding how interactions between states in the international system do not often stop at the state borders but often have direct impacts on states' domestic behavior, as Saddam Hussein of Iraq decision to invade Kuwait and South Africa under apartheid used violence against domestic opposition and mercenaries against the frontline states in southern Africa demonstrate. Here, Alexander Wendt's (1999: 79) critical insights, that first and second-image theory "have the virtue of implying that practices determine the character of anarchy . . . . [And that] . . . only if human or domestic factors cause A to attack B will B have to defend itself," speaks to the intersubjective influence of interactions on agents who find themselves at the intersection between domestic and international structures. Thus, given that "identities are the basis of interests," (ibid. 82) it is the social structure of a system that makes individual (in their different roles) actions possible. This suggests that the architecture of anarchy merely provides a framework for states to interact with other states; learn from each other to shape their actions and reactions based on the observed behavior of other states and non-state actors in the system. And, as Wendt (1995: 76) argues, this shows "how agency and interaction produce and reproduce structures of shared knowledge over time." Thus, international politics is assumed to be both a consequence and a cause of domestic politics, especially for African countries whose postcolonial state structures continue to be impacted by the intersubjective existence of these states with their former colonizers in the same international political and economic structures.

In *Territoriality, Citizenship, and Peacebuilding* (see Kalu et al. 2013), my coauthors and I focused on understanding and explaining the sources of territorial origins of African civil conflicts and ways for mitigating territorially induced conflicts in the continent. As the Cold War ended, the capacity of states in Africa to protect their territorial boundaries, citizens, and resources was called into question in the form of constant civil wars that became problematic in several locations. These conflicts or wars ranged from interstate wars, intrastate conflicts characterized by secessionist movements, irredentism, coups, countercoups, genocide, wars of liberation, to resource-based wars. Although some of the civil conflicts such as those in the DRC, Northern Uganda, Sudan, and Somalia were well-known, others like the civil conflicts in Morocco/Western Sahara, Senegal/Casamance, and several economic and religious-based conflicts in Jos Plateau and Niger Delta in Nigeria, and the several decades-long conflicts involving the Karamajong of Uganda with the Pokot of Kenya over grazing land in the Kenya-Uganda border, are less known to the international community. Understanding the territorial origins of African civil conflicts based on existing empirical measures that define *war* as those involving at least 1,000 battle deaths makes nonsense of the millions of people's lives that have in various dimensions been wasted as a result of territorially induced conflicts/wars in Africa.[17] Although many of the conflicts defy empirical measures, they have a persistent impact on the capacity of states to function and citizens' ability to live normal lives as the cases of those trapped in ongoing conflicts in the Casamance region of Senegal, Western Sahara, against Morocco and Northeastern Nigeria demonstrate.

Indeed, as Furley and May (2006: 3) have noted, based on the use of 1,000 battle-related deaths as a definition of war, only three wars—Somalia against Ethiopia (1977–1978), Ethiopia against Eritrea (1998–2002), and Uganda against Tanzania (1978–1979) qualify as interstate wars in Africa. Thus, while scholarly definitions of interstate conflicts reflect a bias toward major state conflicts whose wars largely reflect territorial battles, these definitions do not help us understand persistent conflicts in Africa, issues of intrastate wars, and opportunistic wars for resource control, instead of the soul of the state, continue unabated. As Carl von Clausewitz states, "war has a chameleon-like character;" it changes its color to a degree in each case, but also has a "remarkable trinity of irrational action, rational action, and chance" (quoted in Furley and May 2006: 4). I argue that in the case of Africa, contemporary civil wars and conflicts are rooted in the territorial contestations that started with European imperial wars over resources in the continent that were ultimately resolved during the Berlin Conference. Those external decisions remain impactful in several intrastate conflicts, for example, in the Democratic Republic of the Congo, and the various mercenaries employed by external entities in Africa. Those externally derived intrastate conflicts are persistent, albeit at a low level of intensity in some states but are all related to the absence of effective mediating and transparent governance institutions and processes embedded with the needs and values of local citizens. This is important because the colonial state institutions and structures bequeathed to Africans at the end of World War II were violent political and economic contraptions designed for continuous exploitation of the new political territories with redrawn geographic boundaries that each European state received at the Berlin Conference in 1884/1885. To be sure, colonial flags and symbols in Africa are formally gone, but colonial flags and symbols are no longer necessary because each state has its indigenous coconspirators who are continuously equipped with guns, access to international markets for guns and mercenaries, and foreign aids for the exploitation of ordinary citizens and resources. In such situations, instability becomes a profitable commodity that is manufactured and distributed locally.

The contemporary history of the African continent is one of the conflicts rooted in European states' imposition of arbitrary and illogical boundaries on various nations and ethnic-nationalities over "macaroons and tea" and discussions on European interests and imaginations over land, that they knew little of, according to Lord Salisbury.[18] While the exercise at the Berlin Conference secured exploitation opportunities for Europeans on the African continent, it also provided an opportunity for Europeans to not resort to war in European heartland with each other and laid the foundation for new, persistent, and varied forms of conflicts in Africa. Analytically, the varied causes of conflicts in the continent's rich social formations are often explained in ethnic terms to include struggles for economic/environmental resources, poor institutions of governance, and issues of identities including religion, language, and racial differences. However, a significant feature of the colonially created and unreformed states is the existence of permissive international political structures within their boundaries that continue to breathe life into civil wars in Africa. As legitimate legacies of the intrastate wars that colonialists initiated and co-opted Africans to fight against each other and other rival colonialists, contemporary Africa's civil wars find historical coherence and ancestral evidence in a handful of the organizations that were used to secure the European states' and private companies' interests during Africa's colonization. Some examples include The King's African Rifles, Royal Africa Corps, West African Frontier Force,[19] and mercenaries[20] and organizations such as the Kulinda Security Ltd in Kenya and Malawi, WatchGuard in Zambia, Compagnie Internationale in the DRC, "Five Commando" in Belgian Congo, Security Advisory Services Ltd in Angola, "Force Omega" in Benin, Executive Outcomes in Namibia, Botswana, and Mozambique, Levdan in Congo-Brazzaville, and Sandline International in Sierra Leone.

Understanding the structural causes of these violent conflicts requires a closer examination of Africa's different regions and states and how external and internal political structures provide opportunities for exploitative relationships and civil wars in Africa. Such an approach is important because it will enable researchers and scholars to move away from analytically perceiving the African continent as one country. Since several European states participated in the colonization project, an objective intellectual "remapping" of the continent will liberate thinking about Africa as culturally monolithic and in turn impact external political, social, and economic perceptions of Africa and Africans, internally and externally. Renewing perspectives will, in turn, enable more effective studies of Africa's civil wars, territorial disagreements, economic, political, and or ideological conflicts which have gone on far longer in some areas than others in different parts of the continent.

Given poor infrastructure across the Sub-Sahara African region and relevant governments' inattention to logistical issues of national development, the likelihood that any given country will be involved in a civil war in Africa is much higher than the likelihood that it will be involved in an international war. Also, most African countries do not have the state capacity to wage effective internal or external wars without external involvement in the form of arms supplies and or hiring of mercenaries and equipment. Indeed, except for six nations' (Rwanda, Uganda, Angola, Zimbabwe, and Sudan) intervention in the DRC in 1996, empire-imposed arbitrary boundaries in Africa have been quite resilient—with only two successful challenges—in Ethiopia and the resulting independence for Eritrea in 1991 and Sudan with the result of political independence for Southern Sudan in 2011. While leaders of South

Sudan plunged the new country into civil war shortly after independence, the Eritrean border with Ethiopia remains restive in 2021 as the central government of Ethiopia is once again involved in a civil war; this time against the Tigrayan rebels whose regional proximity has put Eritreans on alert.

Based on my visits and conversations with citizens in various states in Africa (e.g., Cameroon, Angola, Ethiopia, Kenya, Uganda, South Sudan, Sierra Leone, and Nigeria), the vast majority of the people are hungry to live in peace and stability. Across Africa, ordinary citizens seek collaborative efforts across ethnic, religious, and regional lines to build peaceful nations out of the many ethnic groups cobbled together in the formation of their current states. However, it is the few bad actors with access to powerful weapons, funding from private mining firms, mercenaries, and permissive international political structures that fuel civil wars within "sovereign boundaries" of states led by individuals that are coconspirators in destroying nation-building in Africa. Contextually, state formations out of internal struggles similar to those that created Britain, France, and the United States were able to construct institutions with effective conflict management infrastructure, common national narratives and values, and the capacity to turn different groups into a nation, and build economic and political development institutions that work for the citizens. Contemporary Africa's civil conflicts erupt largely because of the nature of state formation that was imposed by colonizing European states. At independence, those new African states were not reconstituted to serve the local people. Instead, since the African state is a colonial product, both the states and governments have either been slow or, at worst, failed in nation-building across the continent. Against that backdrop, issues of climate change, ethnicity, ideological incongruities, institutional problems, unreformed governance, and economic structures, corruption, and other variables are intervening variables that spark civil conflicts. And depending on the state/territory, these intervening variables intensify civil conflicts into civil wars in the postcolonial African state. In addition to these variables, and under the notion of sovereignty, the skewed international political structure on the continent offers state leaders the opportunity to reign freely. And many in Africa do so illiberally, especially against "perceived enemies of state power." Rather than nation-building, it is such illiberal decisions that often sustain the energies for civil conflicts and wars in the continent.

CONCLUSION

Explaining unsustainable peace after civil wars across Africa and the persistent eruptions of violent conflicts involve understanding the context of the unresolved issues in postcolonial states in Africa. That context is Africa's need to redesign the geographic spaces crafted by the European states and how the permissive structure of the international political system provides opportunities for collaboration between external and internal *destroyers of nation-building* efforts in Africa.

Understanding the colonial state and how its consequent postcolonial character sustains civil violence rather than peace and stability is helpful. One of the realities of the "macaroons and tea" boundaries-mapping exercises in Berlin, Germany, in 1884–1885, is the colonial states that Europeans bequeathed to Africans at independence. The undemocratic processes by which the Europeans created states in Africa are reflected in the illiberal nature of contemporary states in the continent. Generally,[21] the colonial state was effectively organized to act unilaterally on issues of public policy regarding territorial matters. Significant to the illiberal approach, the appointment of individuals to key positions in the public sectors and supporting the control of economic production processes by specific individuals/firms without regard to existing modes of social indigenous relations across Africa. According to Ake (1996: 1–3), the colonial state "attended to the supply of labor, sometimes resorting to forced labor; it churned out administrative instruments and legislated taxes to induce the breakup of traditional social relations of production, the atomization of society, and the process of proletarianization." Educationally, the colonial state ensured that Africans received only minimal training sufficient for performing assigned tasks and "remain steadfast in the performance of their often tedious and disagreeable tasks" (ibid.) Infrastructurally, the colonial state "built roads, railways, and ports to facilitate the collection and export of commodities as well as the import of manufactured goods" (ibid.), without considerations of sectoral and urban/rural linkages. In addition, the colonial states "sold commodities through commodity boards," and "controlled every aspect of the colonial economy tightly to maintain . . . power and domination and to realize the economic objectives of colonization" (ibid).

As the objectives of the colonial state formation in Africa were mainly resources exploitation, very little attention was paid to the political and economic welfare of colonized peoples. Institutionally, there were no sustainable mediating structures established between the state and the people that could be relied on for just settlements of conflicts. In addition, existing traditional religious and cultural institutions for conflicts mediation and violence prevention among community members were not integrated into the evolving colonial or postcolonial state institutions. Thus, at independence, a major legacy of the colonial state was the coercive, exploitative, violence-prone institutions that postcolonial leaders quickly co-opted as tools for competitive advantage against one another in ways that intensified the power vacuum created at decolonization. Consequently, it is difficult to differentiate between the impacts of the institutional processes of colonial and postcolonial states on contemporary Africa and Africans. As Ake(1996: 1–3) notes, the post-colonial state "continues to be totalistic in scope," remains an "apparatus of violence," with a very "narrow social base," and relies on institutions of coercion rather than authority in making and implementing public policy. In many instances, it is as if the colonialists have not left Africa. Consequently, Ake argues that the struggle for political independence, "more often than not . . . was a matter of the colonizers' accepting the inevitable and orchestrat-ing a handover of government to their chosen African successors, successors who could be trusted to share their values and be attentive to their interests" (Ake 1996: 4–5).

And, as indicated above, postcolonial leaders of African states are famil-iar with the lessons that prevailing international structures teach on how to maintain power using security as the synecdoche for national interest. And, "while agitating to overthrow the colonial regime," the nationalists and their various coalitions also worked hard to block one another from appropriating the power of the colonial state. With time, *"their attention turned from the colonial regime to one another* (my italics); and eventually, the competition among these groups came to dominate political life, while the colonial power, now resigned to the demise of colonialism, became a referee rather than the opponent" (ibid.). That change in focus resulted in significant shifts in both the meaning and location of national security. In that regard, to the extent that the interest of former colonial powers was not threatened, they have not impeded the supply of necessary weapons of war, mercenaries, and machines in support of civil wars in states like Angola, the DRC, Libya, Somalia, Ethiopia, Nigeria, South Sudan, Rwanda, and elsewhere in the continent.

Although there are many variables—religion, corruption, ethnic differ-ences, greed, relative deprivation, climate change, and so on—that vie as causal explanations for civil wars in Africa, it is the nature of the unreformed colonial state and the consequent ineffective postcolonial institutions, gov-ernance structures, and processes that continue as triggers and challenges to state authorities in the form of civil wars. Second, while Africa's postcolonial states are accepted and recognized in the international system that privileges "states qua states" decisions, the *laissez-faire* international political and eco-nomic structures, supported by longstanding permissive intrusions into exter-nally weak states like those in Africa. Characterized, from their beginnings, by porous economic borders and politically ungoverned spaces, postcolonial African states present opportunities for non-state actors with access to weap-ons to challenge their power and authority.

Given the undemocratic process by which the postcolonial states in Africa were created, it is important that African states avoid the onset of civil wars by ensuring that the government and its various institutions adopt transparent rules and mechanisms for managing conflicts. That could be achieved by crafting a historical narrative of common goals and visions that will enable citizens to believe in their country and to eschew efforts by internal and external bad actors to initiate civil wars in Africa. A reformed state provides effective services to its people, and its institutions are perceived by the citizens to be fair and just in managing economic, political, religious, and other contested issues. Scholars like Douglas North (1990), Mancur Olson (1993, 1996), and Ghani and Lockhart (2008: 150–151) argue that effective, States "build infrastructure, foster . . . human capital, provide . . . security, establish . . . monetary policy, and govern . . . honestly and transparently. Other measures include the use of tariffs for the protection of infant industries, . . . [and the State also] can . . . step in to provide certain functions that the market is unwilling to perform." Effective states not only provide the infrastructure and human capital needed to run a productive economy, their rules and institutions ensure attention to the protection and smooth function of processes and interests of key players, including labor and capital.

Lastly, effective states in Africa must work persistently to ensure that internal and external agreements that are voluntarily reached between citizens and corporations domiciled in non-African states are implemented in ways that serve the interest of citizens of relevant countries. This is important because privately negotiated agreements, for example, between private individuals from the United Kingdom, the United States, France, and individuals or firms in a given African state, are likely to lead to corruption and, eventually internal violence and civil wars, as the cases of the DRC, Angola, Sierra Leone, and Liberia demonstrate. Indeed, without reforming and strengthening state institutions to act in the interest of the country, leaders cede important decisions to external entities who may not always think in terms of that country's national interests. Though tactically brilliant, some of the mercenaries often fail woefully, leaving the theater with their profits and the mess to the local people to clean up. As Peleman (2000: 158), writes:

> When the then military junta in Sierra Leone, the National Provisional Ruling Council, contacted a number of private military companies to provide assistance, the British company J&S Franklin came up with a strong proposal to train the Sierra Leone military and subcontracted the operation to Jersey-based Gurkha Security Guards. GSG arrived in January 1995 under the command of an American and two British veteran military officers. The American, Bob Mackenzie, was in charge of the operation. . . . his long experience, [included] first in Vietnam and then as a commander in the Rhodesian Special Air Service and some of the crack units of the apartheid South African Defence Force in Mozambique.

In the case of Sierra Leone, the country is still trying to recover from the eleven years of civil war that left legacies of many amputees, civil war babies resulting from rape, destroyed political and economic infrastructure, and with much depleted human capital to reconstruct and run the daily affairs of government.

The interactive external-internal lessons that should have been learned from civil wars in Angola, the DRC, Nigeria, Liberia, Rwanda, Somalia, Sierra Leone, and South Sudan is that, while civil wars are a lucrative business for a few external and internal bad actors, it is destructive, costly in material and human resources, and that post-civil wars leave legacies of distrust that are difficult to overcome. And, for peace and security scholars, paying attention to how the external interactions with the internal factors gel to cause violent civil wars in Africa requires not less but more research with insights from structural theories of international relations within the realist paradigm.

The externally imposed state boundaries that created states in Africa were maintained during the colonial period by violence. The colonial state was effective in carrying out its extractive functions because participating European states were effective in using internal collaborators in various locations in Africa to help do their political, economic, and violent biddings. As enumerated above, these involved several wars between participating European states that also co-opted indigenous Africans in East, West, Central, and Southern African regions. The strategies, weapons, and decisions were crafted by Europeans, and as needed, mercenaries, for example, the Punjabis, the *Rugaruga* fighters, and soldiers from other regions in the continent and ethnic groups were introduced in the wars. For example, the wars between the British and the Germans in Rhodesia and Nyasaland; the Germans, Belgians, and Britain in Tanzania and Zanzibar; and between the British and the French and the British and Germans in West Africa were instances that co-opted Africans' supplemented colonial armies such as the King's Africa Rifles, Royal Africa Corps, and the West African Frontier Force in colonial wars.

Without redrawing the colonial boundaries or reforming the culture of violence that postcolonial states in Africa inherited from the European colonizing schemes, contemporary Africans will continue to exist within an international political system that prolongs the use of longstanding permissive structures to provide access to profit and glory-seeking mercenaries and weapons, enabling autocratic leaders to destroy their countries by waging civil wars against any domestic challengers to their power. Thus, future research on civil wars in Africa must look beyond the state boundaries to the international political-economic structures to identify and explain the connections between external interests and persistent civil war occurrences in Africa. Some questions that could guide such research include What might

Africa's export ledger on minerals and natural resources tell us about previous and ongoing civil wars in the continent? What lessons do African leaders learn from dominant leaders of states that control the international political structures and their willingness to permit access to international markets/banks to deposit ill-gotten wealth from African states, and subsequent use of such wealth for the purchase of arms and mercenaries for more wars? An important connection between external and internal actors and conflicts in Africa documented in Peleman (2000: 157–158) is revealing and worth quoting in detail:

> J.-R. Boulle is a French-speaking, Mauritius-born, British citizen living in Monaco. His mining operations are run through 100 per cent owned Luxembourg-based investment company, MIL Investments, and his principal portfolio manager is based in a small apartment in the Belgian city of Antwerp, the world's main diamond trading centre. Boulle started his career as a buyer for De Beers Consolidated Mines but made his fortune when he began a partnership with another controversial mining investor, Robert Friedland. Friedland is the financial wizard and Vancouver stock exchange guru behind DiamondWorks, the holding company of the Branch Mining and Branch Energy enterprises that pop up whenever and wherever the mercenary companies, Sandline International and Executive Outcomes, are active. His investment company, Ivanhoe Capital Investments, helped DiamondWorks to raise capital for its mining operations. Friedland's brother, Eric, was the chairman and chief executive of DiamondWorks until July 1997. Boulle, in one way or the other, usually heads for the same trouble spots as Robert Friedland. He became seriously rich when he and Friedland started prospecting for diamonds in Canada's Voisey Bay. Their company, Diamond Field Resources, never produced a single carat of diamonds but metaphorically struck gold when it discovered one of the world's richest nickel deposits. In 1995 Diamond Field Resources was sold to Inco, a giant nickel producer, in Canada's biggest ever corporate takeover worth CAN$3.1 billion. Both Boulle's and Friedland's shares were suddenly worth hundreds of millions of dollars. Jean-Raymond Boulle is also a controlling shareholder of the American public company Nord Resources, which has its corporate offices in Dayton, Ohio. Nord owns 50 per cent of one of the world's rare titanium oxide mines, Sierra Rutile Ltd, in Sierra Leone. Boulle bought a considerable part of Nord Resources' shares in early 1996, at a time that the Sierra Rutile mine had already been overrun and was under the control of the rebels of the Revolutionary United Front.

Objectively looking beyond specific state boundaries for the connections between profit-motivated external actors to examine their connections to domestic destroyers of nation-building efforts might help researchers on civil wars in Africa untangle the web weaved by Peleman's narrative above. Both Executive Outcomes (EO) and Sandline International have been associated at different times with mercenary activities in South Africa, Angola, Botswana, Malawi, Mozambique Sierra Leone, Uganda, Zaire, Zambia.[22] To be sure, the ultimate policy responsibility for understanding and ending civil wars and violent conflicts in Africa resides with African states and their leaders. And, even as they disagree on how to evaluate different assumptions, for example, between realists and constructivists, the role of scholars is to shine a light on the issues and ways that will enable policymakers to craft more enabling and productive systems. Overcoming a major part of the challenges of insecurity and civil wars in Africa must include internal state reconstitution that results in nation-building by leaders willing to learn that systems structures and their impacts on decisions for war and peace depend on what such leaders make of it. The fact that weapons and mercenaries are permitted within the international system structures does not mean they are good products for African states. What citizens across many African states are asking for is an effective state whose policies will provide a framework for ongoing conflict management. Such a state would start by building a national narrative of positive possibilities and opportunities and, where appropriate, acquire private property for public purposes. It will build infrastructure, foster human capital development, provide security, have effective monetary policies, and regulate the exploration and exploitation of resources from its land for the benefit of its citizens. Africans are asking for a state that is capable of helping citizens navigate the oceans of the international political economy. Put differently, citizens across the continent of Africa are asking for their governments to govern honestly and transparently. They want states that can step in to provide certain functions that the current market is unwilling or unable to provide (see Ghani and Lockhart 2008: 150–151).

Reconstituting and/or reforming colonial states and their institutions of governance will enhance the capacity of these states to provide security for the citizens, which is most needed for people to go about their economic interests. I am not familiar with ordinary citizens in any African country who are agitating for war and violent repressions. If anything, citizens will follow anything that looks and sounds like peace and stability, not war, which explains what looks like excessive religiosity across the continent. States and institutions that are transparent and just in applying the rule of law that protects citizens' interests and works to provide security are likely to make civil war a thing of the past in Africa. Such states will be effective in the enforcement of institutional constraints on the behaviors of public and private officials and will not accommodate rent-seeking and corruption in public and private spaces (see Mbaku 2004, 2007).

Transcending the problems of Africa's inherited colonial state structures and their consequent weakness within the structure of the international political system requires transparent rules—especially for formal institutions—and norms of social engagement that promote states' institutional effectiveness and politics of inclusion will bring an end to the persistence of civil wars in Africa. For the African states, achieving that would require ambitious, yet practical solutions that reconstruct and reconstitute the structure of the state to provide institutions and judicial structures that (1) minimize political opportunism by state custodians; (2) enhance peaceful coexistence of diverse ethnic-nationalities across relevant countries; (3) provide an enabling platform, for example, protection of physical security and the availability of affordable educational institutions for citizens to engage in productive activities; (4) reduce pervasive state presence by promoting the emergence of a robust civil society that can serve as a check on the exercise of a government agency; and (5) through targeted investments, provide opportunities for citizens to explore and exploit existing resources for the good of their country rather than enhancing the welfare of outside forces. By reconstructing and restructuring the African states on constitutionally based norms and rules of social engagement, hopes for state effectiveness as a platform for ending civil wars can be achieved. Until then, more research from a *modified* structural realist perspective is needed on how interactions between African states and leaders and between major states and non-state actors in the international system are related to the onset and persistence of civil wars in Africa.

NOTES

1. The Correlates of War project and data are available here: www.correlatesofwar.org. For empirical studies on civil war, see Paul Collier, "Doing Well Out of War," Paper Prepared for the Conference on Economic Agendas in Civil Wars, London, 1999, 26–27 April 26–27, 1999. Available at www.worldbank.org/research /conflict/papers/econagendas.pdf; Paul Collier, "Economic Causes of Civil Conflict and Their Implications for Policy," 2000a. Available at www.worldbank.org/research /conflict/papers/civilconflict.pdf; Paul Collier, "Rebellion as a Quasi-Criminal Activity," *Journal of Conflict Resolution*, 44, no. 6 (2000b): 839–853; and Paul Collier and Anne Hoeffler, "On the Incidence of Civil War in Africa," *Journal of Conflict Resolution*, 46, no. 1 (2000): 13–28.

2. While the original speech was published in *The Times* (UK), easily accessible reference is Robert McCorquodale, and Raul Pangalangan, "Pushing Back the Limitations of Territorial Boundaries," *European Journal of International Law*, 12, no. 5 (2001): 867.

3. See "Fighting in Nigeria," *Aberdeen Journal*, January 12, 1909, 5. *British Library Newspapers*, link.gale.com/apps/doc/ID3229775570/BNCN?u=ucriverside&

sid=bookmark-BNCN&xid=13d2a59d. Accessed September 2, 2021. "Natives Repulsed by British and German Troops" is the sub-title of the diplomatic dispatch on the fighting as reported in the Aberdeen Journal.

4. For the full report, see "Nigerian Boundary," *Western Times*, January 13, 1909, 4. *British Library Newspapers*, link.gale.com/apps/doc/EN3220834213/BNCN?u=uc riverside&sid=bookmark-BNCN&xid=04bfbe8d. Accessed September 2, 2021.

5. Ibid.

6. See "In the Cameroons," *Western Daily Press*, December 19, 1914, 6. *British Library Newspapers*, link.gale.com/apps/doc/JL3242436662/BNCN?u=ucriverside& sid=bookmark-BNCN&xid=b7c0415b. Accessed September 4, 2021.

7. For more detailed entries on this type of encounters, see "Can Germans Hold East Africa?" *Dundee Courier*, August 8, 1916, 2. *British Library Newspapers*, link. gale.com/apps/doc/JE3227748351/BNCN?u=ucriverside&sid=bookmark-BNCN&xi d=58476fd9. Accessed September 6, 2021. The Rugaruga referred to in this report were mainly local groups of irregular fighters recruited by Europeans to fight along-side soldiers in East Africa. In essence, they were mercenaries and did not come from a particular ethnic group. For a deeper grasp of the extent colonial and postcolonial interests have used mercenaries in pursuit of their interests, see Musah and Fayemi (cited in note no. 7) and, *Demilitarizing The Mind: African Agendas for Peace and Security*, edited by Alex de Waal (Trenton, NJ: Africa World Press, 2002).

8. Ibid. Also, see Foundation for Security Development in Africa (FOSDA), *FOCUS*: A Quarterly Bulletin (September–December, 2001, with focus on small arms proliferation in West Africa. FOSDA reported that "A shipment of 68 tons of weapons legally sold by Ukraine to Burkina Faso in March 1999 immediately was sent to Liberia and on to the Revolutionary United Front (RUF) in Sierra Leone, countries that [were] under mandatory U.N. embargoes." Also, the activities of Exotic Tropical Timber Enterprise run by Ukrainian arms and diamond dealer, Leonid Minin are well-known to Liberians. But during the civil war in Liberia, the chief player in illicit timber trade was the Oriental Timber CO. (OTC) that controlled 43 percent of Liberia's forests; and the company was implicated in smuggling weapons to the RUF along its timber roads. As Renner notes, "OTC [was] not only engaged in rapacious clear-cutting methods, it . . . also bulldozed through homes and entire villages with little warning and no compensation. Forest management and replanting efforts [were] virtually absent," in the drive for profits without accountability in conflict zones. See Renner, op. cit., 159.

9. For different perspectives on these variables, see Oliver Furley, ed., *Conflict in Africa* (London: Tauris Academic Studies, 1995). Especially, see the contributions on Angola, Liberia and Sierra Leone, Namibia, and Uganda.

10. Ali Mazrui, *The Africans: A Triple Heritage* (Boston, MA: Little, Brown and Co., 1986), 291. Also, see James D. Fearon, and David D. Laitin, "Ethnicity, Insurgency, and Civil War," *American Political Science Review*, 97, no. 1 (2003): 75–90; and, James D. Fearon, and David D. Laitin, "Sons of the Soil, Migrants, and Civil War," *World Development*, 39, no. 2 (2011): 199–211.

11. For relevant quantitative studies on the relationship between the environment and civil wars in Africa, see Muhaydin Ahmed Roble, "Somalia's Famine Contributes to Popular Revolt against al-Shabaab Militants," *Terrorism Monitor*,

9, no. 32 (2011): 3–5; Peter Uvin, "Tragedy in Rwanda: The Political Ecology of Conflict," *Environment: Science and Policy for Sustainable Development*, 38, no. 3 (1996): 7–29; Nils Petter Gleditsch, "Whither or Weather? Climate Change and Conflict." see the special issue of the *Journal of Peace Research*, 49, no. 1 (2012): 3–9; and Cullen Hendrix, Scott Gates, and Halvard Buhaug, "Environment and Conflict," in *What Do We Know About Civil Wars?* edited by T. David Mason, and Sara McLaughlin Mitchell (Lanham, MD: Rowman & Littlefield 2016), 231–246..

12. For a similar argument, see David Strang, "Anomaly and Commonplace in European Expansion: Realist and Institutional Accounts," *International Organization*, 45 (1991): 143–62.

13. In *Theory of International Politics* (New York: Random House, 1979), 91–92, Kenneth Waltz argues that for constructing a sensible theory that richly describes the motivations and actions of states within the constraining structure of the international system characterized by anarchy, one has to assume that "survival is a prerequisite to achieving any goals that states may have." This assumption makes it possible to analyze the behavior of states in trade and or other cooperative policies *as if* such policies are premised on the security need of states.

14. For a focused analysis of realist nonsecurity argument, see Kelechi A. Kalu, *Economic Development and Nigerian Foreign Policy* (Lewiston, NY: The Edwin Mellen Press, 2000).

15. Major states' influence within the international structure is a precursor to the influence that non-state actors with home offices and headquarters in the advanced countries have in their own interactions with leaders from less advanced countries. Thus, non-state actors, like oil companies and natural resources exploration firms, and mercenaries often act on the understanding that they will be protected by their home countries in their interactions with leaders of less advanced countries. This means that individuals carry their state superiority and inequality in their personal interactions with citizens from advanced/less advanced countries.

16. See Alexander Wendt. "Anarchy is What States Make of It: The Social Construction of Power Politics," in *Theory and Structure in International Political Economy*, edited by Charles Lipson and Benjamin J. Cohen (Cambridge, MA: MIT Press, 1999), 75–109. Wendt's original essay was published in *International Organization*, 46, no. 2 (1992): 391–425.

17. This section benefits from my work on the *Territoriality, Citizenship and Peacebuilding* project.

18. See note no. 2.

19. See notes nos. 4 and 6.

20. For a full list of known mercenaries and groups that employed them, see Appendix 1 in *Mercenaries: An African Security Dilemma*, edited by Abdel-Fatau Musah, and J. Kayode Fayemi (London: Pluto Press, 2000), 265–274.

21. This section benefits from my recent work on peace and conflict issues in Africa. See Kelechi Kalu, "Re-Building Peace after Conflicts in Africa," in *Peacebuilding in Africa: The Post-Conflict State and its Multidimensional Crises*, edited by Kelechi A. Kalu and George Klay Kieh, Jr. (Lanham, MD: Lexington

Books, 2021), 1–24. Also, see Claude Ake, *Democracy and Development in Africa* (Washington, DC: The Brookings Institution Press, 1996).
22. See note no. 21. For more specific connections between external individuals and corporations and internal mercenary activities across Africa, see Johan Peleman. "Mining for Serious Trouble: Jean-Raymond Boulle and his Corporate Empire Project," in *Mercenaries: An African Security Dilemma*, edited by Abdel-Fatau Musah, and J. Kayode Fayemi (London: Pluto Press, 2000), 155–168. Also, for a sanitized external involvement in mining activities in Africa with human security consequences for citizens in Africa, see especially chapter 7 on "Finance and Cyanide" in Tom Burgis, *The Looting Machine: Warlords, Oligarchs, Corporations, Smugglers, and the Theft of Africa's Wealth* (New York: Public Affairs, 2015).

REFERENCES

"African Expeditions." 1828, May 23. *Cambridge Chronicle and Journal*, 3421(2): 4. *British Library Newspapers*, link.gale.com/apps/doc/IS3245279922/BNCN?u=uc riverside&sid=bookmark-BNCN&xid=96f20437. Accessed September 6, 2021.
Ake, Claude. 1996. *Democracy and Development in Africa*. Washington, DC: The Brookings Institution Press.
Burgis, Tom. 2015. *The Looting Machine: Warlords, Oligarchs, Corporations, Smugglers, and the Theft of Africa's Wealth*. New York: Public Affairs.
de Waal, Alex. 2002. *Demilitarizing The Mind: African Agendas for Peace and Security*. Trenton, NJ: Africa World Press.
"Fighting in Nigeria." *Aberdeen Journal*, January 12, 1909, 5. *British Library Newspapers*, link.gale.com/apps/doc/ID3229775570/BNCN?u=ucriverside&sid=b ookmark-BNCN&xid=13d2a59d. Accessed September 2, 2021.
Furley, Oliver, ed. 1995. *Conflict in Africa*. London: Tauris Academic Studies.
Furley, Oliver, and Roy May. 2006. *Ending Africa's Wars: Progressing to Peace*. Burlington, VT: Ashgate Publishing.
Ghani, Ashraf, and Clare Lockhart. 2008. *Fixing Failed States: A Framework for Rebuilding a Fractured World*. New York: Oxford University Press.
Gleditsch, Nils Petter, Erik Melander, and Henrik Urdal. 2016. "Introduction—Patterns of Armed Conflict Since 1945." In *What Do We know about Civil Wars?* edited by T. David Mason and Sara McLaughlin Mitchell, 15–32. Lanham, MD: Rowman & Littlefield.
Gourevitch, Peter. 1978. "The Second Image Reversed: The International Sources of Domestic Politics." *International Organization*, 32(4): 881–912.
Gurr, Ted Robert. 1970. *Why Men Rebel*. Princeton, NJ: Princeton University Press.
Kalu, Kelechi A. 2021. "Re-Building Peace after Conflicts in Africa." In *Peacebuilding in Africa: The Post-Conflict State and its Multidimensional Crises*, edited by Kelechi A. Kalu and George Klay Kieh, Jr., 1–23. Lanham, MD: Lexington Books.
Kalu, Kelechi, Ufo Okeke Uzodike, David Kraybill, and John Moolakkattu, eds. 2013. *Territoriality, Citizenship and Peacebuilding: Perspectives on Challenges to Peace in Africa*. London, UK: Adonis & Abbey Publishers Ltd.

Krasner, Stephen. 1985. *Structural Conflict: The Third World Against Global Liberalism*. Berkeley: University of California Press.

Krasner, Stephen. 1992. "Realism, Imperialism, and Democracy: A Response to Gilbert." *Political Theory*, 20(1): 38–52.

Mason, T. David, and Sara McLaughlin Mitchell, eds. 2016. *What Do We Know About Civil Wars?* Lanham, MD: Rowman & Littlefield.

Matthews, Robert O. 1970. "Interstate Conflicts in Africa: A Review." *International Organization*, 24(2): 335–360.

Mazrui, Ali. 1986. *The Africans: A Triple Heritage*. Boston, MA: Little, Brown and Co.

Mbaku, John Mukum. 2004. *Institutions and Development in Africa*. Trenton, NJ: Africa World Press.

Mbaku, John Mukum. 2007. *Corruption in Africa: Causes, Consequences, and Cleanups*. New York: Lexington Books.

Musah, Abdel-Fatau, and J. Kayode Fayemi. 2000. "Africa in Search of Security: Mercenaries and Conflicts – An Overview." In *Mercenaries: An African Security Dilemma*, edited by Abdel-Fatau Musah, and J. Kayode Fayemi, 13–42. London: Pluto Press.

Nathan, Laurie. 2001. *The Four Horsemen of the Apocalypse: The Structural Causes of Crisis and Violencein Africa*. Center for Conflict Resolution, Cape Town University, Track Two, Vol. 10, No. 2.

Nathan, Laurie. 2012. "The Causes of Civil War: The False Logic of Collier and Hoeffler." *South Africa Review of Sociology*, 39(2): 262–275.

North, Douglas C. 1990. *Institutions, Institutional Change and Economic Performance*. Cambridge: Cambridge University Press.

Olson, Mancur. 1993. "Dictatorship, Democracy and Development." *The American Political Science Review*, 87(3): 567–576.

Olson, Mancur. 1996. "Big Bills Left on the Sidewalk: Why Some Nations are Rich, and Others are Poor." *Journal of Economic Perspective*, 10(2): 3–24.

Peleman, Johan. 2000. "Mining for Serious Trouble: Jean-Raymond Boulle and His Corporate Empire Project." In *Mercenaries: An African Security Dilemma*, edited by Abdel-Fatau Musah, and J. Kayode Fayemi, 155–168. London: Pluto Press.

Renner, Michael. 2002. "Breaking the Link Between Resources and Repression." In *State of the World 2002*, edited by Linda Starke, 150–173. New York: W. W. Norton & Company.

Richards, Paul. 1995. "Rebellion in Liberia and Sierra Leone: A Crisis of Youth?" In *Conflict in Africa*, edited by Oliver Furley, 134–170. London: Tauris Academic Studies.

Sikod, Fondo. 2008. "Conflicts & Implications for Poverty & Food Security Policies in Africa." In *The Roots of African Conflicts: The Causes & Costs*, edited by Alfred Nhema & Paul Tiyambe Zeleza, 199–213. Oxford, UK: James Currey Ltd.

Stone, Deborah. 2020. *Counting: How We Use Numbers to Decide What Matters*. New York: W. W. Norton & Company.

Waltz, Kenneth. 1979. *Theory of International Politics.* New York: Random House.

Wendt, Alexander. 1995. "Constructing International Politics." *International Security*, 20(1): 71–81.

Young, Joseph K. 2016. "Antecedents of Civil War Onset: Greed, Grievances, and State Repression." In *What Do We know about Civil Wars?* edited by T. David Mason and Sara McLaughlin Mitchell, 33–42. Lanham, MD: Rowman & Littlefield.

Part II

CASE STUDIES

Chapter 2

Burundi

A Continuum of Civil Wars and Violence

Dawn Nagar

This chapter examines the root causes and forces that led to Burundi's civil wars between the periods 1961 and 2000, and subsequent peace agreements from 2002 to 2006. Numerous scholars and practitioners have over several decades extensively written on Burundi's violent conflicts, which mainly framed the debates in large accounts of in-depth internal ethno-political intra- and interstate regional monstrosities, while skimming over German and Belgian colonization of Burundi and elsewhere in the Great Lakes region. While other scholars start the debate of Africa's colonization as a dependent partner that engages in the systems of their colonizers willingly, with no analyses of how it came about that 10 million people were killed during Belgium's rule during the late 1800s.[1] Nowhere near is any recourse proffered by such progressive scholars, but rather they refrained from advocating action against colonization's masterminds of grotesque rule, except for the singling out of the United States and the World Bank in 1988 for their extensive funding involvement of millions of U.S. dollars and the objection raised by the U.S. House of Representatives with regard to Burundi's violence (Lemarchand 1989: 28). Nowhere near are Burundi's colonizers really called out for their decades of repulsive colonial rule, beset as the very core *problematique* of Burundi's ensuing genocides. Instead, such dialogues begin with the 1966 overthrow of the monarchy, while the roots of disaster are being placed at the doorstep of Burundi's ruling elites solely (Lemarchand Winter 1989).

This chapter underscores that Burundi's horrendous fate was sealed, owing to the colonizers' brutality of oppression, of divide and rule that would become anchored in a deeply rooted divided nation engulfed in hatred for generations to come, with centuries witnessing a continuum of intra- and inter-state wars, the slaughter of hundreds of thousands of children and adults of all ages, and into its foreseeable future. While those who have committed

grave atrocities with impunity remain unchallenged, owing to the negotiations' difficulties experienced during Burundi's fragile 2001 to 2006 peace
agreements, which is an excuse for achieving a "false peace." In order to stop
such horrendous deeds, those who commit acts of genocide must be held
to account; similarly those who have orchestrated decades of ethnic hatred
by capitalizing on ethnic differences, but remain unscathed, must be held to
account for major contributions that led to Burundi's genocides. This chapter
is clear: it is imperative that reparations are paid to Burundi for genocidal
actions, by the agents of colonization and they (the colonizers) be held to
account for their actions as the perpetrators and masterminds of human
injustice, and as the proponents of discriminatory administrative practices,
for their despotic actions in Burundi, and in the Great Lakes that have led to,
and a direct cause of, the hatred and violent clashes that ensued between and
among Burundi's ethnic groups, and within the Great Lakes.

Such acts are the very foundation of Burundi's economic depression felt
today, remaining the poorest country globally with a gross domestic product (GDP) of US$3 billion and gross national income (GNI) per capita of
US$280 in 2018, while colonization's masters remain resource-loaded enjoy-
ing wealth, prosperity, and freedom from civil wars and genocides. It is further imperative that as reparations to Ethiopia was paid by Italy (Nagar 2018:
502), and as Germany has been giving for their accounts in World War I and
among others, so too Burundi should seek reparations for the grievous colonization actions, as well as those international actors who have aided Burundi's
violent conflicts through the training of the country's one-sided military personnel, with reasons given of protecting the country, but en masse killings in
Burundi were pursued by the very same army. These reparations must be an
example that is set and be a deterrent to such powerful actors especially those
largely responsible for Africa's UN peacekeeping missions such as France or
those that use veto power for parochial ends, leading to further oppression of
resource-rich, economically poor fragile states that are forced to be at their
mercy. This chapter is therefore clear that responsibility and accountability of
particularly Germany and Belgium ought to be singled out as direct contributors and accomplices to the violence and ensuing genocides that occurred in
Burundi since 1961, 1965, 1972, 1988, 1993, and smaller scale killings ever
since that must be taken up by the African Union (AU) and by the New-York-
based African Group of Ambassadors at the United Nations (UN) and brought
before the Hague-based International Criminal Court (ICC). The Benjamin
Whitaker Report (1985: 9) of the Commission on Human Rights Sub-
Commission on Prevention of Discrimination and Protection of Minorities at
the UN Economic and Social Council's (ECOSOC) 38th session—an event
that took place over three decades ago pursuant to an ECOSOC Resolution
1983/33 of May 27, 1983—has never really been enacted, regardless of

Burundi's several appearances made at the UN Security Council (UN SC). Nowhere near has any civil servants of the UN secretary-general, nor special envoys or UN Missions (UN doc S/2005/158) and among others, provided real account with clear recourse concerning Burundi's colonial masters but rather skimming accounts that merely indicate that the colonial power has contributed to the "situation" by giving the most important administrative posts to Tutsis rather than Hutus (UN doc S/1995/157 February 24, 1995: 10) nor acutely enacting the Benjamin Whitaker Report (UN doc S/2005/158).

The UN politicking platform – as the highest global throne, is being used as a stage where a careful dance is being conducted by third-world resource-exploited submissive government subjects, who believe that they are the victims of realpolitik; thus dance around, and bows down before, their first-world neocolonial paymasters and carefully tiptoe around Burundi's genocides, while evading the monstrosity of hundreds of thousands of people killed with entire families wiped out, including women, children, infants, and elderly persons, and thrown into latrines; others bound hand and foot and thrown into rivers; others bound and locked up and burned alive, school children and peasant farmers burned alive, while the hatred and bloodthirsty merciless killings are being discussed (UN doc S/1995/157 1995: 21). But, the most important paragraphs that ought to be mentioned are evaded, such as the Whitaker Report (1985: 7), that clearly notes:

Genocide, particularly of indigenous peoples, has also often occurred as a consequence of colonialism, with racism and ethnic prejudice commonly being predisposing factors. In some cases occupying forces maintained their authority by the terror of a perpetual threat of massacre. Examples could occur either at home or overseas: the English for example massacred native populations in Ireland, Scotland and Wales in order to deter resistance and to "clear" land for seizure, and the British also almost wholly exterminated the indigenous people when colonizing Tasmania as late at the start of the nineteenth century. Africa, Australasia and the Americas witnessed numerous other examples. The effect of genocide can be achieved in different ways: today, insensitive economic exploitation can threaten the extinction of some surviving indigenous peoples

THEORETICAL FRAMEWORK

The definition of a civil war supports the main arguments of this chapter, which is viewed as a high-intensity conflict involving regular armed forces that are organized and sustained at a large scale, resulting in a number of casualties, depletion of state resources, economic collapse, with subdued interventions by outside powers (Regan 2000; von Einsiedel 2017). The chapter situates ethnicity and ethno-political discourses in the theories of ethnic conflict, which belongs to the broader category of identity conflict that underscores that ethnic conflict exists in situations where people are mobilized against others on the basis of their ethnic identity, which can result in ethnic mobilization among groups that can lead to genocide (Gurr and Harff 2000).

The flipside of ethnic theories, which is that of modernization theory, argues that greater political and economic interaction among people and widespread communication networks could break down people's parochial identities within ethnic groups and replace those identities with loyalties to national political constituencies. The key proponents of genocide in Burundi (and Rwanda) have been owing to modernization, with the sole purpose of creating division through increasing economic inequality of goods among people, resulting in uneven socioeconomic development, used interchangeably that creates an awareness of socioeconomic differences among ethnic groups, which results in an elevation of differences evident among groups, leading to heightened resentment among groups, and over an extended period of time, result in civil wars (Gurr and Harff 2000).

Moreover, groups victimized by governments would ultimately group together and become politically inclined and involved in an attempt to overthrow the government or a state that could lead to prolonged civil wars in pursuit of power. In understanding ethno-political mobilization and civil wars, five critical precursors could lead to either a genocide or a politicide, which includes persistence of cleavages that exists among ethnic groups; elites having a history of relying on repression to maintain power; elites using their power to reward groups differently for their loyalty; the society had a recent experience of political upheaval, for example, a revolution, or a defeat in war; and exclusionary ideologies that arise defining target groups as expendable. If all five factors are present, ethno-political conflict is likely to have genocidal consequences (Gurr and Harf 2000).

Indeed, Burundi's protracted conflicts are a manifestation of violent interactions between and among different ethnic groups, with a history of oppression experienced by some groups, evolving over two consecutive centuries. These conflicts are deep-rooted in nature, embedded in the deprivation of basic human needs, and structural causes of inadequate weak government institutions. The county's deep-rooted ethnic conflicts make it extremely difficult and almost impossible to resolve. Intrastate conflicts have spiraled into three civil wars since the 1960s, 1980s, and 1990s. Deep-rooted conflict with an ethnic dimension is acutely outlined by John Burton's prevention theories (Burton 1987, 1990). Burton underscores that latent or protracted deep-rooted conflict, when facilitated or managed must address all the conflict actors' basic needs, which include security, identity, autonomy, recognition, belonging, and participation. These needs are much more important than basic needs of food and shelter (Burton 1990) but are ontological, which means that groups in conflict must have them in order to exist peacefully and which must be accommodated effectively when addressing deep-rooted conflicts or disputes. Burundi's deep-rooted conflicts are squarely linked to the deprivation of such basic human needs that have remained unmet for decades, which led to fear, mistrust, and frustrations giving rise to violent conflicts becoming the driving force of interactions.

Burundi's deep-rooted conflicts have thus reached an overt level or stage of conflict that is almost impossible to resolve. Burundi's peace is being challenged, by its spiraling nature, encompassing various dimensions of numerous factors and actors that have been drawn into the conflict, and therefore is persistent. Indeed, the progressive nature in killing off Burundi's population by its own people evolved over two centuries with various actors underpinned by the same discourse of ethnicity and political power struggles of unmet basic human needs—security, identity, autonomy, recognition, belonging and participation, with core socioeconomic and security concerns, as well as political objectives unmet.

Burundi as one of the most densely populated states in Africa comprises three ethnic groups: Hutu (85%), Tutsis (14%), and Twa (1%). Burundi's conflicts have been infused within a myriad of challenges, including a ruthless monarchy heightened by ethnopolitically charged government leaders, using ethnicity, religion, the police, and army as the driving forces to incite violence and remain in power at all costs. Prior to Belgium's invasion in the Great Lakes, Burundi was a kingdom of highly stratified feudal social structures. However, groups remained contented with the system. The Tutsi population of largely pastoral people believed to have migrated from Ethiopia several hundred years ago and followed the arrival of Hutu people. Ethnic superiority was introduced by the Tutsi cattle herders that resulted in the creation of a feudal landholding system (Ubugererwa) (United States Institute of Peace 2004). Of the Tutsi class of cattle owners was a small group inferior to the majority of the Tutsi and more oriented toward pastoralism and not intermarrying with other Tutsi. These divisions marked a precolonial history of ethnic superiority within the Tutsi and a further ethnic superiority between the Tutsi and Hutu people; divisions which the Belgians and Germans would use in their favor during their forced despotic reign (Reyntjens 2000). Then there was a minority group, where intermarriage between the Hutu and Tutsi ethnic groups created a mixed ethnic distinction: the 1 percent of the population of mixed Hutu—Tutsi—the Twa (pygmy) people. The third ethnic group consisting of 85 percent Hutu population is believed to be Bantu-speaking people that migrated to Burundi about 1,000 years ago.

The king (mwami) was chosen from princely dynastic families (ganwa), who appointed local chiefs and wisemen that exercised judicial authority over each hill (Bashinganhaye) (Reyntjens 2000). Some scholars though believe that Burundi's ethnic groups in the anthropological sense do not qualify as ethnic, since the Hutus, Tutsis, and Twa populations are from the same mono-theistic religion and language—Kirundi—and lived in the same territory on hills (Reyntjens 2000). Another belief is that Burundi's ethnic makeup is a myth and the population was segregated by "orders" and not ethnicity. For example, the Hutu people were being subjected to servitude, while the royal Ganwa line of Burundi was considered neither Tutsi nor Hutu people but a separate group, whose essence embodied the nation's identity.[2] The ancient Greek word ethnos refer to people living and acting together, a people or nation within a collective as a manner of being. Aristotle, on the other hand, used ethnos to describe barbarous nations, while Modern Greek uses ethnos to refer to Greeks themselves as a nation (Fortier 1994). These views of what ethnicity really is and whether Hutus, Tutsis, and Twa populations, who lived on the same hill and spoke the same language that had similar religious beliefs, can indeed be defined within ethnic groupings are more clearly out-lined by empirical evidence provided by anthropologist Fredrik Barth (Barth 1969). According to Barth (1969: 9–10),

> First, it is clear that boundaries persist despite a flow of personnel across them. In other words, categorical ethnic distinctions do not depend on an absence of mobility, contact and information, but do entail social processes of exclusion and incorporation whereby discrete categories are maintained *despite* chang-ing participation and membership in the course of individual life histories. Secondly, one finds that stable, persisting, and often vitally important social relations are maintained across such boundaries, and are frequently based pre-cisely on the dichotomized ethnic statuses. In other words, ethnic distinctions do not depend on an absence of social interaction and acceptance, but are quite to the contrary often the very foundations on which embracing social systems are built. Interaction in such a social system does not lead to its liquidation through change and acculturation; cultural differences can persist despite inter-ethnic contact and interdependence. (Barth 1969: 9–10)

Similarly, anthropologist Clifford Geertz (Geertz 1973) defines ethnicity as a personal identity collectively ratified and publicly expressed.

Africa's colonial borders have conveyed a misleading imagery of people's identities and their political identities, which played a key factor in ethnic strife postindependence. Nationalism imparted political salience to ethnicity, which was a major contribution in transforming ethnicity from traditional to Western forms of civilization, with a view to organize and legitimize governments. In conjunction with the modern state, a major rift began forming between present and past cultures, leading to violence and mass mobilization of ethnic groups, while the new culture of nationalism became a means whereby political autonomy could be attained. Such transformations of relevance describes social conflict as having a positive value when it shapes society's norms, values, beliefs, attitudes, and changes myths and belief systems that result in violence (Schellenberg 1996). In other words, social conflict that has undergone transformation through violence is viewed as positive by colonial and neocolonial masters.

Burundi, like several other African states, succumbed to the Berlin conference of 1884–1885—the division and partitioning of Africa. The German administration took over the country in 1889, followed by Belgium in 1918 with their invasion of 1,400 Belgian troops into the country. Belgian control was further supported through the 1923 global territorial policy of the League of Nations (now known as the dysfunctional UN system), authorized Belgium's stronghold over the Ruanda-Urundi territory (Rwanda and Burundi). Belgian colonialism directly ushered in a policy of segregation in Burundi in 1918; political structures that weakened Burundi's monarchy and posed a direct threat to the King system. The Hutu people were mainly cultivators and in some instances the Hutus were appointed as chiefs or councilors to manage the King's royal domains. But, all this changed by Belgium seeking to create later conflicts elsewhere in the Great Lakes, after the despotic reign of its king in the Congo, where Belgium could do with the Congo as it pleased. In addition, over a 23-year period, Belgium silently managed a holocaust, in which, by 1908, one racist Belgian King had the sole power and through his own means killed 10 million Congolese people with no just cause.[3]

In some way or another, the inherent nature of Belgium's intoxication with racism and greed could not save itself from orchestrating brutality and could easily continue where its King had just left off a murderous reign. After twenty-three years of its King's experiential killing and brutality that killed 10 million people, Belgium was undoubtedly, extremely well-informed and very well-versed with the Great Lakes region and its peoples. It is no wonder that Belgium could act decisively and without hesitation, with flawless execution, use "ethnicity" as its very first trump card to sow division, by immediately reorganizing the people of Burundi and radically reducing the system of chiefdoms from 133 to 46.

Ralf Dahrendorf's theory of social conflict acutely posits that social conflict of accessibility of authority, such as the farm laborer who has no authority or property, yet invests much of his/her time on the land of the owner, will legitimize conflict through social means, in the form of strikes and violence (Dahrendor 1959). This reorganization of chiefdoms resulted in

Hutu people losing a considerable amount of positions as local leaders that led to disgruntled groups. Karl Marx's coercion theory, similarly underscores that social conflict that originates in the power structures of certain societies, wherein class division is neatly and tightly spinned in a capitalist society's structure may result in a revolution (Marx 1867). Rwanda and Burundi were thus deliberately targeted by Belgium to create an opposing effect of ethnic hatred in the Great Lakes, by elevating a Tutsi minority over a Hutu majority in both countries, which led to a bloody war in Ruanda in 1959, while in Burundi, countless genocides have occurred since 1965.

GEOPOLITICS: FORCING CIVIL WARS AND GENOCIDES

Burundi has experienced more political crises and conflicts than any former colony in Africa. The decolonization of Africa did end, but it also brought about the contestation of the "superpowers" gaining control and negotiating side deals with despotic African governments unilaterally, feeding greed through Western parochial interests of the United States in its contest with the Soviet Union-led socialist bloc to gaining dominance over resource-rich territories.

Burundi's independence ushered in a discriminatory political discourse anchored on greed over political power fueled by ethnic cleavages of local elites that continued entrenched ethnic exploitative practices as their colonizers did, igniting several civil wars. The consequences of exacerbated ethnic cleavages thus brought about a regional dimension that led to mass migration of people engrossed in ethnic fears and mistrust. The crisscross movements of people formed numerous rebel groups, both within Burundi and in the region, resulting in an exported politics to Burundi. It was impossible to imagine a peace through the numerous peace agreements that all failed Burundi's peace prospects and which instead exacerbated conflicts.

Belgium's rule in the Great Lakes was embodied in the major goal of entrenching ethnic divisions to favor Tutsi people over Hutu people in both Rwanda and Burundi and to create cycles of violent conflicts. Controversially, U.S. involvement in the Great Lakes, which appeared overly zealous to rule out Leopold's reign of terror and his brutality, while the United States was exploiting the Congo's resources also leading to the successful mining of uranium from Congo to create U.S. Hiroshima and Nagasaki bombs that they one after another dropped in Japan in August 1945 (Nzongola-Ntalaja 2011). Although in November 1961 the UN's Fourth Trusteeship Committee of Investigation (UN, A/4494) voiced concern over Belgium's indirect administration, which gave local authorities the title of "burgomasters" that was widening ethnic differences, Africa had no international backing, since international powers were incapable to enact the principles of the 1945 UN Charter proving it meaningless, and too busy exploiting diamonds and gold from Zaire (formerly known as Leopoldville and later known as the Democratic Republic of the Congo [DRC]) and other resource-rich minerals.

The assassination of the Congolese (now the DRC) Prime Minister Patrice Lumumba in January 1961 was enacted by the United States and Belgium through enticement of the UN Secretariat and Lumumba's rivals (Nzongola-Ntalaja 2011). While the UN Secretary-General Dag Hammarsjköld was attempting peaceful negotiations in the Congolese political crisis, his plane suddenly crashed in Northern Zambia in September 1961, with no plausible explanation for the accident (UN doc A/5069/Add.1. 1962).

Congo's 1963 Katanga conflict also resulted in thousands of Congolese fleeing as refugees to neighboring Burundi, Tanzania, and Central African Republic (CAR) (UNHCR 2014). International interests were marred with the intoxication of racism and total disregard for Black Africa and by their greed and corruption without desire to stop the violence and wars in the Great Lakes but ensured their existence through regional destabilization moves, while the diamond-rich Katanga Province in the eastern Congo, Angola's oil and diamonds, and Namibia's diamonds were looted (Nagar 2018: 499–520). The "superpowers" on the UN Security Council, specifically France as the penholder on Burundi, refused to support the mandating missions. This resulted in the sustaining of the strongholds of despots in Burundi. Simultaneously, the "superpowers" were aiding the regional states that were leveraging the necessary support for their interests. Indeed, effective backing was provided by the United States by supporting a despot Joseph Désiré Mobutu (later called Mobutu Sese Seko, who became Congo's President in 1965). This gave Mobutu sufficient clout to oust Kasavubu and Tshombe, thereby forcing them into exile.

In furtherance of such parochial interests, a strongman regime was secured by protecting international economic interests; thus, the United States provided an estimated US$300 million in weapons, while Belgium made available US$100 million in military training to the Mobutu government (Hartung and Moix 2000). Western allies watched as Mobutu looted the country's resources through, for example, diamond-smuggling trade deals with the United States that were conducted via the Kamina Airbase in Southern Zaire and amounted to $5 billion per year.[4]

Similarly, Belgium refused to intervene during the ethnic killings in Rwanda (1959–1962) and Burundi (1961–1965). Burundi and Rwanda were left occupied in wars of ethnic divisions, while Belgium also had deflecting motives in order to loot the Congo's resources (Nagar 2020: 499–520). Rwanda's Hutu revolt and the resulting violent conflict between 1959 and

1961 led to the exodus of 135,000 Tutsi refugees from Rwanda into Burundi. The abolition of Rwanda's monarchy and the establishment of a Republic in 1961 increased the fears of Tutsi people in Burundi. By April 1962, 40,000 Tutsi people were in Burundi, which altered the fabric of Hutu–Tutsi relations in Burundi, as well as 5,000 in Tanzania (formerly Tanganyika), 30,000 in Uganda, and 60,000 in the Kivu Province of the Congo (now the DRC).[5] At the root of Rwanda's Hutu revolt was a "self-fulfilling prophecy": Tutsi people in Burundi believed that Rwanda's Hutu refugees in Burundi were attempting to put in motion a Rwandan republican model with Hutu's becoming victorious to kill off Tutsis as they did in Rwanda. And Burundi's Hutu perceptions of Tutsi politicians were based on enmity (Lemarchand 2006: 41–58; Levine and Nagar 2016). Such exacerbated fears were further entrenched as noted by Khadiagala (2002: 464), when he explains that: "widespread massacres of Hutu in Burundi in 1972 reignited tensions in Rwanda, and led to reprisals against the Rwandan Tutsi" (Khadiagala 2002: 463–98).

THE FIRST CIVIL WAR: A TICKING
TIME BOMB RELEASED, 1961–1966

Demanding Burundi's independence from the Belgians resulted in the creation of the Union pour le Progrés National (UPRONA), a nationalist movement that was formed with the aim to unite ethnic groups and put an end to ethnic division. Led by Prince Louis Rwagasore, UPRONA's mission was in complete opposition to that of Belgium. However, the infusion of class division became more apparent, when the young Tutsi prince married a Hutu woman in 1959. A frustrated Belgium quickly strategized and introduced a perceived democracy under the banner of a "balance of power" against UPRONA by encouraging the formation of a competing party, the Parti Démocratique Chrétien (PDC); the rival party's ideology was infused with Christianity. According to a former Belgian resident Harroy (1987: 399), "The PDC quickly became the bulwark we hoped to use in order to stop the cancerous metastasis of UPRONA's progress."[6] The rival PDC, which was a more conservative Christian party, was led by Belgium's crony, Chief Pierre Baranyanka, who maintained good relations with the Belgian administration. It was at that point in Burundi's history, by playing the political games, that a "time bomb" was set, and soon to be released, with the creation of the PDC prior to legislative elections of September 1961. But, UPRONA won an overwhelming victory in the new National Assembly. The charismatic Rwagasore, unfortunately, had a quick end, when he was assassinated by a PDC assassin, with the involvement of Belgian authorities (Loft and Loft

1988: 88–93), prior to the country's independence. The assassination was designed to incite violence.

Rwagasore's death was the beginning of Hutu and Tutsi divisions, which became engulfed in religion, politics, and ethnicity. The division was acutely felt by the oppressed, along with the legacy of decades of "divide and rule" by Germany and later Belgium. The multiethnic UPRONA party had Catholic elements and Hutu support, further divided into splinter groups of Hutu and Tutsi wings, such as the Jeunesses Nationalistes Rwagasore (JNR). JNR worked as a law enforcement agency in the poor areas of Bujumbura, entrenched in values of a "vicious defense of Tutsi privileges" (Loft and Loft 1988: 90). The JNR creation resulted in the formation of a Hutu group, the Parti du people (the Syndicats Chretiens), which was linked to and associated with a Belgian Catholic trade union. After enough damage was done by the international community, suddenly in June 1962, the UN General Assembly voted for the partition of Ruanda-Urundi, and the independence of Burundi.

But, Bujumbura did not abolish the monarchical system, and power remained vested in the Tutsi King Mwambutsa IV, as the head of a constitutional monarchy that was created in similar fashion to the Belgian system. This independent governmental system had the King as its head of state, who appointed a prime minister; in turn, the prime minister selected his cabinet that received approval by a National Assembly. In addition, Burundi's constitutional monarchy provided for an elected bicameral legislature, an assembly consisting of thirty-three members, including the senate with sixteen members. Furthermore, elections were held every six years. The King ruled by calculated equality by allotting top government posts between Hutus and Tutsis, in attempts to balance competing ethnic interests. However, later on, the King abandoned the political balancing act.

The monarchical system became Burundi's "holy-grail," as the only concluding order with meaning for Hutu and Tutsi people. Again during the 1965 legislative elections, UPRONA won an overwhelming victory in the new National Assembly, with the Hutu people winning fifty-eight seats against the Tutsi people's twenty-two seats that ushered in a Hutu Prime Minister Pierre Ngendandumwe, but he was also killed in January 1965, within fleeting moments of being in office. Following Ngendandumwe's death, King Mwambutsa immediately nullified the Hutu electoral victory, rejected a Hutu Prime Minister as designate, and instead appointed a Tutsi Prime Minister, Léopold Biha. This negligent countermove of the King sparked country-wide violence and revolt in October 1965 and a failed coup attempt and attack on the royal palace. In return, there were mass executions of the entire Hutu political elite (Loft and Loft 1988). The failed coup also resulted in Hutus turning against Hutus, particularly those who were meant to support the revolt and did not (Reyntjens 2000). An estimated 500 Tutsis and 5,000 Hutus were killed (Prunier 1994; Weinstein 1975: 5–24).

The successful assassination of Rwagasore by Belgium, easily triggered the assassination of Ngendandumwe, and the beginning of the first civil war that started in 1965, which became a norm in Burundi: to kill off its leaders, as a natural practice throughout the country's future. The deaths of consecutive Hutu leaders raised entrenched fears, resulting in Hutus' aborting interests in Burundi's political administrative posts and easily handing down their political win to the Tutsi people.

A year later, in 1966, the son of King Mwambutsa, Prince Charles Ndizeye, turned against his father and the King was dethroned. In July 1966, Ndizeye was crowned Tutsi King Ntare V (the last King to be ever crowned) and cunningly used by the army to rid Burundi of King Mwambutsa, only to be dethroned later and the monarchy completely abolished. The mastermind behind the abolition of the monarchy was King Ntare's appointed Tutsi Colonel, Michel Micombero, and his army that finally ended Burundi's monarchical rule. And this led to the beginning of a long-drawn-out Tutsi-dominated army and government.

TUTSI AND HUTU POWER STRUGGLES: VIOLENT ENTANGLEMENT

The intensity of Burundi's intrastate conflicts has been interchangeable, with periods of low to high-intensity wars that culminated several regimes of reinforced patrimonialism, creating a predatory political economic system. Since 1965, the killing of the Hutu political elite and later 300,000 Hutu people in 1972 (UN doc S2005/158: 6), a Tutsi-dominated dictatorship against Hutu opposition would be Burundi's existence for its foreseeable future and included UPRONA, 10 years (1966–1976) led by Michel Micombero; UPRONA, 10 years (1976–1987) a dictatorship led by Colonel Jean-Baptiste Bagaza's religious oppression and detaining political opposition;[7] UPRONA, 5 years (1987–1993) led by Major Pierre Buyoya a Tutsi dictatorship, and 150,000 people massacred. Though, Buyoya's leadership culminated Burundi's New Conventional Government and resulted in elections won by the Hutu people through the: Front pour la démocratie au Burundi (FRODEBU) (an underground organization founded in exile in 1986), a Hutu-dominated party that came into power in 1993 (Boutros-Ghali 1995). Hutu domination would experience a heavy price paid and witnessed the assassinations of two of its presidents and the overthrow of a third Hutu president in systematic fashion. First, Melchior Ndadaye was appointed as Hutu Head of State in July 1993; but his rise to power was short-lived, when he was killed in October 1993, leading to the massacre of 300,000 people (Boutros-Ghali 1995). The assassins of President Ndadaye also took the lives of prominent FRODEBU political leaders and Hutu politicians, who were wiped out for a second time since 1972, included Pontien Karibwami, president of the National Assembly; Gilles Bimazubute, vice president of the National Assembly; Juvenal Ndayikeza, minister of Territorial Administration and Communal Development; Richard Ndikumwami, general administrator of Documentation and Migrations; Euzebie Ntibantunganya, wife of the former minister of External Relations and Cooperation.

Ndadaye's successor, the 39-year-old Hutu president Cyprien Ntaryamira was elected by the Burundian parliament in January 1994; but in less than four months, he too was killed along with Rwanda's president Juvenal Habyarimana (*The Washington Post* 1994). Similarly, the Hutu interim president Sylvestre Ntibantunganya, the official candidate of FRODEBU, was elected by the National Assembly, but overthrown in July 1996 by Pierre Buyoya, making his appearance for a second time as Burundi's leader. By July 1996, the contestation for power in Burundi's political arena was beyond UPRONA and FODEBU's reach and led to the establishment of several parties and organizations, including Shadrack Niyonkuru, president of the Parti du peuple; Ernest Kabushemeye, president of the Parti du rassemblement du people burundais (RPB); Alphonse Rugambarara, president of the Inkinzo-PPO; Vincent Nkikumasabo, president of the Parti social démocrate (PSD); Gaétan Nikobamye, president of the Parti liberal; Mathias Hitimana, president of the Parti pour la reconciliation du peuple; Therence Nsanze, president of the Alliance burundo-africaine pour le salut (ABASA); Vincent Kubwimana, secretary-general of the Confédération des Syndicats Libres du Burundi; and Antonie Nijembazi, vice president of the Association des Employeurs du Burundi (UN doc S/1995/163 1995).

Buyoya's leadership as the head of an interim transitional government, which was in accordance with the Arusha Peace Accords of 2000, commenced in November 2001. In addition, the governance formula was based on consociational democracy, which was designed to regulate Burundi's conflicts: Buyoya (UPRONA) led the transitional government for the first half of the three-year transitional period with Domitien Ndayizeye (FRODEBU) as vice president. During the second half, Ndayizeye took over the presidency and a new vice president was designated from the G-10 Tutsi group (UN doc S/2001/1076 2001). Subsequently, Burundi's 2005 democratic elections brought a rebel group turned political party—a second Hutu party, the National Council for the Defense of Democracy and its armed wing, Forces for the Defense of Democracy (*Conseil National Pour la Défense de la Démocratie(Forces pour la Défense de la Démocratie*)(Burundi) (CNDD-FDD) led by Hutu Pierre Nkurunziza into the political fold, competing against another Hutu-dominated party, FRODEBU. But Nkurunziza's tact-ful maneuvers and convergence of ethnic groups set him up for the highest position in the land as president of Burundi. Nkurunziza was a religious man, with a background as a staunch Catholic. In addition, Nkurunziza's Hutu father was linked to the Burundian royal family, but his mother was a Protestant. Nkurunziza's mixed ethnic lineage created a diverse party that worked beyond the barriers of ethnic divisions easily gathering both Hutu and Tutsi people into its fold. The CNDD-FDD slogan of "God, King and Country" raised concerns that the country might return to a monarchical rule (Miles 2019).

THE SECOND CIVIL WAR: TUTSI-DOMINATED UPRONA GOVERNMENT, 1966–1976

In 1966, Michel Micombero took over the country and proclaimed Burundi a republic but used ethnicity as his main instrument and thus created a Tutsi army. Micombero's victory heralded the National Revolutionary Council (NRC), after dissolving the parliament and constitution, which proceeded a decade of domination. His leadership would create a divisive brand of Tutsi standing up against Tutsi, and Tutsi against Hutu, through Micombero's social and economic inequality policies. His ethnic divide would also resur-face the old fears and heightened colonial experiences of the lowest class of socioeconomic standing that were heavily embedded in favor of a Tutsi bour-geoisie against a proletariat Hutu. The retaliation of Hutus was thus carefully planned over six years, under Micombero's watch, when a group of Hutu extremists killed 3,000 Tutsis. In return, merciless killings ensued headed by Burundi's Interior Minister Albert Shibura, who shot King Ntare and gave orders for the general slaughter of Hutu intellectuals all above primary educa-tion (Prunier 1994: 10). An estimated, 300,000 Hutu people died in the 1972 massacres and thousands of others fled to Tanzania. The displaced Burundian Hutu people later formed rebel movements in their refugee camps to return to Burundi and ignite violence. However, the Hutus never gained power for the next two decades. A U.S. Consulate opened in Bujumbura in October 1960 and became an Embassy in July 1962, but during the 1972 and 1973 mas-sacres, Bujumbura expelled the U.S. Ambassador (U.S. Department of State Bureau of Public Affairs 1988).

International Aid Fueling Micombero's Dictatorship

The reluctance of the international community's attempts at prosecutions undoubtedly promoted a culture of impunity in Burundi. Burundi came out clean with no arrests made for the 1972 massacres. Instead, economics trumped human rights and justice. This was because as a major coffee-producing country, Burundi was welcomed by the United States for its coffee trade surplus. According to Greenland (1975: 3), "No attempt was made by the United States for example, to use the 'coffee weapon' in 1972 against the Burundi government." Micombera could comfortably stage his coup with the firm belief that international aid would not dry up regardless of the violence that ensued. The International Monetary Fund's (IMF) report of 1974 on Burundi's economic position, highlighted by Greenland (1975: 3) revealed that

> The balance of payments position ha[d] improved, coffee earnings [were] good because the quota restrictions ha[d] been lifted, and because the world price is high at present, the 'diversification' of agricultural production into tea and cotton is beginning to pay off, and there are long-term prospects of considerable revenues from the exploitation of nickel deposits. Second, the government can only be encouraged to note that it still receives the tacit-if not active support of other nations. Burundi continued to receive extensive aid from the European Economic Commission [EEC], and from the member countries of the EEC, from UN organizations and elsewhere. It managed to buy all the arms, military aircrafts, and technical expertise which it needs.

The 1972 massacre of the Hutu people included all educated people at various schools and universities, including both staff and students. The massacre was seen as a major victory for keeping the Hutu people out of power, particularly within the military ranks. Micombero thus could comfortably increase the national security budget to benefit Tutsis: from 13.2 percent in 1971 to 22.6 percent of the total budget by 1972. After Burundi's ethnic conflict of 1972, the U.S. government and relief groups contributed almost US$1 million in disaster relief (US Bureau of Public Affairs 1988). But the international aid was only available to the Tutsi victims of the 1972 violence, barring all Hutu survivors from aid and labeling them rebels (Greenland 1975: 3–5)

THIRD CIVIL WAR: UPRONA GOVERNMENT, 1976–1987

Micombero was ousted in November 1976 through a bloodless coup by Colonel Jean-Baptiste Bagaza (Prunier 1994). Under Bagaza's reign, the military was the main perpetrator of human rights violations. Yet, Burundi continued to receive military equipment, communications equipment, and training from France, Germany, Italy, Greece, the Soviet Union, and North Korea.

For its part, the United States provided its military assistance program—the International Military and Education Training (IMET) for Burundi—which began in 1982 primarily for a Tutsi-dominated military regime. Bagaza's human rights record deteriorated. Religious oppression reached new heights: Burundi's church properties were confiscated, arrests and detention of priests and churchgoers occurred on a daily basis, the expulsion of foreign missionaries, and restrictions on the hours available for worship were monitored. Religious groups experienced the brunt of oppression and mainly Seventh-day Adventists and Jehovah Witnesses with harsh conditions during their detention (United States Background Notes 1988).

Burundi's dictators did not shy away from orchestrating violence, while international aid continued to flow at full scale, reaching contribution heights of US$2.5 million by 1988 (United States Background Notes 1988). In addition, Burundi received US$80 million low-interest loan from the World Bank and another for US$7.5 million from the United States (Lemarchand 1989: 27–28). The United States also provided a 1978 development strategy for the Agency for International Development's (AID) program, which was a twofold program that included: (1) increasing agricultural production of improved seeds for corn, wheat, and potatoes; improving health services such as technical and commodity support extended to infant-related health services to promote family planning and (2) training managers and technicians to improve the functioning of public and private sectors.

Regardless of the extensive agricultural aid programs, Burundi faced critical food shortages due to the decades of instability, as well as owing to extreme climatic drought conditions. The United States and its relief agencies moved quickly to secure food and provided US$1 million in disaster relief. Bujumbura's educational program was also bolstered with the implementation of the U.S. African Graduate Fellowship Program (AFGRAD), benefiting Burundi's master's-level students: masters of science degrees in agricultural economics, physiology, and economic planning. Furthermore, the United States introduced the African Manpower Development Program for nondegree training in the fields of agricultural and rural development producing skilled technicians. Meanwhile, the U.S. Information Service (USIS) opened an American Cultural Center in Burundi, offering English language courses. The Fulbright Program, on the other hand, sponsored an exchange of American professors to teach in Burundi. The U.S. Peace Corps provided a technical assistance and support program in March 1983 that focused on Burundi's education, agriculture, and rural development sectors (US Bureau of Public Affairs 1988).

Other major international aid donors for development assistance included the EEC, China, France, Belgium, Germany, the UN, the World Bank, the

Soviet Union, Romania, North Korea, and the Organization of Petroleum Exporting Countries (OPEC). The country's natural resources mainly included nickel, uranium, rare earth oxides, peat, cobalt, copper, and platinum deposits. Burundi's agricultural sector was extensive and included coffee, tea, cotton, and food crops, with 89 percent arable land. Bujumbura's major trade exports in 1986 totaled US$168 million, consisting of coffee, tea, cotton, cigarettes, soft drinks, and beer with the United States and the European Union (formerly the EEC) as the country's major export markets. Burundi's total import trade in 1986 totaled US$202 million and included import partners: Iran, France, Belgium, Germany, and Japan with import trade commodities including cement, asphalt, petroleum, fertilizer, pesticides, and textiles. The country's official exchange rate in 1986/7 was 120 Burundian francs to 1 US dollar. Burundi's 90 percent of the population of subsistence farmers, in 1986 and 1987, concentrated mainly in coffee with a total coffee production of 31,300 tons in 1987, with increases of 40,000 tons by 1988.

The EEC development fund was the donor to tea production and became Burundi's second valuable export market after coffee. Burundi's cotton production was also revived, including diversifying its agricultural products. China was the major international trade partner in Burundi's cotton production, with the 1986 cotton farming production seeing yields of 8,000 metric tons of raw cotton purchased by China's locally built textile factory. Burundi's natural resource and high-grade nickel was excavated by several international firms. These high-grade nickel deposits were discovered in Burundi by the Chicago-based, Amoco multinational corporation (MNC), and expanded its tentacles in Burundi in 1984 and had explorations of hydrocarbons in the northern part of Lake Tanganyika and the Ruzizi Plain (Schissel 1987).

But, Bagaza's enterprise policy changes of an investment code providing only basic guarantees would soon lead to a disgruntled international community and his demise. In 1983, the government began negotiations with the United States for a bilateral investment treaty. Burundi had a majority interest in about 50 mixed enterprises, or "parastatals," with major foreign participation, but Bagaza began implementing reforms that targeted the parastatal sector under the banner of improving increased efficiency and improving performance. These reforms resulted in major divesting occurring particularly in Pirogue on Lake Cohora in the north and increasing government control that moved mixed enterprises from the private sector. Shortly after his meddling of mixed enterprises and diminishing international investment, in September 1987 Bagaza was overthrown by Major Pierre Buyoya in a coup d'état.

FOURTH CIVIL WAR: UPRONA TUTSI-LED
GOVERNMENT 1987–1992

Major Pierre Buyoya overthrew Bagaza and took over the country in 1987, led by UPRONA, and suspended the constitution, dissolved opposition parties, and introduced a thirty-one-member Military Committee for National Salvation (CMSN) to rule the country (US Background Notes 1988). When he took over, Burundi's population of 6 million people had only 1.9 million people employed (US 1988) in a total economy of US$1.3 billion.

Buyoya's 1987 victory brought about renewed hope for Burundi, when he freed all political prisoners—the hundreds that were detained under Bagaza's watch. Religious freedom which was also previously destroyed was restored in a country with 62 percent of the population being Roman Catholic, 5 percent Protestant, 1 percent Muslim, and 32 percent traditional African. Also introduced were sixteen civilians into Buyoya's twenty-minister interim government. Buyoya's reformist regime allowed several movements to serve the country in efforts to promote development and ethnic reconciliation in Burundi. These movements included the Union of Workers in Burundi (Union des Travailleurs du Burundi (UTB); the Union of Burundi Women (Union des Femmes Burundaises [UFB]); the Union of Revolutionary Burundi Youth (union de Jeunesse Revolutionnaire du Burundi); and a children's group, the Pioneers (US Background Notes 1988).

Extensive international aid assisted Buyoya who was regarded as a dramatic improvement from Bagaza and seen as a lesser evil that improved the human rights situation in Burundi (US 1988). The implementation of a judicial mechanism assisted several thousand Burundi refugees who had previously fled the 1972 massacres to the DRC and Tanzania and now to return to their land. Burundi was divided into fifteen provinces, each headed by a governor, with further subdivisions of communal subsectors of zones, and groups of hills or collines (which were traditionally organized along family lines) (US 1988). Buyoya appointed more Hutu ministers and governors into his government. Buyoya also introduced changes to the new central committee comprising of forty-one Hutu, thirty-eight Tutsi, and one Twa, while the army remained untouched and Tutsi-exclusive (Prunier 1994). Given the traumatic ethnic history and decades of violent conflict, Buyoya's biggest mistake and double-standard was the discrimination in the army. The Tutsi-dominated military remained intact for over two decades, since Micombera and Bagaza regimes, but nevertheless, continued receiving international backing, viewed by the international community as crucial to maintaining law and order. International military aid included IMET's US$176,000 in 1987 and sending Burundi military officers for professional and technical training courses in the United States. Burundi's military training was also extended to the U.S. Army and Air Force base in Kinshasa (U.S. Department of State Bureau of Public Affairs 1988).

Several Hutu people gained access to state institutions that demonstrated a remarkable difference to previous regimes. The international community thrived in Burundi. China built a cotton textile mill that exceeded national needs with major prospects for international cotton trade. China constructed the Mugere hydroelectric dam supplying hydroelectrical power to Bujumbura. The Amoco Corporation continued its oil exploration program in Burundi, beginning in 1984. And by 1988, Amoco's foreign oil production exceeded its total U.S. output, with 25 percent of its earnings gained largely through Egypt. In addition, further drilling rights were secured in the Congo, Gabon, Kenya, Liberia, Madagascar, Morocco, Mozambique, Sierra Leone, Tanzania, and Tunisia (Rosenheim 1985).

A year later, in 1988, a Hutu revolt broke out in the north of the country, staged by a group, the Liberation of the Hutu People (Palipehutu), which was formed in 1980, in the Tanzanian refugee camps. The rebel group returned to Burundi to carry out retaliation for the previous massacres. The group slaughtered hundreds of Tutsi in the northern towns of Ntega and Marangara. In response, the Tutsi-led army retaliated and massacred 20,000 Hutus (UN doc S/1994/1039 1994). A total of 150,000 people were killed (U.S. Background Notes: 1988), Also, 60,000 people, mainly Hutus, fled to Rwanda. The 1988 killings by the Palipehutu resulted in a quick reshuffle of the government by Buyoya, who saw the wrath of Burundi's deeply entrenched ethnic discrimination (Prunier 1994). Buyoya moved quickly in October 1988 and ensured that a new Hutu Prime Minister was appointed—Adrien Sibomana, the first Hutu politician, after the assassination of Ngendandumwe in 1965. These events followed a commission that was established to prepare a report for a new constitution on the democratization of national institutions and political structures. The Commission for National Unity, which comprised equal numbers of twelve Hutus and twelve Tutsis, was tasked to investigate the massacres and the importance of national unity.[8] This report was published in April 1989, and subsequently led to the institutionalization of Burundi's Charter of National Unity and Bill of Rights that included banning discrimination.[9] In September 1991, a parliamentary forum was created to function in conjunction with a presidential system of government; a renewable five-year presidential mandate; proportional representation; freedom of the press; guarantees of human rights; and a system of controlled multi-partyism, for political groupings seeking legal recognition to comply with ethnic, regional, and religious impartiality and acceptance of the Charter on National Unity (UN doc E/CN.4/1996/4/Add.1 1995).

Owing to Burundi's violent conflicts and instability, the country was viewed as a high-risk, by international community; therefore, while securing aid, also secured were effective mitigating risks of a transportation system in cases of emergencies and evacuation of the international community. Burundi was home to over 4,500 Europeans.[10] Burundi's transportation system included a World War I German navy steamer transporting passengers and cargo around Lake Tanganyika. Several flights to and from Burundi included regular direct flights between Burundi and Europe that were scheduled several times per week—with Burundi's upgraded airport allowing the use of jumbo jets, as well as several flights connecting Bujumbura with Nairobi, Dar es Salaam, and Kinshasa. In 1988, Burundi also introduced a bus system between residential districts and its city center (U.S. 1988). While the air transport system was an effective mitigating risk for the international community to evacuate Burundi during violent conflict, the bus system, on the other hand, became an effective mechanism in gaining quick and easy access around the country for perpetrators of mass violence.

FIFTH CIVIL WAR: UPRONA WEAKENED—HUTU DOMINANCE 1993–2005

Meanwhile, a Hutu Burundi refugee, Melchior Ndadaye, who was exiled in Rwanda, returned to Burundi with a group of militants from the FRODEBU. The organization was established in 1986 as an underground movement. Since the commission's report on national unity pushed by Buyoya, the subsequent referendum, resulted in the promulgation of a decree-law on political parties that led to the introduction of a multiparty political system, and thus provided FRODEBU the credentials to establish itself as a political party and easy entry into Burundi's political space. With an 85 percent Hutu population that was given an opportunity to express their democratic rights in a national election for the first time after decades of oppression, Hutu people undoubtedly swayed the pendulum in favor of FRODEBU. On the other hand, Burundi's Tutsi population was likened to South Africa's pre-1994 apartheid white government's black racism and their oppression against black people, therefore, Tutsis would not accept a Hutu president and Burundi's fate of violence was sealed as it entered its 1993 democratic era.

Burundi's multiparty presidential elections took place on June 1 and 29, 1993. The first presidential poll included the main parties: FRODEBU in support of Melchior Ndadaye and UPRONA aligned with Buyoya. FRODEBU claimed 71 percent of the votes and 65 of the 81 seats; UPRONA 21.4 percent of the votes and secured the remaining 16 seats. Ndadaye was elected as the Hutu head of state with his new twenty-three-member council of ministers to end Tutsi domination which commenced during German and Belgian colonialism. Although Buyoya accepted defeat, an attempted coup was staged shortly after the elections on July 3, by disgruntled UPRONA military dissidents (UN doc E/CN.4/1996/4/Add.1). Ndadaye's extensive army reform measures were a major trigger, because they posed a threat to the majority Tutsi-led army, which had been in power since the 1960s (UN doc 1995: 26; World Bank 1994). Instead of uniting the country, Ndadaye divided Burundi and its people and disregarded ethnic fears of civil war and massacres. He was killed only four months after ascending to power, through assassination by troops of the Tutsi-dominated army on October 21, 1993. And the very next day, the perpetrators and murderers of Ndadaye, forcefully instituted François Ngeze a Hutu from UPRONA, as the president of their National State Security Council (UN doc S/1994/1039: 3). Ndadaye's death led to Burundi's fourth civil war, during which about 300,000 people died and 700,000 were displaced.

Burundi's festering of major root causes of the county's long history of ethnic strife with a Tutsi minority holding the most senior state administrative positions, including the army, education, and business, that could not let go of their economic and social privilege. President Ndadaye thus made several errors in the spirit of shared power. For examples, he extended an open invitation to all exiled Burundi people to return to Burundi, which created fear for the Tutsis in Burundi, who had occupied the land belonging to Hutu refugees and other properties for two decades since 1972; his invitation also sparked renewed fear among the Hutu, who observed the return of Tutsi army refugees and other belligerents, as well as former despots, including the former president Bagaza, who went into exile in Libya after the 1987 coup (Prunier 1994). Ndadaye was not only opposed by UPRONA but also by the PALIPEHUTU underground organization. The reform plans too, quickly introduced by Ndadaye in reorganization of the central and local administration, left many Tutsi governors and local administrators jobless (UN doc S/1995/157 1995).

Three months later, Ndadaye's successor, President Cyprien Ntaryamira, was elected on January 13, 1994, by the Burundian parliament, without holding presidential election; but instead, Article 85 of the Burundian Constitution was adjusted. Subsequently on December 23, 1993, Sylvestre Ntibantunganya was elected as the president of the new Bureau of Burundi's parliament. Pursuant to high-level AU and UN interventions of special envoys and secretary-and under-secretaries general, Burundi's new government was installed on February 7, 1994. FRODEBU and its allies received 60 percent of ministerial posts, and 40 percent was allotted to the opposition. Three months later on April 6, 1994, President Ntaryamira' was killed together with the Rwandan President Juvénal Habyarimana, when their plane was shot down in a rocket attack in Kigali (UN S/1994/1039: 3). The mass killings in Bujumbura continued while in Rwanda 800,000 people were slaughtered by Hutu militiamen and the country's gendarmerie. Astonishingly, after Ntaryamira's death, the Constitutional Court of Burundi declared his election unconstitutional anyway, since his election to the presidency was not made through popular vote.

Based on the ruling of the Constitutional Court of Burundi and the negotiations conducted by the high-level delegations from the Organization of African Unity (OAU)(now the AU) and the UN, Burundi was compelled to retain Hutu leadership. Thus, Sylvestre Ntibantunganya was sworn in as the interim president of Burundi, in accordance with its constitution, since he was serving as the speaker of parliament. Meanwhile, as the interim presidency was being conferred upon Ntibantunganya in April 1994, Leonard Nyangoma, a former minister in President Ndadaye's government, formed a new party called the National Council for the Defense of Democracy (CNDD-FDD) and its armed wing, the Forces for the Defense of Democracy (*Conseil National Pour la Défense de la Démocratie–Forces pour la Défense de la Démocratie*) (Burundi) (CNDD-FDD). Former president Bagaza also organized a new political party, the Parti Pour le redressment national (PARENA).

AVOIDING A SIXTH CIVIL WAR: DIPLOMATIC EFFORTS, 1994–1995

The June 1994 negotiations among Burundi's major political parties ensued with the assistance of the former UN secretary-general Boutros Boutros Ghali's former special representative Ahemdou Ould Abdallah, with the intention of establishing procedures for the restoration of the elected presidency (UN doc S/1994/1039). Following the coups of 1993 and 1994, a UN fact-finding mission was led under Boutros-Ghali's former special representative Ibrahim Gambari, a former permanent representative of Nigeria to the UN. The Great Lakes remained volatile, while the UN closed its "Operation Turquoise." France deployed its military in Rwanda to stop the massacres, but the military force aborted its mission, resulting in 800,000 deaths in Rwanda in 1994. The security situation and the genocide of 1994 in Rwanda led to massive exoduses of Burundi people fleeing from Rwanda back to Burundi. Included in the exodus to Burundi were the Rwandese Patriotic Front (RPF) forces, which exacerbated Burundi's civil war. Moreover, the mass movements of displaced persons also included forces of the interahamwe militia and former soldiers of the Rwandese government, among refugees fleeing to Burundi and along Burundi's border during and after the 1994 Rwanda genocide.

Through Gambari, inclusivity of all people and main actors in Burundi was the success factor that resulted in achieving the equal representation of ethnic groups throughout government and administrative institutions. These mediated efforts led to Burundi's successfully establishing the "Forum of the Negotiations," which was led by representatives of civil society, religious groups, as well as recognized political parties. Such interventions effectively resulted in the first agreement on power-sharing reached on September 10, 1994, signed by thirteen political parties, including in the main, Jean Minani, president of FRODEBU, and Charles Mukasi, president of UPRONA. The modalities of the power-sharing negotiations included an appointed president for a four-year transitional period; the appointment of a prime minister from among the opposition, who would countersign the president's decisions; and the creation of a National Security Council of ten members equitably divided between FRODEBU and the opposition (UN doc S/1994/1152).[11] Subsequently, the appointment of a new president on September 18, 1994, was reached and signed by all political parties with the exception of the Parti PARENA, headed by former president Bagaza, including Nyangoma's CNDD Party, and the Palipehutu Party leaders were also absent from the power-sharing negotiations. Ntibantunganya, as the official candidate of FRODEBU, was elected by the National Assembly by sixty-eight votes to one and sworn in for a second time as Burundi's president on October 1, 1994; and the Tutsi, Anatole Kanyenkiko (UPRONA,) as prime minister on October 3, 1994, resulting in a new coalition government constituted on October 5, 1994 (UN doc S/1994/1152).

ETHNOPOLITICS AND POWER FITS OF UPRONA

The new coalition government proved ineffective. Burundi's conflicts were thus again sparked by six small opposition parties who did not manage to obtain posts in the government. Bujumbura's politics had dramatically changed the political scene, with ethnic groups infused into parties which became the dominant forces. UPRONA lost the first government seat and made a mockery of the new coalition government and its legislature, and also used it as a platform to gain power by fighting old and new battles and calling to book those who had committed atrocities during 1993. UPRONA demanded that Jean Minani be removed as speaker of the Assemblée nationale and accused him of inciting violence during the attempted coup of 1993 (UN doc S/1994/1152). UPRONA further threatened its withdrawal from the new coalition government and the legislature. Three months later, Minani was replaced by Léonce Ngendakumana of FRODEBU. But soon after Minani's dismissal, UPRONA created further infighting and conflict within government, demanding that Prime Minister Antole Kanyenkiko too should resign. UPRONA's leader, Charles Mukasi, was determined to resolve the coalition government, threatening to overthrow the government should Kanyenkiko refuse relinquishing his post. Kanyenkiko was being accused of behaving too moderately during the failed 1993 coup and should thus resign in solidarity with his party. Kanyenkiko's refusal resulted in his expulsion from UPRONA. Infighting within Burundi's political parties became common (UN doc S/1994/1152).

THE RETURN OF BUYOYA IN 1996

The return of Buyoya brought about an imminent change once again to Burundi's political arena. Buyoya was instrumental in ushering in Burundi's constitutional change in 1991 that brought Hutus back to power. Buyoya's coup also ushered in a firm response from external actors with stringent economic sanctions on Burundi. Buyoya completely miscalculated the regional and international responses, which was to be different than his 1987 coup when he ousted Bagaza. Preceding Buyoya's latest coup, between the period 1993 and 1996, after graciously stepping down and losing to his electoral opponent Ndadaye, Buyoya worked on "democracy programs" in Burundi. Astonishingly, in 1994, Buyoya received a total of US$145,000 from the Clinton administration's AID claimed for the use of promoting democracy. In addition, the U.S. grants to Buyoya's Foundation for Unity, Peace, and Democracy totaled US$2,500 (to be an election observer to South Africa in April 1994). In 1995, Buyoya also received US$25,000 for a project on how to assist Burundian Tutsis in exile or those who had fled into the bush; US$3,000 to attend a conference in Benin on "Democratization and the Role of the Military." In 1996, Buyoya received an additional US$51,250 to study "Institutional System Adapted to Burundi" and US$12,580 for a refugee "Reinsertion Action Program" in the Bururi Province. Bill Hagelman, an official of USAID, noted that the Buyoya foundation grants were not cut because they were covered under a program called "Democratic Governance" (Drogin 1996). Buyoya was thus in good shape to stage a coup d'état in July 1996, which overthrew the interim Hutu President Ntibantunganya, who went into hiding, fearing for his life, thereby allowing easy gains and entry into Burundi. Buyoya was sworn in as self-proclaimed interim president and attempted at all costs to reinstate his Tutsi Party. However, Buyoya's efforts were futile, because he had to toe the line of the AU and UN.[12]

MULTILATERAL INTERNATIONAL
DIPLOMATIC INVOLVEMENT

The 1996 period was unlike the 1960s–1980s and early 1990s, when multilateral international involvement in Burundi was minimal. With several genocides and civil wars, continental and international instruments of human rights and international humanitarian laws proved to be more forceful, albeit without the use of a military force. Burundi was thus held to account, and external actors did not hesitate to intervene. Burundi is a member-state of several regional, continental, and international organizations, including the UN, the AU (formerly known as the OAU), Kagera River Basin Organization (KBO), the Non-Aligned Movement (NAM), the Group of 77 African, Caribbean, and Pacific Group of States (ACP); the Preferential Trade Agreement for Eastern and Southern Africa (PTA) (now the Common Market for Eastern and Southern Africa), the East African Community (EAC), the International Conference on the Great Lakes Region (ICGLR), and a member of the ICC. Subsequently, Burundi returned its instruments to the Hague and withdrew as a member in 2016. Tanzania's former president, Julius Nyerere took a very strong stance against the military coup staged by Buyoya in July 1996, and so did the leaders of the Great Lakes Region (Uganda, Rwanda, and DRC, which led to economic sanctions against Burundi).[13] During Buyoya's despotic return, the Burundian courts imposed 220 death sentences on the perpetrators of the 1993 genocide. The UN Human Rights Commission Special Rapporteur on Burundi provided several scathing reports of the violence in Burundi. During the Special Rapporteur's fourth visit to Burundi in December 1997, thousands of innocent civilians were killed by rebels, consisting mainly of militia and former Rwandan and Zairian soldiers at the Gakumbu Military Camp, and the international airport at Bujumbura in the District of Mutimbuzi, the zone of Rukaramu Province of Bujumbura. The killings were linked to the CNDD-FDD and Palipehutu rebel groups.[14] Two years later, Buyoya was still in power and was met with more stringent sanctions from the international community.

These harsh sanctions forced Buyoya to commit to a new era for Burundi and the beginning of a power-sharing government under the Arusha Peace negotiations of June 1998. But, the Arusha negotiations that began in 1998 also brought about the emergence of several factions through the infighting within political parties, pushing for power and gains from the Arusha processes. The Arusha negotiations thus led to degrees of violence throughout the country. In 1998, a fall-out among the members of the CNDD-FDD Party ensued, and Nyangoma broke away from CNDD-FDD and maintained the political wing, CNDD, while his counterpart, Jean-Bosco Ndayikengurukiye, led the bulk of the party—CNDD-FDD. The Arusha 2000 Peace Accords gave actualization to both rebel groups and government to have a stake at the high table of Burundi. The economics of war led to several rebel groups forming in Burundi participating in the Arusha Peace and Reconciliation Agreement of August 28, 2000. At the apex of Burundi's transitional government, the humanitarian suffering in Burundi continued unabated. And this resulted in 500,000 Burundian refugees, and more than 800,000 people, about 12 percent of the population, being internally displaced (UN doc SC/7155, 2001).

THE ARUSHA NEGOTIATIONS AND THE BURUNDI POWER-SHARING GOVERNMENT MODEL, 1998–2004

The Arusha Peace Accords were signed by seventeen parties and the transitional government of Burundi. These events led to the appointment of a twenty-nine-member Monitoring Committee of the Arusha Agreement on Peace and Reconciliation, as well as the installation of the transitional leadership on November 1, 2001. This agreement meant that Buyoya led the country for the first half of the three-year transitional period with Domitien Ndayizeye of FRODEBU as vice president, from 2002 to 2005. During the second phase, Ndayizeye assumed the presidency, and a new vice president was designated from the G-10 group of Tutsi parties. The Arusha negotiators brokered an agreement among the G-7 group of Hutu parties and G-10 group of Tutsi parties on a transitional government. Thereafter, the cabinet members were nominated in accordance with the agreed quotas: 60 percent for the G-7 and 40 percent for the G-1. Thereafter, there were several positive developments, including that "Buyoya and the G-7 group agreed on the legal framework for the composition of the cabinet, the structure of government, and the transitional National Assembly. The composition of the senate as well as the selection of the president of the senate were determined by the G-10" (UN doc. S/2001/1076 2001: 1). While the agreement for the transitional government was being finalized, Burundi was still at war with the CNDD-FDD and the Palipehutu-FNL because the two political parties chose to remain outside of the Arusha Peace negotiations and the transitional governance processes. Burundi had a powerful military of 80,000 soldiers, while CNDD-FDD had a rebel force of 30,000. Meanwhile, the critical processes that emerged from the Arusha 2000 Accords were the Comprehensive Ceasefire Agreements, which were signed in 2002, 2003, and 2006. These agreements provided rebel groups outside of the Accords an opportunity to lay down their arms and commit to the disarmament, demilitarization, and demobilization (DDR) processes, as well as allowing their integration into the security sector reform processes of Burundi's military and police. In October 2002, Ndayikengurukiye's CNDD-FDD, and Alain Mugabarabona's Palipehutu-FNL were the first to sign the comprehensive ceasefire agreement. Pierre Nkurunziza's CNDD-FDD only came to the negotiating table in November 2003 and signed, which preceded his tactics of pushing for the reorganization of the military structure of a power-sharing defense and security model to suit

CNDD-FDD.[15] This agreement marked a political and military victory for the CNDD-FDD. On the other hand, Palipehutu-FNL led by Agathon Rwasa continued its acts of aggression, and only came to the negotiating table three years later, in September 2006, to sign the comprehensive ceasefire agreement with the government (UN doc S/RES/1545; UN doc S/2006/994).

ETHNIC INCLUSIVITY: A TRUMP CARD FOR CNDD-FDD

Burundi had seventeen parties around the negotiation table during the Arusha Accords of 2000. But the resulting transitional government of November 2001 left out the smaller and insignificant parties within the G-7 Hutu and G-10 Tutsi. The quotas were 60 percent for the G-7 Hutu parties and 40 percent for the Tutsi G-10 parties for cabinet members; the allocation of cabinet posts was determined through negotiations among the participating signatories. This became problematic, because the various allocated positions went to the elite groups within the parties. The facilitation team of the 2000 Arusha Accords did not involve themselves with the correct allocation of seats; they left this to the parties. However, the former deputy president of South Africa, Jacob Zuma, who served as the chief facilitator of the peace process, raised several major issues regarding the allocation of the positions and the marginalization of the smaller political parties:

Differences have, however, arisen within the G-7 (Hutu) and G-10 (Tutsi) political families. The differences within G-7 have been between FRODEBU and the smaller Hutu parties, and within G-10 between UPRONA and the smaller Tutsi parties. The smaller parties complained that they are not properly consulted when decisions are taken in the name of the groups, and that they have not been given their fair share in the distribution of government posts. Some parties opposed to the Transitional Government and to the Arusha Agreement have become more vocal at a time when ceasefire negotiations are being conducted at the highest level. This has resulted in the arrest, in October 2002, of Charles Mukasi, leader of UPRONA wing opposed to the Arusha Agreement, and the house arrest early in November 2002 of former President Jean-Baptiste Bagaza, leader of the Party for National Recovery (PARENA). So far, the differences among and within parties, as well as the subversive campaigns against the transitional institutions led by extremist parties are not expected to scuttle the peace process. (UN doc S/2002/1259 2002: 13)

Daniel Sullivan, and several other scholars attempted to fit the Arusha 2000 Accords into a negotiating model based on Arend Lijphart's theory of consociational democracy, by assessing whether Burundi's Arusha negotiations were flawed leading up to the end of the civil war in 2006 (Reyntjens 2006; Sullivan 2004). Consociational democracy defines a power-sharing model of a grand coalition that includes the participation of leaders of all segments in the cabinet within a parliamentary system, based on proportionality. Such cooperation occurs when the country endures persistent violent conflicts in a continually fragmented society, which leads them to consciously and rationally take remedial actions. The consociational democracy theory outlines four sequential critical steps, which ought to build on each other for success: a grand coalition, autonomy for the segments of society, minority overrepresentation or parity, and a minority veto (Sullivan 2005: 78–79).

Through the consociational democracy model, a deeply divided society of ethnic and political cleavages of a technically constructed power-sharing model simply erased the ethnic issue. During the Mandela 2001 negotiations, the G-10 Tutsi group insisted that political-ethnic affiliations should be considered, meaning that Tutsi would have to belong to a Tutsi party, but that too was rejected by the facilitators (Reyntjens 2006). While the ethnic balance was only relevant with regard to the quotas agreed to in the 2000 Arusha Peace Accords, nothing prevented either Tutsi or Hutu from joining a political party. Ethnic inclusivity was thus made use of when Nkurunziza and his CNDD-FDD Hutu party entered the political arena and immediately used the weakness of the nonethnic position, by encouraging both Hutus and Tutsis to join CNDD-FDD. After the signing of the Protocol on Political Power-Sharing, Defense, and Security in Tshwane (Pretoria) on October 8, 2003, between the transitional government and CNDD-FDD, Nkurunziza immediately became minister of state in charge of good governance and the general inspection of the state. Nkurunziza had two years to gather both Tutsis and Hutus to create a strong position in the 2005 national elections against his fellow Hutu party and opposition FRODEBU. Indeed, in 2004, over fifty MPs crossed the party line over to CNDD-FDD. The 2005 election results proved the interethnic nature of the CNDD-FDD, with 30 percent of its elected MPs being Tutsi (Reyntjens 2006).

CONCLUSION

Burundi's civil wars have been a culmination of several factors and actors. The overarching factors are rooted in German and Belgian colonialism. For example, the cultural, political, and socioeconomic structures and systems developed by the colonizers and retained by the postindependence regimes in Burundi caused the violent conflicts in 1959, 1961, 1965, 1972, 1988, and 1993. However, from 2005 to 2018, the nature of the political violence has changed from the earlier days that were based on the mass killings of Hutus and Tutsis to targeted ones directed at the leaders and members of the major opposition parties, with Imbonerakure, the youth wing of the ruling party, as the chief perpetrator.

Burundi's low-intensity wars fought between 2006 and 2019 have remained embedded in a perceived democracy of greed over political power in the hands of a strongman despot and the dominance of a single-party system woven into political and military ideals, which acutely pursues the absence of, and denialism for, democratic governance. Ultimately, its existence can only be sustained by four infused causal factors that must be present to feed off one another, which in turn gives rise to power for, and the existence of, the despot. First, manipulated and distorted political democratization processes that involved a militarized, autocratic, and repressive system. Democracy thus made a return with a strongman system in the hands of rebel leaders and former warlords—made political actors—to gain support from neighbors— the DRC, Rwanda, and Uganda—resulting in further regional destabilization and a protracted intrastate conflict in Burundi. The conflict therefore had a positive value to sustain the despots' political power.

Second, the mismanagement of multicultural and multinational values of citizens, and the marginalization of large segments of the populations in Burundi and those of its neighbors, led to the mass exoduses of disgruntled people in the Great Lakes and the formation of rebel groups turned political actors. This contributed to the phenomenon of recycled violence by rebel group, entanglements within and among rebel groups, within and among opposition parties, within the Burundian government, among rebel groups and opposition parties. In turn, this created a diversion from the autocratic nature of the regime and led to the creation of confusion about the real conflict factors and actors. Therefore, conflict had a positive value for the despot, as well as the rebel groups and opposition parties, which were sustained through an institutionalized predatocracy by both internal and external allies, backed by a regional predatory system, from which they received both the legitimacy and parts of the dividends—notably through the looting of natural resources.

Third, the absence of inclusive growth, and the crises of underdevelopment of a postconflict state plagued with low-intensity wars have continued unabatedly, while grandiose macroeconomic policies, such as the 2005 Priority Goals and the 2019 National Development Plan, have enticed multilateral organizations within the international community in postconflict reconstruction efforts to assist a government that lacks socioeconomic responsibilities to its people.

Fourth, the country's diversity has been continuously used as an opportunity to intentionally sow ethnic discord among the population, among the opposition and within governmental structures, to ignite violence that inevitably led to a weakened economy that is devoid of any poverty reduction possibilities, amid the continuous misplaced World Bank and UN peace-building funding. The funding from these multilateral institutions was not used, for example, to address issues such as mass poverty and chronic unemployment among vulnerable groups such as women and the youth.

In addition, the ongoing instability in the eastern DRC and other neighboring countries to Burundi poses a continuous threat, owing to the Great Lakes region's natural resources profiting rebel groups exiled in neighboring eastern DRC. The Arusha Processes proposed several mechanisms to be put in place to support Burundi in achieving and sustaining peace. For example, security sector reform processes led to Burundi's Tutsi-dominated military transforming and reducing its size from 80,000 to 30,000. Similarly, 22,000 ex-combatants were integrated into the police.

In further assistance to Burundi's security sector reform processes, Burundi's soldiers were welcomed into peacekeeping missions by the AU and received compensation totaling US$18 million. For example, the AU's Mission in Somalia (AMISOM) pays each soldier US$1,028 per month. But, all this has changed, which led former President Nkurunziza to express his disappointment in the AU's decision to withdraw 1,000 troops from AMISOM (Fröhlich 2019). By February 2019, the withdrawn contingent of 1,000 Burundi soldiers from AMISOM returned to Bujumbura (Kaneza 2019). Such a move provides a potent cocktail for a disaster with a strong potential of a military coup, given Burundi's track record of military coups.

The absence of effective justice mechanisms as well as the proposed truth, justice, and reconciliation processes, suggested during the Arusha 2000 Accords, remain hanging in the balance, with many crimes unaddressed. For example, those who committed these crimes were never dealt with, thereby providing perpetrators with the continuous advantage of violence in pursuit of power and victims the disadvantage of a weak justice system (UN doc S/2019/837 2019). Thus, vitriolic human rights violations and atrocities committed during gender-based violence continued. Thus, rape continues to be used as weapon of war, mainly by national security forces and the intelligence service.

The persistence of autocracy in Burundi gives warning signs of red alert for potential civil war in the country. Since the 2005, 2010, and 2015 elections, the CNDD-FDD has ruled Burundi as a one-party state, using ethnicity as its trump card, while successfully bypassing ethnic quotas and appointing cronies loyal to the CNDD-FDD and placing them in key government posts. Such a practice of patronage within the ruling CNDD-FDD is intentionally done to create instability within and among opposition parties. In turn, this can only lead to several splinter groups forming within the opposition, with the great potential of exacerbating conflicts in an already fragile country. In May 2020, the UN's Human Rights Commission (UNHRC) raised alarm perturbed by the gross violations of human rights. This was caused by the engagement in acts of violence by both the Burundi's government and opposition in the continued contestations over state power (UNHRC Commission of Inquiry on Burundi 2020).

Burundi's metamorphosis into a "rogue state" has been particularly apparent during its preelection processes, with total disregard for life and the well-being of the population. Amid the mass deprivation, President Nkurunziza was given US $500,000 and a luxury villa for stepping down in 2020 (Kiruga 2020). The May 2020 elections marked a second time in Burundi's independent history, when a president willfully transferred presidential power to the winner of an election—Nkurunziza transferred power to his CNDD-FDD compatriot, General Évariste Ndayishimiye, nicknamed Neva, for a seven-year term. The first was the 1993 elections which witnessed the first democratic transfer of power from Buyoya to the Hutu majority FRODEBU party's candidate Ndadaye. However, the main opposition party, National Council for Liberty (CNL) headed by Agathon Rwasa, cried foul and challenged the results in Burundi's Constitutional Court.[16]

There are no quick fixes in a broken society with weak state institutions and the continuation of human rights atrocities being committed with no recourse. As the 2020 elections forged ahead, the UN Human Rights Council's Commission of Inquiry on Burundi remained greatly perturbed by the extent of human rights violations committed since September 2019 by the CNDD-FDD's youth league, the Imbonerakure.[17] In a March 2020 report, the commissioners leading Commission of Inquiry on Burundi asserted that "Burundi election countdown amid 'deteriorating' human rights situation [. . .] the Imbonerakure members of a youth league linked to President Pierre Nkurunziza's ruling party—and to multiple attacks against opposition politicians and their families. They have continued to carry out 'killings disappearances, arbitrary arrests and detentions, acts of torture and ill-treatment and rape against actual or alleged political opposition members'" (UN Human Rights 2020). Burundi, however, continues to receive full support of US$114 million to assist in the country's humanitarian response to climate change (UN doc S/2020/232), regardless of the ongoing acts of aggression.

Burundi's violent conflicts would only end if its government is willing to adopt an inclusive approach and enact a power-sharing model among its politicians. One of the major postelection developments was former President Nkurunziza's sudden death on June 8, 2020, from a heart attack (Richardson 2020). Has Nkurunziza's death turned the tables for Burundi's violent conflicts? Has the former president's sudden passing placed a sealed lid on the heinous crimes of human rights committed by Nkurunziza's

Imbonerakure members? With a deafening silence coming from the AU since the passing away of Nkurunziza, it appears that his Imbonerakure compatriots will remain unpunished. What is the AU to do at this junction of Burundi's politics? Will the AU forge ahead and hold accountable those who committed human rights violations? Also, will the AU turn another sealed eyelid and ignore Burundi's security issues or provide necessary security force for imminent peace-building deployment, instead of misplaced hopes on the UN to deploy a force that will never be forthcoming, except to ensure a perceived peace through the continuation of government-funding packages?

NOTES

1. See for example René Lemarchand, "Patterns of State Collapse and Reconstruction in Central Africa: Reflections on the Crisis in the Great Lakes Region," *Africa Spectrum*, 32, no. 2 (1997): 173–193; Rene Lemarchand, *Rwanda and Burundi* (New York and London: Pall Mall Press and Frederick Praeger, 1970); Rene Lemarchand, *Burundi: Ethnic Conflict and Genocide*. (New York: Cambridge University Press and Woodrow Wilson Center Press, 1995); Filip Reyntjens, *Rwanda: Trois jours qui ont fait basculer l'histoire* (Brussels and L'Harmattan: Institut Africain/CEDAF, 1995); Jean-François Bayart, and Stephen Ellis, "Centenary Issue: A Hundred Years of Africa," *African Affairs*, 99, no. 395 (2000): 217–267; and Devon Curtis, "Development Assistance and the Lasting Legacies of Rebellion in Burundi and Rwanda," *Third World Quarterly*, 36, no. 7 (2015): 1365–1381. Authors largely from the West proffers no recourse to be considered by the World Body with regard to Africa's colonization autocratic Tsars, instead, huge analyses are provided on their worrisome debates of the internal dynamics of Burundi and its donor dependencies of political parties; while some see the African citizen as the trickster during colonization, with no recourse proffered, but the innocence of colonial masters.

2. Gérard Prunier, "The Myth of the Hutus and Tutsis," *Le Monde diplomatique*, February 2016. For further views on Burundi's historical trajectory, see Francis Loft, "Background to the Massacres in Burundi," *Review of African Political Economy*, 15, no. 43 (1988): 88–93; Jeremy J. Greenland, "Black Racism in Burundi," *New Blackfriars*, 54, no. 641 (1973): 443–451; see also Filip Reyntjens, "The Proof of the Pudding is in the Eating: The June 1993 Elections in Burundi," *Journal of Modern African Studies*, 31, no. 4 (1993): 563–583.

3. Adam Hochschild, *King Leopold's Ghost* (New York: Harper Collins, 1998). *See also The Guardian*, "The Hidden Holocaust," May 13, 1999.

4. Georges Nzongola-Ntalaja,"Patrice Lumumba: The Important Assassination of the 20th Century," *The Guradian*, January 17, 2011. Nzongola-Ntalaja notes in this article that: "This heinous crime was a culmination of two inter-related assassination plots by American and Belgian governments, which used Congolese accomplices and a Belgian execution squad to carry out the deed."

5. UN High Commissioner for Refugees (UNHCR), January 1, 1963. https://www.refworld.org/docid/3ae68c400.html. Accessed September 30, 2019.

6. An account of Belgian colonialism in Burundi is provided by the last Belgian colonial Resident: see Jean-Paul Harroy, *Burundi 1955–1962* (Brussels: Hayez, 1987), 399. *Cited in* Prunier, *Burundi a Manageable Crisis* (United Kingdom: Writenet: 9, October 1994).

7. UN Report of the Security Council Mission to Burundi. August 13 and 14, 1994, UN doc. S/1994/1039; see also Rene Lemarchand, "Social Change and Political Modernization in Burundi," *The Journal of Modern African Studies*, 4, no. 4 (1966): 401–33.

8. UN Economic and Social Council, Commission on Human Rights, UN doc. E/CN.4/1996/4/Add.1, July 24, 1995.

9. Economic and Social Council, UN Commission of Human Rights. UN doc. E/CN.4/1996/4/Add.1. http://hrlibrary.umn.edu/commission/country52/4-add1.htm. Accessed October 30, 2019.

10. United States Department of State, Bureau of Public Affairs, *Burundi Post Report* (Washington, DC: Office of Public Communication, March 1987).

11. See also UN Rapporteur, "12th Supplement 1993–1995: Chapter VIII," https://www.un.org/french/docs/cs/repertoire/93-95/CHAPTER%208/AFRICA/item09-%20Burundi.pdf. Accessed October 20, 2019.

12. United States Human Rights Report on Burundi, 1997. https://1997-2001.state.gov/global/human_rights/1997_hrp_report/burundi.html. Accessed October 25, 2019.

13. UN Press Release, "Press Conference by Foreign Minister of Burundi," March 17, 1998. https://www.un.org/press/en/1998/19980317.BURUNDI.html. Accessed October 25, 2019.

14. UN High Commissioner for Human Rights (UNOHCR). January 6 and 7, 1998. "Special Rapporteur on Burundi Strongly Condemns 'Unspeakable Acts' near Bujumbura," UN doc. doc. HR/98/1, 1. https://newsarchive.ohchr.org/en/NewsEvents/Pages/DisplayNews.aspx?NewsID=4531&LangID=E. Accessed October 25, 2019.

15. Pretoria Protocol on Burundi's October 2003 Power Sharing Agreement on Defense and Security with the Transitional Government and Pierre Nkurunziza. https://peacemaker.un.org/sites/peacemaker.un.org/files/Burundi_Protocol%20on%20Outstanding%20Issues_2003.pdf. Accessed October 30, 2019.

16. France24. May 25, 2020. "Burundi Expected to Announce Results of Presidential Election Monday;" May 25, 2020. See also Aljazeera, "First Democratic Transfer in 58 Years," May 25, 2020.

17. Security Council Report, "May 2020 Monthly Forecast," April 30, 2020.

REFERENCES

Aljazeera. 2020. "First Democratic Transfer in 58 Years." May.

Barth, Fredrik. 1969. *Ethnic Groups and Boundaries: The Social Organization of Culture Difference.* Boston: Little Brown.

Bayart, Jean-François, and Stephen Ellis. 2000. "Centenary Issue: A Hundred Years of Africa." *African Affairs*, 99(395): 217–267.

Boutros, Boutros-Ghali. 1995. *UN docs S/1995/157: 11*. February.

Curtis, Devon. 2015. "Development Assistance and the Lasting Legacies of Rebellion in Burundi and Rwanda." *Third World Quarterly*, 36(7): 1365–1381.

Drogin, Bob. 1996. "Burundi Coup Leader Received U.S. Funds." *Los Angeles Times*, July 27. https://www.latimes.com/archives/la-xpm-1996-07-27-mn-28410 -story.html. Accessed October 20, 2019.

Economic and Social Council, UN Commission of Human Rights. 1996. *UN doc. E/ CN.4/1996/4/Add.1*. http://hrlibrary.umn.edu/commission/country52/4-add1.htm. Accessed October 30, 2019.

Fortier, Anne-Marie. November 1994. "Ethnicity." *Paragraph: A Journal of Modern Critical Theory*, 17(3): 213–223.

France24. 2020. "Burundi Expected to Announce Results of Presidential Election Monday." May 25.

Geertz, Clifford. 1973. *The Interpretation of Cultures*. New York: Basic Books.

Greenland, Jeremy. 1973. "Black Racism in Burundi." *New Blackfriars*, 54(641): 443–51.

Greenland, Jeremy. 1975. "The Two Options Now Facing Burundi." *Issue: A Journal of Opinion*, 5(2): 3–5.

Harff, Barbara, and Robert Gurr Ted, eds. 2000. *Ethnic Conflict in World Politics*. 2nd ed. London: Routledge.

Harroy Jean-Paul. 1987. *Burundi 1955–1962*. Brussels: Hayez.

Hartung, William, D. and Bridget Moix. 2000. *Report: U.S. Arms to Africa and the Congo War*. World Policy Institute, January. http://www.worldpolicy.org/projects/ arms/reports/congo.htm. Accessed May 30, 2017.

Hochschild, Adam. 1998. *King Leopold's Ghost*. New York: Harper Collins.

Independent(United Kingdom). 1994. "Obituary: Cyprien Ntaryamira." April 8.

Khadiagala, Gilbert. 2002. "Implementing the Arusha Peace Agreement on Rwanda." In *Ending Civil Wars: The Implementation of Peace Agreements*, edited by Stephen John Stedman, Donald Rothchild and Elizabeth M Cousens. Boulder, CO: Lynn Reinner, 463–498.

Lemarchand, René. 1966. "Social Change and Political Modernization in Burundi." *The Journal of Modern African Studies*, 4(4): 401–33.

Lemarchand, René. 1970. *Rwanda and Burundi*. New York and London: Pall Mall Press and Frederick Praeger.

Lemarchand, René. 1989. "Burundi: The Killing Fields Revisited." *Issue: A Journal of Opinion*, 18(1): 22–28.

Lemarchand, René. 1995. *Burundi: Ethnic Conflict and Genocide*. New York: Cambridge University Press and Woodrow Wilson Center Press.

Lemarchand, René. 1997. "Patterns of State Collapse and Reconstruction in Central Africa: Reflections on the Crisis in the Great Lakes Region." *Africa Spectrum*, 32(2): 173–193.

Lemarchand, René. 2006. "Burundi at a Crossroads." In *Security Dynamics in Africa's Great Lakes Region*, edited by Gilbert M. Khadiagala. Boulder, CO and London: Lynne Rienner, 41–58.

Levine, Daniel, and Dawn Nagar, eds. 2016. *Africa's Region-Building: Politics and Economics*. New York: Palgrave Macmillan.

Loft, Francis, and Frances Loft. 1988. "Background to the Massacres in Burundi." *Review of African Political Economy*, 15(43): 88–93.

Marx, Karl. 1867. *Daz Kapital*. Hamburg, Germany: Verlag von Otto Meisner.

Miles, Tom. 2019. "UN Warns of Burundi Atrocities As 'Divine' Ruler Eyes 2020 Elections." *Reuters*, September 4.

Morris, Kiruga. 2020. "Burundi: WHO Reps Expelled Ahead of Polls Set to Go, Despite COVID19." *The Africa Report*, May 18.

Nagar, Dawn. 2018. *Africa and the World: Bilateral and Multilateral International Diplomacy*. New York: Palgrave Macmillan.

Nagar, Dawn. 2020. *Politics and Pan–Africanism: Diplomacy, Regional Economies and Peacebuilding in Contemporary Africa*. London: I.B. Tauris.

Nagar, Dawn. 2021. *Challenging the UN Peace and Security Agenda in Africa*. New York: Palgrave Macmillan.

Nzongola-Ntalaja, Georges. 2011. "Patrice Lumumba: The Most Important Assassination of the 20th century." *The Guardian(United Kingdom)*, January 17. https://www.theguardian.com/global-development/poverty-matters/2011/jan/17/patrice-lumumba-50th-anniversary-assassination. Accessed June 30, 2017.

Pretoria Protocol on Burundi's October 2003 Power Sharing Agreement on Defense and Security with the Transitional Government and Pierre Nkurunziza. 2003. https://peacemaker.un.org/sites/peacemaker.un.org/files/Burundi_Protocol%20on%20Outstanding%20Issues_2003.pdf. Accessed October 30, 2019.

Prunier, Gerard. 1994. *Burundi a Manageable Crisis?* United Kingdom: Writenet: 9.

Prunier, Gérard. 2016. "The Myth of the Hutus and Tutsis." *Le Monde diplomatique*, February.

Regan, Patrick M. 2000. *Civil Wars and Foreign Powers*. Ann Arbor, MI: University of Michigan Press.

Reyntjens, Filip. 1995. *Rwanda: Trois jours qui ont fait basculer l'histoire*. Brussels and L'Harmattan: Institut Africain/CEDAF.

Reyntjens, René. 1993. "The Proof of the Pudding is in the Eating: The June 1993 Elections in Burundi." *Journal of Modern African Studies*, 31(4): 563–83.

Reyntjen, René. 2000. *Burundi: Prospects for Peace*. London: Minority Rights Group International.

Reyntjens, Filip. 2006. "Briefing: Burundi: A Peaceful Transition After a Decade of War?" *African Affairs*, 105(418): 117–135.

Richardson, Paul. 2020. "Burundi Leader Dies after 15 Years of Turbulent Rule." *Bloomberg*, June 9.

Rosenheim, Daniel. 1985. "Amoco: Once again a Star on the World Stage." *Chicago Tribune*, May 13.

Schissel, Howard. 1987. "AMCO Expands African Oil Search." *Journal of Commerce. Com*, July 26. https://www.joc.com/amoco-expands-african-oil-search_19870726.html. Accessed September 30, 2019.

Security Council Report. 2020. "May 2020 Monthly Forecast." April 30.

Sullivan, Daniel. 2005. "The Missing Pillars: A Look at the Future of Peace in Burundi
    Through the Lens of Arend Lijphart's Theory of Consociational Democracy." *The
    Journal of Modern African Studies*, 43(1): 75–95.
The Washington Post. 1994. "Two African Presidents are Killed in Plane Crash."
    April 7.
UN. 1994. *Report of the Security Council Mission to Burundi*. August 13 and 14,
    1994.
UN. 2001 "Installation of Burundi's Transitional government on 1 November
    'Turning Point' in peace process says Security Council." *UN doc. SC/715,5.*
    https://www.un.org/press/en/2001/sc7155.doc.htm. Accessed October 25, 2019.
UN. 2005. *Doc. S/2005/158*. March 11.
UN Economic and Social Council, Commission on Human Rights. 1995. *UN doc. E/
    CN.4/1996/4/Add.1*. July 24.
UN Economic Social Council (ECOSOC). 1985. *Doc. E/CN.4/Sub.2/1985/7*.
UN High Commissioner for Human Rights (UNOHCR). 1998. "Special Rapporteur
    on Burundi Strongly Condemns 'Unspeakable Acts' Near Bujumbura." *UN doc.
    HR/98/1, 1*. January 6 and 7. https://newsarchive.ohchr.org/en/NewsEvents/Pages/
    DisplayNews.aspx?NewsID=4531&LangID=E. Accessed October 25, 2019.
UN High Commissioner for Refugees (UNHCR). 1963. *Doc UNCHR*, January.
    https://www.refworld.org/docid/3ae68c400.html. Accessed September 30, 2019.
UNHCR. 2014. *Congolese Refugees: A Protracted Situation*. https://www.unhcr.org
    /558c0e039.pdf. Accessed October 30, 2019.
United Nations. 1962. *(UN) doc. A/5069/Add.1*. April 24.
United Nations. 1994. *UN doc. S/1994/1039*. September 9.
United Nations.1995. *UN doc. S/1995/157*. February 24.
United Nations. 1995. *UN doc. E/CN.4/1996/4/Add.1*. July 24.
United Nations. 1996. *UN doc. E/CN.4/1996/4/Add.1*.
United Nations. 1998 "Press Conference by Foreign Minister of Burundi." *Press
    Release*, March 17. https://www.un.org/press/en/1998/19980317.BURUNDI.html.
    Accessed October 25, 2019.
United Nations. 2001. *UN doc. S/2001/1076*. November 14.
United Nations. 2004. *UN doc. S/RES/1545*. May 21.
United Nations. 2005. *UN doc. S2005/158: 6*.
United Nations. 2006. *UN doc. S/2006/994*. December 18.
United Nations. 2020. *UN doc. S/2020/232*. March 25.
United States. 1997. *Human Rights Report on Burundi*. https://1997-2001.state.gov/
    global/human_rights/1997_hrp_report/burundi.html. Accessed October 25, 2019.
United States Department of State, Bureau of Public Affairs. 1987. *Burundi Post
    Report*. Washington, DC: Office of Public Communication.
United States Department of State, Bureau of Public Affairs. 1988. *Burundi
    Background Notes*. Washington, DC: Office of Public Communication. July.
United States Institute for Peace (USIP). 2004. *Burundi Report*, January 13. https://
    www.usip.org/sites/default/files/file/resources/collections/commissions/Burundi
    -Report.pdf. Accessed September 2019.

UN Rapporteur. "12th Supplement 1993–1995: Chapter VIII." *Doc Repertoire.* https://www.un.org/french/docs/cs/repertoire/93-95/CHAPTER%208/AFRICA/ item09-%20Burundi.pdf. Accessed October 20, 2019.

von Einsiedel, Sebastian. 2017. *Civil War Trends and the Changing Nature of Armed Conflict.* Occasional Paper. Tokyo: UN University.

Weinstein, Warren. 1975. "Burundi." In *Civil Wars and the Politics of International Relief,* edited by Morris Davis, 5–24. New York: Praeger.

Chapter 3

Civil War in Cameroon

Avitus Agbor

In the context of a protracted political crisis, marked by gross violations of human rights, an exhaustive discourse on constructing a postconflict society requires, inter alia, a careful introspection on the legal and political arrangements that fomented, in the first place, the eruption of such conflicts and what must be done to ensure guarantees of nonrepetition. Like it has happened in most societies that were once called conflict and postconflict societies, the ongoing conflict in Cameroon, precisely in the English-speaking region therein, provides an opportunity for many questions to be asked. In light of the gross violations of human rights that have occurred during this conflict, could one consider the possibility of transitional justice arrangements in post-conflict Cameroon?

This chapter seeks to expound this idea: it starts by looking at the historical evolution of Cameroon and how the regimes of Ahidjo and Biya introduced and reaffirmed systemic discrimination against a linguistic minority, the exploitation of economic resources in that region, which, unfortunately, were not countermatched by socioeconomic development of the region. The chapter then reflects on the nature of political violence in Cameroon, highlighting its regular recurrence while drawing unique features of the Anglophone crisis. The chapter then mentions some of the dynamics of the conflict and then proceeds to discuss in detail the notion of transitional justice.

HISTORICAL DEVELOPMENT

In order to better comprehend the crisis in Cameroon, it is important to look at historical developments and how the country's colonial history as well as the system of administration instituted by the former and current presidents

97

contributed thereto. On the African Continent, Cameroon stands out as a glaring example of a country whose internal politics and linguistic rifts remain attributable, in most part, to its pre-1961 history: a colonial past that saw the country undergo the tutelage of three European countries. First, the Germans, and then followed by the British and the French. The Berlin Conference that took place from 1884 to 1885, resulted in the annexation of Cameroon by Germany, which ruled the colony until 1919. Known as German *Kamerun* during this time, the British and the French, per Article 22 of the Covenant of the League of Nations, took over as a mandated territory (Ngoh 1996). The British administered one-fifth of the territory (as an annexure to Nigeria which was already its colony) and was known as British Cameroons (currently former West Cameroon). On the other hand, the French administered four-fifths of the territory in what would be called East Cameroon.

The two administered territories obtained independence on different dates and ways: for the French-administered Eastern Cameroon, independence was obtained on January 1, 1960, with the name *République du Cameroun* (roughly translated it will read Republic of Cameroon) (Ngoh 1996: 167). For the British-administered West Cameroon, a plebiscite was sponsored by the United Nations on February 11, 1961. The aim of this plebiscite was to offer the people therein to determine if they wanted to achieve independence by either joining the already independent French-speaking *République du Cameroun* or with Nigeria (Fonge 1997: 39). The results showed that the preference was to join the already independent *République du Cameroun*. Southern Cameroons achieved its independence by uniting with the already independent French-speaking Cameroon on October 1, 1961 (Fonge 1997: 234; Takougang and Krieger 1999: 3–4). There were numerous internal political developments sequel to this, which undoubtedly have contributed to the current Anglophone Cameroon conflict. A referendum was held across the national territory in which Cameroonians voted to shift from a federal state system to a unitary one, earning the official appellation the "United Republic of Cameroon" on May 20, 1972 (Fonge 1999: 40). In 1984, the formal adoption of unitary state features was completed, and the word "United" was deleted from its name, with a return to Republic of Cameroon as the French-administered territory was earlier known (Takougang and Krieger 1999).

THE POSTCOLONIAL ERA: THE AHIDJO AND BIYA REGIMES

In the ensuing decades, both the Ahidjo and Biya regimes have exploited unconscionably and without account the economic resources of the Anglophone region, without the corresponding development of basic infrastructure.

Internal political arrangements and socioeconomic structures and priorities have revealed systemic discrimination perpetrated by the French-speaking Cameroonians (the majority, linguistically) against the English-speaking Cameroonians (the linguistic minority). Employment preferences and opportunities, development-related projects, political appointments, recruitment into public service, access to public services, and a gradual but progressive suffocation of Anglophone culture by the Francophone, such as educational curricula and legal practices, became conspicuous vexing issues that fuelled anti-Francophone sentiments over time.

These negative sentiments hit the crescendo in October 2016 when teachers and practicing lawyers in the Anglophone region asked for systemic reforms that would bring to par official recognition of Anglophone cultures and curricular for schools in the region and the complete removal of French and French-speaking judges and prosecutors in the courts in the English-speaking region. From civil disobedience to protests, the crisis gradually gained momentum, with the government taking no concrete effort to bring it to an end. Eventually, the crisis grew larger than the architects had foreseen: it degenerated to calls for a new political order: secession, federation, or retaining the status quo.

THE CURRENT CIVIL WAR

Meadow (2009: 232) postulates a captivating definition of a conflict society as "one that is characterized by a lack of consensus on governance, questionable legitimacy of governing institutions, or unresolved and ongoing religious, racial, or ethnic cleavages." Commonly, such conflict is manifested through civil war, guerrilla conflicts, domestic terrorism, or domestic military campaigns.

Political developments in Cameroon since the second half of 2016 suffice to warrant Cameroon as a conflict-torn society as its history since then has been dotted by incidents of politically motivated violence perpetrated by government officials and armed groups. This is for the purpose of furthering divergent and conflicting political agendas, demands, and in the hope that such will alter the current political status quo. Unprecedented and turbulent waves of sporadic acts of barbarism have characterized the protracted internecine conflict in which ethnic and linguistic minorities of the English-speaking areas (Anglophones) are demanding, among other things, for secession from the French-speaking side (Francophones).

The conspicuous political volatility has engineered the commission of gross human rights violations with responsibility thereof attributable to both the forces of government and recognized armed groups. Within this realm of political violence, heinous human rights violations have been committed: from random arrests and prolonged detentions; abductions; summary executions; murders; extermination; extrajudicial killings; enforced disappearances; to false imprisonment and other inhumane acts, Cameroonians have witnessed the perpetration of these in a systematic way that has resulted in large-scale victimization. In addition, surreptitious killings of masterminds of political protests and campaigns; assassinations of political leaders; mass murders of unarmed children and women; indiscriminate arrests and prolonged detentions without trials of protesters; arraignment of civilians before military tribunals; torture; use of batons and teargases to disperse political rallies and other covet operations have been reduced to the ordinary. Unfortunately and undoubtedly, the utilization of these tactics of repressing citizens' participation in government is not new: many a time in the political history of Cameroon the government has resorted to these strategies as a means of slowing down the momentum, curtailing public participation as ways of retaining its grip on political power. Schools have been vandalized; business entities set ablaze; villages shattered and their residents forced to leave. Hitherto, these were committed with impunity as they were often done on the instructions or directions of the government. The magnitude of victimization added to the systemic nature of these crimes; it speaks to the broken relationship between the victims of these violations and the government who ought to safeguard its people as well as respect, promote, and protect their rights.

The Dynamics of the Civil War

Undeniably, political violence is not a new phenomenon in the country's political history. Even though a glimpse at history reveals that such political tactics have become the modus operandi of the government, a few are worth mentioning: in 1990, the quest for *multipartyism* as a gateway to democracy and democratization turned sour as political violence was meted to the protesters who took to the streets (Konings 2010: 244–265). In 1991, demands for a sovereign national conference that would serve as a platform for public accountability from occupants of public offices were rejected by the ruling party, and the country slipped into chaos as ghost town operations halted businesses and civilians victimized by military and paramilitary personnel, including the police (Konings 2010: 244–265). In 1992, the first contested multiparty presidential elections would lead to the imposition of a state of emergency in Bamenda, the capital of the then-North-West Province, characterized by numerous human rights violations in which individuals were targeted for their political beliefs.

On a regular basis, different individuals are rendered victims simply because they engage in conduct that is perceived as offensive by the government. Political ideologies and actions that question the government, expose their misdeeds, or interrogate the competence and integrity of occupants of public offices are responded to with victimization of the individuals in question, and oft, their relatives and friends. As such, victimization of individuals based on their political ideologies and actions have been a way of conducting politics in Cameroon. While in previous instances the victimization has been across the nation, the current civil war in Cameroon seems very different: targeting Anglophone Cameroonians for their demands to end decades of marginalization and discrimination, serious human rights violations have been committed by the government of Cameroon, as well as other armed groups that have emerged therein for the purpose of fostering and winning their agendas which include, among other things, the adoption of a ten-sate federation or complete secession from the French-speaking Cameroon.

Unlike previous instances of political violence, the current political conflict is very distinct in many dimensions. First, political "conflicts" in Cameroon do not get protracted like this one which has spanned beyond two years. Second, the political demands that are made come from people who share a common linguistic background (English-speaking) based on their colonial heritage. Third, the conflict is limited to the English-speaking regions where elements thereof have made some political demands perceived as untenable by the French-speaking Cameroonians. Fourth, the scale of victimization and the organized nature of the human rights abuses now bring to focus the impact of this political violence as it has ruptured the tense relationship between the Anglophones and Francophones, on the one hand; and the victims and the perpetrators, on the other hand.

These instances, past and ongoing, unfortunately, do share some commonalities: the complete absence of any form of accountability, whether administrative or judicial (civil and criminal), for perpetrators of these heinous human rights violations. Irrespective of the gravity of human rights violations committed, they have been sanctioned with impunity. The perpetrators in this instance, as mentioned earlier, include both government officials and armed groups in the Anglophone Cameroon. In shaping the future political and legal landscape of Cameroon, the past must be confronted. This means that these abuses must be investigated, the truth obtained and documented, the perpetrators held accountable through criminal prosecutions, reparations awarded to victims of these violations and specific guarantees of nonrepetition put in place to ensure that the country does not relapse to its past. All these actions constitute the fundamental pillars of transitional justice which do include establishing the rule of law as an antithesis to rule by law, by implementing political and legal reforms and putting the affected communities and country on the path to peace and reconciliation.

Transitional Justice

The conflict, however, is ongoing, and that makes it difficult to prescribe with persuasiveness any befitting transitional justice mechanism, as there is a possibility, like any given conflict, of it escalating to unimaginable proportions which changes its character. In addition, transitional justice mechanisms have never been contemplated or introduced to Cameroon in the aftermath of a ravaging political violence or conflict. Considering any transitional justice mechanism, in the light of the above, is a delicate exercise that requires the involvement of the government, the civil society, the relevant stakeholders in the conflict, and the global community as well. The tasks to be fulfilled by such a mechanism and the goals to achieve will be enormous, ranging from punitive justice; seeking peace, unity, and reconciliation; obtaining the truth; memorialization of victims; the awarding of reparations to victims; to a change in the political and legal culture that permitted the commission of these human rights violations. These violations, as argued below, need to be outlined and appreciated in order to underscore the need for transitional justice mechanisms in the aftermath of the conflict.

Anglophone Cameroonians residing in the designated regions have been reduced to hapless victims of atrocities committed within the remit of contentious politics that has gone sour. The worrying issue about these atrocities is the gravity and intent underlying their commission. So far, it is beyond doubt that the crimes are systematic in their planning, preparation, and commission. The scale of victimization is now widespread. When atrocities of this nature are systematically planned, prepared for, and committed, or the scale of victimization is widespread, then, they become suggestive of the commission of serious crimes in international law. In addition, if such atrocities, such as the killings, are perpetuated with an intent to destroy, in part or in whole, a protected group of people such as an ethnicity, then, that may also be a genocide in the offing.

As has been witnessed, the massive deployment and utilization of state-owned and instructed law enforcement operatives under the direction of the state are partly responsible for what is taking place. No official denials have been recorded as the victims are unarmed and not in any combat. The scale of victimization, added to the organized nature of these crimes, put them beyond the threshold of normally acceptable violence within a state. In other words, the crimes, so far, do now exude a gravity that should earn the concerns of the international community as they suggest that crimes against humanity are currently being committed: murder; extermination; torture; rape and other forms of sexual violence; random arrests and prolonged detentions; enforced disappearances and other inhumane acts have been committed within the framework of a widespread and systematic attack directed against a civilian population and with knowledge of the fact that there is an attack within which these crimes are committed.

In addition to the commission of crimes against humanity, it is also highly suspected that the intent of the Francophone-led government is to perpetrate these crimes with the intention to destroy, in part or in whole, one of the protected groups contemplated in the United Nations' Convention on the Prevention and Punishment of the Crime of Genocide (the Genocide Convention): an ethnic group. It should, however, be noted that these crimes in themselves do not attract the severity that they get: it is the framework within which they are committed that does. In this instance, they are made serious because they fall within the definitional elements of what constitute serious crimes in international law: for the crime of crimes against humanity, there is clearly a widespread or systematic attack that is directed against a civilian population and the crimes are committed with knowledge of such an attack. For the crime of genocide, the killings are done with the intent to destroy, in part or in whole, a protected group of people.

In my view, the aforementioned crimes are not ordinary crimes that can be ignored. They constitute serious crimes in international law. As serious crimes of grave concern to mankind, there is a duty to investigate and prosecute these crimes whenever they are committed or suspected to have been committed (Obura 2011). This duty is clearly stipulated in international instruments, and partly has evolved over time through customary international law as well as international human rights law (Obura 2011).

Imputing a Genocidal Intent?

Major onslaughts launched against Anglophone Cameroonians across the nation based on their ethnicity and linguistic backgrounds and on Anglophone territories in Cameroon have been systematic in nature as they are organized, planned, ordered, directed, and perpetrated by the government. Police officials, paramilitary, and military personnel, including the gendarmes, have been used to bombard villages, shatter shelters, disrupt civilian lifestyle, and perpetrate egregious human rights violations. Added to the systematicity of these atrocities is the scale of victimization: the toll of these on human lives and civic liberties continue to skyrocket on a daily basis.

Based on reports from credible human rights bodies, the documented instances of loss of human lives speak of about 5,000, inclusive of state officials and agents consumed in this decimating conflict. Inasmuch as there is reason to suspect the commission of crimes against humanity given the fact that these atrocities such as murder, extermination, arrests and detention (false imprisonment), torture and other inhumane acts are committed as part of a widespread or systematic attack launched against a civilian population, it might also be indicative of an implied genocidal intent. Absent official papers that could confirm or refute this suspicion, the killings of Anglophone Cameroonians based on their ethnicity are aimed at, at least, the partial destruction of the people of Anglophone Cameroon as a result of their ethnic and linguistic origins and traits.

MOVING BEYOND A CONFLICT-TORN CAMEROON: THE NEED TO SHAPE THE FUTURE

Amid this prolonged political imbroglio, numerous questions are asked: How do we end this ravaging political conflict? How do we shape a new legal and political order for Cameroon? Watered down to more individualistic questions, victims (both direct and indirect) of human rights violations are asking themselves questions that reflect their disappointment, woundedness, and hope for justice: Who killed my son? How did my brother disappear? What has happened to my husband since his abduction? When will the youths in the vicinity be released from detention? Who ordered the execution of my comrades? What was the underlying motive behind these atrocities? If we seek to find answers to these questions, then, there must be at least a national mechanism that is put in place in order to foster such an exercise, be it a truth commission, fact-finding commission, or commission of inquiry.

The tales and narratives told by both direct and indirect victims; the witnesses; the perpetrators; the other individuals who bear some form of responsibility for these atrocities are vital not only in the national healing process but also in understanding how the society slipped to that level of inhumanity and bestiality; the possibility of memorializing the victims; the award of reparations; and the setting into motion any form of accountability for these perpetrators. It also affords the country the opportunity to auto-examine its history and identify its fault lines, asking questions such as how did it get to this abysmal state: poor administration; corruption that is rife; the absence of the rule of law; weak political and legal institutions; high levels of unemployment; dysfunctional political institutions that are domineered by an overarching executive; abject poverty; weak judicial system; and a dangerous ideology that democracy is about how the majority wields control and not how minorities are protected within the system.

The pursuit of justice, it is hoped, may help in dismantling this failed and unsustainable system of Cameroonian politics that has been cancerous to the entire national psyche. In addition, it may put in place credible political culture and institutions in which everyone is respected, protected, and promoted. In this case, as the entire nation atones for its sins, guarantees of nonrepetition should be put in place. Moreover, the pursuit of accountability may lead to some form of victim catharsis of what they have endured over time: the pain of losing a loved one without knowing why; the degree of grief suffered by such a victim; and how their lives have been devastated by such a loss.

Lastly, investigating and prosecuting perpetrators of these atrocities, it is hoped, will deter others from taking a role in the commission of such atrocities in the future. As mentioned earlier, the tactic of victimization and intimidation is typical of Cameroon's Francophone-led government that is fostered through sporadic and intermittent cruelties that target specific individuals and groups of people. Its nascent democracy has been stagnated and tainted by severe curtailments on expressions of citizenship participation. These curtailments have, often, been violent and repressive, some spanning over longer periods of time. Even though they constitute massive violations of human rights, impunity has been their aftermath. Therefore, pursuing any form of justice for these atrocities now will signal the end of that era of impunity, replacing it with accountability as those responsible for their planning, preparation, and commission will be identified, exposed, and prosecuted.

Cameroon is gradually and progressively tethering toward the path of a devastating intra-state, ethnolinguistic, and tribal conflict that pits its demographics against one another: Anglophone against Francophones, the young versus the old, and so on. The need for the establishment of the rule of law, and confront the past and present human rights violations committed particularly by the state, is very urgent. Cameroon's broken judicial and political institutions; an inept and corrupt criminal justice system that thrives on the whims and caprices of the political elite; the debunked and nonsensical philosophies upon which its democracy and democratization rest; the endemic corruption; abused resources; diminished security; a fragmented population; internecine suspicion that has increasingly eroded the trust the people have in government officials; and a culture of impunity that serves as the official reward for those who take part in human rights violations—these do provide a partial silhouette of the saddening contextual background but also some of the daunting challenges that need to be confronted and overcome in the identification, design, and implementation of an appropriate transitional justice mechanism.

Based on the evidence documented in societies that have experienced large-scale human rights violations, especially under repressive regimes or intra/interstate armed conflicts, promoting peace and reconciliation in the long term requires the establishment of an effective governing system of administration and justice that is built on the respect for the rule of law and the protection of human rights. Even though the notion of transitional justice is not new as many countries across the globe have considered and implemented different mechanisms, such has never been the Cameroonian experience. Yet the stories of past abuses would have justified the consideration and implementation of transitional justice mechanisms.

For reasons of space, this chapter cannot fully map out the most appropriate transitional justice mechanism that will befit the Cameroonian context. However, given the nature of the ongoing conflict, it recommends the first step toward the path to national unity and reconciliation: the need for an institutional mechanism that seeks the truth, reveals the perpetrators, discloses the underlying motives, and paves the way for accountability. In my view, the establishment of a truth (and reconciliation) commission will be priceless in this regard. In the long run, this mechanism, if implemented and properly executed, will contribute to ending the culture of impunity and establishing the rule of law in the context of building a peaceful society that practices democratic governance. It offers a state which, hitherto, was the theater of human rights violations the opportunity to lay and build the pillars of human rights protection. The respect for promotion and protection of human rights becomes the core of its new political construct, and accountability for their violations a routine norm. The establishment of a truth (and reconciliation) commission, as a key transitional justice mechanism, will serve multifaceted purposes, some of which will include bringing to an end the continuous human rights violations; an investigation into past human rights violations; holding perpetrators (both state and nonstate actors) accountable for these human rights violations; the imposition of appropriate sanctions on both natural and juristic persons who bear responsibility for these human rights violations; the provision of reparations to direct and indirect victims of these human rights violations; preventing such violations from occurring in the future through the implementation of guarantees of nonrepetition; overhauling the entire criminal justice system and putting the country on the path to peace and reconciliation at individual, societal, and national levels.

The truth (and reconciliation) commission, unfortunately, will not be the sole transitional justice mechanism: it becomes the key game starter and changer which transmits to offenders, victims, and civil society the need to move beyond the past by confronting it, as the nation shapes the future. As such, different mechanisms may be put in place, as long as they play a role in fulfilling the goals of transitional justice: establishing the truth of what has happened; providing a public platform to the victims; holding perpetrators accountable; strengthening the rule of law; providing reparations to victims; effecting institutional reform; promoting reconciliation; and promoting public deliberations. In this regard, designing and implementing additional transitional justice models should obviously capture the aforementioned aims and objectives and must take a holistic approach that encompasses criminal prosecutions; a truth (and reconciliation) commission; reparation programs; reform of the security sector; and memorialization of victims, whether as individuals, groups, or communities.

In the past few decades, numerous societies across the globe have increasingly embraced the enforcement of international human rights norms. As such, there has been greater accountability for human rights violations committed during previous regimes' repressive rule, political transition, or armed conflicts (both international and domestic). Examples of these abound, which do provide a blueprint for Cameroon. They include South Africa, the former Yugoslavia, East Timor, Iraq, Rwanda, Sierra Leone, Chile, Mexico, Argentina, and Colombia. Irrespective of the aims and objectives of what kind of transitional justice mechanism to be adopted and implemented in Cameroon, account must be taken of factors such as the local context in which the crimes or human rights violations were committed; the cultural practices of the people; economic realities; political philosophies and cultures; institutions and influences. This requires extensive consultations with the local communities in Cameroon so that they inform the design, implementation, and evolution of such mechanisms and policies. This is key to the effectiveness and success of any such mechanism.

CONCLUSION

This chapter has provided a contextual background to the problem that is ongoing in Cameroon. Hoping that the conflict comes to an end, there will be a need for the nation to confront those (past) abuses in order to shape a peaceful future where there is national unity and cohesion among the different demographics. To ignore the past will be a dangerous path to consider as different victims have endured various depths of woundedness and bitterness. There is a severe and deep lack of trust in the government as these have now become their way of doing politics.

In order to shape the future, the government, aided by the international community, must consider addressing the past abuses in order to identify the systemic cracks that contributed to this dismal history. The first step toward this end is the establishment of an independent and credible mechanism that offers the platform for the entire nation to witness and document the narratives of the victims of the experiences they encountered during these violations. The provision of a platform for such individuals, where names will be called and details of violations disclosed, will be priceless in reconstructing a peaceful Cameroon that is founded on national reconciliation and unity.

REFERENCES

Fonge, F. P. 1997. *Modernization Without Development in Africa: Patterns of Change and Continuity in Post-Independence Cameroonian Public Service*. Trenton, NJ: Africa World Press.

Konings, P. J. J. 1996. "The Post-colonial State and Economic and Political Reforms in Cameroon." In *Liberalization in the Developing World – Institutional and Economic Change in Latin America, Africa and Asia*, edited by A. E. Jilberto, F. Jilberto, A. Mommen, 244–265. London: Routledge.

Meadow, R. G. 2009. "Political Violence and the Media." *Marquette Law Review*, 93: 231–240.

Ngoh, V. J. 1996. *History of Cameroon Since 1800*. Limbe: Presbook.

Obura, K. 2011. "Duty to Prosecute International Crimes Under International Law." In *Prosecuting International Crimes in Africa*, edited by C. Murungu and J. Biegon, 11–31. Pretoria: PULP.

Takougang, Joseph M., and M. Krieger GER. 1999. *African State and Society in the 1990s: Cameroon's Political Crossroads*. Boulder, CO: Westview Press.

Chapter 4

Posttraumatic Stress Disorder and Conflict

A Study of the Tuobodom Chieftaincy in Ghana

Sabina Appiah-Boateng, Stephen B. Kendie,
and Kenneth Aikins

Although Ghana is perceived to be a peaceful nation, one of the many issues confronting the nation is the menace of ethnic and communal conflicts. Each one of the sixteen regions in Ghana suffers one or more conflicts. What makes the conflicts unique in Ghana is the fact that they do not have a collective cause that will result in national involvement (Achampong 2010; Kragelund 2008). These communal conflicts and their associated violence have penetrated the fabric of the country's economy which normally arise from different value systems, aggressive competition for environmental resources, and ethnic/identity crises, among others.

Of all the types of conflicts that occur in Ghana, Aganah (2008) declares that the most recurrent and potentially violent forms of conflict are the chieftaincy conflicts. Chieftaincy, which revolves around culture, is generally considered the traditional form of governance. In Ghana, power is transferred to these leaders to exercise in their various territories. Nyaaba (2009) seems to agree with this when he stated that traditional leaders/rulers are individuals who occupy communal political leadership positions. According to him, these positions are sanctified by cultural norms and values. Chieftaincy systems are normally marked as the embodiment of the spirits of the ancestors, as well as the living community. It is recognized that the institution of chieftaincy is one of the oldest traditional institutions in Ghana. It has its resilience and cultural value systems (Abotchie et al. 2006). Conflicts in the chieftaincy system occur when there are disputes between rival claimants to the traditional political office of "chief" in a given traditional area. Conflicts also arise from this system knowing the benefits associated with it such as prestige, power, reputation, resources, among others.

According to Collier (2003), the impacts of conflicts are complex and wide-ranging. They are not limited to countries at war. They ripple outward from the initial violence, spreading from individuals and communities to countries and regions. Conflicts cause widespread insecurity due to forced displacement, sudden destitution, the breakup of families and communities, collapsed social structures, and the breakdown of the rule of law. This insecurity can persist long after the conflicts have ended as internally displaced persons (IDP), refugees, and asylum seekers try to adjust to new circumstances around them, cope with loss, and regain a sense of normalcy.

From this assertion by Collier, it is clear that conflicts have lots of negative effects on people. The effects may be classified into social, psychological, economic, political, and cultural dimensions. These effects can also be classified as tangible or intangible (Collier 2003; Pouligny 2010). The latter (intangible) classification, of which posttraumatic stress disorder (PTSD) is an example, is the gap for this study. It appears there have not been studies that sought to present how the protracted conflict in Tuobodom has affected residents and probably resulted in PTSD among them.

This chapter seeks to investigate whether or not residents in the Tuobodom community experience posttraumatic stress disorder from the civil conflict, using the Impact of Event Scale, Revised Edition. Also, the study examines whether any differences existed between males and females concerning the possibility of PTSD among them as well as their age differences.

PROBLEMATIZING POSTTRAUMATIC STRESS DISORDER

Posttraumatic stress disorder (PTSD) has been defined in Diagnostic and Statistical Manual- Fourth Edition (DSM-IV) as the development of characteristic symptoms following a psychologically traumatic event that is generally outside the range of normal human experience (Davidson and Foa 1991). Andrews et al. (2000) examined and pointed out that the outcome of PTSD seems to have been interrelated with the history of warfare. Based on this premise, several studies have examined PTSD following a range of traumatic experiences including accidents of all kinds, violence, sexual abuse, disasters, crime, among others (McFarlane 1987)

According to the DSM-IV, the cluster of PTSD, which includes intrusion, avoidance, and hyperarousal symptoms, changes over time. Intrusion refers to the penetration into the consciousness of thoughts, images, feelings, and nightmares about the trauma and to a variety of repetitive behaviors. Avoidance reflects the tendencies of psychic numbing, conscious denial of meaning and consequences of the trauma, behavior, inhibition, and counter-phobic activities related to the traumatic event. Hyperarousal is an abnormal state of activation that occurs in the wake of traumatic or highly stressful events. Intrusion is generally the initial phase, followed by avoidance (Davidsonand Foa 1991; Horowitz 1993).

The symptoms in these criteria include the re-experiencing traumatic symptoms such as flashback in which the individual relives the event. The individual can have repetitive nightmares. The individual also has intense psychological distress in response to reminders and reacts physiologically to reminders of the traumatic event. The avoidance symptoms in the criteria include the victim's persistent effort to avoid thoughts, feelings, or conversations connected with trauma or avoiding activities, places, or people that arouse recollections of the trauma. Hyperarousal symptoms in these criteria include sleep disturbance, hypervigilance, and exaggerated startle response (Horowitz 1993).

Several empirical studies have been done on exposure to traumatic events and the developments of PTSD. Dagbah (2010) found out that indirect exposure of persons to a traumatic event even develops PTSD. Green et al. (1991) also examined PTSD among survivors at the collapse of Buffalo Creek and found out that females experienced higher PTSD symptoms. Similarly, they also examined the individual subscale on PTSD and gender. Though there was no significant difference between women and men on the criterion intrusion symptoms, women had high levels of criterion hyperarousal and criterion avoidance symptoms (Carmassi et al. 2014).

There appears to be more empirical studies on PTSD and gender than age. Thompson et al. (1993) examined age differences in the psychological consequences of Hurricane Hugo and found that younger people exhibited the most distress in the absence of a disaster, whereas middle-aged people exhibited most distress in the presence of a disaster. The authors examined the effects of age on PTSD in a cultural context and compared the effects of age after similar disasters in three different parts of the world. The findings showed no consistent effect of age on PTSD. Therefore, it was concluded that PTSD depended upon the social, economic, cultural, and historical context of the disaster-stricken setting more than it depended on age. They found inconsistent results among respondents from the United States, Mexico, and Poland, where the most distressed were the middle-aged, the young, and the old, respectively. Thus, the age differences in PTSD prevalence tend to show some cultural variance. Forstmeier and Maercker (2008) found a substantially higher prevalence of PTSD among participants in the age range of 60–93 years compared to the participants below 60 years of age. Thus, the results showed a linear increase in the prevalence of PTSD. In this chapter, we sought to examine PTSD and violent chieftaincy conflict in Tuobodom on age and gender using a mixed-method design.

METHODOLOGY

The study purposively selected Tuobodom as the case study. This followed the selection principles that it has the longest-standing chieftaincy conflict, the relapsed and violent nature, and the rate of media reports. The study sampled 300 males and females 15 years and above that were directly and indirectly affected by the conflict. Stratified sampling was used to sample 135 and 165 dwellers from Krotia and Abromanmu, respectively. The lottery type of the simple random sampling technique was employed to sample individual respondents for the study.

The sources of data collected for the study were primary and secondary. The study employed the sequential explanatory mixed-method design using an interview schedule and interview guide. Questions on the interview schedule were items on the Impact of Event Scale-Revised (IES-R) by (Creamer et al. 2003). The IES-R is a psychological instrument used to assess posttraumatic stress disorders among people who have experienced traumatic events.

The IES-R is a short instrument that has twenty-two questions and it is an appropriate instrument to measure the subjective response to a specific traumatic event, especially in the response sets of intrusion, avoidance, and hyperarousal. IES-R yields a total score ranging from 0 to 88 and a score of 33 as scientifically cutoff score for a probable diagnosis of PTSD. The quantitative data collected were analyzed using SPSS version 18 for descriptive presentation, t-test, correlation, and multiple regression. The qualitative data were analyzed manually, and narratives from respondents backed the quantitative data.

THE CIVIL CONFLICT IN TUOBODOM

Tuobodom is one of the high-income-generating communities in Ghana. It is said to be one of the leading tomato and pepper production communities in Ghana. However, from 1924 till now, the community has suffered a protracted chieftaincy conflict. It is a conflict between two rival chiefs and the causes range from power struggle, ethnic crisis, competition over land, and allegiance issue. The two chiefs, Barima Obeng Ameyaw I, who owes allegiance to the Techiman Stool in the Brong-Ahafo region, and Nana Baffour Asare II, whose allegiance is to the chief of the Asante Kingdom

(Asantehene), Otumfuo Osei-Tutu II in the Ashanti region all live in the same community, Tuobodom. As stated by Gyamera et al. (2018) in Ghana, land and chieftaincy are linked.

The size of a chief's land determines his power and authority, and this explains the competition over land resource between the two chiefs in the community. While the descent of the Brong-Ahafo region form the Bono lineage, and they are people of Abromanu in the Tuobodom community, the Asantes are the Krotia people in the community. The actors in the conflict have formed ethnic lines which they use to uniquely distinguish themselves from their opponent. The triggers of the Tuobodom chieftaincy conflict include kidnapping and arrest of Nana Asare Baffour II by some youth alleged to have been ordered to do so by the Paramount Chief of Techiman, when Nana Baffour II attempted to celebrate the annual yam festival (Prah and Yeboah 2011).

In a study by Appiah-Boateng (2014), couples who have intermarried from Krotia and Abromanmu and have marital issues and reported to their families stretched the issues to involve larger rival community factions. The people of Abromanmu and Krotia are known to have the backings of the New Democratic Congress Party and New Patriotic Party, respectively. And during almost every election cycle when there are electoral disputes, these escalate and reignite the communal conflict.

The conflict in Tuobodom is fortified by the psychocultural conflict theory which says that conflicts are prolonged because of the culturally induced concepts. It tells how human attitude and actions create enmities as a result of what they have learned from the early stages of growth. Deep-seated emotions are also factors for the protracted nature of conflicts. Emotions play a role in the meaning we ascribe to power, social status, identity, and relationships, and this displays so well during conflicts (Bloomfield et al. 2006; Lewicki et al. 2003)

RESULTS

The chapter explored the gender and age distributions of the respondents in the Tuobodom community. The gender distribution of the respondents revealed that majority of the respondents were males. Table 4.1 shows the means and standard deviation of participants' responses with their sex distribution. However, performing an independent sample test, Levene's test with equality of variance, operating at a confidence level of 95%, revealed that the difference between males and females was not significant with a t-value of .66 and p-value of .77.

$t_{(444)} = .66;$ p-value = .77

Table 4.1 Gender Distribution and PTSD Scale

Sex	N	Mean	Std. Dev.
Male	180	57.71	17.69
Female	120	56.7	19.99
Total	300		

Source: Author created.

Table 4.2 The Means of IES-R Subscales Concerning Respondents' Gender Distribution

Sex	Intrusion	Hyperarousal	Avoidance	Total Means
Males	23.98	15.39	18.33	19.23
Females	23.80	15.86	17.075	18.394

Source: Author created.

Table 4.3 Age Distribution of Respondents

Age	Frequency (N)	Percentage (%)
Below 18 years	1	.3
18–34years	136	45.3
35–59 years	128	42.7
60 years and above	36	12.0
Total	300	100

Source: Author Created.

There was no significant difference between males and females.

Table 4.2 presents the means of IES-R subscales with respondents' sex distribution. It revealed that both males and females experienced high intrusion, hyperarousal, and avoidance symptoms.

Table 4.3 reveals the age distribution of the respondents. It appeared from the study that most of the sampled respondents for the study were between the ages of 18–34 years and 35–59 years. However, respondents between 18 years to 34 years were the majority.

The results in table 4.4 revealed the age distribution of respondents on the IES-R subscale. It emerged that residents within the age bracket 35 years and 59 years experienced high posttraumatic stress, followed by those aged 60 years and above. Residents below 18 years were the least traumatized. The residents within the age bracket 35–59 years experienced high intrusive thoughts and would want to do everything possible to avoid symptoms of the conflict. They also displayed most hyperarousal symptoms, such as feeling startled, jumpy, and irritability.

Table 4.5 depicts the age distribution of the respondents on the Impact of Event Scale, Revised edition by computing one-way analysis of variance test. To know whether the differences that existed between the age brackets were

Table 4.4   Age Distribution and IES-R Subscales

Age	Intrusion	Hyperarousal	Avoidance	Means
Below 18years	17	6	27	16.66
18–34 years	22.20	14.43	16.69	17.77
35–59 years	25.42	16.59	19.03	20.34
60 years and above	24.92	16.61	17.33	19.62

Source: Author created.

Table 4.5   ANOVA: Age Distribution and IES-R Subscales

Subscale	F	Sig.
Intrusion	10.784	.000
Hyperarousal	8.111	.000
Avoidance	3.364	.006

Source: Author created.

significant, one-way analysis of variance test was performed, and it emerged that the differences that existed among all the age brackets were significant. The intrusive and hyperarousal symptoms between the youth and the older adults were highly significant.

DISCUSSION

Although male respondents were more than females, the results from table 4.1 revealed that there was no significant difference between males and females with a t-value of .66 and p-value of .05. The result could be attributed to the fact that most of the casualties in Tuobodom have been men. It was possible that the high number of male respondents may be because many females fled the community out of fear leaving the majority of the males behind. Although there was no significant difference between males and females, both sexes reported high posttraumatic stress disorder with a mean score of 57.71 (males) and 56.7 (females).

This result contradicted findings by Hassan and Shafi (2013) and Green et al. (1991) who found out that there were significant differences in PTSD between women and men. In the case of Green et al. (1991), the differences could be attributed to sampling. Again, it could be that many women were present, but in the case of the Tuobodom chieftaincy conflict, it was affected by the whole community. This conclusion was made possible as Creamer et al. (2003) suggested a mean score of 33 and above as indicative of PTSD. The IESR instrument was usable in the Tuobodom community research as it reported in a high Cronbach alpha of .95

The study further observed the sex distribution in relations to the means of IES-R subscales. The mean calculated score for each subscale included intrusion (13.6), hyperarousal (10.2), and avoidance (13.6) Creamer et al. (2003). From table 4.2, both males and females experience high symptoms of intrusion, hyperarousal, and avoidance. That is, they all suffered severe PTSD.

In this study, most of the residents had conflict scenes penetrating their consciousness and affecting their emotions. A female respondent from the Krotia faction recounted:

> I am a direct victim. In 1996, I was pregnant but had a miscarriage because news got to us at home that my uncle was shot at the lorry station and the perpetrators had cut his penis and put it into his mouth. These thoughts keep coming into my mind that makes me hate the Abromanmu people. They are wicked people.

The majority stated that flashbacks of the events during the conflict keep haunting them. This was what a respondent said: "The presence of police, the introduction of guns and the burning of the houses . . . they come to my mind and I'm always afraid" (A respondent from Abromanmu faction).

The results obtained on the intrusion category reflect that the people of Tuobodom are experiencing extreme intrusion syndromes of the chieftaincy conflict. In similar studies, Dyregrov et al. (2000) made comparable observations that people find themselves in traumatic states, especially when the conflict happens to be characterized by violent situations on a sustained basis as in the case of the Tuobodom chieftaincy conflict. They suffer intrusion symptoms such as trouble staying asleep, flashbacks of reminders, pictures popping into memories, and experiencing terrible dreams.

Majority of the respondents in Tuobodom said that they felt extremely watchful and on-guard. This often affected them in their ability to complete tasks as they always become alert and vigilant in their everyday dealings. Most of them said that feeling watchful and on-guard was not a problem at all. Hyperarousal manifests itself as a tendency to be startled easily, even in response to minor cues like low noise, irritability, restlessness, explosive anger, and feeling of guilt exist among residents of Tuobodom community. This is how a respondent puts it:

> Sister, it is Christmas time but our children cannot even play with fireworks because the noise keeps frightening us. We are always attentive and on guard. I am a seller in the market and I always tie my money on my cloth so that when the Tuobodom trumpet sounds, me and my children can escape. (A respondent at the marketplace)

The study revealed that both old adults and youth suffered posttraumatic stress during and after the conflict. The finding agrees with that of Forstmeier and Maercker (2008) who found out that substantially higher prevalence of PTSD develops among participants in the age range of 60–93 years compared to the participants below 60 years of age.

This is how an old man aged 74 put it:

> Tuobodom previously wasn't like this though once a while the two chiefs fight. Now the youth know their right and because they don't have any work to do, they want to fight. The Krotia youth engage in the conflict with all their strength because they don't want to lose a property given to them by their ancestors. However, when it occurs, we the old ones get so worried. I feel my heartbeat, have heart attack . . . we don't want them to fight. The government should come and intervene.

Generally, the conflict has created feelings of detachment among residents of the community. Residents demonstrate this in the form of their refusal to talk about it. Nonetheless, many others have difficulty taking it from their memories because of the loss of close relatives and friends. They expressed deep-seated emotions and memories about the negative repercussions of the chieftaincy conflict. By and large, it can be said that the residents of Tuobodom are experiencing extreme posttraumatic stress disorders with the empirical cases above.

POLICY IMPLICATIONS

The result of the study implies conflict management and psychological counseling. The deep-seated emotions, pains, irritability, fright, among other symptoms when not psychologically handled, can in themselves revive the conflict. This calls for collaboration between researchers in the field of conflict studies and clinical psychologists in Ghana to help in this direction. Again, since almost all the regions suffer one form of violent conflict or the other, we recommend that similar studies are done in all these areas to inform policy-making and policy implementation about the psychological implications of violent conflict and the need for conflict victims to receive psychological care.

The Ghana Education Service should implement trauma healing programs in schools' curriculum to support the mental health of pupils and students who may be secondary victims of the conflict. This study also echoes strongly to policymakers to evaluate the nexus between Goal 3 (health and well-being) and Goal 16 (promotion of peace and inclusive society) of the United Nations' Sustainable Development Goals (SDGS).

CONCLUSION

The Tuobodom chieftaincy conflict in Ghana has a long history, and it is underpinned by modern systems of governance and colonization. The study investigated the posttraumatic stress disorders associated with the violent chieftaincy conflict in Tuobodom. It is evident from the study that the protracted nature of the Tuobodom chieftaincy conflict has affected the people psychologically. The majority of respondents claimed that they suffered from posttraumatic stress disorders anytime the conflict erupts.

They experienced flashbacks of gunshots and the death of their family members and loved ones. These pictures pop into their minds anytime there are reminders. They have challenges falling and staying asleep. They have problems avoiding reminders about the conflict and trying to take it from their memories. The youth, as well as the aged, were reported to experience high intrusive thoughts and do all they can to avoid thoughts about the violence. As a result, many have become hyperaroused where they easily become startled, irritated, jumpy, and angry.

REFERENCES

Abotchie, Chris, Albert Awedoba, and Irene K. Odotei. 2006. "Perceptions of Chieftaincy." In *Chieftaincy in Ghana: Culture, Governance and Development,* edited by Irene K. Odotei and A. K. Awedoba. Legon: Sub-Saharan Publishers, 103–116.

Achampong, Osei Benjamin. 2010. *Chieftaincy, Conflict, and Women in Ghana.* Unpublished MPhil Thesis. University of Oslo. Oslo.

Aganah, Gamel A. M. 2008. *The Effects of Chieftaincy Conflicts on Local Development: The Case of the Bawku East Municipality.* Master's Thesis, Universitetet Tromsø. Tromsø.

Andrews, Bernice et al. 2007. "Delayed-Onset Posttraumatic Stress Disorder: A Systematic Review of the Evidence." *American Journal of Psychiatry*, 164, no. 9: 1319–1326.

Appiah-Boateng, Sabina. 2014. *An Evaluation of the Psychosocial Effects of the Tuobodom Chieftaincy Conflict on the People of Tuobodom in the Brong-Ahafo Region.* Unpublished MPhil Thesis. University of Cape Coast. Cape Coast, Ghana.

Bloomfield David et al., eds. 2006. "Social Change and Conflict Transformation." In *Berghof Handbook for Conflict Transformation Dialogue Series.* Issue 5. Berlin, Germany: Berghof Research Center for Constructive Conflict Management,

Carmassi, Claudia, et al. 2014. "Gender Differences in DSM-5 versus DSM-IV-TR PTSD Prevalence and Criteria Comparison Among 512 Survivors to the L' Aquila Earthquake." *Journal of Affective Disorders*, 160: 55–61.

Collier, Paul. 2003. *Breaking the Conflict Trap: Civil War and Development Policy.* Washington, DC: World Bank Publications.

Creamer, Mark et al. 2003. "Psychometric Properties of the Impact of Event Scale—Revised." *Behaviour Research and Therapy*, 41(12): 1489–1496.

Dagbah, Francis E. Klutse. 2010. *Ethnic Conflicts and Symptoms of Post-Traumatic Stress in Children: A Study of Children from Bawku in North-eastern Ghana.* Master's thesis. University of Oslo. Oslo.

Davidson, Jonathan R., and Edna B. Foa. 1991. "Diagnostic Issues in Posttraumatic Stress Disorder: Considerations for the DSM-IV." *Journal of Abnormal Psychology*, 100(3): 346–355.

Dyregrov, Atle et al. 2000. "Trauma Exposure and Psychological Reactions to Genocide Among Rwandan Children." *Journal of Traumatic Stress*, 13(1): 3–21.

Forstmeier, Simon, and Andreas Maercker. 2008. "Motivational Reserve: Lifetime Motivational Abilities Contribute to Cognitive and Emotional Health in Old Age." *Psychology and Ageing*, 23 (4): 886–899.

Green, Bonnie L. et al. 1991. "Children and Disaster: Age, Gender, and Parental Effects on PTSD Symptoms." *Journal of the American Academy of Child & Adolescent Psychiatry*, 30(6): 945–951.

Gyamera, Ebenezer Ankomah et al. 2018. "Land Acquisition in Ghana: Dealing with the Challenges and the Way Forward." *Journal of Agricultural Economics, Extension and Rural Development*, 6(1): 664–672.

Horowitz, Mardi J. 1993. "Stress-Response Syndromes." In *International Handbook of Traumatic Stress Syndromes*, edited by John P. Wilson and Beverley Raphael. Boston: Springer, 49–60.

Kragelund, Peter. 2008. "The Return of Non-DAC Donors to Africa: New Prospects for African Development." *Development Policy Review*, 26(5): 555–584.

Lewicki, Roy, Barbara Gray, and Michael Elliott. 2003. *Making Sense of Intractable Environmental Conflicts: Concepts and Cases.* Washington/Covelo/London: Island Press.

McFarlane, Alexander Cowell. 1987. "Posttraumatic Phenomena in a Longitudinal Study of Children Following a Natural Disaster." *Journal of the American Academy of Child & Adolescent Psychiatry*, 26(5): 764–769.

Nyaaba, Ali Yakubu. 2009. *Transformations in the Chieftaincy Institution in Northern Ghana From 1900–1969: A Case Study of Navrongo and Sakot.* PhD Thesis. Kwame Nkrumah University of Science and Technology. Kumasi., Ghana.

Pouligny, Béatrice. 2010. *State-Society Relations and the Intangible Dimensions of State Resilience and State-Building: A Bottom-Up Perspective.* EUI Working Paper No. 33, Robert Schumer Center for Advanced Studies, European University Institute, Florence, Italy.

Prah, Mansah, and Alfred Yeboah. 2011. "Tuobodom Chieftaincy Conflict in Ghana: A Review and Analysis of Media Reports." *The Journal of Pan African Studies*, 4(3): 20–33.

Thompson, Martie P. et al. 1993. "Age Differences in the Psychological Consequences of Hurricane Hugo." *Psychology and Aging*, 8(4): 606–616.

Chapter 5

Liberia's Civil Wars

George Klay Kieh Jr.

Liberia was unaffected by the wave of civil wars that swept across the African Continent beginning in the 1950s, with the civil war in Sudan and subsequent civil wars in other African states in the 1960s, 1970s, and early 1980s (Ali and Matthew 1999; Williams 2016). This was because unlike the civil war affected African states, the underlying civil conflict in Liberia had not reached its crescendo, the sine qua non for the transition from conflict to war. In other words, although the Liberian polity was plagued by similar crises that plagued the civil war afflicted African states, these crises had not run their course.

However, the April 14, 1979, mass uprising in Liberia was a major signal that the Liberian civil conflict was on the trajectory of escalation (Kieh 2008, 2012a; Sawyer 1992). The mass uprising was organized by a coalition of national social movements—the Movement for Justice in Africa (MOJA) and the Progressive Alliance of Liberia (PAL)—and the student movement, including the Liberian National Student Movement (LINSU), the University of Liberia Student Union (ULSU), and the Student Unification Party (SUP), the ruling party, to protest the country's perennial problem of socioeconomic and political crises (Cordor 1979; Kieh 2008, 2012a; Sawyer 1992). Importantly, the Tolbert regime was gravely concerned about its security, as well as the prospects for a wider conflagration. Hence, the Tolbert government requested and received a contingent of troops from neighboring Guinea under the rulership of President Ahmed Sekou Toure, a close friend of President Tolbert (Liebenow 1980).

About a year later, the Tolbert regime and the dynasty of the ruling True Whig Party were deposed in a military coup (Kieh 1982, 2004, 2008, 2012a; Sawyer 1986, 1992). The coup brought to power the People's Redemption Council (PRC), the military junta, headed by Master-Sergeant Samuel K. Doe.

Then, about a decade later, Liberia imploded into its first civil war, when the Charles Taylor-led National Patriotic Front of Liberia (NPFL) attacked the country from its bridgehead in neighboring Cote d'Ivoire, beginning in Nimba County in the north-central region of the country (Huband 1998). After almost eight years of mayhem, including deaths, injuries, internal displacement, a refugee crisis, and destruction, as well as sixteen failed peace accord, the first civil war ended in 1997 with the signing of the Abuja II Peace Accord, the seventeenth peace agreement, by the warring parties and the transitional government of Liberia, with the Economic Community of West African States (ECOWAS) as the mediator (Kieh 2011a). Subsequently, presidential election was held on July 19, 1997, and Charles Taylor, the leader of the NPFL, the main rebel group, was elected the president of Liberia (Harris 1999; Kieh 2011b; Lyons 1998). Barely two years after the end of the first civil war, Liberia again descended into armed conflict, when the Liberians United for Reconciliation and Democracy (LURD), an amalgam of the leaders of some of the erstwhile warlordist militias, launched a military attack from its base in neighboring Guinea, thereby starting the second civil war (Kieh 2009a; Brabazon 2003). After almost four years of deaths, injuries, internal displacement, a refugee crisis, and destruction, the war ended with the signing of the Comprehensive Peace Agreement (CPA) or the Accra Peace Accord under the leadership of ECOWAS on August 18, 2003. Thereafter, a transitional government was established that governed the country for two years (2003–2005). Then, in October 2005, presidential and legislative elections were held to choose a new government (Harris 2006; Kieh 2006, 2011c; Sawyer 2008).

What were the major causes of Liberia's two civil wars? Who were the internal and external forces or actors that shaped these two civil wars? These are the two major questions this chapter will seek to address. In order to address the questions, the chapter is divided into three parts. The first section examines the factors and forces that shaped the first Liberian civil war. In the second part, the root causes and the internal and external actors that shaped the wars are interrogated. Finally, the chapter draws some major conclusions.

THE FIRST CIVIL WAR (1989–1997)

The Major Causes of the War

The Liberian State

The multidimensional crises of underdevelopment—cultural, economic, political, and social—generated by the peripheral capitalist Liberian state were the root causes of the country's first war (Kieh 2008). The peripheral capitalist Liberian state and its multidimensional crises have evolved in two major phases: the settler and peripheral capitalist phases. The former spanned the period 1822–1926, while the latter commenced in 1926 and is ongoing even after the country's two civil wars.

The Settler Phase

The settler phase commenced in 1820 with the repatriation of freed black slaves from the United States. The repatriation project was designed to address the emergent race problem in the United States (Smith 1972). That is, with the obtaining of freedom by some blacks from the American plantation-based slavery, the American ruling class was quite concerned about the potential adverse impact a growing black population would have on its power (Beyan 1991; Kieh 2008; Sawyer 1992; Smith 1972). Hence, after the examination of various options, the American ruling class made the determination to repatriate the freed blacks to Africa, the land of their ancestral origins. In this vein, the American Colonization Society (ACS), which was organized in 1816 by some of the prominent members of the American ruling class, including Henry Clay and Bushrod Washington, was designated by the American government to implement the repatriation plan with the state's financial and military support (Beyan 1991; Kieh 2008, 2102a; Sawyer 1992). Initially, the repatriated blacks were sent to Shebro Island in Sierra Leone (Beyan 1991). However, after an outbreak of malaria, the repatriation project was relocated to the Grain Coast (now Liberia) (Kieh 2008).

When the freed blacks arrived on the Grain Coast, they met several African ethnic groups occupying the area (Beyan 1991; Dunn and Tarr 1988). Each of the African ethnic groups had established polities replete with their own cultural, economic, political, social, and religious systems (Dunn and Tarr 1988; Kieh 2008, 2012a; Sawyer 1992). However, rather than forging bonds of unity with their African kin, the repatriated blacks exuded a sense of hubris that was based on what Brown (1941: 10) refers to as a "slave psychology." Because they had lived in the United States, howbeit as slaves, the repatriated blacks believed that they were superior to the Africans, who they met occupying the Grain Coast (Brown 1941; Cassell 1970). The myth of the so-called "superiority" of the repatriated blacks found expression in their professed goals of "civilizing" and "Christianizing" the Africans, who they met on the Grain Coast (Dunn and Tarr 1988; Kieh 2018; Sawyer 1992). In addition, the repatriated blacks under the suzerainty of the ACS and backed by American military might was able to acquire land from the various African polities through sundry means, including brigandry (Beyan 1991; Movement for Justice in Africa 1980). These actions on the part of the repatriated blacks set into motion a series of conflicts between them, on the one hand, and various African polities, on the other hand (Levitt 2005). Given the advantage of

American military might, the various African ethnic groups were subdued during these wars. However, the territorial expanse of the Liberian state remained relatively small during the colonial, commonwealth, and initial years of the postindependence epochs of the settler state phase. Thus, the Liberian state in its various iterations coexisted with various African ethnic polities.

Furthermore, the ACS established a caste-like system as the centerpiece of the political economy of the colonial Liberian state (1822–1837). Under the emergent social structure, an individual's station in the society was determined by ancestral origins and skin pigmentation (Burrowes 1982; Kieh 2008, 2012a, 2017). In this vein, the functionaries of the ACS occupied the upper stratum of the social order. The middle tier was occupied by the light-skinned repatriated blacks. The lowest rung comprised the dark-skinned repatriated blacks, the Congos (the recaptives, who were liberated en route to slavery), and the members of the various African ethnic groups, who were under the jurisdiction of the colonial Liberian state. During the commonwealth era (1837–1847), the composition of the various tiers changed: The light-skinned repatriated blacks, who were given administrative control over the affairs of the state, graduated to the upper echelon of the social order. The dark-skinned repatriated blacks became the occupants of the middle tier. The Congos and the members of the various African ethnic groups, who were under the jurisdiction of the Liberian state, comprised the lowest stratum.

Importantly, motivated by the desire of the light-skinned repatriated blacks to fully control state power, they declared Liberian an independent state in 1847, amid the underlying multidimensional crises. However, instead of designing the modalities to address the contradictions and crises, the resulting vision, design, and operation of the independent Liberian state exacerbated and increased the contradictions and crises. Politically, the emergent independent state was an exclusionary one that did not include people, who did not belong to the repatriated black stock. This meant the members of the various African ethnic groups, who constituted the majority, were excluded from participating in the state. For example, the Declaration of Independence only recognized the repatriated blacks (Declaration of Independence of Liberia, 1847). This meant that the Liberian state was created only for them. Similarly, the delegates to the constitutional convention were drawn exclusively from the repatriated black stock (Beyan 1991; Kieh 2008). The resulting constitution granted citizenship only to the repatriated blacks and their descendants. This excluded the members of the various African ethnic groups and the Congos (the members of the various African groups gained partial citizenship in 1907 and full citizenship in 1947). However, in a classic demonstration of "taxation without representation," the members of the various African ethnic groups were required to pay taxes (Kieh 2008). In addition, the members of the various African groups were compelled to perform sundry duties in the area of civil works (Kieh 2008). Cumulatively, the vagaries of the "apartheid-like system" led to continued conflicts, including wars, between the Liberian state and various Africans and African ethnic groups (Levitt 2005).

Culturally, the "clash of civilizations" continued, as the functionaries of the Liberian state and ordinary citizens from the repatriated Africans stock sought to impose the parody of the American way of life on the members of the various African ethnic groups (Kieh 2008). For example, traditional values were subordinated to the so-called "American ones" (Kieh 2008). Ostensibly, the repatriated Africans were desirous of transforming the members of the various African groups into "Americans." However, the paradox was that the repatriated Africans were never recognized as "Americans" themselves. In addition, the repatriated Africans observed the American way of life in bondage. Thus, it was quite interesting that the repatriated Africans would endeavor to superimpose a cultural system that they did not understand. Notwithstanding, the repatriated Africans' ill-informed quest to Americanize the members of the various ethnic groups contributed to various civil conflicts, including violent ones (Levitt 2005).

Economically, the caste-cum-class structure led to, among other things, inequalities in wealth and income. For example, the members of the upper stratum, including entrepreneurs and state managers, amassed disproportionate shares of the wealth and income (Kieh 2008). In addition, the members of the various African ethnic groups, who were denied citizenship, correspondingly lacked access to employment opportunities. And this adversely affected their material well-being. For example, employment in the public sector was monopolized by the members of the repatriated African stock. The situation was made worse after 1869, when the state became the principal sources of employment (Kieh 2008). That is, after the collapse of the autonomous capitalist development model, as a result of the collapse of local businesses due to the competition from well-resourced European firms, jobs in the public sector became premium. Hence, since the members of the African ethnic groups lacked the rights of citizenship, they were denied access to jobs in the state bureaucracy.

Socially, access to education, health care, and other social services was determined by both citizenship and an individual's status in the caste-cum-class structure. This meant the members of the upper tier had the greatest access, followed by the members of the middle level. As for the members of the various African ethnic groups, who were relegated to the lowest rung because of their ancestral origins, they had minimum access to social amenities. For example, in the area of education, the children from various families within the African ethnic groups stock became the wards of families within the repatriated Africans from the United States stock, as the major pathway to attending school (Sawyer 1992). In addition, other children from the various African ethnic groups lived with American Christian missionaries, who went to Liberia to spread variants of American Christianity (Kieh 1991). Furthermore, various American Christian denominations established educational institutions in Liberia. And these served as avenues for children from the lowest stratum of the caste-cum-class structure to acquire education.

The Peripheral Capitalist Phase

Origins

Liberia's final incorporation into the world capitalist system in 1926 heralded a major shift in the country's socioeconomic structure: The establishment of the Firestone Plantations in Liberia's rubber sector represented the opening of the Liberian economy to foreign investments.[1] Importantly, wage labor was introduced as a mainstay of the emergent peripheral capitalist political economy (Kieh 2008, 2012a; Mayson and Sawyer 1979; Sawyer 1992). Similarly, class became ascendant over ancestral origins and skin pigmentation (Kieh 2008, 2012a). That is, an individual's relationship to the major means of production became the dominant determinant of her or his socioeconomic status (Kieh 2008, 2012a). However, ancestral origins and skin pigmentation, the major levers of the caste system, remained significant because they had not run their course (Kieh 2008, 2012a). In other words, class and caste continued to overlap; however, class became the more dominant (Kieh 2008, 2012a). Significantly, with the extension of Liberian citizenship to the members of the various African ethnic groups in 1947 (Pailey 2021), some of them ascended to the emergent new local ruling class (Kieh 2008, 2012a).

The emergent peripheral capitalist Liberian state assumed a dual orientation: external and internal. David (1984: 58) provides a summation of the duality:

> [The Liberian state as a peripheral capitalist formation] straddle[s] not one but two levels of articulation: between the world capitalist economic system and the peripheral social formation as a whole, and within the social formation . . . The peripheral state as a unit of economic reproduction . . . is required to play a "central"(interventionist) role in the process of capital accumulation.

Furthermore, as an appendage of the world capitalist system, the structure of the political economy of the peripheral capitalist Liberian state is determined by the former (Ziemann and Lanzendorfer 1977: 45). As Amin (1974: 8) argues, "the underdeveloped countries form part of a world system, that the history of their integration into the system forged their special structure—which henceforth has nothing in common with what prevailed before their integration in the modern world."

Portrait

Cumulatively, the peripheral capitalist Liberian state developed a portrait reflective of its duality. In terms of its nature, the peripheral capitalist Liberian state is exclusionary, because it does not represent the totality of the historical-cultural experiences of Liberia's major cultural streams—African ethnic groups, the Congos (those who were liberated en route to slavery), people of African descent from the Caribbean, and Africans from other African states, especially in the West African region (Kieh 2008, 2012a, 2018). Instead, the Liberian state represents only the historical and cultural experiences of the repatriated Africans from the United States cultural stream (Kieh 2008, 2012a, 2018). And this is reflected in the Declaration of Independence and the country's national symbols and awards such as the flag, motto, and seal (Kieh 2008, 2012a, 2018; Nyanseor 2014, 2015).

The state's mission is twofold. One is to create an enabling environment in which metropolitan-based multinational corporations and other businesses can accumulate capital through various predatory means, including paying workers "starvation wages" (Kieh 2008, 2012a, 2021; Mayson and Sawyer 1979). When the workers protested against low wages and horrendous working conditions, the Liberian government did not hesitate to use the coercive instruments of the state, including the police and the military, to inflict violence on them (Kieh 2008, 2012a). For example, during the labor strikes on the Firestone Plantations Company in 1961 and 1964, the army and police were dispatched to brutalize the workers (Kieh 2008). In fact during the 1997 strike, workers were killed and scores of others wounded by the military and the police (Miller 2015). The other aspect of the state's mission is to create propitious conditions for the members of the faction or fraction of the local ruling class that controls state power to engage in primitive accumulation (Kieh 2017, 2021). This entails the use of the agency of their respective offices in the state bureaucracy to enrich themselves through the use of sundry illegal means, including bribery, extortion, the stealing of public funds and fraudulent procurement schemes (Kieh 2017, 2021). This is why the contestations over the control of state power are virtual "life and death battles" between the competing political factions and fractions (Kieh 2008, 2012a, 2017, 2019, 2021).

The state has a multidimensional character. As Agbese (2007: 45) argues, "the African state [is] a composite of an oppressor, a terrorist, a criminalized entity, a criminal enterprise, and a beggar or client state of a foreign power." For example, the Liberian state displays its "criminalized" character when it creates a conducive environment in which state managers can use their respective positions as license to pillage and plunder public financial and other resources. Similarly, the "negligent" dimension of the state's character is revealed, when the state refuses to invest in education, health care, decent housing, food security, sanitation, and access to clean drinking, among others. This recurrent practice has and continues to adversely affect the material conditions of the subalterns.

The Crises of the State

Background

Over time, the portrait of the peripheral capitalist Liberian state produced multidimensional crises—cultural, economic, political, and social. Over time, the cumulative effects of these crises eroded the legitimacy of the state and its various regimes. Ultimately, the conditions were created for the state to implode into a civil war, as was the case in 1989, with the eruption of the country's first civil war.

The Cultural Crises

In the cultural realm, the *ancien* conflict between the descendants of the repatriated Africans from the United States and the African ethnic groups continued. Although, class had become ascendant as the fulcrum of the emergent political economy, the descendants of the repatriated Africans from the United States continued to dominate the class structure (Kieh 2008, 2012a). The Tubman (1944–1971) and Tolbert (1971–1980) regimes took steps to address the enduring conflict between the two stocks. In the case of the Tubman regime, it took several steps. One was the granting of full citizenship to the members of all the African ethnic groups. Another was the enunciation of the "Unification and Integration Policy" in 1954. According to President Tubman, the policy's chief architect, the policy was designed, among other things, to

> destroy all the ideologies that tend to divide us. Americo-Liberianism must be forgotten and all of us must register a new era of justice, equality, fair ideology, and equal opportunities for everyone from ever part of the country regardless of tribe, clan, section, element, creed or economic status. (Lowenkopf 1976: 55)

However, President Tubman undermined his "Unification and Integration Policy" by, among other things, creating the "Most Venerable Order of the Knighthood of the Pioneers" as the country's highest award. The central problem with the award was that it was established exclusively to honor the memory of the forebears of the repatriated Africans from the United States stock (Kieh 2018). In so doing, it excluded the contributions of the other major stocks—African ethnic groups, the Congos, Africans, who migrated from the Caribbean, and Africans from various countries in the West African region—that constitute the country's cultural "mosaic" (Kieh 2018). Furthermore, four new counties—Bong, Grand Gedeh, Lofa, and Nimba—were created out of the existing central, eastern, and western provinces. These regions were occupied predominantly by the members of some of the African ethnic groups such as the Kpelle, Krahn, Belle, Gbandi, Kissi, Lorma, Gio, and Mano. Ostensibly, the purpose was to help create structural balance in the country's local government structure by placing the regions that were occupied by these African ethnic groups on par with the other regions of the country.

Similarly, the Tolbert regime formulated and implemented various policies that were also designed to address the cultural crises. A key one was the establishment of the positions of First and Second Deputy Speakers of the House of Representatives (Kieh 2008, 2012a). The position of First Deputy Speaker was allocated to the "old counties" the political terrain of the repatriated Africans from the United States and the Second Deputy Speakership to the "new counties" the political base of the African ethnic groups (Kieh 2008). In the same vein, the positions of First and Second National Chairs of the ruling True Whig Party (TWP) were created. The First National Vice Chairmanship was allocated to the "old counties," and the one of Second Vice National Chair to the "new counties." Clearly, the allocation formula that was used for the changes in both the House of Representatives, and the ruling TWP exacerbated the ethnocultural schism between the African ethnic groups and the repatriated Africans from the United States by accentuating the subordination of the "new counties" to the "old counties." In addition, President Tolbert created the "county quotas" as the basis for making cabinet appointments. The purpose was to ensure that at a minimum a cabinet minister was appointed from each of the country's regions.

In contradistinction to the Tubman and Tolbert regimes, the Doe regime (1980–1990) did not even attempt to promote national unity (Kieh 2008; Sawyer 1992). Once the erosion of his regime's legitimacy reached a crescendo in 1982, as a result of what the Lawyers' Committee for Human Rights called "a promise betrayed" (Berkeley 1986: 1), Doe resorted to the use of the instrumentalization of ethnicity (Kieh 2008, 2012a; Sawyer 1992): Doe constructed an "ethnic conflict" between the Krahn ethnic group (his kin and kith) and the Gio and Mano ethnic groups—the classic "us against them." At the core of this contrived "ethnic conflict" was Doe's postulation that the Gio and Mano ethnic groups posed grave threat to the Krahn ethnic group, and by extension, his regime (Kieh 2008; Sawyer 1992; Wonkeryor 1985). In this vein, the Doe regime commenced the implementation of its "ethnic strategy" by dismissing scores of members of the Gio and Mano ethnic groups from various positions in the state bureaucracy, including the military and

security apparatus (Kieh 2008: 140; Wonkeryor 1985). This was followed by
Doe's decision to demote General Thomas Quiwonkpa, the most prominent
government official from the Gio and Mano ethnic group, from his position
as commanding-general of the Armed Forces of Liberia, to the ceremonial
position of secretary-general of the ruling PRC, the military junta (Kieh
2008; Wonkeryor 1985). General Quiwonkpa refused to accept the demotion.
Consequently, the Doe regime undertook a campaign of political persecution against the members of the Gio and Mano ethnic groups, especially the
former government officials (Kieh 2008; Wonkeryor 1985). This led General
Quiwonkpa and several prominent members of the Gio and Mano ethnic
groups, including former government officials, to flee the country and seek
refuge in various countries (Kieh 2008; Wonkeryor 1985). Significantly, after
the abortive November 1985 coup led by General Quiwonkpa, the Doe regime
undertook retaliatory "scorch the earth" campaign, known as the "Nimba
Raid" against the home region of General Quiwonkpa (Human Rights Watch
1990a; Kieh 2008; Wonkeryor 1985). Consequently, scores of people were
killed and injured, and houses and other properties destroyed (Human Rights
Watch 1990a; Kieh 2008; Wonkeryor 1985). The post-"Nimba Raid" era
witnessed the development of animosity between the members of the Krahn
ethnic group, on the one hand, and those of the Gio and Mano ethnic groups,
on the other (Kieh 2008).

The Economic Crises

Economically, the crises found expression in various spheres. One revolved
around the inequalities and inequities in wealth and income. By 1980, for
example, about 4 percent of the population owned and controlled about 60 percent of the wealth (Movement for Justice in Africa 1980). This meant that about
96 percent of the population, the overwhelming majority, owned and controlled
40 percent of the national wealth. Similarly, by the end of the Doe regime,
about 5 percent of the population, constituting the new expanded local wing of
the ruling class, amassed about 70 percent of the wealth (Kieh 1997: 27).

Further, the distribution of income was skewed. For example, in 1960,
the upper class, comprising about 4 percent of the population, owned about
60.4 percent of the national income (National Planning Office, Liberia 1961).
By 1980, the share of the national income for the upper class increased to
about 65 percent (Ministry of Planning and Economic Affairs, Liberia 1981).
Similarly, five years later, the upper class, representing about 5 percent of the
population, owned and controlled about 68 percent of the national income
(Ministry of Planning and Economic Affairs, Liberia 1986).

As for unemployment, in 1970, for example, the rate stood at about 40
percent (National Planning Office, Liberia 1971). Interestingly, the high rate
of unemployment existed amid the influx of foreign-based multinational

corporations and other businesses, as a result of the Tubman regime's "open door policy." During the Tolbert regime, for example, the unemployment rate burgeoned to about 50 percent in 1980 (Ministry of Planning and Economic Affairs, Liberia 1981). This was due to the confluence of global and domestic factors, including recession and the resulting impact on the profits of businesses operating in the Liberian economy. By the end of the Doe regime, the unemployment rate rose to more than 60 percent, fueled by the labor retrenchment schemes of the major multinational corporations, such as the Firestone Plantations Company, the Bong Mining Company, and the Liberian American Swedish Mineral Company (LAMCO) (Kieh 2008; Ministry of Planning and Economic Affairs, Liberia 1989).

Amid the sordid state of the material well-being of the members of the subaltern classes, the members of the local wing of the Liberian ruling class engaged in the primitive accumulation of capital through the use of various illicit means (Kieh 2017, 2021). For example, during the Tubman, Tolbert, and Doe regimes, it was commonplace for state managers to use the agency of their respective official positions to accumulate wealth through various corrupt means such as bribery, extortion, and fraudulent procurement schemes (Kieh 2017, 2021). Moreover, the permissive "culture of impunity" rooted in the absence of the "rule of law" encouraged and sustained corruption. For example, at the end of the Doe regime in 1990, it was estimated that he and his supplicants siphoned off more than $300 million in public funds through sundry corrupt means (Ballah 2003: 11).

The Political Crises

The Governance System

At the core of Liberia's political crises was the type and nature of the governance system. When the country gained independence in 1847, the emergent governance system was an apartheid-like liberal democratic model (Kieh 2008, 2009b, 2012a; Sawyer 1992). While the model had the major elements of a liberal democratic governance system, the members of the various African ethnic groups were not allowed to participate in the political process (Kieh 2008, 2009b, 2012a; Sawyer 1992). This was because the 1847 Constitution did not grant citizenship to them (Constitution 1847). Even though the governance system became fully liberal democratic in 1847, with the granting of full citizenship to the members of the various African ethnic groups, the repatriated Africans from the United States stock continued to dominate the polity in virtually every sphere (Kieh 2008, 2012a; Sawyer 1992).

However, in 1951, the governance system experienced another major change: The Tubman regime embarked upon a campaign of closing the "political space," by, among other things, "muzzling opposition political parties" (Wreh 1976). A major example was the outlawing of the opposition Reformation Party and the subsequent exiling of Didho Twe, its presidential candidate, during the heat of the 1951 presidential election (Wreh 1976). The transition from a liberal democratic governance system to an authoritarian one was completed in 1955, when the Tubman regime arrested, imprisoned, and publicly humiliated scores of opposition leaders (Wreh 1976). Thereafter, Tubman institutionalized authoritarianism by, *inter alia*, prohibiting the exercise of constitutionally guaranteed political rights and civil liberties, including freedoms of association, assembly, of the press, and of speech. In addition, a *de facto* one-party system emerged with the ruling TWP as the sole political party (Kieh 2008, 2012a; Sawyer 1992; Wreh 1976).

With Tolbert's ascendancy to the presidency, after President Tubman's death in 1971, he undertook a campaign of political liberalization that was designed to jettison the country's authoritarian governance system (Kieh 2008, 2012a, 2015; Sawyer 1992). Among other things, the liberalization efforts created an enabling environment for the establishment of two national social movements—MOJA and the PAL. Collectively, these two national social movements played pivotal roles in waging the struggle for democratic reforms (Kieh 2008, 2012a, 2015; Sawyer 1992). However, pressured by the dominant hardline wing of the ruling TWP, the Tolbert regime abandoned its liberalization efforts and reverted to authoritarianism (Kieh 2008, 2012a; Sawyer 1992). For example, the Sedition Law (revised) was enacted in 1978 that made it a crime to criticize the Liberian government (Kieh 2008, 2012a). The return to authoritarian governance witnessed the emergence of conflicts between the Tolbert regime, on the one hand, and various reform groups, including the two national social movements, the labor and student movements (Kieh 2008, 2012a, 2015). The apex of these conflicts was the April 14, 1979 mass demonstration against the Tolbert regime (Cordor 1979; Kieh 2008, 2012a; Sawyer 1992).

The April 12, 1980, military coup was greeted with enthusiasm and high expectations by most Liberians, who entertained the hope, among others, that Doe and the ruling PRC would provide the requisite leadership in terminating the perennial authoritarian governance system and replacing it with a democratic one (Berkeley 1986; Kieh 2004, 2008, 2012a; Liebenow 1987; Sawyer 1987, 1992). However, barely a month after the occurrence of the coup, it became clear that the Doe regime would retain the country's authoritarian governance system. This was evidenced by, for example, the holding of "kangaroo trials" and subsequent execution of prominent officials in the Tolbert regime and the ruling TWP (Freedom House 2021). Subsequently, the Doe military regime (1980–1986) and its civilianized variant (1986–1990) developed and institutionalized a militarized authoritarian governance system. For example, on August 22, 1984, Doe ordered the military in his notorious "move or be removed order" to invade the campus of the University of Liberia and quell the demonstration of students, who were demanding the release of Amos Sawyer, the Dean of Liberia College (Humanities and Social Sciences), and George Klay Kieh Jr., lecturer of political science, who were arrested and detained by the Doe regime on the charge of treason (Kieh 2008, 2012a, 2012b; Liebenow 1987; Sawyer 1992; Williams 2006). Consequently, scores of individuals were killed and wounded as the result of the wanton abuses committed by the military (Kieh 2008, 2012a, 2012b; Liebenow 1987; Sawyer 1992; Williams 2006).

The "Hegemonic Presidency"

The "hegemonic presidency" has been, and continues to be, the foundation of authoritarianism in Liberia (Kieh 2008, 2012a, 2012c, 2017, 2020; Liebenow 1971, 1987; Lowenkopf 1976; Sawyer 1992). The phenomenon has its roots in the "Barclay Plan" of 1904, which gave the presidency sweeping powers in various spheres (Sawyer 1973, 1992). The sphere of presidential appointive powers covering local governments under the "Barclay Plan" was derived from the 1847 Constitution (Constitution of Liberia 1847). Similarly, the 1986 Constitution gives the president expansive appointive powers in the executive and judicial branches (Constitution of Liberia 1986). For example, the president appoints cabinet ministers, deputy and assistant ministers, judges, magistrates, sheriffs, and bailiffs (Constitution of Liberia 1986). As Sawyer (2005: 3) observes, "The President of Liberia has sweeping constitutional powers of appointment of executive and judicial officials."

Another major contributing factor to the maintenance of the "hegemonic presidency" is a compliant legislature (Wreh 1976). This has been demonstrated in various ways. A major one was the enactment of laws, such as the Sedition Law (revised) and the Emergency Power Act, that gave the president of Liberia carte blanche authority to violate the constitutionally granted rights of freedoms of assembly, association, press, and speech (Kieh 2008, 2012a; Sawyer 1992). For example, under the Emergency Power Act, the president could ban organizations and order the arrest of those, who he determined "posed threat" to political stability (Kieh 2008, 2012a). The profundity of legislative obeisance to the presidency and the resulting implications for fostering authoritarianism led Wreh (1976: xi) to lament: "there was no countervailing power from the people or the constitutionally created National Legislature . . . [an institution] which should provide the checks and balances to the executive branch."

The Violation of Political Human Rights

The violation of political human rights was a mainstay of the Liberian state project from its inception. As has been discussed, for example, although the members of the various African ethnic groups were denied citizenship from 1847 to 1907 (granted partial citizenship in 1905, and full citizenship in 1947), they were required to pay taxes and perform sundry other tasks (Kieh 2008, 2012a; Pailey 2021).

Furthermore, during the King regime (beginning in 1929), hundreds of Liberians (mainly from the various African ethnic groups) were shipped to Fernando Po, a Spanish colony, to work as slave laborers on the plantations (Sundiata 1980). The gravity of the slave labor crisis led the League of Nations to appoint the Christy Commission in 1929 to investigate the matter (Sundiata 1980). In its findings, the Christy Commission laid the responsibility for the slave labor crisis at the doorsteps of President King and several of the top officials of his regime (Sundiata 1980). Consequently, President King and Vice President Yancy were forced to resign in 1930 (Sundiata 1980).

During the Tubman regime (beginning in 1951), the thrust of the violation of political human rights focused on individuals and groups, who are seen as opponents of the regime. For example, as has been discussed, the opposition Reformation Party was banned in contravention of the constitutionally granted freedom of association. Similarly, the Tubman regime concocted a "fake coup" in 1955 and used it as a pretext to arrest and imprisoned prominent opposition leaders (Wreh 1976). In addition, S. David Coleman, the chair of the main opposition party, was killed (Wreh 1976).

In the same vein, during the Tolbert administration, the regime engaged in sundry human rights violations after the end of its "political liberalization" efforts in 1973. As has been discussed, a revised version of the Sedition Law was enacted in 1978 that made it a criminal offense to criticize the regime or a government official (Kieh 2008, 2012a). Furthermore, on April 14, 1979, upon the orders of President Tolbert, the police and security forces opened fire on peaceful citizens, who were demonstrating against decades of political repression and socioeconomic malaise (Cordor 1979; Kieh 2008, 2012a; Sawyer 1992). As well, in 1980, the opposition Progressive People's Party (PPP) was banned and its leaders arrested and imprisoned on the charge of treason (Kieh 2008, 2012a; Sawyer 1992).

Like its immediate predecessors, the Doe regime also engaged in the vitriolic violation of political human rights. For example, in 1982, the Doe regime arrested and imprisoned several leaders of the student movement for criticizing the regime (Press 2015; Reuters 1982). Subsequently, the student leaders were tried and found guilty by the military tribunal and sentenced to death by a firing squad (Press 2015; Reuters 1982). However, the wave of domestic and international pressure forced the Doe regime to release the students from prison (Press, 2015; Reuters 1982). Two years later, the Doe regime issued Decree #88A that criminalized the criticism of the regime (Messing 2005).

In addition, in 1986, the Doe regime prohibited the major opposition political parties from forming a coalition (Liebenow 1988).

The Social Crises

Socially, the basic services such as education, health care, access to clean drinking water and sanitation were woefully inadequate. In the area of education, for example, access was quite limited because there was inadequate number of schools, especially in the rural areas (Kieh 2008, 2012a). Hence, by the end of the Doe regime, only about 32 percent of the school eligible students were enrolled in school at the primary level (Government of Liberia 2004: 20). Similarly, staffing, instructional materials, and resources, as well as equipment were inadequate (Kieh 2008, 2012a).

In the area of health care, by 1985, for example, only 35 percent of the citizens had access (Ministry of Planning and Economic Affairs, Liberia 1986). Another major problem was the inadequacy of staffing (for a population then of about 3 million people). In 1989, for example, there were about 3,526 healthcare workers in the public health sector (World Health Organization 2003: 2). Of this number, about 237 were physicians and specialists, 656 nurses and nurse midwives, 2782 trained traditional midwives, and 1,381 supporting personnel (World Health Organization 2003: 2). In addition, there was the inadequacy of hospitals, health centers, equipment, and drugs (medical) (Kieh 2008, 2012a).

As for access to clean drinking water and acceptable level of sanitation, they, too, were inadequate. For example, in 1985, only about 23 percent of rural dwellers had access to safe drinking water (United Nations Development Program 1990). This meant that about 77 percent, the vast majority, got their water from unsafe sources, including various bodies of water that were contaminated with human refuse, among others. This made them vulnerable to contracting various water-borne diseases, including typhoid. Similarly, during the same period, more than half of the population did not have access to acceptable sanitation (United Nations Development Program 1990). The resultant effect was that the majority of the country's population was vulnerable to contracting various diseases, including malaria.

The Major Forces

Background

As has been discussed, the country's perennial multidimensional crises of underdevelopment had two major resulting adverse effects. One was that it eroded the legitimacy of the state and its various regimes. Consequently, the majority of Liberians became alienated from the state and its various regimes, because they were considered irrelevant to their lives (Kieh 2008, 2012a). The other negative effect was that the crises of underdevelopment sowed and nurtured the seeds of civil conflict. Importantly, the failure of the postcoup Doe regime to provide the requisite leadership in addressing the crises of underdevelopment provided the trigger or proximate cause for the outbreak of the country's first civil war on December 24, 1989.

The first civil war was shaped by several domestic and external forces. In the case of the former, they were the conflicting parties that fought the war. As for the latter, they served two major roles as peacemakers and supporters (Kieh 1992). In this section, the major domestic and external actors that shaped the first civil war will be discussed.

The Internal Forces

The Doe regime was the main target of the military incursion that was carried out by the NPFL that eventually led to the outbreak of the war on December 24, 1989 (Kieh 1992). The overarching purpose of the NPFL's incursion was to overthrow the Doe regime. Concerned about regime survival, the Doe regime used the Armed Forces of Liberia (AFL), the national military force, to repel the NPFL's military incursion. In so doing, the AFL committed atrocities against civilians, especially the members of the Gio and Mano ethnic groups (Human Rights Watch 1990b, 1991). This was because the overwhelming majority of the NPFL's fighters were members of the Gio and Mano ethnic groups (Human Rights Watch 1990b).

The NPFL was the main rebel group that launched the military incursion that culminated in the first civil war. The group was organized by Charles Taylor, the former director-general of the General Services Agency (GSA) in the Doe regime (Adebayo 2002; Ellis 2001; Geddes 2013; Huband 1998). In 1982, Taylor was dismissed by Doe for allegedly defrauding the Liberian government through a fraudulent procurement scheme that he established as the head of the GSA (Kieh 2008). Subsequently, Taylor was fired as the head of the GSA (Kieh 2008). Fearing that he might be arrested and imprisoned, Taylor fled Liberia and went to Ghana where he was arrested and detained but later released (Kieh 2008). He then went to the United States, where he had previously lived for many years, prior to the 1980 coup in Liberia. Upon the request of the Doe regime based on the extradition treaty between Liberia and the United States, Taylor was arrested and imprisoned, pending his extradition to Liberia (Huband 1998). However, in 1985, Taylor reportedly escaped from prison in the United States and fled to Cote d' Ivoire.[2] In Cote d'Ivoire, he met some of the participants in the abortive November 1985 coup against the Doe regime that was led by the late General Quiwonkpa (Huband 1998). Subsequently, he succeeded in recruiting some of them to constitute the core of his warlordist militia (Huband 1998). Thereafter, Taylor and his core fighters, including Prince Johnson, received military training in Libya from the Gaddafi regime that had an adversarial relationship with the Doe government (Huband 1998; Kieh 1992, 2008). Thereafter, Taylor and his core fighters went to Cote d'Ivoire, where they received support from the Boigny regime that was hostile to Doe (Huband 1998; Kieh 1992, 2008). Thus, Cote d'Ivoire was used as the launchpad for the military incursion that commenced on December 24, 1989 (Huband 1998; Kieh 1992, 2008). During the war, the NPFL, like the Doe regime, committed atrocities mainly against civilians (Human Rights Watch 1991),

The Independent National Patriotic Front (INPFL) was a breakaway faction from the NPFL that was organized in 1990 by Prince Johnson, one of Taylor's former core fighters (Adebayo 2002; Kieh 1992). Johnson broke away from Taylor, because, according to him (Johnson), Taylor deviated from the original "principles" of the NPFL (Kieh 1992, 2008). With the INPFL's entry into the war, the conflict became three-sided involving the AFL and the NPFL. The INPFL established its military base in Cadwell, a suburb of Monrovia, the capital city (Kieh 2008). On September 10, 1990, Johnson and a squad of his fighters captured President Doe at the Freeport of Monrovia, where Doe had gone to visit General Albert Quanoo, the commander of the peacekeeping force of the ECOWAS (Henry 1990).[3] Subsequently, Doe was publicly humiliated by Johnson, tortured, and brutally murdered thereafter (*LA Times* 1990). In addition, the INPFL also committed atrocities against civilians, usually upon Johnson's orders (Human Rights Watch 1990b). In 1996, Johnson was rescued from his Cadwell Base by ECOMOG, the ECOWAS peacekeeping force, amid an imminent attack by the NPFL (Kieh 2008). The attack was against the backdrop of Johnson allegedly double-crossing Taylor, after agreeing to the formation of an alliance between the NPFL and INPFL to launch "Octopus," a military attack against Monrovia. Johnson was subsequently taken to Nigeria for safety (Kieh 2008). Consequently, the INPFL collapsed, and its fighters joined the various emergent warlordist militias.

The United Liberation Movement of Liberia for Democracy (ULIMO) was organized in 1991, in Sierra Leone by some former officials of the Doe regime, after the collapse of the Liberian government in September 1990 (Adebayo 2002; Enro 1995; Kieh 2004). From its inception, ULIMO was plagued by internal conflicts between and among its various factions over the leadership of the militia (Enro 1995; Kieh 2004). These conflicts led to two major adverse outcomes. First, General Albert Karpeh, the head of the group, who served as the Minister of Defense in the Doe regime, was killed under mysterious circumstances (Enro 1995; Kieh 2004). Second, in 1994, the militia splintered into two major factions: ULIMO-J led by Roosevelt Johnson, and ULIMO-K led by Alhaji Kromah, the former director-general of the Liberian Broadcasting System (LBS) and the former minister of information in the Doe regime (Enro 1995; Kieh 2004). ULIMO-J recruited the bulk of its fighters from the Krahn ethnic group, while ULIMO-K drew its recruits mainly from the Mandingo ethnic group (Kieh 2004). Subsequently, the two factions fought against one another, and the NPFL (Kieh 2004). The two militias, like the NPFL and the AFL, committed egregious acts against civilians (Human Rights Watch 1990b, 1991). In addition, ULIMO-J formed an alliance with the remnants of the AFL. On the other hand, ULIMO-K formed a temporary alliance with the NPFL in 1996, in launching "Octopus" (Kieh 2004). After the failure of "Octopus," the alliance ended, as the NPFL resumed its attacks against ULIMO-K.

The Liberian Peace Council (LPC) was organized in 1993 by George Boley, who held several positions in the Doe regime, including minister of state for presidential affairs (Adebayo 2002; Enro 1995; Kieh 2004). LPC recruited its fighters mainly from the Krahn ethnic group that was the major target of the NPFL (Kieh 2004). Operationally, LPC coordinated its military activities with the AFL and ULIMO-J, given the ties of their leaders as former functionaries of the Doe regime and the major targets of the NPFL (Kieh 2004).

The External Forces

Cote d'Ivoire played several major interlocking roles in the civil war. A key one, as has been discussed, was the launchpad for the NPFL's military incursion into Liberia, beginning on December 24, 1989 (Kieh 1992). Another was serving as a sanctuary for Taylor and his major supporters. In addition, it served as the NPFL's conduit for its (NPFL's) international activities, including the purchase of arms and the illicit sale of Liberia's natural resources (Kieh 1992). Furthermore, it served as the NPFL's chief regional patron, protector, and defender in the West African region. For example, Cote d' Ivoire led the opposition to the intervention of ECOMOG, the peacekeeping force of ECOWAS, in the first Liberian war (Kieh 1992).

Libya's central role, as has been discussed, was the provision of military training and weapons to the NPFL. Taylor and his core fighters were trained by the Gaddafi regime's military (Huband 1998; Kieh 1992). In addition, Libya provided the initial batch of weapons to the NPFL that the latter used to launch the military incursion into Liberia on December 24, 1989 (Huband 1998; Kieh 1992). Gaddafi regarded Doe as a client of the United States, his (Gaddafi's) principal enemy (Kieh 1992). The animosity between Gaddafi and Doe was vividly demonstrated during the 19th Summit of the Organization of African Unity (OAU): Doe threatened to engage Gaddafi in a fistfight, if he (Gaddafi) had criticized the United States during the meeting (Liberia Data Project 2021).

Nigeria was the lead country for ECOWAS' peacemaking and peacekeeping efforts during the first Liberian civil war (Adebayo 2002; Kieh 1992; Vogt 1992). In the peacemaking area, Nigeria led the regional efforts to end the war through the use of mediation and negotiation. Significantly, it was Nigeria's pivotal role that led to the implementation of the Abuja II Peace Accord in 1996 that finally ended the war, after sixteen failed peace agreements (Kieh 2011a). In addition, Nigeria undertook efforts to help de-escalate the war after the failure of the NPFL-led military operation dubbed "Octopus" in 1986: As has been discussed, Nigeria took and granted Prince Johnson, the leader of the INPFL, sanctuary. The major resulting effect was the collapse of the INPFL, and thereby the removal of a major faction from the war. In terms of peacekeeping, Nigeria provided the bulk of the financial and military resources for ECOMOG (Adebayo 2002; Vogt 1992). In addition, after the capture and the murder of President Doe in September 1990, Nigeria took over the command of the regional peacekeeping force (Adebayo 2002; Vogt 1992).

The United States played various roles in the civil war. A key one was mediation. After initially adopting a "hands-off" approach during the regime of Bush '41, based on the rationale that Liberia was no longer important to American national interests, the new Clinton administration undertook its own mediation efforts (Kieh 1996, 2007a). The purpose of the mediation was to help end the war. However, the American mediation efforts were hamstrung by the mistrust between the NPFL and the United States, which had its roots in Taylor's arrest, imprisonment, and "escape or release" from prison in Massachusetts (Kieh 1996, 2007a). As part of its mediation efforts, the United States made arrangements with the Togolese Government to grant President Doe asylum (Krauss 1990). However, Doe rejected the offer, insisting, among other things, that he had to take the entirety of his presidential guards with him into exile in Togo (Krauss 1990). The other role was using Prince Johnson and the INPFL to capture Doe, thereby removing him as the major factor in the civil war (Tango Tango Video 1990). However, the capture and subsequent murder of Doe by Prince Johnson and the INPFL did not end the civil war. On the contrary, as has been discussed, it led to the emergence of new warlordist militias—ULIMO, then ULIMO-J and ULIMO-K and LPC.

The ECOWAS was the lead organization in the quest to end the civil war. In this vein, ECOWAS undertook two interrelated sets of activities: peacemaking and peacekeeping. In the case of the former, ECOWAS mediated seventeen peace accords (Kieh 1992, 2011a). The initial sixteen peace agreements failed to end the war, because Taylor reneged on each of them after the signing (Kieh 1992, 2011a). However, the Abuja II Peace Accord, the seventeenth peace agreement, ended the war (Kieh 1992, 2011a). This was because it provided for punitive actions against any party that reneged on the implementation of the terms of the accord, including enforcement mechanisms (Kieh 1992, 2011a). Clearly, this pressured Taylor and the NPFL to abandon their perennial "spoiler's role" (Kieh 1992, 2011a). The other instrument used by ECOWAS was peacekeeping (Adebayo 2002; Kieh 1999, 2000; Vogt 1992). Amid opposition from Cote d' Ivoire and the NPFL, ECOWAS deployed ECOMOG as a peacekeeping force, the first military intervention in a member-state in 1990 (Adebayo 2002; Kieh 1999, 2000; Vogt 1992). Furthermore, ECOWAS provided security for the sections of Liberia that were not under the control of the NPFL. As well, ECOWAS supervised the presidential election in July 1997. Also, after the termination of the war, ECOWAS undertook a failed attempt to restructure the Liberian military. The effort was rejected by the Taylor regime, which claimed that as a sovereign state, Liberia had the right to undertake its own security sector reform, including the restructuring of the military (Ebo 2015).

The OAU played a supportive role in the civil war. Essentially, as a classic case of subsidiarity, the OAU deferred to ECOWAS' leadership as the regional organization closest to the theater of the war (Howe 1996; Mortimer 1996). Against this backdrop, the OAU undertook two major complementary activities. One was the support of ECOWAS' mediation efforts through the OAU's Special Representative for the Liberian Civil War. The other was the provision of troops from Senegal and Tanzania to supplement ECOMOG (Howe 1996; Mortimer 1996). The OAU took this action in response to Taylor and the NPFL complaint that ECOMOG was biased against them; hence, they needed troops from "neutral African countries" to disarm their fighters under the Cotonou Peace Accord (Howe 1996; Kieh 2011a). However, the involvement of the Senegalese and Tanzanian peacekeepers did not lead to the NPFL disarming. Instead, the NPFL attacked the Senegalese and Tanzania troops in the latter's efforts to disarm the fighters from the former (Howe 1996; Mortimer 1996). Consequently, some of the troops were captured and detained by the NPFL for a period of time ((Howe 1996; Mortimer 1996). Ultimately, the NPFL's belligerent action led to the withdrawal of the Senegalese and Tanzanian contingents from the peacekeeping force (Howe 1996; Mortimer 1996).

Like the OAU, the United Nations (UN) deferred to ECOWAS' leadership on the first Liberian civil war (United Nations Security Council 1993). That is, the UN assumed a supportive role. In this vein, under UN Security Council, Resolution 866 (1993) authorized the deployment of a peace observation mission, pursuant to the provisions of the Cotonou Peace Accord (Cotonou Peace Accord 1993). Accordingly, a peace observation mission was deployed in Liberia comprising a total of 652 military and civilian observers (Kieh 2009b; United Nations 1993). The mandate of the peace observation mission was fourfold. First, the mission was authorized to monitor and verify the ceasefire under the Cotonou Peace Accord (United Nations 1993). Second, the mission was empowered to monitor compliance with the arms embargo (United Nations 1993). Third, the mission was authorized to disarm, encamp, and demobilize all combatants (United Nations 1993). Fourth, the mission was given the responsibility to monitor and investigate human rights violations. In terms of an assessment, the mission was hamstrung by three major factors. A key one was that the UN allotted limited resources to the mission (Kieh 2009c). Another was the mission's inability to investigate the egregious human rights abuses that were committed against unarmed civilians by the warring factions. Furthermore, the Taylor-led NPFL remained wedded to playing the role of the "spoiler" in the peace process (Kieh 2011a). Hence, the NPFL refused to abide by the terms of the Cotonou Peace Accord (Kieh 2011a).

The End of the First Liberian Civil War

As has been discussed, the first Liberian civil war ended in 1996, with the signing of the Abuja II Peace Accord (Kieh 2009a, 2011a). This was followed by the disarmament and demobilization processes, which lasted from November 26, 1996, to February 7, 1997 (Kieh 2009a; Tanner 1998). However, both processes were incomplete, because the warring factions, especially the NPFL, were not fully disarmed (Tanner 1998). In other words, the combatants kept some of their weapons. As Tanner (1998: 137) observes, "The fighters that queued in the demobilization centers were not the factions more reliable troops." In addition, the combatants who were disarmed were not rehabilitated (Kieh 2009a). Hence, they were reintegrated into their various communities suffering from a plethora of war-related psychological and related problems (Kieh 2009a).

In spite of the incomplete DDRR processes, the presidential election was held amid what Lyons (2004: 36) characterized as the "militarization of politics." That is, with the NPFL's "military machinery" still intact, Charles Taylor, the standard bearer of the National Patriotic Party (NPP), the political offshoot of the NPFL, used the threat of the use of military force to intimidate the other presidential candidates, as well as the Liberian electorate (Lyons 1998; Tanner 1998). For example, Taylor's "military apparatus" was used to harass some of the other presidential candidates as they campaigned in various regions of the country (Kieh 2009a; Liberia Data Project 2021). Similarly, Taylor threatened the electorate that if he did not win the presidential election, he would revert to war (Human Rights Watch 2000: 50). Fearful of another round of war, the majority of the electorate capitulated to Taylor's threat in a "vote for security" (Lyons 1998). Thus, Taylor won the presidential election with more than 75 percent of the votes (Harris 1999; Kieh 2011b). Thereafter, Taylor was inaugurated as the president of Liberia on August 6, 1997.

Significantly, as has been discussed, after the election, the new Taylor regime reneged on the agreement for ECOMOG to supervise the creation of the new Liberian military. Using the sovereignty argument as a pretext, the Taylor regime undertook the establishment of the new military, police, and security establishment (Human Rights Watch 1997; Kieh 2009a). In turn, this created a sense of insecurity among the former warlordist militias and contributed to sowing the seeds for the second civil war (Human Rights Watch 1997; Kieh 2009a).

THE SECOND CIVIL WAR (1999–2003)

The Major Causes of the War

Background

The second Liberian civil war commenced on April 21, 1999, with an armed attack by the LURD, using neighboring Guinea as launchpad (Yangbeh 2006). The war was caused by two major interlocking factors: the failed postconflict peace-building project and the resulting nonreconstitution of the authoritarian peripheral capitalist Liberian state. The resultant effect was state failure—cultural, economic, political, security, and social. In turn, state failure led to a crisis of regime legitimacy, and the resulting second civil war.

Cultural Failure

The centerpiece of cultural failure was the Taylor regime's use of "ethnic scapegoating:" Faced with the crisis of legitimacy due to the horrendous failure of his regime to provide the requisite leadership in building durable peace through the democratic reconstitution of the Liberian state, the Taylor regime resorted to blaming the Krahn and Mandingo ethnic groups for its sordid performance (Kieh 2009a). The two ethnic groups had closed ties with the Doe regime. Thus, the Taylor regime tried to develop the narrative that the remnants of the Doe regime were plotting to topple the former. Three major cases are instructive. One was the arrest and imprisonment of Hassan Bility, a Liberian journalist, who hailed from the Mandingo ethnic group (Kieh 2009a, 2012a; U.S. Department of State 1999). The Taylor regime accused Bility of being the mastermind of the propaganda dimension of the orchestrated multifaceted efforts by the Mandingo ethnic group to undermine his regime (Kieh 2009a, 2012a). During his detention, Bility was tortured and subjected to other forms of inhumane treatment (U.S. Department of State 1999).

The other example was the "Camp Johnson Road Mini-War." In waging its campaign of persecution against the members of the Krahn ethnic group, the Taylor regime attempted to arrest and detain Roosevelt Johnson, the former leader of ULIMO-J, the warlordist militia, and a prominent figure from the Krahn ethnic group, in September 1997 (Kieh 2008, 2009a, 2012a). The resulting "tugs and pulls" led to a "mini-war" between the remnants of the Johnson-led ULIMO-J and the Liberian military (Kieh 2008, 2009a, 2012a). Consequently, some people were killed and wounded. In addition, the Taylor regime failed to achieve its ultimate objective of arresting Johnson: He escaped and fled to Cote d' Ivoire.

In October 1998, the Taylor regime arrested and imprisoned thirteen members of the Krahn ethnic group, including Bai Gballah, who was a friend of Taylor during their stay in the United States prior to the April 12, 1980, coup (Kieh 2009a, 2012a). The accused were tried, convicted, and sentenced to ten years in prison (Kieh 2009a, 2012a). The trial was a mockery of due process (Kieh 2009a, 2012a).

Economic Failure

One of the glaring manifestations of state failure found expression in inequalities and inequities in wealth and income between the emergent new local wing of the ruling class led by President Taylor and the subaltern classes. In terms of wealth, Taylor established a stranglehold over state revenues. For example, the revenues (U.S. Dollars) that were generated on a daily basis from major public corporations like the National Port Authority and the Liberian Petroleum Refining Corporation (LPRC) were deposited in a vault located in Taylor's private home nicknamed "White Flower" (Liberian Data Project 2021). Then, as what Lowenkopf (1976: 51) refers to as a "Tammy Boss," Taylor used the state's revenues to enrich himself, and to share portions with the members of his inner circle (Liberia Data Project 2021). In sum, the wealth of the state was monopolized by Taylor and the members of his inner circles. Similarly, in terms of income, the average civil servant was paid $15.00 per month, while Taylor and the top government officials received thousands of dollars (Liberia Data Project 2021). Cumulatively, the gross inequalities and inequities in wealth contributed to abject mass poverty. By 1998, for example, about 80 percent of the population was living on less than US$1 a day (United Nations Development Program 1990).

In the area of employment, job opportunities in the private sector were quite scarce. One of the major reasons was that private investors were concerned about the excesses of the Taylor regime and the resulting adverse impact on political stability and profit-making. However, although new positions were created in the public sector, they were filled by the members of the Taylor-led NPP (Liberia Data Project 2021). In addition, even the bloating of the state bureaucracy was inadequate to meet the employment needs of the citizens. By 1999, the unemployment rate stood at about 90 percent (Liberia Data Project 2021).

Amid mass abject poverty, Taylor and the leading members of his regime engaged in the primitive accumulation of capital through the agency of their respective offices in the state bureaucracy using sundry illegal means such as bribery and extortion (Kieh 2012a, 2017; Sandy 2008). As Sandy (2008: 5) asserts, "[The Taylor regime] became one of the most corrupt governments in the history of Liberia . . . Taylor's Liberia was a rogue state where there existed no system of accountability." By 1998, for example, Taylor's personal wealth, which was accumulated through illegal means both as a warlord and president, was estimated at $450 million (Human Rights Watch 1999).

Political Failure

Authoritarian Governance System

President Taylor retained the authoritarian governance system that was one of the major crises of the legitimacy of the state that led to the first civil war. Specifically, like his immediate predecessor, Samuel Doe, Taylor militarized the authoritarian governance system: threat and the military force were used as instruments to cow down the population, especially to force the regime's critics into submission. For example, as will be discussed in the section on the violation of political human rights, the Taylor regime used the military recurrently to inflict repression on civil society organizations (Human Rights Watch 1997, 1998, 1999). In addition, Taylor was a quintessential autocrat, who, among other things, exercised unbridled suzerainty over the entire government without any oversight (Human Rights Watch 1997, 1998, 1999).

The "Hegemonic Presidency"

President Taylor further entrenched the "hegemonic presidency" and the resulting dominance of the presidency. As Human Rights Watch (2002: 65) asserts, "President Taylor's government functioned without accountability, independent of an effective judiciary and legislature that operate[d] in fear of the executive." In effect, the legislative and judiciary branches were subordinated to the presidency.

Several major cases are instructive. One was the recurrent issuance of threats by President Taylor to the members of the National Legislature, especially from his ruling NPP, that he would remove them from office if they did not oblige to his edicts (Liberia Data Project 2021). Similarly, President Taylor insisted that there was no "separation of powers." Hence, all powers resided in the presidency (Human Rights Watch 2002). Furthermore, In June

1999, President Taylor instructed the Supreme Court of Liberia to suspend its ruling in a case involving a local bank, pending what he termed "executive review" (Radio Veritas 1999).

Political Human Rights

In terms of political human rights, the Taylor regime violated them in several cases. For example, the Taylor regime violated the constitutionally guaranteed freedom of assembly. A major case was on September 7, 1997, when the Taylor regime dispatched a contingent of security personnel to the Firestone Plantations Company to violently quell a labor strike (Liberia Human Rights Campaign 1998). The workers were protesting the company's decision to deduct 37.5 percent from their salaries toward the repayment of an undisclosed amount of money that was stolen from the company's vault during the first Liberian civil war (Liberia Human Rights Campaign 1998: 2). Several workers were killed and scores of others were injured (Liberia Human Rights Campaign 1998).

As for the freedom of the press, the Taylor regime routinely muzzled the independent press (Human Rights Watch 1999). Several cases are noteworthy. In 1997, for example, some journalists from the *Inquirer Newspaper* were arrested and detained by the Taylor regime for publishing a story that was deemed critical of the regime (Human Rights Watch 1998: 1). Another case was on December 21, 1997, when state security forces abducted and detained Alex Redd, a journalist from the Ducor Broadcasting Corporation, and held him captive for two days (Human Rights Watch 1998). In 1998, the Liberian press was banned by the Taylor regime from placing information about the government on the internet (African Faith and Justice Network 1998: 2).

The Taylor regime also committed politically motivated murders. For example, on November 28, 1997, Samuel Dokie, a former confidante of Taylor, was murdered by the Special Security Service upon President Taylor's order (Human Rights Watch 1998). Cumulatively, from 1997 to 1999, the Taylor regime committed about 357 politically motivated murders (U.S. Department of State, 1997, 1998, 1999, 2000).

Security Failure

One of the major tenets of the Abuja II Peace Accord that ended the first Liberian civil war was the requirement that the new Liberian government collaborate with ECOWAS in reforming the country's security sector that has had a long history of politicization (Bah 2006). However, upon assuming the Liberian Presidency after the election and inauguration, President Taylor violated the security sector provision of the Abuja II Peace Accord. Instead, he transformed his rebel warlordist militia, the NPFL, into the country's new security establishment comprising the military, police, and security establishment (Human Rights Watch 1997). In addition, the Taylor regime established special units within the military and police. In the military, the Executive Mansion Special Unit (EMSU) and the Anti-Terrorist Unit (ATU) were established. The EMSU served as the presidential guard akin to similar units in countries like Burkina Faso under Blaise Compaore. The ATU, which was headed by Chuckie Taylor, President Taylor's son, had the responsibilities to operate the checkpoints that were established throughout the country as major elements of the emergent "garrison state" (Laswell 1941). As the *Perspective Magazine* (2003: 1) observes, "For one thing, Liberian security checkpoints [were] notorious for their behavior. And no issue [was] more emblematic of the [Taylor] regime's damaged credibility than its scandalous support for the murderous security apparatus." The other function was as the Taylor regime's death squad (Liberia Data Project 2021). The ATU was responsible for murdering the regime's political opponents, both real and imagined (Liberia Data Project 2021). As for the police, the Special Operations Division was established for the purpose of terrorizing media outlets and civil society organizations that were designated as opponents of the Taylor regime (Liberia Data Project 2021)).

Another major example of the failed security sector reform was the lack of professionalism and discipline among the ranks of military, police, and security establishment (Human Rights Watch 1998). For example, these security units, especially the EMSU, ATU, and SOD committed various human rights violations, including beatings and other forms of torture, harassment, and arbitrary arrests of citizens (Amnesty International 1998; Human Rights Watch 1998). Similarly, the Special Security Service (SSS), which was primarily responsible for protective services for the president, vice president, and other high officials of government, was also used as an auxiliary death squad (Liberia Data Project 2021). For example, it was a unit of the SSS that President Taylor used to murder Samuel Dokie, a one-time confidante of President Taylor, and his relatives (The Analyst Newspaper 2008).

Further, the Taylor regime used the AFL as a partisan military force. As has been discussed, for example, in September 1997, President Taylor deployed a contingent of the AFL on Camp Johnson Road in Monrovia, the capital city. The purpose of the military operation was to arrest Roosevelt Johnson, the leader of ULIMO-J, one of the former warlordist militias. The major resultant effect was the outbreak of a mini-war in which scores of people were killed and wounded. Ultimately, the military operation failed to achieve its objective because Roosevelt Johnson escaped and fled the country (Kieh 2009a).

Significantly, the failure of the Taylor regime to reform the security sector as was required by the Abuja II Peace Accord coupled with the Camp Johnson

Road mini-war developed a profound sense of insecurity in the former rival warlords and their major supporters (Kieh 2009a). Their collective fear was based on the fact that Taylor could easily deploy his partisan military, police, and security forces to inflict harm on them. In addition, the failed arrest of Roosevelt Johnson was perceived as an ominous harbinger of their imminent arrest and imprisonment (Kieh 2009a). Accordingly, several of the former warlords and some of their major supporters fled Liberia and sought refuge in neighboring Guinea (Brabazon 2003). Subsequently, the former warlords and others organized the LURD for the sole purpose of waging an armed rebellion against the Taylor regime (Brabazon 2003).

Social Failure

Education

The Liberian educational system was plagued by several major challenges after the first civil war. A key problem was the woeful inadequacy of schools, especially in the rural areas that bore the brunt of the destruction brought by the war (Liberia Data Project 2021). The destruction of school buildings worsened the country's perennial problem of the inadequacy of school buildings (Liberia Data Project 2021). The major resulting effect was that thousands of students could not attend school (Liberia Data Project 2021).

Another problem was the inadequacy of school personnel, especially administrators and teachers. This problem was made worse by the "brain drain" experienced when the majority of the qualified personnel fled the country for safety in other countries during the first civil war (Liberia Data Project 2021). One of the major resultant effects was the employment of untrained and unqualified teachers (Liberia Data Project 2021). This action seriously undermined the teaching and learning processes, because, among other things, a large cadre of unqualified teachers was expected to constitute the instructional core of the country's post–first civil war educational system. In terms of student learning, for most part, students failed to acquire the requisite knowledge base and skills sets that were coterminous with their academic levels (Liberia Data Project 2021).

Similarly, instructional materials such as textbooks were woefully inadequate (Liberia Data Project 2021). Against this background, the teaching and learning processes were dependent upon course notes that were prepared by the teachers, including the large pool of untrained and unqualified teachers. Several major problems emerged. One was the fact that some unqualified and untrained teachers also prepared the course notes. This meant the quality of the information contained in the course notes was highly suspicious. Another issue was the commercialization of the course notes (Liberia Data Project 2021). Teachers sold the course notes to the students, and this was particularly challenging for the students given the very high rate of poverty and deprivation (Liberia Data Project 2021). In addition, the lack of textbooks militated against the students' capacity to prepare adequately for the various course sessions, especially the development of their critical thinking skills. Furthermore, the students relied exclusively on the course notes as the only sources of readings for the various courses.

Equipment and other important materials that were central to the teaching and learning processes were also inadequate. For example, laboratories for courses in the natural sciences at various institutions lacked the scientific equipment and materials to conduct experiments and engage in other activities related to scientific inquiry (Liberia Data Project 2021). Also, schools had inadequate seating. In some instances, students had to sit on blocks, if they could not afford to purchase their own desks (Liberia Data Project 2021).

Health Care

The Taylor regime failed to invest in both the construction of new healthcare facilities and the repair the few existing ones that were damaged by the first civil war (Liberia Data Project 2021). Given the inadequacy of healthcare facilities during the pre–first civil war era, it was expected that the Taylor regime would have constructed new healthcare facilities, especially in the rural areas, where these facilities are virtually nonexistent (Liberia Data Project 2021). As well, against the backdrop of the devastating effects the first civil war had on an already inadequate physical healthcare infrastructure, it was expected that the damaged hospitals and health centers would have been renovated by the Taylor regime. But, characteristically, no such investment was made (Liberia Data Project 2021).

In terms of health personnel, including doctors and nurses, several of them fled the country during the first civil war (Liberia Data Project 2021). However, the majority of them did not return to the country after the first civil war ended in 1997 (Liberia Data Project 2021). Hence, the numbers of doctors, nurses, and other health professionals were inadequate to cater to the needs of the population (Liberia Data Project 2021). To make matters worse, the Taylor regime failed to invest in the training of healthcare professionals (Liberia Data Project 2021). For example, the College of Medicine at the University of Liberia, the country's flagship institution, was underfunded as an integral part of the Taylor regime's policy approach to health care and education (Liberia Data Project 2021).

Another major challenge was the overwhelming majority of Liberians did not have access to health care (Liberia Data Project 2021). The problem was mediated by the state of disrepair of the existent hospitals and health centers and the failure of the Taylor regime to make health security a national priority. This was evidenced by the failure to repair the existing healthcare facilities that had been destroyed by the first civil war and to construct new ones. Overall, the Taylor regime relied on metropolitan-based nongovernmental organizations (NGOs) in the health sector to cater to the health needs of the citizens (Liberia Data Project 2021).

Importantly, the sordid state of the country's health sector had profound adverse effects. A major one was that in 1999 the life expectancy was about 43 years (United Nations Development Program 1999). In addition, only about 44 percent of the population (less than half) was expected to reach 40 years of age (United Nations Program 1999: 21).

The Major Forces

Background

Two major sets of forces—internal and external—shaped the second Liberian civil war. In the case of the former, the Taylor regime through its military (the AFL), the LURD, and the Movement for Democracy in Liberia (MODEL) were the protagonists. Unlike the first Liberian civil war in which the warlordist militias attacked the forces of the Liberian government (up till 1990), and one another, LURD and MODEL, formed an alliance against the Taylor regime. Hence, the Taylor regime was the only target for the two militias.

In terms of the external forces, the major ones were Guinea, Cote d'Ivoire, the United States, ECOWAS, and the UN. The locus of Guinea's role revolved around its support for LURD (Brabazon 2003). And this was evidenced by Guinea allowing LURD to use its territory as a bridgehead from which it attacked Liberia (Brabazon 2003). For its part, Cote d'Ivoire was the principal external patron for MODEL (Brabazon 2003). In terms of the United States, it played key roles in pressuring President Taylor to resign and peace stabilization. In the case of ECOWAS, it played the lead role in peacemaking and peacekeeping efforts. As for the UN, it was responsible for postwar termination peacekeeping and security in Liberia.

The Internal Forces

As has been discussed, the Taylor regime was the primary target of the second Liberian civil war. That is, both LURD and MODEL, the two rebel groups, were desirous of toppling the Taylor regime through the use of military force (Brabazon 2003). For its part, the Taylor regime relied on the partisan AFL, which was dominated by former fighters of the Taylor-led NPFL (Human Rights Watch 2003).

The LURD was organized in July 1999, in Freetown, Sierra Leone by a group of Liberian exiles, who were opposed to the Taylor regime (Brabazon 2003). The overarching goal of LURD was to dislodge the

Taylor regime from power through military means (Brabazon 2003). The emergent adversarial relationship between the Taylor regime and LURD was informed by two major factors. One was the partisan nature of the Taylor regime. The related factor was the partisan nature of the post civil war recomposition of the military, the police, and the security services. Rather than restructuring the security sector as per the decision under the Abuja II Peace Accord that ended the first civil war, the Taylor regime made the decision to impose the ex-fighters of the NPLF as the members of the country's new military, police, and services (Brabazon 2003; Kieh 2009a). The other factor was the Taylor regime's campaign of political persecution waged against the leader and members of the ULIMO-J, a former rival warlordist militia, as well as targeted members of the Krahn and Mandingo (Kieh 2009a). Based on the actions of the Taylor regime, they were fearful that their physical security was in peril (Brabazon 2003; Kieh 2009a). Against this background, on April 21, 1999, LURD launched an armed attach against Liberia from its sanctuary in neighboring Guinea (Brabazon 2003; Kieh 2009a).

The MODEL was organized in 2003, by Liberian exiles living in refugee camps in the Cote d'Ivoire (Kaihko 2018). The Liberian exiles were associated with some of the former warlordist militias—LPC and ULIMO—that fought during the first Liberian civil war (Kaihko 2018). These exiles fled Liberia because they were quite fearful that the Taylor regime posed grave danger to their physical security (Kaihko 2018; Kieh 2009a). Their fear was confirmed by various actions of the Taylor regime, including its attempt to arrest Roosevelt Johnson, the leader of ULIMO-J, and the persecution of the members of the Krahn ethnic group from which the bulk of the members of MODEL hailed (Kaihko 2018; Kieh 2009a). Given its shared interest with LURD of toppling the Taylor regime, MODEL joined the war in March 2003 (Pham 2004). MODEL opened a second front of the war against the Taylor regime as a complement to the first front, which was launched by LURD (BBC Radio 2003).

The External Forces

Cote d'Ivoire was the chief external patron of MODEL (Frontline World 2005; Kaihko 2018). Initially, it sponsored the formation of MODEL as a progovernment militia in the Gbagbo regime's war with various rebel groups in Cote d'Ivoire in 2002 (Kaihko 2018). In this vein, the Ivorian government provided MODEL with weapons and other logistics (Kaihko 2018). Then in 2003, MODEL was transformed into a Liberian rebel group against the Taylor regime (Kaihko 2018). The shift in MODEL's mission was necessitated by the Taylor regime's support for two antigovernment rebel groups in Cote d'Ivoire-The Popular Movement of the Ivorian Great West (MJP) and the Movement for Just and Peace (MJP) (The New Humanitarian 2021). Clearly, the Gbagbo regime's support of MODEL in its quest to topple the Taylor regime was a retaliatory act. Frontline (2003: 1) provides the following summation of the Gbagbo regime's *raison d'etre*: "Taylor backed rebellion in Guinea, the Ivory Coast, and Sierra Leone. Guinea and the Ivory Coast countered by supporting rebel groups inside Liberia."

In the case of Ghana, its major role in the war was peacemaking. This was done in two major ways. One was through the effort to persuade President Taylor to reach an agreement with LURD and MODEL that would lead to the termination of the war. The most prominent example was the peace conference that was convened in Accra, Ghana, on June 4, 2004. However, the meeting was overshadowed by the issuance of a writ of arrest for President Taylor for his role in the Sierra Leonean civil war (Special Court for Sierra Leone 2021). The other way was Ghana played host to the peace talks that ended the civil war culminating in the signing of the Accra Peace Accord or the CPA by the belligerents and political parties.

Guinea served as LURD's chief patron by, among other things, providing the rebel group with a base from which it launched the attached that morphed into Liberia's second civil war (Brabazon 2003). Guinea supported LURD for two major reasons. One was an act of retaliation against the Taylor regime for supporting a Guinean rebel group that was desirous of ousting the Conte regime from power (Frontline 2003). The other was a personal reason: Ayesha Conneh, a Guinea citizen, who was the "principal spiritual adviser to Lasana Conte, the [then] President of Guinea" intervened for the support of LURD by the Guinean government (Brabazon 2003: 2).

In the case of Nigeria, it played several major roles. A key one was in helping to organize ECOMIL, the peacekeeping force of ECOWAS, which was deployed in Liberia to help stabilize the country (Oshewolo 2019). The other was the pivotal role played in helping to convince President Taylor to resign as the best option for the termination of the war (Kieh 2010). Furthermore, Nigeria agreed to provide President Taylor asylum, after the latter's resignation (Oshewolo 2019). Taylor lived in Calabar, Nigeria, until he was later arrested by Nigerian security officers and handed over to the new Liberian government (Polgreens 2006). In turn, the Sirleaf regime turned Taylor over to the Special Court for Sierra Leone, pursuant to the writ of arrest that was issued by the court for his role in the Sierra Leonean civil war (Boisbouvier 2021).

After its initial reluctance to get involved in the second Liberian civil war, the United States changed its policy, amid an avalanche of domestic and international pressure (Kieh 2010; Matthews 2003; O'Connor 2004; The New York Times 2003). The American intervention took several major forms. One was the support for ECOWAS' "stabilization project" in Liberia (Kieh

2010: 131). The assistance took the forms of training, finance, and logistics. Another was the demonstration of American military power as leverage to pressure President Taylor to resign (Pham 2006). Specifically, the United States deployed "three warships with 2,300 marines . . . initially deployed off the Liberian coast" (Pham 2006: 38). Taylor resigned on August 11, 2003, and left Liberia for exile in Nigeria.

As for ECOWAS, it played the leadership role in the international community that led to the termination of the second Liberian civil war. And this was done in several ways. For example, in the area of peacemaking, ECOWAS led the efforts that culminated in the signing of the Accra Peace Accord or the CPA (Kieh 2007c, 2011a). Similarly, ECOWAS deployed ECOMIL, its peacekeeping force, to stabilize the security situation in Liberia (Kieh 2010; Oshewolo 2019). This was critical to creating an enabling environment for the provision of humanitarian assistance, the seating of the transitional government headed by the late Gyude Bryant, and the deployment of the United Nations Mission to Liberia (UNMIL).

As for the United Nations, after playing a supportive role to ECOWAS, it assumed the responsibility for Liberia's postwar security (Farrell 2012). Under United Nations Security Council Resolution 1509, the UNMIL was established. It commenced operations on October 1, 2003. In addition, UNMIL was composed of 15,000 personnel. The major elements of UNMIL's mandate were:

1. The protection of civilians;
2. Reform of justice and security institutions;
3. Human rights promotion and protection;
4. The provision of public information; and
5. The protection of United Nations personnel (United Nations Security Council 2003).

The mission lasted for about fifteen years. It ended on March 30, 2018, following Liberia's third post–second civil war presidential election (United Nations Mission in Liberia 2021). Overall, the mission achieved its cardinal objective of helping prevent the reoccurrence of civil war, even mid the "tugs and pulls" that have attended Liberia's second postconflict peace-building project.

The Termination of the Second Civil War

The termination of the second Liberian civil war proceeded in three major stages. First President Charles Taylor resigned on August 11, 2003. This was a major precondition established by LURD and MODEL for ending the war. Particularly, President Taylor was pressured to resign amid the threat of the use of military force against his regime by the U.S. Government (Kieh 2010). In addition, the decision by the Nigerian government under President Olusegun Obasanjo to grant Taylor asylum in Nigeria helped shape Taylor's willingness to resign.

The second phase was the deployment of ECOMIL the peacekeeping force of ECOWAS. ECOMIL stabilized the security situation in Liberia by, among other things, establishing security corridors that allowed for the continued delivery of humanitarian assistance to civilians (the UN assumed the peacekeeping and national security roles after the signing of the Accra Peace Accord or the CPA).

Third, LURD, MODEL, the remnants of the Taylor regime and the political parties, negotiated a peace accord (Accra Peace Accord or the CPA) under the aegis of ECOWAS. The peace accord had several major provisions, including the establishment of a government of national unity, and the holding of democratic elections in 2005 (Comprehensive Peace Agreement 2003). Subsequently, the transitional government was established, and its tenure lasted from October 1, 2003, to January 16, 2006 (Comprehensive Peace Agreement 2003). On January 16, 2006, the new Sirleaf regime assumed power, along with the elected members of the Senate and the House of Representatives.

CONCLUSION

The second Liberian civil war was caused by the failure of the Taylor regime to democratically reconstitute the authoritarian peripheral capitalist Liberia state. In addition, the Taylor regime exacerbated the multidimensional crises of the state by its horrendous performance, including the maintenance of the authoritarian governance system, class inequities, and social malaise. In sum, the Taylor regime had the opportunity to shepherd a postconflict peace-building project based on democratic state reconstitution but failed to do so.

Taylor's campaign of destabilization in the West African region, which was driven primarily by his penchant for the primitive accumulation of wealth through the use of various illicit means, including violence, was quite pivotal to the decisions of Guinea and Cote d'Ivoire to support LURD and MODEL respectively. In other words, the Taylor regime's actions ultimately proved to be detrimental to its survival, as evidenced by the civil war on two fronts. If the Taylor regime had promoted a policy of good neighborliness, it would have been quite difficult for LURD and MODEL to have launch pads from which to attack Liberia.

Importantly, the cumulative effects of peacemaking and peacekeeping led by ECOWAS ultimately culminated in war termination. In other words, the war would not have ended if the international community under ECOWAS' leadership did not play a pivotal role. This was because given the intransigent positions of the Taylor regime, on the one hand, and LURD and MODEL, on the other, it would have been impossible to end the war. Instead, the warring parties would have engaged in a protracted conflict with its resulting calamitous effects, including displacement, deaths, injuries, and the destruction of both public and private properties.

Finally, while war termination is important because it creates an enabling environment for postconflict peace-building, it is not the panacea to the prevention of the recurrence of war. Instead, it is the nature and dynamics of the postconflict peace-building project that are the determinants for the building of durable peace. Accordingly, in the Liberian case, the travails of the post–second civil war peace-building project, which commenced in October 2003, will ultimately determine the country's quest for the building of durable peace. In this vein, for example, if the regimes that have ascended to power since 2006 fail to democratically reconstitute the Liberian state, including addressing the multidimensional crises that provided the roots for the second civil war, then durable peach stability will become elusive.

NOTES

1. The Firestone Plantations Company was established in 1926 and was purchased by Bridgestone, a Japanese corporation, in 1975.

2. According to Taylor's account, he was released from prison based on the intervention of the U.S. Central Intelligence Agency (CIA), and sent to West Africa and eventually Liberia, to topple the Doe regime (Kieh 2010).

3. Prince Johnson has stated that he was requested by the U.S. Embassy in Liberia to capture Doe, as a way of helping to end the war. Against this background, Johnson also claimed that the U.S. Embassy provided him with intelligence about Doe's visit to the Freeport of Monrovia. There is video recording that shows Prince Johnson trying to communicate with the U.S. Embassy after Doe's capture (Tango Tango Video 1990).

REFERENCES

Adebayo, Adekeye. 2002. *Liberia's Civil War: Nigeria, ECOMOG, and Regional Security in West Africa.* Boulder, DO: Lynne Rienror Publishers.

Africa Faith and Justice Network. 1998. *Human Rights Watch's Letter to President Charles Taylor.* Washington DC: AFJN.

Agbese, Pita Ogaba, 2007. "The African State: A Political Economy." In *Beyond State Failure and Collapse: Making the State Relevant in Africa*, edited by George Klay Kieh, Jr., 22–48. Lanham, MD: Lexington Books.

Ali, Tasier and Robert O. Matthews, eds. 1999. *Civil Wars in Africa: Roots and Resolution*. McGill-Queens University Press.

Amin, Samir. 1974. *Accumulation on a World Scale*. New York: Monthly Review Press.

Amnesty International. 1998. *World Report*. London: Amnesty International.

Ballah, Henrietta, 2003. *Ethnicity, Politics and Social Conflict: The Quest for Peace in Liberia*. University Park, PA: McNair Scholar Program of the Pennsylvania State University.

Bah, Mamadou Diouma.2006. *Peacebuilding Through Informal Channels: A Comparative Analysis of Liberia and Mozambique*. Master's Thesis. University of Tromso.

BBC Radio. 2003. "Interview with Joe Wylie." April 9.

Berkeley, Bill. 1986. *Liberia: A Promised Betrayed*. New York: Lawyers Committee for Human Rights.

Beyan, Amos. 1991. *The American Colonization Society and the Creation of the Liberian State*. Lanham, MD: University Press of America.

Boisbouvier. 2021. "Liberia: 15 Years Later, We Remember the Long Hunt for Charles Taylor." *theafricanreport*, March 29, 1–3.

Brabazon, James. 2003. *Liberia: Liberians United for Democracy and Reconciliation*. London: The Royal Institute for International Affairs. Armed Non-State Actors Project Briefing Paper No. 1.

Brown, George. 1941. *Economic History of Liberia*. Washington, DC: Associated Publishers.

Burrowes, Carl Patrick. 1982. *The Ruling Class Thesis in Liberia: A Reconsideration*. Occasional Paper. Chicago, IL.

Cassell, C. Abayomi. 1970. *History of the First African Republic*. New York: Fountainhead Publishers.

Comprehensive Peace Agreement. 2003. *Agreement Between the Government of Liberia and the Liberians United for Reconciliation and Democracy (LURD) and the Movement for Democracy in Liberia (MODEL) and Political Parties*. Accra, Ghana. August 18.

Constitution of Liberia. 1986. Monrovia: Government Printing Office.

Cordor, Henry. 1979. *The April 24 Crisis in Liberia*. Occasional Paper. Monrovia, Liberia.

David, Magdalene. 1984. "The Love of Liberty Brought Us Here: An Analysis of the Development of the Settler State in 19th Century Liberia." *Review of African Political Economy*, 11(31): 57–70.

Declaration of Independence of Liberia. 1847. Monrovia, Liberia.

Dunn, D. Elwood and Byron Tarr. 1988. *Liberia: A Polity in Transition*. Metuchen, NJ: Scarecrow Press.

Ebo, Adedeji. 2015. *The Challenges and Opportunities of Security Sector Reform in Post-Conflict Liberia*. Occasional Paper No. 9. Geneva Center for the Democratic Control of the Armed Forces.

Ellis, Stephen. 2001. *The Mask of Anarchy: The Destruction of Liberia and the Religious Dimension of an African Civil War*. New York: New York University Press.

Enro, Comfort. 1995. "ECOWAS and Subregional Peacekeeping in Liberia." *The Journal of Humanitarian Assistance*. www.tufts.edu/jha.archives. Accessed July 26, 2021.

Farrall, Jeremy. 2012. "Recurring Dilemmas in a Recurring Conflict: Evaluating the UN Mission in Liberia (2003–2006)." *Journal of International Peacekeeping*, 16(1): 306–342.

Freedom House. 2021. *Freedom in the World*. Washington, DC: Freedom House.

Frontline World. 2003. *Liberia: No More War*. May. www.pbs.org. Accessed July 26, 2021.

Geddes, Felix. 2013. *Civil War and State Formation: The Political Economy of War and Peace in Liberia*. Frankfurt, Germany: Campus Verlag.

Harris, David. 1999. "From 'Warlord' to 'Democratic President:' How Charles Taylor Won the 1997 Liberian Elections." *The Journal of Modern African Studies*, 37(3): 431–455.

Harris, David. 2006. "Liberia 2005: An Unusual African Post-Conflict Election." *The Journal of Modern African Studies*, 44(3): 375–395.

Henry, Neil. 1990. "Liberian Report Says Doe Shot, Captured." *The Washington Post*, September 10.

Howe, Herbert. 1996. "Lessons of Liberia: ECOMOG and Regional Peacekeeping." *International Security*, 21(3): 145–176.

Huband, Mark. 1998. *The Liberian Civil War*. London: Frank Cass.

Human Rights Watch. 1990a. *Flight From Terror*. New York: Human Rights Watch.

Human Rights Watch. 1990b. *Liberia: A Human Rights Disaster*. October 25.

Human Rights Watch. 1991. *Liberia: The Cycle of Abuses: Human Rights Violations Since the November Ceasefire*, October 21.

Human Rights Watch. 1997. *Liberia: Emerging From the Destruction*. New York: Human Rights Watch.

Human Rights Watch. 1998. *World Report*. New York: Human Rights Watch.

Human Rights Watch. 1999. *World Report*. New York: Human Rights Watch.

Human Rights Watch. 2002. *World Report*. New York: Human Rights Watch.

Human Rights Watch. 2003. *World Report*. New York: Human Rights Watch.

Kaihko, Ilmari. 2018. "The MODEL Structure of Armed Group: From Liberian Refugees to Heroes of Cote d' Ivoire and Liberators of the Homeland." *Small Wars and Insurgency*, 29(14): 776–800.

Kieh, George Klay. 1982. *The Causes of the Military Coup in Liberia*. Master's Thesis. Northwestern University.

Kieh, George Klay. 1991. "The Roots of Western Influence in Africa: The Conditioning Processes." *Social Science Journal*, 29(1): 7–19.

Kieh, George Klay. 1992. "Combatants, Patrons, Peacemakers, and the Liberian Civil Conflict." *Studies in Conflict and Terrorism*, 15(2): 125–143.

Kieh, George Klay. 1996. *Ending the First Liberian Civil War: Implications for United States Policy Toward West Africa*. Monograph No. 1. Washington, DC: TransAfrica.

Kieh, George Klay. 1997. "The Crisis of Democracy in Liberia." *Liberian Studies Journal*, 22(1): 23–29.

Kieh, George Klay. 1999. "The Economic Community of West African States, Conflict Management and the Liberian Civil War." *Low Intensity Conflict and Law Enforcement*, 8(2): 129–150.

Kieh, George Klay. 2000. "Civil War and Peacekeeping in the West African Subregion: The Case of ECOWAS' Intervention in Liberia." *Journal of Third World Spectrum*, 7(1): 39–58.

Kieh, George Klay. 2004. "Irregular Warfare and the First Liberian Civil War." *Journal of International and Area Studies*, 11(9): 55–77.

Kieh, George Klay. 2006. "Elections and Voting Behavior: The Case of the 2005 Liberian Election." *UMOJA*, 1(2): 1–17.

Kieh, George Klay. 2007a. "The United States and the First Liberian Civil War." *Africa Quarterly*, 46(1): 24–35.

Kieh, George Klay. 2007b. "The Economic Community of West African States, Peacemaking and the Second Liberian Civil War." *Liberian Studies Journal*, 32(1): 67–83.

Kieh, George Klay. 2008. *The First Liberian Civil War: The Crises of Underdevelopment*. New York: Peter Lang Publishing.

Kieh, George Klay. 2009a. "The Roots of the Second Liberian Civil War." *International Journal of World Peace*, 26(1): 7–30.

Kieh, George Klay. 2009b. "New Visions of Constitutionalism and Governance in Africa: Lessons from Liberia." In *Socio-Political Scaffolding and the Construction of Change: Constitutionalism and Governance in Africa*, edited by Kelechi Kalu and Peyi Soyinka Airewele, 59–90. Trenton, NJ: Africa World Press.

Kieh, George Klay. 2009c. "The United Nations Peace Observation Mission and the First Liberian Civil War." *Peace Studies Journal*, 1(2): 45–59.

Kieh, George Klay. 2010. "United States Foreign Policy and the Second Liberian Civil War." *African Journal of International Affairs*, 13(1–2): 121–144.

Kieh, George Klay. 2011a. "Peace Agreements and War Termination: Lessons from Liberia." *African Journal on Conflict Resolution*, 11(3): 53–86.

Kieh, George Klay. 2011b. "Warlords, Politicians and the Post-First Civil War Election in Liberia." *African and Asian Studies*, 10(1&2): 88–99.

Kieh, George Klay. 2011c. "The First Post-Conflict Legislative Election in Liberia." *Liberian Studies Journal*, 36(2): 1–28.

Kieh, George Klay. 2012a. *Liberia's State Failure, Collapse and Reconstitution*. Cherry Hill, NJ: Africana Legacy Publishers.

Kieh, George Klay. 2012b. "Neocolonialism: American Foreign Policy and the First Liberian Civil War." *Journal of Pan-African Studies*, 5(1): 164–184.

Kieh, George Klay. 2012c."Hegemonic Presidency and Post-Conflict Peacebuilding in Liberia." *African Journal of Peace and Conflict*, 5(2): 14–26.

Kieh, George Klay. 2013. "Liberia's Second Post-Conflict Presidential Election." *Journal of International Studies and Development*, 3(1): 123–141.

Kieh, George Klay. 2015. "The Travails of Democracy in Liberia." In *National Democratic Reforms in Africa*, edited by Said Ademujobi, 23–62. New York: Palgrave.

Kieh, George Klay. 2017. "The Janus-Faced Liberian State." *Liberian Studies Journal*, 43(1&2): 36–72.

Kieh, George Klay. 2018. "Rethinking Liberia's National Symbols." *Liberian Studies Journal*, 43(1&2): 31–57.

Kieh, George Klay. 2019. "The Travails of the Liberian State." In *Liberia in the Twenty-First Century: Issues and Perspectives*, edited by George Klay Kieh, Jr., 31–64. Hauppauge, NY: Nova Science Publishers.

Kieh, George Klay. 2021. "Capital Accumulation in Liberia's Rubber and Iron Ore Sectors." In *Africa and the Global System of Accumulation*, edited by Emmanuel Oritsejafor and Allan Cooper, 54–69. New York: Routledge.

Krauss, Clifford. 1990. "Liberia Officer Is Said to Desert," *The New York Times*, July 5, Sec. A., 11.

LA Times. 1990. "Liberian Rebels Display Doe's Body, Reports Say." September 11.

Lassell, Harold. 1941. "The Garrison State." *American Journal of Sociology*, 46(4): 455–468.

Liberia Data Project. 2021. *Cultural, Economic, Environmental, Political, Religious, Security and Social Data on Liberia.* Texas: Cypress.

Liberia Human Rights Campaign 1998. *Some of the Human Rights Abuses During the Early Part of Charles Taylor's Regime.* October.

Liebenow, J. Gus. 1980. *Liberia: The Dissolution of Privilege.* Part II. American Universities Staff Report No. 40.

Liebenow, J. Gus. 1987. *Liberia: The Guest for Democracy.* Bloomington, IN: Indiana University Press.

Liebenow, J. Gus. 1988. "Liberian Political Opposition in the Post-Election Period." *Liberian Studies Journal*, 13(2): 240–254.

Levitt, Jeremy. 2005. *The Evolution of Deadly Conflict in Liberia: From Paternalism to State Collapse.* Durham, NC: Carolina Academic Press.

Lowenkopf, Martin. 1976. *Liberia: The Conservative Road to Development.* Stanford, CA: Hoover Institution of War.

Lyons, Terrence. 1998. *Voting for Peace: Post-Conflict Elections in Liberia.* Washington, DC: The Brookings Institution Press.

Lyons, Terrence. 2004. "Post-Conflict Elections and Process of Demilitarizing Politics: The Role of Electoral Administration." *Democratization*, 11(3): 36–62.

Massing, Michael. 2005. "How Liberia Held 'Free Elections'." *The Nation*, October 13, 1.

Matthew, Mark. 2003. "White House Weighing Options for U.S. Involvement in Liberia." *The Seattle Sun*, July 1.

Mayson, Dew Tuan-Wleh and Amos Sawyer. 1979. "Labor in Liberia." *Review of African Political Economy*, 6(14): 3–15.

Miller, T. Christian. 2005. "Firestone and the Warlord." *ProPublica*, March 12,

Ministry of Planning and Economic Affairs. 1986. *Economic Survey of Liberia.* Monrovia: Government Printing Office.

Ministry of Planning and Economic Affairs. 1989. *Economic Survey of Liberia.* Monrovia: Government Printing.

Mortimer, Robert. "Senegal's Role in ECOMOG: The Francophone Dimension of the Liberian Crisis." *The Journal of Modern African Studies*, 34(2): 293–306.

Movement for Justice in Africa. 1980. *The Situation in Our Country*. Monrovia, Liberia: Movement for Justice in Africa.

National Planning Office, Liberia. 1961. *Annual Report*. Monrovia, Liberia: Government Printing Office.

National Planning Office. 1971. *Annual Report*. Monrovia, Liberia: National Planning Office.

Nyanseor, Siahyonkrohn. 2014. "The Review of Our National Symbols: Another Good for Nothing Exercise." *The Voice of Liberia*, July 7, 1–2.

Nyanseor, Siahyonkrohn. 2015. "The Liberian Flag: Designed or Copied?" *Liberian Dialogue*, September 2, 1–2.

O'Connor, James. 2004. "Here Interest Meets Humanity: How to End the War and Support Reconstruction in Liberia, and the Case for Modest American Leadership." *Harvard Human Rights Journal*, 17(1): 208–247.

Oshewolo, Segun. 2019. "Unpacking Nigeria's Peace Efforts During the Second Cycle of the Liberian Conflict." *Austral: Brazilian Journal of Strategy and International Relations*, 8(15): 258–277.

Perspective Magazine. 2003. "The Cold Bloody Murder of Kaare Lund, Emmanuel Sharpolu and Musa Keita." March 17, 1–2.

Pham, John Peter. 2004. "A Nation Long For Lorn: Liberia's Journey From Civil War Toward Civil Society." *International Journal of Non-Profit Law*, 6(4): www.icnl.org. Accessed March 2, 2021.

Pham, John Peter. 2006. "Re-inventing Liberia: Civil Society, Governance, and a Nation's Post-War Recovery." *The International Journal of Not-For-Profit Law*, 8(2): 38–54.

Polgreen, Lydia. 2006. "Liberian Warlord Charles Taylor Caught in Nigeria." *The New York Times,* March 26.

Press, Robert. 2015. *Ripples of Hope: How Ordinary People Resist Repression Without Violence*. Amsterdam, The Netherlands: Amsterdam University Press.

Radio Veritas. 1999. *News Broadcast*. Monrovia, Liberia. June 19.

Reuters. 1982. "6 Reprieved in Liberia." January 29.

Sandy, Moses. 2008. "Corruption: A De facto Way of Life in Liberia." *Liberian Journal*, December 23, 5.

Sawyer, Amos. 1987. *"Effective Immediately:" Dictatorship in Liberia, 1980–1986: A Personal Perspective*. Working Paper. Bremen, Germany: Liberia Working Group.

Sawyer, Amos. 1992. *The Emergence of Autocracy in Liberia: Tragedy and Challenge*. San Francisco, CA: Institute for Cultural Studies Press.

Sawyer, Amos. 2005. "Liberating Liberia: Understanding the Nature and Needs of Governance." *Harvard Journal of International Affairs*, 27(3): 1–6.

Sawyer, Amos. 2008. "Emerging Patterns in Liberia's Post-Conflict Politics: Observations From the 2005 Elections." *African Affairs*, 107(427): 177–199.

Smith, Robert. 1972. *United States Policy Toward Liberia, 1822–1971*. Monrovia, Liberia: Providence Publications.

Special Court for Sierra Leone. 2021. *The Prosecutor Versus Charles Ghankay Taylor.* www.specialcourtforsierraleone.org. Accessed March 2, 2021.

Sundiata, Ibrahim. 1980. *Black Scandal: America and the Liberian Labor Crisis, 1929–1936.* Philadelphia, PA: Institute for the Study of Human Issues.

Tanner, Victor. 1998. "Liberia: Railroading Peace." *Review of African Political Economy*, 25(75): 133–147.

The New York Times. 2003. "America's Role in Liberia." July 24, A 18.

The New Humanitarian. 2021. "Global Witness Accuses Liberia of Destabilizing Neighbors." www.thehumanitarian.org. Accessed July 26, 2021.

The Tango, Tango Video. 1990.

United Nations. 1993. *Security Council Resolution 866.* New York: United Nations.

United Nations. 2003. *Security Council Resolution 1509.* New York: United Nations.

United Nations Development Program. 1990. *Promoting Good Governance in Liberia: Towards the Formulation of a National Framework.* New York: UNDP.

United Nations Development Program. 1999. *Liberia's Governance Program.* New York: UNDP.

United Nations Mission in Liberia. 2021. *Background.* www.unmil.org. Accessed July 26, 2021.

United States Department of State. 1997. *Liberia: Human Rights Report.* Washington, DC: U.S. State Department.

United States Department of State. 1998. *Liberia: Human Rights Report.* Washington, DC: U.S. State Department.

United States Department of State. 1999. *Liberia: Human Rights Report.* Washington, DC: U.S. State Department.

United States Department of State. 2000. *Liberia: Human Rights Report.* Washington, DC: U.S. State Department.

Vogt, Margaret, ed. 1992. *The Liberian Crisis and ECOMOG: A Bold Attempt at Regional Peacekeeping.* Lagos, Nigeria: Gabumo Publishing Company.

Williams, Gabriel. 2006. *The Heart of Darkness.* Bloomington, IN: Trafford Publishing.

Williams, Paul. 2016. *War and Conflict in Africa.* 2nd ed. London: Polity.

World Health Organization. 2003. *Liberia: Health/Nutrition Sector Report.* Brazzeville, Congo: WHO.

Wonkeryor, Edward Lama. 1985. *Liberia Military Dictatorship: A Fiasco Revolution.* Chicago: Strugglers Press.

Wreh, Tuan. 1976. *The Love of Liberty Brought Us Here.* New York: C. Hurst.

Yangbeh, Varney. 2006. "Liberia's Security and Foreign Policy Dilemmas." *African Policy Journal*, 1(1): www.apj.hkspublications.org. Accessed March 2, 2021.

Ziemann, W., and M. Lanzendorfer. 1977. "The State in Peripheral Societies." *Socialist Register*, 14(3): 145–177.

Chapter 6

Personality Conflicts and the Nigerian Civil War

Michael Ediagbonya

Personality conflicts in Nigerian politics actually started in the pre-independence era and finally culminated in the Nigerian civil war in 1967. The chapter will examine the contributions of personality conflicts to the occurrence of the Nigerian civil war. In the pre-independence era, the political class used ethnic nationalism to cause disaffection in the country. A great deal of ethnic consciousness and hostility in Nigeria was created by competing politicians exploiting their own ethnic background in order to build up a following. Hence, Lloyd (1970: 1–13) argues, "Nigeria's problems do derive in large measure from the tensions which have arisen between the large ethnic groups and that the hostility derives not from the ethnic differences but from competition between peoples for wealth and power."

Even the intense ethnic rivalry also manifested in the way Dr. Azikiwe was prevented from going to the House of Representatives in 1951. Again conflict of interest was clearly displayed in the constitutional crises from 1914 to 1951 in the country. According to Ezera (1960: 22), the Nigerian Council of 1914 consisted of thirty-six members, including six Nigerian nominated to represent the coastal districts and the interiors of the country. It must be said that this council did not in any way meet the hopes and aspirations of Nigerians especially as it was not a legislative council but mere advisory, hence strong criticism came from the educated elites.

Although the elective principle introduced by Sir Clifford Constitution of 1922 was cherished by the nationalists, because it provided four Nigerians to be elected into the legislative council, but it was criticized because the governor had veto power and the members of the executive council were predominantly white. Ojiako (1981: 11) notes that "Sir Clifford called such politicians, among them, late Herbert Macaulay and Eric Moore as coastal agitators, who depended even for their existence on British magnanimity."

Sir Richards's Constitution of 1947 was again criticized by the nationalists as it was seen by many that the constitution had very little or nothing to give Nigerians in terms of constitutional advancement or progress (Ediagbonya 2020). The Nigerian nationalists also condemned Sir John Macpherson's constitution of 1951, because Nigerians were made ministers without ministries. The constitution collapsed because the northern delegates in the central legislative council refusal to support the motion by Chief Anthony Enahoro of Action Group in 1953 that Nigeria should be self-governed by 1956. So personality conflicts in Nigeria politics have records of long history.

The personality discontent and conflicts became more complex and complicated as a result of the sociopolitical events that took place in Nigeria between 1960 and 1966 which included corruption, unemployment, personality conflict between Chief Akintola, the premier of western region and Chief Obafemi Awolowo the leader of Action Group, 1963 census, federal election of 1964 and the western regional election of 1965. This 1965 election produced more violence than had ever been witnessed before because of election riggings and thuggery. In such a chaotic situation, Nigerians were not surprised when Major Nzeogwu announced the coup of January 15, 1966.

The Nigerian civil war which started on July 6, 1967, and ended on the January 12, 1970, was an avoidable collision which occurred when the Nigerian and the Biafran troops exchanged salvoes, inside the Republic of Biafra (Oluleye 1985). Judging from the numerical strength of the Nigerian army and the inferiority of the Biafran Army in all respects, neither side expected a prolonged war (New Nigeria 1967). On the other hand, the Biafran troops believed that the level of killing of the Ibos in northern Nigeria after the January 15, 1966, coup and the countercoup of July 29, 1966, was enough justification for them to fight with tenacity of purpose in order to jealously defend Biafra where their wives and children were living.

The bloody civil war could have been avoided if General Yakubu Gowon, Lt. Col. Odumegwu Ojukwu, General Aguiyi Ironsi, and Usman Kastina were matured, tactful, and diplomatic enough in handling the issues that led to the war. Such contentious issues include January 15, 1966, coup and the countercoup of July 29, 1966, the promulgation of Decree No. 34, the massive killings of the Ibos in the north, the creation of twelve states, and the declaration of the Republic of Biafra, and so on.

Tekeno (1989: 2) observes, "It is not yet possible to give an accurate figure of war casualties, dead and wounded, soldiers and civilians with several hundreds of deaths a day among children from starvation, malnutrition, disease, several millions of families had traumatic experiences which in turn affected their morale during the war effort."

This war was avoidable if not for the personality conflicts of the military leaders that led to the war, who were particularly ambitious and wanted to taste the affluence and sweetness of power to enable them display their heroic arrogance. Finally on January 10, 1970, General Ojukwu and his aides fled to Ivory Coast, when the self-defense was impossible to continue, leaving the second-in-command behind, General Philip Effiong, to announce the end of secession (Ene 2011).

PERSONALITY CONFLICTS IN NIGERIAN POLITICS IN THE PRE-INDEPENDENCE ERA

First and foremost, it may be necessary to examine the concept "conflict." Conflict is seen as opposition to another or each other; disagree Kesterner and Ray see conflict as social factual situation in which at least two parties (individuals, groups, states) are involved and strive for goals which can only be reached by one party and/or want to employ incompatible means to achieve a certain goal (Kesterner and Ray 2002). Thus, a conflict refers to a disagreement or differences in opinion as to how certain objective could be achieved.

On the strength of this understanding, the personality conflicts in Nigerian politics can now be examined. The first bone of contention in the pre-independence era was ethnic nationalism. It is the interactions among members of different ethnic groups that produce ethnicity. Unevenness in development sharpened the awareness of group differentiation which in turn intensified Nigerian intergroup competition and tensions. This episode of ethnicity witnessed the employment of ethnic propaganda which laid the foundation of ethnic assertiveness that was built upon by others. Between the period 1941 and 1950, the unhealthy rivalry between the Ibo and Yoruba was intensified. According to Ezera, the Ibos usually referred to by the Yoruba as Kobo-Kobo which means backward ones made what looked like a serious effort to narrow the gap between them and the Yoruba (Ezera 1970: 90).

The return of Dr. Azikiwe to Nigeria from the United States compounded the problems of Yoruba people. In fact when Azikiwe returned to Lagos, his impact on journalism and society was extra ordinary. The general public admired him but not those politicians and nationalists who felt challenged and threatened by his ambitions. His newspapers, *Daily Comet* and *West African Pilot*, caused panic and tension among the Yoruba people. He was resisted by some politicians of Yoruba and Hausa origin because of his bright political fortunes. Chief Awolowo soon became the champion of Yoruba nationalism as the leader of the Action Group. Also the presidential address by Dr. Azikiwe at the first Ibo State conference did not help matters. In the address, he said, "It would appear that the God of Africa has created Igbo nation to lead the children of Africa from the bondage of the age" (West African Pilot 1949). This clearly epitomized the upsurge of Ibo nationalism.

This very unhealthy ethnic rivalry which was first limited to the south soon extended to the north, so that it soon became the north/south rivalry. The processes of drawing up the Macpherson constitution of 1951 provided the opportunity for extending the ethnic mess to the north. The starting point which was the general conference at Ibadan in 1950 in which major questions confronted the conference marked the beginning of the north in ethnic struggle. The north demanded 50 percent representation at the central legislature but the southern delegates were opposed to it. The northern delegation won on the issue of representation at the center and demanded to redraw the boundaries between the regions. This marked the beginning of northern domination in the political scene of the country which the south continues to protest until the army struck in January 15, 1966 in sympathy of the southern agitation.

Even the intense ethnic rivalry manifested in the way Dr. Azikwe was prevented from going to the House of Representative in 1951. The majority party in the region has the power for selecting representative from the regional houses to the House of Representative. Dr. Azikiwe won on the platform of NCNC to the Western House of Assembly, an assembly predominantly comprising of Action Group members. The Action Group was able to use this advantage to prevent Zik from becoming a member of the House of Representatives.

Zik's ambition was to represent this constituency in the House of Representatives (Ediagbonya 2007). By the new constitutional arrangements, Lagos was administratively part of the western region, and in accordance with the principle of regional nomination to the House of Representatives, Azikiwe had to obtain the endorsement of the West House of Assembly. Azikiwe appeared to have been outmaneuvered, and he failed in his attempt to go to the Central Legislative House.

Azikiwe's movement from the western region to the eastern region in 1953 marked the final chapter of the evolution of ethnic politics and regional nationalism in Nigeria. This was interpreted by supporters of Zik as attempt to destroy the political influence in the country. This was why Kalu Ezera noted that Azikiwe was defeated because he was an Ibo, since his party colleagues who were selected were all Yorubas (Ezera 1970).

There was the issue of constitutional controversy. The personality conflicts can be seen in the Nigerian council established by Lord Lugard, who was the governor-general of Nigeria between 1914 and 1919. The six nominated Nigerians into this council were two Emirs from the north, the Alafin of Oyo, one member each from Lagos, Calabar, and the Benin-Warri (Federal Information Service 1955). These members rarely attended the council meeting and most of them could not understand the official language, English. The educated elites were not represented in the council; hence, they strongly criticized it and argued that they were not true representatives of the people of Nigeria. It was not a surprise that the Nigerian council was quickly replaced by the 1922 constitution established by Sir Clifford who took over as the new governor of Nigeria in 1919. This constitution of 1922 made provision for four elected Nigerians to be included into the Legislative Council in Lagos. Three seats were allotted to Lagos and one seat allocated to Calabar. Although the elective principle in the constitution was cherished by the nationalists, because it encouraged the formation of political parties and newspapers, it was highly criticized because the governor had veto power. Again the executive council was predominantly whites and the northern delegates were not represented, as the north was governed by the proclamation of the governor.

This was discontent and mistrust between the governor and Nigerians because Sir Clifford doubted the capacity and capability of the Nigerian to rule his own country. Our nationalists disagreed on this and advocated for more constitutional development.

Sir Richard's constitution came into effect in 1947. He was appointed by the British Government to replace Sir Bernard Bourdillon as the governor of Nigeria. Oyediran (1998: 12) remarks that the constitution aimed "to promote the unity of the country; to provide adequately within that unity for the diverse elements that make up the country; and to secure for the Africans greater participation in the decision of their own affairs." Ojiako notes that out of the forty-five members for the whole of Nigeria, twenty-eight of the members were Nigerians of whom four were elected and the remaining twenty-four nominated (Ojiako 1998). Unfortunately, the constitution was strongly criticized by the nationalists in Nigeria. The National Council of Nigeria and Cameroon (NCNC) spearheaded the campaign against the constitution. The party expressed disappointment over the unilateral way which the governor drafted his constitution without consulting Nigerians. Nigerians agitated that the constitution should be withdrawn. Hence, a national campaign was organized throughout the country to expose the ills of the constitution and to raise money in order to send a powerful delegation to London to protest to the Secretary of States for the Colonies, Arthur Creech Jones. Although Creech Jones rejected their request to withdraw the constitution, the speed at which a new governor was appointed to replace Sir Richard is suggestive that the British government was mindful of the criticism or agitation against the constitution (Ediagbonya 2020).

The name of the new governor was Sir John Macpherson. Again, the Nigerian nationalists also condemned the constitution established by Sir John Macpherson in 1951 because Nigerians were made ministers without ministries, and the position of prime minister was vacant. The constitution collapsed because the northern delegates in the central legislative council refused to support the motion moved by Chief Anthony Enahoro of Action Group in

1953 that Nigeria should be self-governed by 1956. While the members in the south saw it as eventful and historic, the northern members saw it as an attempt by the south to set in motion political hegemony. Hence, Sarduana of Sokoto, Sir Ahmandu Bello added to the motto as soon as it is practicable. It was said that excited crowds outside the House of Representatives in Lagos showed their disapproval of the northern stand by booing and insulting the northern members hence they swore never to come to the south for any meeting again (NERC 1978).

Another point of personality conflicts in the pre-independence era was in the 1957 conference, where the demand for the creation of states by the minorities came to focus. The 1957 constitutional conference took place in London under the chairmanship of Allan Lennox-Boyd. The issue of creation of states was so complex that the conference could not resolve it, hence it was decided that a commission of inquiry be appointed to handle the issue and propose means of allaying those fears. At a point in Nigeria, there was fear of the minorities from the major ethnic groups. A four-man commission of inquiry under the chairmanship of Sir Henry Willinck was set up. This issue was only resolved in 1958 conference when the commission recommended that no state should be created, instead a long list of fundamental human rights should be entrenched in the constitution to protect Nigerian citizens (Report by the Resumed Nigeria Constitutional Conference 1958). From the foregoing, it is established that the personality conflicts and its effect on the body polity of Nigeria is not novel rather it is deep in our history. The atmosphere was already charged before independence.

PERSONALITY CONFLICTS IN NIGERIAN POLITICS IN THE FIRST REPUBLIC, 1960–1966

Personality conflicts in the First Republic among the leading politicians in Nigeria created serious problems. It may be imperative to examine the events in the country which created conflict and crisis situation from the period of 1960, when the nation got independence, to 1966 when the military coup dismissed the democratically elected government.

Nigeria obtained her independent status from Britain on October 1, 1960. This was a result of the relentless efforts of our nationalists who fought for the independence after making many sacrifices for their fatherland. The attainment of independence saw the emergence of Nigerian elites assuming powers over the affairs of their country. After independence, there were high hopes for Nigerians who had lived many years of despair under the turpitude of the colonial rule. However, the hopes and aspirations became dashed when the country started facing serious economic, social, and political problems.

The most unfortunate aspect was that the promises given to the citizens by the leaders at independence became mere mirage between 1960 and 1966. The political situation in Nigeria became tense. The seeds of disturbances and discord had been sown. Many problems which disturbed the stability of the First Republic could have been avoided, had those at the helm of affairs been motivated more by their loyalty to a United Nigeria than by tribalism and self-interest. Efforts were directed toward regional rather than national interests.

First was the issue of corruption. Olav (1970: 47–48) argues that extensive corruption in almost every field of public affairs had discredited the government parties and the politicians at large. The political leaders use their political office to accumulate immense wealth. The holding of political office now came to mean to the common man as well as the soldiers the quickest means of getting rich. It is therefore not surprising that soldiers who have the means to capture political office and power by force of arms cannot resist the temptation indefinitely. Supporting this assertion, Isichei affirms that in both the regional governments and at the center, politicians who became notorious for their extravagance and corruption aroused the hostility of the more politically conscious masses who came to wonder what independence was all about (Isichei 1969).

In the same vein, the ring leader of the first coup of January 15, 1966, Major Nzeogwu, commenting on the gravity of corruption in the first Republic said:

Our enemies are the political profiteers, swindlers, the men in high and low places that seek bribe demand ten percent, those that seek to keep the country permanently divided, so that they can remain in office as ministers and VIPs of waste, the tribalists, the nepotists, those that make the country look big for nothing before international circle. (Ibid. 306)

Second was the issue of unemployment. This was a problem during the period under focus. The governments were confronted with the problem of large number of school leavers without jobs. This discontent was widespread and a serious challenge to government without providing solution. Unemployment is a disease no matter any angle we want to look at it. A situation where many youths in a country are unemployed results in social vices like thuggery, armed robbery, frustration, and so on. In the First Republic of Nigeria, unemployment rate was very high and unacceptable. It was felt that the politicians were responsible for this state of affairs because it was the general opinion that the politicians misappropriated the wealth of the country instead of using it to create opportunities for employment for the people, especially youths. It was therefore not a surprise that Ken Post and M.

Vickers (1972: 534–535) comment that: "If revolutions come in West Africa, it is from this group that they will draw their rank and file."

Again was the issue of 1962 and 1963 census. The census controversy was a very serious problem during this period. The politicians were very much aware of the significance of census as it determines the numerical strength of each region in the federal legislature. In addition to that, it determines the revenue which each region collects from the federation account or from the central distributable pool. Ojo maintains that one of the political issues that arose from census figures in Nigeria has always been that they determine the relative numerical strength of each region or state in the federal parliament and that the eastern region issued its first secession threat over the 1963 census controversy (Ojo 2006). The year 1959 was a glaring example when the northern region got the largest number of parliamentary seats, 174 out of 312 in the Federal House of Representative because of the population census of 1952–1953. The eastern region had only seventy-three while the western region had sixty-two and Lagos got three as a result of the 1952–1953 census. When the result of the 1962 census came out, in July 1962, the figures showed that the population of the eastern region rose from 7 million to 12.3 million and that of the western region increased by 70 percent from 6.08 million. The figures of the north dropped which they highly resisted. The tension created by claims and counterclaims compelled the prime minister to cancel the 1962 census results, and he ordered a recount. The 1963 census created more confusion and tension. When the result came out in February 1964, the north had 29.7 million, east had 12.4 million, west had 10.3 million, while Lagos had 0.75 million and midwest had 2.5m (Ibid., 88–89).

The 1963 census became very imperative because it is going to enable the Federal Electoral Commission allocate parliamentary seats to each of the regions on the basis of their population for the 1964 federal elections. The most surprising aspect of the census result of 1963 is that it affirms the population of the north was more than that of the east, west, midwest, and Lagos combined. Hence, the large-scale condemnation in southern Nigeria, while the NPC accepted the result as a true reflection of what took place, the premiers of eastern and midwestern regions, respectively. Dr. Okpara and Dennis Osadebey rejected the result. In an editorial of February 27, 1964, the *Nigerian Tribune* described the results of the census as a mixture of surprise and riddle (*The Nigerian Tribune* 1964). Dr. Michael Okpara went further to institute a law suit to invalidate the census figures and threatened to pull the eastern region out of the federation if the northern figure was not cancelled (West African Pilot March 11, 1964). Dennis Osadebey dismissed the census as the most stupendous joke of our age (Ojo 2006). Although the figures were accepted as a result of the acceptance of the NPC, the most powerful and ruling party, the seeds of discord were already planted hence Nigerians were not surprised when the first military coup took place announcing the termination of Tafawa Balewa government. It would be recalled that this census issue led to the collapse of the coalition government between the NCNC and NPC. At the same time, it promoted the unity of purpose between the Action Group and the NCNC for the first time forming an alliance called the United Progressive Grand Alliance (UPGA) to contest the 1964 federal election against Nigerian National Alliance (NNA).

The personality conflict between Akintola and Awolowo in 1962 was another volatile challenge in the political arena in Nigeria. Ojo observes that as a result of the devastating attacks to which the opposition subjected virtually every program and policy of the government, the federal government was bent on annihilating the opposition in western region particularly Chief Awolowo, the opposition's arrowhead (Ojo 2006).

That opportunity came when there was rift between Premier Akintola and the leader of the opposition in the Federal House of Representatives Chief Obafemi Awolowo. When Awolowo decided to move from the western region to the federal legislature, there was disagreement within the party over who should succeed him as premier, against Awo's wish. Akintola became the premier and soon after began to take control of decision-making in the western regional government without consulting with Awolowo. This misunderstanding started from the prime minister's opinion of government of national unity through the formation of a coalition government by the three major parties. While Akintola supported the idea, Awolowo was against it. Chief Awolowo opposition was based on the fact that he was the leader of the opposition in the federal legislature. He became very popular in the country because of his series of attacks on major issues mostly on colonialism, the economy, and corruption. In the real sense, since we were practicing democracy, it was very necessary to have official opposition to check and balance the policies of the government. Absence of official opposition promotes despotism, tyranny, and oppression. Hence, it was very surprising that the prime minister was muting an idea of all embracing government without opposition.

Indeed because of the pro-NPC and pro-north posture of Akintola, Sir Ahmadu Bello called on "all men of goodwill throughout Nigeria to rally round him" (*Daily Times* 1962). Action group as a party addressed this issue at an AG party conference held in Jos in May 1962. Chief Akintola was found guilty and replaced with Alhaji S.A Adegbenro as premier of western region. This resulted to riots in the Western House of Assembly by the supporters of Akintola and Chief Obafemi Awolowo, as the new premier as Adegbenro attempted to commence his role as the premier. The federal government did not waste time to declare a state of emergency on the west which lasted for six months with a new administrator, Dr. M.A. Majekodunmi, appointed by the federal government. It is necessary to put on record that the federal government did not conduct fresh election at the expiration of the emergency period instead adopted jungle justice by reinstating Akintola as the premier of western region in order to prevent the opposition from coming to power. Ojo (2006: 128–129) argues "that it was Chief Akintola"s desperate attempt to hold on to power that sparked off the unprecedented violence in Western Nigeria in the last quarter of 1965."

Another challenge was in 1964 when the federal election was conducted in the country. By the time of the General Election of 1964, the pattern of alliances had changed. Two major alliances were eventually formed to contest the election of 1964 which were NNA, the Nigerian National Alliance made up of NPC, NNDP, Midwest Democratic front, and Dynamic Party of Dr. Chike Obi and UPGA, the United Progressive Grand Alliance, made up of the NCNC, the AG, NEPU, and the United Middle Belt Congress. In July 1964, NCNC abandoned its coalition with the NPC and declared its decision to campaign jointly with the AG in the forthcoming federal elections (Eluwa et al. 2005: 258–260). This latest action of NCNC was partly as a result of the way and manner in which the NPC manipulated the census result of 1963 which already gave them undue advantage in the allocation of seats in the Federal House of Representatives which in a way demonstrated the permanent political domination of the north over the south. In reaction to this in August 1964, NNA was formed. In October 1964, UPGA was equally formed.

The 1964 federal election witnessed high level of irregularities as the election was not free and fair, far from being credible. There were incidents of thuggery and intimidation. Much hooliganism and violence were displayed. At the end of the election, the NPC wing of the NNA had won 162 of the 167 seats in the north which by implication means, without merging with any other political party, it could on its own form a government at the federal level. The newly formed Nigerian National Democratic Party under the Leadership of Chief Akintola won thirty-six seats in the west which was additional boost to the NNA as it increased the electoral strength of the alliance. This electoral victory of NNDP in the western region was not as a result of the general acceptance of the party by the electorates, it was partly due to UPGA leaders who asked their supporters to boycott the election and the high level of rigging by the government in power. By the rules of the game, it was the duty of the president to appoint as prime minister the leader of the political party that had the majority in the House of Representatives. Dr. Azikiwe threatened that he would resign than to call on a person like Sir Tafawa Balewa to form a government. The issue became complex when the prime minister refused the advice of the president to set aside the results of the election. This resulted in the absence of government for three days for the first time in the Nigeria's political history. Anglin (1965: 173) argues that the "1964–1965 elections has often been referred to as a classic case of the politics of brinkmanship and that it was during these elections that the first plot for a military coup d'etat by some members of the Nigerian army was planned."

The western regional election of 1965 created more problems for the country. In fact it was the last straw that broke the camel's back. The desperation and inordinate ambition of Chief Akintola to remain in power in the western region which was challenged by the people resulted in unmitigated disaster which will be discussed from generation to generation. This incident was the last in the chains of events that eclipsed the Nigerian First Republic. This October election in 1965 provided the golden opportunity for the people of western Nigeria to vote for the restoration of regional government. It was an election which was supposed to showcase the party really in power in the western region, all things being equal. This election unfortunately produced more violence than had ever been witnessed before. The electoral officers suffered greatly, so there was collapse of the electoral administration. Serious riot broke out in many parts of the region on Election Day. In some areas, police opened fire and killed innocent civilians. Due to election rigging and federal government support, Akintola and his party NNDP formed the government, after much intimidation and killing of political opponents. It is possible to say that because he never properly faced the electorates and also because he thought he might lose in a free and fair election, Akintola used every political and administrative control at his disposal to ensure his continued stay in office. Much more thuggery, violence, and arson occurred. A common feature of that election was the serious riot and violence between the supporters of the NNDP and the UPGA. Many were killed and properties destroyed. Again one could have expected the federal government to declare a state of emergency hence there was a total breakdown of law and order. Based on emotion, sentiment, and political consideration, the government allowed the situation to degenerate to such a disgraceful and dangerous state because the federal government was more interested in preserving Chief Akintola as the premier of the region than to restore law and order. This situation was more pathetic when considered against the background that the federal government remained adamant despite the appeal from the students of the University of Ibadan, Labor Unions, Civil societies, and other elites. In fact the 1965 western regional election was a national disgrace. Ballot papers were distributed to government supporters while the opposition members were denied even driving them from the polls by local government policemen. The votes were falsified in favor of the ruling party. In such a chaotic situation, Nigerians were not surprised when Major Nzeogwu announced the coup of January 15 1966, one of the factors that led to the Nigerian civil war in 1967.

Unfortunately, this coup was later misinterpreted in some quarters in Nigeria especially in northern Nigeria and tagged as Ibo-intended Coup. It may be correct to assume such position because of the nature of the killings which affected top politicians and army officers in the north and west. On a constructive ground, considering the level of the anarchy, chaotic situation, ethnic sentiments, corruption, unemployment, election rigging, and thuggery associated with the First Republic in Nigeria, it may be wrong to ascribe bias, prejudices, malice, and ethnic coloration to that coup. Hence, there was wide jubilation and celebration across the country when the coup was first announced.

PERSONALITY CONFLICTS IN THE POST-JANUARY 1966 MILITARY COUP ERA

Military rule in Nigeria started in 1966 after the abortive coup of January 15, 1966. Most military administrations in Nigeria have been found to be promoting their own interests and encouraging corruption, nepotism, inefficiency, tribalism, and political instability. This point was made by Odetola who notes that military is, by definition and tradition, an institutionalized conservative force untrained in the tactics and strategies of civilian rule and political management (Odetola 1982). Their misconduct clearly epitomized the altruism that they were only ambitious and wanted to taste the affluence and sweetness of power to enable them display their heroic arrogance.

The Nigerian civil war between 1967 and 1970 gave a strong lesson that the military cannot effectively manage the affairs of this country. The bloody civil war could have been avoided if General Yakubu Gowon and Lt. Col. Odumegwu Ojukwu were tactful in handling the issues that led to the war.

In the first place, the January 15, 1966, coup which terminated not only the Nigerian First Republic but also the lives of a good number of its leading politicians was the climax of a five-year crisis-infected political journey (Ojo 2006). It must be established that there were several evidences to the 1966 disaster but the politicians willfully ignored them displaying lukewarm attitude to such sensitive issues which became counterproductive. A group of majors based in Kaduna staged a coup on the night of January 14–15, 1960, in which the federal prime minister, the premiers of the north and west, the federal minister of finance, and most of the senior army officers were killed. Unfortunately, a serious problem was already created in the country as the coup plotters led by Major Nzeogwu did not succeed in taking over the government as they failed to kill the head of the army, Major-General J.T.U. Aguiyi Ironsi. Hence, the surviving officers led by Aguiyi Ironsi were able to put down the coup and restore their control of the army. The problem of what to do with the coup plotters became a burning issue and highly contentious.

This military coup of January 15, 1966, during which many northern and western leaders were murdered, started the descending process down the ladder of worsening relations between Ibos and other Nigerians. Initially this coup was widely accepted and welcome in the country as a relief from the chaos and corruption of the civilian regime. The political parties, trade unions, and student organizations pledged total loyalty to the new regime.

In his broadcast to the nation on January 28, 1966, Major-General Aguiyi Ironsi outlined the policies and programs of his government as stated below:

Fellow citizens, tonight I wish to outline the policies and programs of my Government for the Republic. All Nigerians want an end to regionalism. Tribal loyalties and activities which promote tribal consciousness and sectional interests must give way to the urgent task of national reconstruction. The National Military Government will preserve Nigeria as a strong nation. We shall give firm, honest and disciplined leadership. There are a number of urgent problems now facing us. In solving them I shall count on your continued co-operation and hard work. (Aguiyi Ironsi 1966)

In this new spirit of a United Nigeria, one of the first steps he took was to reorganize the four regional federal structures. Instead of continuing with the regional system, Ironsi divided Nigeria into groups of provinces. This action of Aguiyi Ironsi created discord and conflict between leaders of the northern and eastern parts of the country. A military governor was appointed to each of the group of provinces in accordance with his new unitary system of government. On Tuesday, January 15, he named his four regional military governors. Lieutenant Colonel Odumegwu Ojukwu was appointed the military governor of eastern Nigeria, Lieutenant Colonel Adekunle Fajuyi for the west, Lieutenant Colonel David Ejoor for midwest, and Lieutenant Colonel Hassan Usman Katsina for the north.

It must be said that Ironsi's preference for a unitary structure instead of a federation shows clearly that he has poor understanding of the political nature of the country, especially the purpose for the adoption of the federal system of government. Decree No. 34 was promulgated to empower a unitary system of government for Nigeria. By this arrangement, from May 24, 1966, Nigeria ceased to be a federation but the Republic of Nigeria. The Federal Military Government was to be known as the National Military Government. The regions would be referred to as a group of provinces. The northerners interpreted this as an attempt to bring the northern region under southern control and Igbo domination. This decree had the unfortunate effect of confirming to the northerners who could not see themselves competing effectively for government jobs on the basis of merit with the more educationally advanced southerners, their worst fears of a masterplan to dominate them (Golden

City Post 1966). Again, it should be pointed out that the north believed and maintained that the coup has an ethnic regional intention because most of the Ibo politicians like Dr. Azikiwe, Dr. Okpara, all escaped and survived while in the north, their notable politicians like Sir Tafawa Balewa, Sir Ahmadu Bello, and some top military officers like Brigadier Zakari Maimalari, Col. Kur Mohammed, and others were killed. To compound the strained political relationship in the country, the composition of the coup plotters call for serious questioning. The coup was led and most probably initiated by seven army officers, six were Ibos. Hence, it was difficult to convince the north that the January 15, 1966 coup was free from ethnic bias and partisan orientation.

There were violent anti-Ironsi demonstrations in several towns in northern Nigeria between May 28 and 31, 1966, in which many people were killed. An official statement from the military governor's office in Kaduna in June put the number of dead at ninety-two, but the eastern military governor, claiming to be quoting police reports, put the number at 3,000 at a press conference in Enugu on October 11, 1966 (Drum 1966). Golden City post comments that bloody riots in northern Nigeria four weeks ago led to the massacre of some 600 southerners by the northern Hausas. They cut the throats of the Ibos like sacrificial animals (Golden City Post 1966). The killing of the southerners in the north raised the issue of lip services. The head of state Major-General Aguiyi Ironsi was the commander-in-chief of the armed forces fully in charge of security. He had no excuse that these killings went on without intervention by the government. Especially his brothers and sisters were the people directly involved. It was even said that within a few months of his assuming office, he paid visits to the north without visiting the other regions. All efforts were done by him to placate the north. Almost all the former politicians in the east, west, and midwest were on his orders placed in detention, but politicians of northern Nigeria were left undisturbed. The northern politicians were even rapidly absorbed in strategic positions in the native administrations in the region (Drum 1967).

Major-General Aguiyi continued to commit one political blunder after the other because of his inexperience. It is also possible to say that the military governor of the north, Lieutenant Colonel Hassan Katsina, lacked national feeling in the whole episode. He was also paying lip services to this killing of the Ibos in the north. A strong commitment by the head of state and the military governor of north could have stopped this national embarrassment and disgrace. The military governor of the northern region, Lt. Col. H. U. Katsina underestimated the military capability of the Biafran troops by saying that "The federal army could crush the East in a few hours if the supreme commander gave the go ahead" Oluleye (1985: 53). Considering this unfortunate situation and regrettable massacres of the Ibos in the north, can anybody blame Lieutenant Colonel Ojukwu for taking decisive action to prevent the further killings of his people by ordering the Ibos to return from the north to their region for safety one may ask? As the military governor of eastern Nigeria, he saw it as a moral justification to intervene. Even before his order to his people to return home, they were already fleeing the north for their safety.

REACTIONS TO THE FATE OF COUP PLOTTERS

This was a contentious issue during this period under focus. These coup plotters were seen as heroes by some Nigerians in leading the overthrow of the corrupt politicians of the First Republic. That was not the reaction of north who saw the killing of the top politicians and military officers as a serious calamity. To the north, particularly the military, they were of the opinion that they should be tried according to military tradition. Unfortunately, they also found that although the coup plotters were detained in prison, they were paid their regular salaries and other allowances. How can one be placed in the prison yet be receiving salaries and allowances. It is possible to see this as a typical example of inhumanity, hence a charged and explosive point was reached.

In a statement issued by Major Kaduna Nzeogwu on January 19, 1966, he said:

> He had submitted to the country's new military regime, five conditions under which he and his men would submit to its authority, Major-General Johnson Aguiyi Ironsi, now ruling the country, had virtually accepted, the term, are: Safe conduct for himself and all his officers and men. A guarantee of freedom from legal proceedings now or later. An assurance that the politicians they fought to remove would not be returned to office. Compensation to be paid to the families of officers and men killed in the up risings. All his officers and men arrested in Western Nigeria to be released. (Nzeogwu' 1966)

The above statement from the ring leader of the January 15, 1966, Coup Major Nzeogwu confirmed that some persons in Nigeria saw them as heroes. Also the acceptance of the conditions under which they will submit to the military head of state, Major-General Aguiyi Ironsi, is quite unfortunate. It goes to show vividly that the military can never succeed in political governance because they are insensitive to the general will of the people. This is supported by Dare (1989: 11–19) when he argues: "If the deposed civilian administration has performed poorly, the initial acceptance of the military may be high but this may not detract from the pervasive feeling that the military rule is illegitimate."

Ordinarily the military tradition points to the fact that the inability to succeed in military coup is punishable by death. This is why soldiers are always very careful and skeptical in participating in military coup because of the severe consequences which Major-General Aguiyi Ironsi cannot claim ignorance. So it is not an exaggeration to say that the ineffective, poor, and inefficient handling of affairs by Major-General Aguiyi Ironsi during his six months administration in Nigeria was a factor that led to personality conflicts and Nigerian civil war. With this tensed and harsh political climate between the north and east, crisis was inevitable.

PERSONALITY CONFLICTS IN THE POST-JULY MILITARY COUP ERA, JULY 29, 1966, COUP

Another sad event in the history of this country was the countercoup of July 29, 1966. This coup was organized by the aggrieved northern soldiers to revenge the killings of their top politicians and army officers in the January 15, 1966. This coup led to the death of Major-General Aguiyi Ironsi, the head of state on a visit to Ibadan. His host the military governor of western Nigeria was also killed by the mutinous soldiers of the Nigerian army. It was such a solemn occasion that most Nigerians cannot forget in a hurry.

Also many officers of the Nigerian army and innocent civilians of Ibo origin were killed. The coup was directed against the Ibos. Many Ibo officers and soldiers were shot down in their barracks.

Lt. Col. Ojukwu representing his people was now against the rest of Nigeria. Tamuno (1989: 8–9) argues that in "May, July and September, 1966 ethnic murders and other forms of brutality and barbarism assumed alarming proportions in parts of the Federal Republic." The resultant reign of terror became a major feature of Nigeria's era of bad feeling which tested the utmost endurance of leaders, military, and civilian (Ibid 8-10).

When the rate of killings of civilians increased from May 1966, the aggrieved Igbos felt insecure in parts of the country other than eastern Nigeria. Commenting on this issue, Oluleye (1995: 39) observes that "the coup leaders of July 29, 1966 made it clear that their main aim was to avenge the death of the Northerners killed on January 15, 1966." These sporadic uprisings against the Ibos in the north was a bad omen for the country as, after July 29, 1966, it witnessed one form of disaster or the other every two months. Hence, this continued assassination of the Ibos in the north hardened their hearts against the federation especially as many of the Ibos in the north were repatriated to east losing all their means of livelihood. In such a chaotic and pathetic situation, no right-thinking person can blame Lt. Col. Ojukwu for supporting his people against the federal government that could not make serious effort to stop the killings. Especially when Olav maintains that people from the south without the Yoruba tribal marks were indiscriminately killed by the rioters, their property being looted and their homes burned (Olav 1970). In Kano, in particular, soldiers who had returned from eastern Nigeria participated in the massacres. The killings of the Ibos in the north led to reprisal attack against Hausa traders in the eastern region. Even the military governor of eastern Nigeria, Lt. Col. Ojukwu after July 29, 1966, observed that Ibos and soldiers from the north could no longer share the same barracks. Hence, he took the decision to disarm the officers and soldiers from their regions and to escort them out of the region.

It is important to put on record that most of the actions and decisions unilaterally taken by Lt. Col. Ojukwu were done without consultation. It is instructive to say here that they were taken by him without considering national interest. Patriotism, nationalism, and understanding are key virtues of unity which were lacking in Ojukwu at this critical period as he was consumed by ethnic feelings, tribalism, and nepotism. This massive massacre of the Ibo military officers and innocent civilians in the north, and the failure of both federal and northern governments to intervene, points to the fact that civil war in Nigeria could not be avoided.

THE EMERGENCE OF GENERAL YAKUBU GOWON AS HEAD OF STATE AND THE REACTIONS OF LT. COL. OJUKWU

When Lt. Col. Yakubu Gowon came to power, there was much anxiety and uncertainty about the continuous existence of Nigerian state partly due to the serious disruption caused by the disturbances in the north to avenge the death of their politicians and senior military soldiers in the January 15, 1966, coup. The Second Military coup of July 29, 1966, compounded the already strained relationship between the northern and eastern Nigeria. The signposts or the probability of a civil war was already manifesting. Oluleye states that from the time of kidnapping of Major-General Aguiyi Ironsi on the morning of July 29, 1966, till July 30, 1966, the country witnessed an interregnum (Oluleye 1985). He posits further that the whole populace was confused until August 1, 1966, when the newly appointed head of state, Lt. Col. Yakubu Gowon, removed the veil of mystery about the former head of state and his host to the nation (Ibid).

The first heated controversy between Lt. Col. Yakubu Gowon and Lt. Col. Ojukwu started with the emergence of General Yakubu Gowon as the new head of state of Nigeria. Before this appointment, he was the army chief of staff. With the assassination of Brigadier-General Aguiyi Ironsi, the next in rank was Brigadier Babafemi Ogundipe. Unfortunately, he was not able to assert his authority over the troops for obvious political and ethnic reasons. Although the chief of staff, Supreme Headquarters, Brigadier B.O. A. Ogundipe made some announcements to calm the public during the interregnum, the voice was not that of a king (Ibid). While the appointment of General Yakubu Gowon was accepted by governors of the northern region, Lt. Col. H.U. Katsina, western region, Colonel R. A. Adebayo, Lt. Col. D.A. Ejoor of midwest region, and the administrator of Lagos, Lt. Col. Ojukwu representing his people was against the appointment. Even other members of Supreme Military Council like Commodore J.E.A Wey, chief of naval staff and Mr. Kam Salam, the inspector-general of police all pledged their unalloyed and unflinching loyalty and support for the Gowon-led Federal Military government. Ojukwu''s argument was that Lt. Col. Gowon was not the most senior officer, and therefore had no right to that position. Hence, he refused to recognize it and was not ready to take orders from Gowon who he considers his military mate. Again because of fear and concern for his safety, Ojukwu from then refused to attend any meeting in Lagos so there was communication gap between Lagos and Enugu. This was a serious political mistake on part of Ojukwu because it was not in the best interest of national unity.

Particularly, Lt. Col. Ojukwu, the military governor of East Central State, refused to accept General Gowon as the head of state, for any reason, which was unpatriotic. This was against the background that Brigadier Ogundipe was not able to assert control over the army. It is true that in line with military tradition, he was supposed to be rightful successor to Aguiyi Ironsi but that was the thinking of the coup plotters of July 29, 1966. The stand of the top northern military officers was for a northerner to take that position in order for the north to claim back the leadership of the nation. Lt. Col. Ojukwu, the first master's degree holder to enlist into the Nigerian army in addition to his vast knowledge of military coup cannot claim ignorance of the fact that the coup was organized by ambitious northern soldiers who wanted an end to southern domination in the affairs of the country, particularly Ibos. Against that background, there could have been no way for them to favor Brigadier Ogundipe to take over the affairs of the country. On being told about the coup, Brigadier Ogundipe failed to exert his authority through a challenge, and he made a dramatic escape using amphibious transportation means to Cotonou in the Republic of Benin. His departure paved the way to leadership tussle between two lieutenant colonels which later translated into the civil war (Ibid. 38). Since the most senior military officer in Nigeria at the time, Brigadier Ogundipe escaped thereby creating a vacuum in government which lasted for three days and General Gowon was the person approved by the army, it could have been necessary for Lt. Col. Ojukwu to recognize that position in the interest of national unity. This he did not do thereby creating another problem, for this attitude created the seeds of discord and acrimony between the two. Again as a matter of fact, within the caucus of the northern officers, Lt. Col. Yakubu Gowon was the most senior, and he was their choice. This nonacceptance of Yakubu Gowon by Lt. Col. Ojukwu as the new head of state worsened the relationship between the federal and eastern governments.

THE GOWON-OJUKWU PERSONALITY CONFLICT AND THE NIGERIAN CIVIL WAR

The personality conflicts manifested much in the Aburi Conference between the federal government and Lt. Col. Ojukwu, the military governor of eastern region. This disagreement between Lt. Col. Ojukwu and the federal government led by General Yakubu Gowon was one of the immediate factors that led to Nigerian civil war. Several diplomatic activities with the encouragement of the British and the Americans culminated in the Aburi meeting of early January 1967 (Abdullahi 1989). By the end of December 1966, it was becoming very clear that the civil war in Nigeria was inevitable, as both sides of the conflict were preparing gradually for war. The Aburi conference which took place in Ghana in early January, 1967, came to a close on January 5, 1967, when a communiqué was signed by the delegates representing the federal government and the eastern region. Tribute must be accorded to the Ghana head of state, General Ankrah, who offered to mediate in order to find a peaceful resolution so as to promote peaceful coexistence in the country.

Walson (2012: 89) remarks that "it was during the Aburi conference that the Nigerian military leaders realized that political prowess was a tactical skill which is much more than being experts at the trigger and that it was the first time after independence that the country's dirty 'Linens' was washed not only in the public but also shamefully spread in the clear view of their former colonial masters and other nations who might have laughed in derision."

This ad hoc conference was purely an intramilitary affair. It was an attempt by the Ghanaian head of state to resolve the problem which the military had plugged Nigeria into and were not able to resolve. The conference obviously exposed the military's incapability to handle critical political issues because of their high level of administrative immaturity. This conference was the last opportunity to avert the civil war. So the interpretation given to the decisions of the conference differed on arrival in Nigeria. The conference failed to produce desirable results and so the civil war in Nigeria started in 1967. The military leaders saw it as opportunity to display eloquence and insulting idioms in order to showcase their strength, unnecessary pride, arrogance, heroism without considering the interest of innocent Nigerians that will be killed should the war commences. No consideration was given to national interest and unity. Nigerians were happy to hear that the Supreme Military Council's meeting which was very difficult to convene in the country was at last held in Ghana. Many were hopeful that the outcome will be positive and the war averted. It was very frustrating to many Nigerians that nothing tangible was achieved instead more complications set in from that point; it was now certain that Nigeria was going to war.

According to Walson (2012: 89), the Ghanaian mediating team was able to impress on the Nigerian military leaders to agree among other things that:

> The army was to be administered by the supreme military council. The chairman of which was the Head of the Federal Military Government and commander in Chief of the Armed Forces. A military headquarters in which each region was to be represented was to be set-up under a chief of staff. In each region was to be established an area commander. The SMC was to deal with all matters of appointment and promotions of persons in executive posts in the Armed forces and the police. Military Governors for the duration of the military Government were to have control over area commander in their regions for the purpose of internal security.

It was quite unfortunate that the military leaders at the conference on getting home gave selfish and ethnic interpretation to what was arrived at the summit. To Lt. Col. Ojukwu, what was agreed on was extreme decentralization which will give the eastern region full control of its affairs. To the federal government, led by General Yakubu Gowon, it was a federation. Streamau (1977: 49) states that "Gowon was invited to Accra to review the issue and was advised on the need to placate the rebels." Again General Ankrah also secured Gowon's permission to send a high-level fact-finding delegation directly to Ojukwu's headquarters in Enugu (Ibid). It was said also that the Ghanaian military leaders also hastily sought to arrange a West African mini-summit to discuss the Nigerian conflict in advance of the O.A U meetings in Kinshasa, Zaire (now the Democratic Republic of the Congo). All these bold efforts of Ghana to provide a lasting solution to the conflict to avert war proved abortive. Hence, the war started on July 6, 1967. With this conflicting interpretation and understanding, it was evident that the two soldiers, General Yakubu Gowon and Lt. Col. Ojukwu, were heading for a destructive war which would engulf the whole nation. According to Prof. Eliagwu, Aburi's resolutions and reactions to it later were indicative of the military's weakness in political system Walson (2012: 92–92).

THE CREATION OF TWELVE STATES

The national broadcast of General Yakubu Gowon on May 27, 1967, aggravated the already tensed political situation in the country. In that broadcast, he
proclaimed a national state of emergency and divided the country into twelve
states: three in the east, six in the north, the west and midwest remained as
they were, and the federal capital Lagos was constituted into the twelfth state.

> I am therefore proclaiming a state of emergency throughout Nigeria with
> immediate effect. I have assumed full powers as Commander-in-Chief of the
> Armed forces and Head of the Federal Military Government for the short period
> necessary to carry through the measures which are now urgently required. In
> this period of emergency, no political statements in the press, on the Radio and
> Television, all public media or any other political activity; will not be tolerated.
> The military and police are empowered to deal summarily with any offender.
> To ensure justice, these states are being created simultaneously. To this end
> therefore, I am promulgating a Decree which will divide the Federal Republic
> into twelve States. East Central State comprising the present Eastern Region
> excluding Calabar, and Ogoja provinces. River State comprising Ahoada, Brass
> Degema, Ogoni and Port Harcourt Division. (Gowon 1967)

Such a statement from General Gowon did not help; instead, it provoked
Ojukwu to declare the Republic of Biafra three days later. Since he has
started the peace process which many peace-loving Nigerians applauded,
there was no need for such a show of power and strength, as it later became
counterproductive. Again his creation of states was another area that needs
serious examination. According to General Gowon, I am satisfied that the
creation of new states as the only possible basis for stability and equality is
the overwhelming desire of vast majority of Nigerians (Ibid). Again he said:
"It is true that the country has a long history of well-articulated demands for
states. This is as a result of the fears of minorities against majority domination
in the country" (Ibid).

However, the timing was wrong. It was interpreted by many as an attempt
to disunite and destabilize the eastern region, thereby making it less powerful
in the event of secession. A period when the situation in the country could be
described an era of uncertainty and instability, such creation of states would be
suspicious. Again the Ibos saw the creation of River and southeastern states as
a way of depriving them of the much-needed support they could have received
from these minorities in their region. By giving them their states, which they
have been agitating for since 1950s, they were very grateful to the federal
government. It is also clear that they will support the federal government in
any conflict between it and the Ibos in order to reciprocate the kind gesture of

the federal government. More especially the eastern regional government did not support the creation of new states in the region since the agitations for state creation started in the 1950s. Ojukwu used these miscalculations and the inordinate ambition of General Gowon to quickly declare the Republic of Biafra on May 30, 1967, three days after General Gowon created the twelve states.

GENERAL GOWON AND LT. COL. OJUKWU'S AMBITIONS

Inordinate ambition of Gowon came out clearly in his broadcast in October, 1974, that "it would be unrealistic to handover power to a civilian government because the politicians had learned nothing and forgotten nothing" (Gowon 1974). In the *Daily Times* comment of August 6, 1975, the regime of Gowon was accused of lack of consultation, indecision, indiscipline, and neglect (*Daily Times* 1975). This was when General Gowon became intoxicated by the power and spoils of office and wanted to renege in his promise to quit office in 1976. This was very sad indeed because he did this with military fiat without consultation. Gowon's desire for power came out clearly in his national broadcast of May 27, 1967.

For Lt. Col. Ojukwu, he was a man of inordinate ambition and has strong desire to acquire power. His actions and activities before and during the Nigerian civil war demonstrated this feature in him. Even before the declaration of the Republic of Biafra, Ojukwu and his team, according to General Gowon in his nationwide broadcast on May 27, 1967, "disrupted the direct movement of oil products from the refinery near Port-Harcourt to the northern region. They have hindered the transit of goods to neighboring countries and have even seized goods belonging to foreign countries. Only recently they committed the barbaric crime of hi-jacking of a plane bound for Lagos from Benin" (Gowon's Broadcast, October 1974). General Gowon also pointed that "certain vehicles of the post and telegraphs department which went to the east on resumption of services have been illegally detained in the Region" (Ibid). This was collaborated by Chief Anthony Enahoro, the Nigerian Federal Commissioner of Information and Labor, when he said.

> The Enugu Regime seized more than one-third of the rolling stock of the Nigerian Railways, including 800 wagons and 115 oil tankers. It obstructed the movement of oil products from the Refinery owned by all the Governments of Nigeria. It seized an aircraft of Nigerian Airways and hi-jacked another in the Mid-West region. It seized property belonging to a foreign government of the Republic of Chad. It expelled all non-Easterners from the East. (Tamuno 1989: 8)

No responsible government can allow such unilateral decisions which were illegal in the first place; hence, the federal government of Nigeria took some drastic measure to bring down Ojukwu regime. Again the ambitious Ojukwu refused to participate in peace conferences in an effort to avoid the war. This was unacceptable to Lt. Col. Ojukwu because it did not accept secession. His main focus was the acceptance of a separate sovereign Republic by the federal government. The resolution of peace meeting convened by National Conciliation Committee in order to find a lasting solution was rejected by Ojukwu. This committee was made of bishops, judges, and reputable political leaders. In fact they were distinguished citizens of this country. At the end of the meeting, recommendations were submitted to both sides involved in the conflict. These included the reciprocal abrogation of economic measures taken by the Federal Military Government and the seizure of the Federal Statutory Corporations and Federal Revenue by the Eastern government. (Ibid) These reciprocal actions were to be implemented within one week, that is, by May 25, 1967. "I accepted the recommendations and issued instructions effective from Tuesday, May 23, 1967, the response of the East has been completely negative and they have continued their propaganda and stage-managed demonstrations for independence" (Ibid).

In an attempt to frustrate any peace move by the federal government, the eastern government led by Lt. Col. Ojukwu would always insist that Nigeria should recognize the breakaway state and conclude a peace treaty with him as head of a foreign state which no responsible government that is worth its salt can accept. "It must be clear that by accepting such a suggestion, the Federal Government of Nigeria would have been the first Government to recognize the so-called Republic of Biafra which up till today has not been recognized by any Government or international organization" (Federal Government 1967). It is necessary to also add that the western region warned that if the east succeeds then the west follows.

Lt. Col. Ojukwu was an ambitious seeker for political power at any cost. This desire affected most decisions he took which sustained the Nigerian civil war. The personality conflict was more complicated among the actors of the civil war because of Ojukwu's attribute of nonflexibility and nondynamism, a man who tends to be static in decision-making. He was fully ready to crush top military officers in the Biafra and federal army and political leaders who were directly and indirectly challenging his authority. Gowon was compelled to say thus:

He was even ready to sacrifice some of his federal power if this could appease Ojukwu and his war- mongering advisers in the East. The famous decree No. 8 virtually gave the regions unprecedented autonomy. Military Governors in the regions could make certain vital decisions without reference to him. Ojukwu had won all that was possible in a loose federation. But this was not enough, Ojukwu proceeded in spite of this demonstration of good intentions to national-ize federal agencies and corporations in the east. Even when many people said this was the stage to attack, Gowon still tried to avoid worsening the situation. Then suddenly, on May 30, 1967 Ojukwu went on the air at Enugu and declared his Republic of Biafra. (Tamuno 1989: 8)

Tamuno (1989: 9) argues that "Ojukwu, on the other hand, did not disguise his interest in such matters like seeking high political office, seemed ambi-tions and sought to reach the very top of his profession." So it is possible to say that Ojukwu saw Gowon as blocking his path to further progress in Federal Nigeria hence he was not ready to listen to voices of reasoning.

Another typical example was the relationship between him and Kaduna Nzeogwu because of his idea of one Nigeria and New Nigeria Army. Even many saw his death, at the very early part of the civil war while on the Biafra side in July 1967, as mysterious and highly suspicious. After the military coup of January 15, 1966, a sharp difference existed between both heroes. Both of them distrusted each other. Solarin comments about his visit to Enugu in 1967, thus:

Nzeogwu took me first to Lt. Colonel Ojukwu's office, but he would not go in with me when I asked why not, he told me that two of them did not see eye to eye on the question of fighting for succession. He was not on talking terms with Ojukwu. He however went with me to Colonel Banjo's office, which was next door to Ojukwu. You have no doubt heard a lot of rumors about my relations with Ojukwu. He is worried about my popularity among his own people. I was to be put back in prison, but he was afraid of repercussions. Right now. I am not allowed contact with troops nor am I permitted to operate on the staff. One gentlemen's agreement we have is that I can carry on with whatever pleases me. (Nzeogwu 1967).

The conflict of interest between both went to the extent that people specu-lated that Ojukwu was involved in the death of Nzeogwu, an allegation he denied! According to Lt. Col. Ojukwu; "It is convenient for some people now to start telling lies than the truth about what actually happened. That fatal patrol that Nzeogwu mounted, he did in the company of my brother Tom Biggar. They both died in the same action side by side in that death part of me died" (Ene 2011: 5).

This development between the two of them took place primarily because of Ojukwu"s perceived idea that Nzeogwu was capable of challenging his authority anytime and anywhere. Dr. Chike Obi was not spared by Lt. Col. Ojukwu political hegemony. According to him, he was detained by Ojukwu for daring to oppose his idea of secession (Drum, June 15, 1970). "People who were no more than human skeletons fought over food, the cell was worse than hell (Ibid)." George Okoro, writing for a Nigerian daily newspaper tried to paint the picture of how one man fooled 12 million people (Ibid). Supporting the view that the ambition of Ojukwu led the nation to war, Dr. Nnamdi Azikiwe, who went on a nationwide tour to the northwestern and north central states to see things for himself, said:

I find it very difficult to understand the stand of Ojukwu. For the mere fact that I got up in London and appealed to him to retract their steps, go to the conference table and negotiate for a just and honorable settlement. I was called names and they have mounted polemics against me day and night for the past two weeks. I don't mind. (Azikiwe 1969)

Another area of concern was his courage in the execution of top military officers in the Biafran army based on his ambition. Many brilliant professional soldiers of military distinction were victims of this assault. He blamed his serious miscalculations on the capture of midwest on some of his gallant soldiers like Major Sam Agbamuche, Major Philip Alale, Col. Banjo, and Major Emmanuel Ifeajuna. It is an irony of history that August 9, on which the people of the midwest celebrate the anniversary of the creation of their state was the day rebel troops from the Republic of Biafra invaded the territory.

On the pre-dawn hours, more than 100 lorries carrying several thousands of rebel troops crossed the bridge from Onitsha to Asaba. There, the troops split into three columns. One headed for Sapele, Ughelli and Warri, the second moved to Agbor and Auchi and the third to Benin City, the capital. They gained control of the Midwest by disarming loyal federal troops. In Benin City the rebels seized the Armory, Magazine, Nigerian Broadcasting Station, the Central Bank, Government House, Post and Telegraphs office and took over other key points in the city. (Handbook of Midwest State 1967)

Fortunately, through the courage and bravery of Col. Murtala Mohammed and the efforts of the federal troops, midwest was recaptured from Biafran soldiers on September 30, 1967. The entire episode of the midwest invasion was a very costly venture and total failure. In order to quickly eliminate these great military officers, recognized all over the country, they were accused of treason. Instead of blaming them and pointing out areas where they failed, they were tried by a court-martial and found guilty of treason. They were all executed the same day. That goes to demonstrate that absolute power corrupts absolutely. By this development, all those likely to challenge his authority were gone.

OJUKWU DECLARATION OF THE
REPUBLIC OF BIAFRA

The last straw that broke the camel's back was Ojukwu declaration of the Republic of Biafra. This was an eloquent testimony that peaceful resolution was no more possible, hence the war began on July 6, 1970. First and foremost, it may be necessary to define the concept "Biafra" for proper understanding of the issue under focus. Lord Milverton saw Biafra as a name invented by the rebel leader to cover the eastern region, as if it was one natural tribally united area because he claimed to carry with him by force several reluctant minority tribes numbering about 5 million people and the reason why he had to force them into the rebellion was that the seaport of Port Harcourt and the bulk of the oil were in their territory and not in Ibo land (*Daily Telegraph* 1968).

It is important to establish the fact that Lt. Col. Ojukwu was not the first person to invent the term "Biafra." The British first used Biafra to describe the heart of the Ibo land and called it the Bight of Biafra just as we also have the Bight of Benin. However, today Biafra is synonymous with Ojukwu because it became so popular and a household name after Ojukwu"s declaration.

Much ground was prepared by the eastern region for secession before the final declaration of the Republic of Biafra. On May 30, 1967, Olav listed the following actions and activities as preparation to secede from the federation. They are:

1. Constitutional proposals from the federal government were rejected by Ojukwu, who also declined to participate in the federal executive organs.
2. He refused to accept Gowon as his military superior.
3. He suggested that under the existing conditions, the regional units of Nigeria ought to pull apart.
4. He took some unilateral decisions which include (a) the release on March 12, 1967, of army officers who had participated in the January coup including the leader of the Coup Major Nzeogwu against protests from Lagos (b) Publishing a white paper to maintain that the regions should have full control over their own resources
5. When the Lagos government on March 31, 1967, published its budget statement not taking account of the claims of the Enugu government that the regions themselves should have control over regional resources, the Enugu government published an edit stating that all revenues from eastern Nigeria which had gone into the federal treasury were now to be paid to the eastern region treasury and the revenue collection would be subject to control by the regional government. This edict was explicitly presented by eastern region authorities as the first step toward secession

and was immediately turned down by the federal government which maintained that the edict was illegal and contrary to the constitution. A new edict published by the eastern region government on April 18, 1967, continued this process by proclaiming the take-over of ten federal corporations and installation situated in the eastern region (Olav 1970: 53).

It can be argued that the declaration of the Republic of Biafra considering the prevailing circumstances in the country is inevitable. Lt. Col. Ojukwu was looking for any possible utterances from the federal government which could be considered as inimical to the interest of the Ibos. That opportunity came when Lt. Col. Ojukwu summoned a joint meeting of erudite civilians and military officers where it was obvious in the emotion-laden address that Ojukwu was appealing to the leaders of eastern Nigeria to mandate him to declare at the earliest practicable date, eastern Nigeria as an independent state by the name and title "Republic of Biafra" (Ibid). That was the final push in an attempt by Lt. Col. Ojukwu to declare the Republic of Biafra. It is against this background that one tends to see the radio broadcast to the nation on May 27, 1967, as not constructive and diplomatic enough. That broadcast gave Lt. Col. Ojukwu the justification to declare the Republic of Biafra finally. Part of its reads:

> "The citizens of Nigeria have not given the military regime any mandate to divide up the country into sovereign states and to plunge them into a bloody disaster. "Furthermore, he announced the reorganization of the country into 12 states 3 of which were carved out of the Eastern Region. (Gowon 1967)

Lt. Col. Ojukwu, a very intelligent soldier, who saw himself as far above his fellow officers and who suspected the motives and moves of fellow officers, saw the danger in this address, especially creating three states from the eastern region reacted quickly. He addressed the people of eastern Nigeria on May 30, 1967.

> Fellow country men and women, you the people of Eastern Nigeria: conscious of the supreme authority of Almighty God over all mankind, of your duty to yourselves and posterity: Aware that you can no longer be protected in your lives and in your property by any Government based outside Eastern Nigeria; believing that you are born free and have certain inalienable rights which can best be preserved by yourselves, determined to dissolve all political and other ties between you and the former Federal Republic of Nigeria; prepared to enter into such association, treaty or alliance with any sovereign state within the former Federal Republic of Nigeria and elsewhere on such terms and conditions as best to subserve your common good. Affirming your trust and confidence

in me; having mandated me to proclaim on your behalf and in your name, that Eastern Nigeria, be a sovereign Independent Republic, now, therefore, I Lieutenant colonel, Chukwuemeka Odumegwu Ojukwu, military governor of Eastern Nigeria, by virtue of the authority, and pursuant to the principles, recited above, do hereby solemnly proclaim that the territory and region known as and called Eastern Nigeria together with her continental shelf and territorial waters shall henceforth be an independent sovereign state of the name and title of "The Republic of Biafra" and I do declare that all political ties between us and the Federal Republic of Nigeria hereby totally dissolved. (Ojukwu 1967)

The first reaction of General Gowon was to announce to the nation that Lt. Col. Ojukwu had been dismissed from the Nigeria Army and relieved of his post as the military governor of the eastern region. Therefore, it was not surprising that on July 6, 1967, war broke out between federal troops and Biafra forces when the federal government stated that it was taking action to end the rebellion in the eastern region. By July 6, 1967, federal forces invade the east and took Nsukka after days of fighting. Ogoja in the southeastern state was liberated on July 15, and Bonny was captured by federal forces on July 26, 1967. This war continued until 1970 when it ended.

CONCLUSION

The personality conflicts in Nigerian politics date back to pre-independence era. Initially, it took the form of ethnic nationalism and crisis arising from tribal identity. Between 1914 and 1958 was a period of serious constitutional crises which aggravated the personality conflicts among those in the political class on the one side and crises of interest between our nationalists and the colonial officials on the other.

Between 1960 and 1966, the salient issues involved in the personality conflicts were corruption, unemployment, conflict of interest between Chief Akintola and Chief Obafemi Awolowo, the 1962/1963 census crisis, the 1964 Federal Election, the 1965 western regional election, and the military coup of January 15, 1966. It was during the 1964–1965 elections that the first plot for a military coup d' etat by some members of the Nigerian army was planned.

The Nigerian civil war eventually broke out on July 6, 1967, because of the inability and lack of capability on part of General Aguiyi Ironsi, General Gowon, and Lt. Col. Ojukwu to manage the issues effectively that led to the avoidable war. What was considered by the head of states, General Yakubu Gowon, as a mere police action to arrest Lt. Col. Ojukwu to end the rebellion and the threat by the governor of the northern region, Lt. Col. H. U. Katsina, that the federal army could crush the east in a few hours if the supreme commander gave the go-ahead later turned out to be a full scale or total war, which only ended after thirty months.

In the military coup of January 15, 1966, led by Major Kaduna Nzeogwu, the government of the federation was overthrown with much violence in which many top military officers and political leaders especially from the north and western Nigeria were killed. In spite of the general acceptance of the coup as an end to the regime of the corrupt politicians who were more possessed with regional inclinations instead of national interest, the policies of the head of state, Brigadier-General Aguiyi Ironsi convinced the north that it was an Ibo plot to eliminate them from the corridors of power and to establish Igbo hegemony. Hence, some top army officers of northern origin organized a countercoup on July 29, 1966, in which Brigadier-General Aguiyi Ironsi and his host Fajuyi were killed. Many Ibos military officers in the barracks and innocent civilians were killed. The conflict of interest demonstrated in the military coups of 1966 points to the fact that civil war in Nigeria was unavoidable.

In May, July, and September 1966, ethnically motivated murder and other forms of brutality, especially against the Igbos, assumed alarming dimensions. At this time, Nigeria was at the brink of total collapse. The last opportunity came when the Ghanaian head of state, General Ankrah, agreed to mediate in order to find a peaceful settlement to the issues at stake. The meeting took place in Aburi, Ghana in the month of January 1967. Unfortunately, the decisions reached in that conference was interpreted differently when they returned to Nigeria. To Gowon and other federal government delegates, it was a federation, while Ojukwu saw it as a confederation. Since the Aburi conference could not provide a settlement, the eastern region led by Ojukwu was now fully set to declare the Republic of Biafra.

The last straw that broke the camel's back was the radio broadcast by General Gowon on May 27, 1967, dividing Nigeria into twelve states with the eastern region divided into three states. The Eastern Nigeria Consultative Assembly reacted the same night by passing a resolution empowering Ojukwu to declare the eastern region independent. Thus, on May 30, 1967, Ojukwu went on the air at Enugu and declared the Republic of Biafra. General Gowon reacted by dismissing Ojukwu from the Nigerian army and was relieved of his post as military governor of the eastern region. On July 6, 1967, war officially broke out between federal troops and Biafran forces.

The thirty months civil war in Nigeria officially ended on January 12, 1970. On January 10, 1970, General Ojukwu had his last meeting with his cabinet and military advisers where he informed them of his decision to leave (New-Nigeria January 12, 1970). General Ojukwu fled Biafra on January 11, 1970, to Ivory Coast and left the Republic of Biafra in the hands of Major-General Philip Effiong who was the second-in-command in the Biafra army to announce the end of Biafra rebellion. The end of the civil war was followed by Gowon's astute speech of "No Victor, No Vanquished" and his refusal to punish war prisoners or dissidents and his efforts of reconciliation, rehabilitation, and reconstruction deserve commendation. The destroyed bridges and burned markets, cement factories, oil location, roads, railway lines, and health centers received fast attention in the eastern part of the country in particular and Nigeria in general. This demonstrated to the world that the propaganda of genocide against the Ibos may have been exaggerated. The Nigerian civil war was inevitable considering the personality conflicts in Nigerian politics from the pre-independence era to the post–July 29 military countercoup.

REFERENCES

Abdullahi, Mahadi. 1989. "The Roles of Neighboring Countries in the Nigerian Civil War." In *Panel on Nigeria Since Independence*, edited By T. N. Tamuno and S. C. Ukpabi. Ibadan, Nigeria: Heinemann Educational Books, 112–115.

Aguiyi-Ironsi, J. T. U. 1966. *Broadcast to the Nation on the Policies and Programs of His Government*. January 28.

Anglin, D. G. 1965. "Brinkmanship in Nigeria: The Federal Election of 1964–65." *International Journal*, 20(2): 173–188.

Coleman, James S. 1958. *Nigeria: Background to Nationalism*. Berkeley: University of California Press.

Daily Times. 1962. March 20.

Daily Times. 1975. August.

Drum. 1967. January 25.

Drum. 1970. June 15.

Ediagbonya, Michael. 2020. "Nigeria Constitutional Development in Historical Perspective, 1914–1960." *American Journal of Humanities and Social Sciences Research*, 4(2): 289–314.

Effiong, P. 1970. *A Declaration by Lt. Col. Phillip Effiong that Biafra Has Ceased to Exist*. Federal Ministry of Information Press Release No. 46. January, 15.

Eluwa, C. I. C. Nwachukwu, U. N. Nwaubani, A. C. and Ukagwu, M. O. 2005. *A History of Nigeria*. Onitsha, Nigeria: Africana First Publishers, Limited.

Ene, J. C. 2011. *In the Beginning*. Port Hartcourt, Nigeria: E. C. Bosco Integrated Services.

Federal Government of Nigeria. 1967. *Federal Government's Response to the Request of Lt. Col. Ojukwu that "Nigeria should recognize the breakaway state and conclude a peace Treaty with him as Head of a foreign state in a peace meeting."*

Guardian. 1967. January 18.

Golden City Post. 1966. July 17.

Gowon, Yakubu. 1967. *Broadcast to the Nation*. May 27.

Gowon, Yakubu. 1968. *An Address on the Progress of the War*, August 31.

Gowon, Yakubu. 1970. *His Response to the Address of Lt. Col. Philip Effiong Address*. January 15.

Gowon, Yakubu. 1970. *Midnight Broadcast.* January 31.

Gowon, Yakubu. 1971. *Broadcast to the Nation.* October.

Handbook of Midwest State. 1967. Federal Republic of Nigeria.

Isichei, Elizabeth 1969. *History of West Africa Since 1800.* New York: Macmillan.

Lloyd, P. C. 1970. "The Ethnic Background to the Nigerian Civil War." In *Nigerian Politics and Military Rule,* edited By S. K. Painter Brick. London: Institute of Commonwealth Studies.

New Nigerian. 1970. January 13.

Nigerian Tribune. 1964. February 27.

Nzeogwu, Kaduna. 1967. *Kaduna. Letter to Obasanjo,* June 17.

Odetola, Olatunde. 1982. *Military Regimes and Development: A Comparative Analysis in African Societies.* London: Allen and Unwin.

Odetola, Olatunde. 1989. *The Praetorian Trap: The Problems and Prospects of Military Disengagement.* Lecture Delivered at Obafemi Awolowo University Ile-Ife, April 18.

Ojiako, J. O. 1981. *Nigeria: Yesterday, Today and...* Onitsha, Nigeria: African Educational Publishers (Nigeria) Ltd.

Ojo, E. O. 2006. *Aspects of Nigerian History.* Lagos: King Julius Educational Publishers.

Ojukwu, Odumegwu. 1967. *Except from Ojukwu's Declaration of Secession.* May 30.

Olav, Stoke. 1970. *An Introduction to the Politics, Economy and Social Setting of Modern Nigeria.* Uppsala, Sweden: Soderom and Finn.

Oluleye, J. J. 1985. *Military Leadership in Nigeria.* Ibadan: Ibadan University Press.

Osiruemu, E. O. 1995. *The Labor Movement Under the Military Rule in Nigeria.* University of Benin, Ph.D. Thesis.

Post, Kenneth and Michael Vickers. 1972. *Structure and Conflicts in Nigeria.* London: Heinemann.

Stremlau, J. J. 1977. *The International Politics of the Nigerian Civil War, 1967–1970.* Princeton, NJ: Princeton University.

Tamuno, T. N. 1989. "Introduction: Men and Measure in the Nigerian Crisis, 1966–1970." In *Panel on Nigeria Since Independence,* edited By T. N. Tamuno and S. C. Ukpabi. Ibadan, Nigeria: Heinemann Educational Books, 2–10.

Chapter 7

On Rwanda's Civil War (October 1, 1990–April 6, 1994)

Assessing the International Determinant

Fiacre Bienvenu

Scholarship on origins and dynamics of war in Africa has not yet connected to factors beyond immediate security borders. Armed conflicts in the region are generally constricted to the interiors of territorial boundaries and not plausibly explored as a process that is exteriorly defined. That analytical framework is flawed in that it fails to consider the totality of domestic, international, and corporation constraints on territorial actors. Therefore, examining any conflict in Africa outside the international dimension is to leave out a key mechanistic explanation to the workings of conflicts.

This chapter examines the external determinants of the Rwandan civil war of the 1990s. It attempts to trace them to the time as far back as before the inception of the republic. The chapter specifically assesses, how did ingredients so external to both the state and the actors become so prevalent that they shaped, maintained, dominated, and conditioned the war and the behavior of conflicting actors? Examining this question through the three genes of war—ideology, logistics, and geopolitics—I posit that the originating rudiments of the Rwandan conflict are located in the colonial design that made the state a zero-sum end—that the effects of such a design created a pervasive paramountcy of geo-colonial powers (France and Belgium) in national security regulation and that domestic state actors—rather than challenging, correcting, or balancing that order—enabled it, without which the catastrophe would not have happened.

CIVIL WAR IN RWANDA AND THE THEORY

Buzan and Waever (1998, 2003) have systematized security issues that are otherwise too vast to delineate. Their regional security complex theory

193

(RSCT) universalizes security aspects and makes common rules for examining them across the globe. It contends that armed conflicts in peripheral states are shaped by territorial *regions* they occur in, but not by global powers. Buzan and Waever (2003) posit that security is a cluster of dynamics that are always regionally structured and that the *regional* structure—*not external* factors—is the proper principle of arrangement for how bounded territoriality and distribution of power affect security outcomes in conflicts.[1] Central to this theoretical architecture is that threats tend to travel more easily over short distance than over a long one, and therefore security interdependence patterns are something that should be located in regionally based clusters, hence the terminology "security complex." However, that approach to security dynamics is limiting and does not provide tools for determining origins of ideas that war actors depend on in their quest to control a state. RSCT also confines security paradigms within closed territorial boundaries, ignoring the significance of supraregional materials in shaping local security dynamics. To the extent that no state operates in a vacuum, and that actors are not exclusively impelled by their personal instincts or desires about power (Migdal 2001: 47–51), but by a host of constraints around the state, some near others stemming from far away (Malloy 1977; Modelski 1978, 1979), then for a war to be fought and won, some logistical, ideological, and external conditions must be met. These three genes of war—ideology, material, and geopolitical configurations—determine security dynamics of a country, as well as the behavior of battling actors.

Using the case of Rwanda's civil war in the early 1990s, this chapter examines the extent to which internal security dynamics were a direct result of a political order set up by external actors. Specifically, I seek to determine the extent to which the ideology and the logistics that defined the beginning and the end of the war in Rwanda were rooted in configurations outside the Rwandan actors. I intend to tease out the extent to which ideas, material power, and alliances developed by external powers gave impetus to the breakout and the end of the war in the 1990s.

The central argument is that Rwanda's insecurity in the 1990s (and after) was a direct result of patterns of power competition designed by the colonial powers. I contend that the patterns of insecurity in Rwanda (and, to a large extent, of the African Great Lakes region) were indelibly formed during its first encounter with Belgium and the succeeding tutelage provided by France. I contend further that without the systematization (by Belgium and later reinforced by France) of what had long been fluid and artificial standards of identity into a set of fixed identity categories, it would have been impossible for the civil war to occur.[2] I challenge the RSCT tenets that colonialism was only an innocuous "interlude" and a bland "overlay" in the formation of patterns of amity and enmity in the Sub-Saharan region (Buzon and Weaver 2003:

219–223). The patterns out of which Rwanda's logic of civil war sprouted defy that security logic. And failing to consider the colonial institutional legacies for the war is to omit a crucial component in the compound that defined the dynamics of insecurity in Rwanda and in its regional neighbors.[3] In the next sections, I will discuss the relevance of such external conditions in Rwanda's civil war in the 1990s. I will demonstrate that international actors were the most significant determinants—both ideologically and materially— along the trajectory of Rwanda's conflict before, during, and after the war.

The *ideology* component (by which I mean acceptance of the view usually labeled as "narrative") provides a description of how the conflict was shaped discursively by opposed domestic actors for legitimacy and morale during the war. It is the discursive narrative that each actor used to create, justify, and legitimize their action. I examine the securitization strategy used by each side during the war and assess the extent to which each side's narrative, in design, invoked internal or external imaginings about the opponent to justify their own behavior. I pay attention to the origins of each side's discursive constructs, where they came from, when, and why they came about. The material analysis of the war (by which I mean "logistical power") describes how the balance of power was deterministically shaped by international actors. I contend that the logistical edge that the government received from France, its international ally, did not translate into material advantage or prompt rapid end of the war. Rather, it exacerbated the conflict and without it the war would have been much shorter and produced a less severe outcome in terms of human losses. The geopolitical analysis uncovers the extent to which Rwanda's civil war involved great power struggles and took precedence over domestic dynamics.

Given the interconnectedness of events in Rwanda, it would be, must I clarify, incorrect to treat the civil war as a separate and independent episode in the nation's postcolonial conflict history. The war is one element in the wider context that led to the genocide against the Tutsi. It preceded and even overlapped with the genocide. Therefore, this chapter ends at the early moments of the genocide, but I solely focus on the war that spanned the period of October 1, 1990, through April 6, 1994. This timeframe is only meant to conform to the goal set in this volume, that is, to provide various comparative perspectives on civil wars, peace, and security dynamics in Africa.

THE IDEOLOGY: HOW THE INTERNATIONAL DYNAMICS SHAPED THE RWANDAN CIVIL WAR

The conflict began as ethnic in nature. But ethnicity, in and of itself, that is, as a typology and a category of difference, did not alone produce the conflict.

It is the ideas and the reification of ideas built in ethnicity that engendered the patterns of amity and enmity in Rwanda that led to it. The origins, the evolution, and the institutions that matured such ideas up were rooted in the "truth" produced by the colonial governance about ethnic differentiations, which became the basis upon which the battling parties waged the war. Local actors were not objectively independent, as the RSCT would suggest, in birthing, reifying, and exploiting those identity ideas and their implications for power control. Rather, out of the Belgian design of rule system derived overriding ingredients that incepted the state as an organization whose security depended on ostracizing one "ethnic" group while the other enjoyed monopoly of governance. That us-without-them-in power foundation as well the political culture it produced became the new norm in town that subsequent political actors practiced on until the outbreak of the war in 1990. So, how did all that begin and which ideas about identity existed before the Belgian rule that changed as a result of colonial redesign of power?

Long before Rwanda became an independent republic, in 1962, social relations and patterns of power competition had already been indelibly redesigned by the Belgian colonial rule. Both symbolically and substantively, Hutu and Tutsi had coexisted for centuries as two fluid and fungible social groups. But the colonial power systematized what was otherwise prolific, varying, and temporal in meaning and practice and turned it into fixed and permanent standards of identity. Yet, as Des Forges (1995: 44–45) once described it, these two groups (Hutu and Tutsi along with the third, Twa) represented their own forms of social elitism, not racism, before being transformed. Individuals could, and indeed did, toggle across these social categories as a result of the then economic order. But a deliberate colonial policy transformed the old, dynamic social categories into distinctly unequal castes opposing *Hutu* to *Tutsi* (and peripheralized *Twa* in relation to the other two) as though they had never had anything to do with each other before. That identity redesign engendered a new thought system of how conflicts and political order would subsequently be imagined. It set new norms for power competition in the new political landscape.

The Effects of Colonization on Rwanda's Security Dynamics

Precolonial Rwanda had different notions of identity which had been grounded and also more open, malleable, and interlocked. Such notions included *umuryango* (kinship groups), *imiryango* (a larger social group, or clan), and the versatile concept of *ubwoko*, "race, species, family, order" (Chrétien et al. 1995: 333; Vansina 2004: 33–38). Clan, the umbrella term for such larger social groups, superseded all other identity sobriquets in practice. At least twenty-seven total clans existed across precolonial Rwanda and subsumed all other subsidiary identity levels, including the social categories of Tutsi, Hutu, and Twa. When Belgian rulers arrived in Rwandan in the early 1900s, they worked with the existing monarchy and within the existing identity order. Local rulers came from the group called *Nyiginya*, one of the many clans that also overlapped with the group of Tutsi.[4] But seeking to consolidate its power, the colonial administration restudied, reclassified, and limited the collective identity to just a three-category typology of Hutu, Tutsi, and Twa.

To seal it off into practice, the administration also introduced the identity card system in the 1930s, inscribing *de facto* those new ideas into the formal institutions of the state. That policy bestowed upon every citizen a categorical, exclusive attribution. Each citizen's ID would hence bear only one of the three categories and was left with no choice, except what was inscribed on the official ID card. The first census—establishing the foundation for the notions of pluralistic power balance and differences—sanctioned that Hutu were 84 percent, Tutsi 14 percent, and Twa less than 1 percent.[5] The traditional clan system disappeared as a result, at least in the power system. Not as a result of organic processes but as a conscious design of the colonial power, the internal patterns of socioeconomic and sociopolitical relations changed forever.

As those changes took place, the clergy—leaders of the Catholic Church—worked as the right hand of the colonial administration. The church acted as "a contractor" of the colonial rule, in that it prescribed and delivered every social service, including health care, education, agriculture, and so on, in addition to converting members into Christians (Gaud 1995: 3–4). The then king of Rwanda even dedicated his now Christian nation to "King Jesus," shortly after World War II. Hutus were, based on the recent census results, the majority in the country. By virtue of plurality, Hutus filled up churches more than Tutsis. But because the colonial rule had found *Aba-Nyiginya* (who became permanently subsumed into the new brand of Tutsi) in power and propped them up first. Local members, church leaders, as well as other auxiliary leaders in the congregation were also Tutsi. When the alliances of Belgians and Tutsi elite began to dwindle—primarily as the later questioned, resented, and resisted the ultimate colonial intentions—a new campaign to *democratize* the nation began.

Undergirding the call for a new political change was the logic that throughout its existence, the majority (Hutu) had been unjustly dominated by a minority (Tutsi) and that it was time to balance history. The church supported this *Hutu* nationalist campaign in the 1950s. It did so by supporting the birth of the Party for Emancipation of Hutu Populace (PARMEHUTU), which promptly spread nationally with one goal: to advance the cause of Hutu members and to bring them to development, power, and self-determination. At the same time, the church was an active and effective influencer of virtually all social spheres including the sociodemocratic platforms. The church—now acting as a hybrid democratic-Christian defense entity—seemed unbothered at all that PARMEHUTU's primary agenda was principally rooted in ethnically divisive motives. For the newly groomed members of the Hutu elite, the priority was to nab power from Tutsi and place it where it was supposed to be, on the majority side.

Concomitant with that vision, a narrative about Tutsi had to be conjured up and seeded in the public imaginary to justify these abrupt changes. Otherwise, it made no sense that a trivial minority had ruled the kingdom of Rwanda for so long, so effectively, and so autocratically without being challenged by the *vox populi*. An effective discourse about Tutsi's ascendance to power and the subsequent "subjugation" of a majority had to be explained in such a way that ousting them from power at that time seemed only judicious. That change had drawn from the knowledge produced and popularized by the colonial administration about the Tutsi rulership.

Belgian rulers—products of the scientific racism era—had extensively studied and documented the Rwandan governance system. That was necessary or they would not have been able to control it. They understood well the workings of the *Nyiginya* monarchical system but were puzzled by both its origins and the endurance of its establishment. Therefore, they created a discourse that connected it to a foreign provenance to justify how one group of Africans had been able to successfully govern another for that long. To Belgian rulers, *Nyiginya* rulers ought to have stemmed from non-African origins. The documented narrative had it that *Nyiginya* people (also called Tutsi) were long descendants of the Ham lineage who had come from Abyssinia or Egypt to profit from the *Aba-Hutu*.[6] The colonial narrative contended that Tutsi were too intelligent to derive from the Bantu people, from which Hutu belonged. The newly developed Hutu elites quickly embraced and propagated that Tutsis were foreigners and conquerors. And for both the Belgian Church leaders and the Hutu elite, reclaiming power from Tutsi through revolutionary means was a legitimate democratic action. While bringing about democracy—a principle in which the will of the majority ought to prevail—was paramount, it also meant that the principle of respecting the minority was less important and hence ignored.

The year 1959 would become the turning point in materializing both the Belgian objectives and the newly groomed Hutu elites' promised change. On the day which became widely known as *"La Toussaint Rwandaise"* (Rwandan Lent), the nation witnessed the beginning of what would officially be branded the "social revolution." But it was, in reality, the first massacre of Tutsi in the history of the nation (Chrétien 1991: 113; Lemarchand 1970a: 216; Reyntjens 1985: 466; Schimmel 2011). Between 20,000 and 100,000 were killed in a slaughter that the British philosopher Bertrand Russell then described in *Le Monde* as "the most horrible and systematic massacre we have had occasion to witness since the extermination of the Jews by the Nazis" (quoted in Eltringham 2004: 43; see also Goose and Smyth 1994: 88). The massacre forced additional 150,000 to 350,000 Tutsi to exile in the neighboring Uganda, Burundi, Tanzania, and Zaire (Africa Watch 1993; Des Forges 1999: 40; Ndahiro and Rwagatare 2015: 30; Watson 1991). There is no indication that the Belgian rulers were taken aback by the consequences of their disseminated ideas and enforced policies. With the colossal economic, social, political, and military clout they still held over the new administration—even after independence—the colonial community did not recommend or advocate for corrective measures.

In Uganda, Tutsi *Banya-rwanda* and their descendants suffered—socially and politically—under the tyranny of dictators, including Milton Obote and Idi Amin. They lived in refugee camps and were subjugated, discriminated against, and lacked citizenship and legal residence. In these countries, "they were vulnerable to deportation, displacement, and harassment" (Smyth 1994: 585). Back home, paradoxically, none of the consecutive Hutu governments tried to correct the very vice of exclusive and ethnic-based rule that they had accused their Tutsi predecessors of. Different post-1959 Hutu governments did not show the compunction of their discriminatory identity policies nor the willingness to repatriate their exiled (Tutsi) compatriots. Instead, in a series of on-and-off episodes, governments continued to massacre Tutsi in Rwanda since the "revolution" that ousted the monarchial rule. These recurring state-sanctioned killings were often referred to as "work" or "clearing the bush" (Eltringham 2004: 34–38; quoted in Gourevitch 1995; see also Huggins 2009: 184). They were sporadic and seasonal and went on until the Rwandan Patriotic Front (RPF) members decided to launch a major invasion on October 1, 1990, against the current government.

In the early 1980s, at least 2,000 young Tutsi exiles had joined a Ugandan guerrilla movement led by a former defense minister, Yoweri Kaguta Museveni, to oust the autocrat Milton Obote. Those Rwandan refugees had joined a foreign insurgency with the hope that once it seized power and restored social and political equality in Uganda, then that new power system would, in return, help them achieve the same objectives in their country of origin, Rwanda. Subsequently, in October 1982, the Ugandan autocrat Obote expelled 80,000 Rwandan refugees whom he accused of siding with his opponents; Habyarimana of Rwanda, arguing that the country was overpopulated, expelled them back into Uganda (Gaud 1995: 24). In 1986, Museveni's guerrilla ousted Obote and became the new leader of Uganda. A year later, the RPF, a political movement composed of regionally exiled Rwandans, was founded and established against the Habyarimana government. Again in 1986, President Habyarimana of Rwanda compared the eventual return of

Tutsi exiles to pouring another drop into an already-full glass, implying that there was no extra room left in the nation to house regional refugees Huggins (2009: 185); (Kayihura and Zukus 2014: 36). He also conducted policies that nefariously singled out Tutsi and discriminated against them. One such policy was the *quota* system which ensured that no more than 9 percent of seats in public services and higher education be given to Tutsi; the goal for the policy was to weed out "surplus" students (Eltringham 2004: 21; Gourevitch 1995; Huggins 2009: 184).

When the RPF launched the armed invasion through Rwanda's northern border with Uganda in October, it sought to (a) put an end to the exclusivist *Hutu Power* rule, (b) repatriate the exiles, and (c) institute an inclusive political order. The civil war claimed 4,500 lives, both combatants and noncombatants, and internally displaced about an additional million, or at least one out of seven civilians (Human Rights Watch 1994: 4).

On the government side, the national conversation about the war was developed along purely ethnic lines and was rooted in the same rhetoric of the 1959 "social revolution" (Eltringham 2004: 44–45; Gourevitch 1995; Huggins 2009: 185–186). The reference to 1959 supported that "the feudal-monarchical" minority, "the Tutsi," had oppressed "the Hutu" and the so-called *peuple majoritaire* (a code phrase for Hutu) had successfully implemented its "popular" or "democratic will" by rising up against "the Tutsi" who were now returning to obliterate that order by means of war. Therefore, as the official discourse had it, the "country" was at war against *Inyangarwanda* (renegades of Rwanda), and the time now called for the *peuple* to "embrace the just cause," to "vehemently defend the nation" once again, to guard "the gains of the 1959 revolution," and to quell the "the oppressor" whose intention was to suppress the republican institutions; and in order to do so, "the Hutu must stop having pity on the Tutsi!" (Chrétien 1991: 116–119).[7] In this incendiary rhetoric campaign, members of the RPF were publicly cast as *Inyenzi* (cockroaches) who, whether outside or inside Rwanda, deserved to be fought with all means and *uprooted-ly* (*inkundura*). The subsequent logic was that the Tutsi on the war front along with their internal *ibyitso,* "accomplices" (along with any Hutu opposing that nationalist Hutu ideology), were deemed enemies of the country. At the same time, as the government recruited and armed Hutu youth militias for "civil defense," massacres of Tutsi and assassination of Hutu oppositionists proceeded with regularity across the nation.

In August 1993, the war was at its peak. President Juvénal Habyarimana faced pressure from both the members of his inner circle and the RPF insurgency. But as he even signed a power-sharing peace accord with the RPF in Arusha, Tanzania, extremist Hutu members in his inner circle began to speculate that he himself had become an accomplice (Gourevitch 1995; Huggings

2009: 200).[8] Political campaigns had also polarized across that same ethnic ideology. Anti-Tutsi propaganda took a crescendo and was broadcast on national media and published in journals and magazines days and nights. "Let whatever is blistering burst," *Kangura*, a Hutu extremist newspaper, advised in January of 1994, clarifying that "at such a time, a lot of blood will be poured" (cited in Gourevitch 1995). In March 1994, *Kangura* ran a new headline that read "Habyarimana will die in March," explaining that the assassins would be Hutus bought by the cockroaches (idem.).

THE MATERIAL COMPOSITION OF THE WAR: HOW INTERNATIONAL ACTORS BUILT IT UP

In this conflict, the parties needed both numerical superiority and more firepower of its army to prevail. But to the extent that the parties were poor and marginal in composition, their military superiority was externally mobilized. An edge in military capabilities was therefore sought from preexisting alliances. On the one hand, the Habyarimana government had Mobutu, the president of then Zaire from whom he received substantial troops to help fight the RPF. But those troops were ill-equipped, ill-trained, and were not even well-treated or incentivized at home. The Zairian troops, therefore, lacked a fundamental stake in the Rwandan conflict. They were not a force Habyarimana could rely on to prevail over the blitzkrieg RPF who was driven and determined to the core. For that, Habyarimana sought mightier combat troops, equipment, and strategy that he could not find in the region. He turned to Belgium and France with whom he had long and close ties.

On the other hand, the RPF had Uganda and Britain, but unlike the Habyarimana allies, none of these two allies actually sent their own troops to the battlefield. When the RPF launched its insurgency against the government of Rwanda through the northern border with Uganda, more than half of its initial troops and all of its officers were drawn from Uganda's National Resistance Army (NRA). They all had Rwandan original roots and had served in the NRA in Uganda. The idea of launching an attack against the government they decried was their own in both design and human capital requirements. Over the following years, the RPF recruited and expanded out of Rwandan diasporic exiles scattered in the region (Tanzania, Burundi, Zaire, and Uganda).

What is noticeable about the dynamics of those alliances and the leverage they provided is how they differed in origins, volume, and outcome. One would have thought that regional dynamics would be sufficient to bequeath logistical superiority upon one side over the other and therefore shape the outcome of the war, but remarkably they were not. The support to the

Habyarimana government came almost exclusively from his international allies, France and Belgium. Materially, Great Britain offered no support to the RPF, or if there ever was one, it was absolutely invisible. In the region, Zaire and Uganda had been directly connected to Rwanda's war, each supporting one side and such support continued throughout the war but fulfilling different outcomes. On the Habyarimana government's side, it was France—not Zaire—that gave it the material leverage it needed. France played the role of logistical furnisher, strategic overseer, and the *de facto* guarantor of the government's security. But France's support to the Habyarimana government also obviated the rules of the international system and ultimately led to deleterious results in this conflict. Conversely, Britain was not materially tutelary to the RPF. Its support to the RPF was hardly noticeable (be it in London or on the battlefield), and if there ever was one, Uganda was the proxy actor. Museveni provided a training ground for the RPF soldiers and was their immediate *de facto* protector, but not to the level commensurate with that of France to the Habyarimana government.

France's Overreach in the Conflict

At the outbreak of the war, the government of Rwanda drew from its existing stock of Belgian automatic rifles and French-armored vehicles. But Rwanda quickly noticed it was understocked, under siege, and needed to amplify itself as mightily and quickly as the fast advancing RPF troops prompted. Its 5,000 army troops rapidly rose to 40,000; the RPF's was estimated at 3,000 and had, by end of the war, grown to 8,000. Until then, Belgium—Rwanda's former colonial power—had been its main trade partner, political ally, and military patron. But Belgium had an explicit policy against providing lethal arms to a country at war. Following the RPF attack, Belgium continued to provide military training, boots, and uniforms to the Rwandan army but did not provide arms.[9] However, France did and provided far more than just arms even in stark defiance and violation of international norms.[10] A government-sanctioned weapons contract signed on March 30, 1992, indicated, "the BUYER and the SUPPLIER agree not to show the content of this contract to third parties" (documented in Smyth 1994: 586). Rwanda was the buyer and Egypt the seller. It was a $6 million transaction to procure Egypt-made Kalashnikov rifles, antipersonnel mines, plastic explosives, mortars, and long-range artillery to Rwanda. More documents indicated that the sale was financed by a "first-rate international bank approved by" Egypt (idem). The government of Rwanda paid $1 million in cash up front, promised to pay the next $1 million with 615 tons of reserve tea, and the balance would be paid at the rate of $1 million over the next four years. The "first-rate international bank" guaranteed Rwanda's payment of full $6 million. Few commercial banks—traditionally profit-driven institutions—would take on such a risk at that time. But "Crédit Lyonnais" did. It was a nationalized bank of France at the time of the transaction. As Smyth (idem) surmises, the sale was *ipso facto* a secret military assistance from France to Rwanda. In the following period, it morphed into a subsidy given to the Rwandan government by France. Quite unexpectedly though, those arrangements were quickly upset when the RPF captured the Mulindi tea factory and the plantation surrounding it later that month. The harvest did not happen, and the tea was spoiled. "Our economy was already ailing in 1990, and of course the war has not resolved anything," President Habyarimana declared in October 1992.

But to understand France's obsession over Rwanda's security control, as well as the significance of its power during the war, one must revisit the events harking to long before the *Crédit Lyonnais's* illicit arms sponsoring and its cover-up. Only two days after the war had broken out (October 3rd, 1990), François Mitterrand, the French president, ordered *Opération Noroît*, a special force of 680 men, to help Habyarimana repel the RPF troops who had come just less than 15 miles to Kigali, the capital city (Gregory 2000: 439; Guichaoua 2020: 156–158; Thomann 1998: 138).[11] Within less than three months, there were eighty seasoned French military advisers based in Rwanda, availed by the *Elysée*, coordinating daily operations with President Habyarimana and his senior commanders (Smolar 2011). On the ground and outside of Rwanda, French officials continued to collect intelligence on and for the war, advising, and supplying more weapons to the government of Rwanda (Soudan 2015: 42). In three years, the French troops in Rwanda had grown to 3,000. Jean Christophe Mitterrand, the son of the French president and the head of African policy unit at the *Elysée*, was the permanent focal point official bridging the two governments as he intensified the support to the Rwandan government throughout the wartime.

As French officials procured more weapons and trainings, the troops on the ground stood by and watched the Rwandan presidential guard organize *Interahamwe*, the Frankenstein monsters that carried out the systematic murders of innocent men, women, and children because—on the basis of *Tutsi*-ness—they had become the state's enemies along with the RPF troops (Gregory 2000: 439–442; Wallis 2006). Amidst these murders, French officials rushed to defend the record of the Habyarimana regime instead. "Civilians were killed as in any war," said Colonel Cussac, the French military attaché, to journalists in Kigali at that time. During a short press conference, Colonel Cussac declined to give his first name and was defiant with a disdainful attitude toward those who pressed him on France's role in this conflict. "Are you saying that the provision of military assistance is a human rights violence?" (idem) he retorted, appealing to old sentiments. "France and the United States have a common history—for example, in Vietnam" (idem).

Yet, all non-French Western diplomats in Kigali were critical of France's role. Those diplomats along with other relief workers were all aware and publicly voiced their concerns over France providing artillery support for the Rwandan government infantry troops and that French advisers had been attached to Rwandan high commanders (Smyth 1994: 587).

It is unclear whether "Cussac" was his real identity, but it is clear that the information on the Rwandan war that the French officials were sharing with the public differed and contradicted what they shared among themselves. Recently declassified files revealed that on October 12, 1990—less than two weeks into the war—a certain Colonel Galinié, the head of military operations in Kigali, had alerted, in a telegram, his superiors in Paris to the fact that the Habyarimana government had been committing murders against Tutsi civilians. "It is to be feared that this conflict may wind up into an ethnic warfare" (quoted in Smolar 2011), the telegraph noted. Next day, Ambassador Georges Martres of France in Kigali, the superior of Colonel Galinié, reiterated the killings in another report: "organized by the MRND (party of the President), Hutu civilians have ramped up the hunting of Tutsi suspects in hills. Mass killings have been reported in the area of Kibilira," adding that the presidential loyalists were "increasingly taking part in military actions through self-defense groups who are armed with bows and arrows and machetes" (idem.). But in spite of unequivocal signs that a government they supported was targeting innocent civilians, French officials did not review or rescind that backing. Nor did they use their influence to impugn Habyarimana and constrain him to end the ongoing massacres of Tutsi civilians. Quite to the contrary, the French support increased over the following years.

In the near term, the French military intervention helped the *Forces Armées Rwandaises* (FAR) regain control of the territory they had previously lost. It reinvigorated their morale on the battlefield and reduced their fear to lose to the RPF. For the government, the presence of French troops on their side meant that winning the war against a rowdy but less comparable insurgency—one that had started with 3,000 fighters—was certainly possible. Fighting from the wings of the might of French arsenal provided the government troops with prevailing guarantees. But France's direct involvement in the conflict meant more than just material superiority, and to both sides. In the first place, France's siding with the FAR legitimized the behavior of Rwandan officials and troops, including the assassinations of Tutsi civilians. When the French officials and troops expressed no concerns or sanctions over the killings of innocent civilians but went on to supply and support the regime even further, it encouraged the latter to expand the killings across the country. It meant that there were no serious consequences the government would face from major powers or that France would otherwise continue to defend it and the cause its officials were advancing. In the second place, France joining the

FAR in the war also conveyed a message of capital importance to the RPF. The overzealous boost bestowed upon the government troops by France reinforced RPF's convictions that it had every good reason to fight the oppressive regime to the last ounce of strength. For the RPF officials, the choice was clear: to either duck and slide back into the perpetual plight of exile life or to pursue self-determination in the homeland even if all odds appeared stuck against them. France directly combating the RPF troops in Rwanda meant that unless they too stepped up the fight, no other actor in the international system was coming to the rescue of *Tutsi* civilians under assault domestically and those in exile. France's involvement in this conflict reshuffled and reshaped calculation strategies of both the government of Rwanda and the RPF, and ultimately contributed to the loss of hundreds of thousands of victims during and after the war.

France's Calculations in the War

For the *Elysée*, the primordial objective was first and foremost to stop the RPF from disrupting the France-Africa order that Habyarimana guaranteed in the region. Therefore, the prevailing strategy into this war was "tit for tat" by upping the "Rwandan capabilities" (Smolar 2011). For France, the urgency called for defending Habyarimana at all cost as the only way to stop the expanding English-speaking influence in the region that Britain was pushing for through Uganda, the supporter of a Tutsi-led insurgency. In the logics of French foreign policy, Rwanda ought to remain in the bloc of 21 Francophone African nations at all cost.

To achieve its foreign policy objectives, France went to great length to rally a mighty military complex (material, strategic, and infantry) around the Habyarimana government, its military, and its militias. In just the first few hours of the war, France rushed in 60 mm, 81 mm, and 120 mm mortars and 105 mm light artillery guns. Within the first month into the war, France provided seasoned advisers and four companies of 680 combat troops to the government. It also concocted unlawful financial operations to descend more arms into the hands of the Rwandan government troops. France was also involved in conducting media campaigns on the behalf of the Habyarimana government. But all those efforts were not winning the war that France had banked on to maintain Rwanda in its African geopolitical sphere. Quite surprisingly, the RPF was winning the war against the French and the Habyarimana coalition. When the civil war had practically ended with almost no recourse left to salvage that Rwando-French coalition, France decided to deploy even a much larger military operation in Rwanda. The RPF had upset the existing geo-colonial order that France had maintained in the region since the 1960s. French officials understood it well but persisted with the thought that somehow a reversal was possible. They cast *Opération Turquoise* as a purely humanitarian intervention with one mission, to create a "safe zone" in the southwestern region of Rwanda. But both the timing and the volume of the mission contradicted the humanitarian basis it purported.

The Washington Post expressed skepticism about the renewed French intervention in Rwanda casting doubt on its initial humanitarian goal. "Such impartiality is in contrast to the military, economic and diplomatic support France has provided the government of President Juvenal Habyarimana" (Randal 1994). Again, just earlier, between October 1, 1990, and April 1994, France had deployed over 3,000 troops in Rwanda. But this time, between June 23 and August 22, 1994—the duration of *Opération Turquoise*—France deployed additional 3,400 ground force troops, 1,000 armored vehicles, 120 mm marine mortar battery, 600 other vehicles, 8 Super Puma (heavy) helicopters, 2 light Gazelle helicopters, 4 Mirage F1CT ground attack aircraft, 4 Mirage F1CT reconnaissance aircraft, 4 Jaguar strike/fighter aircraft, 6 C-130 tactical-lift aircraft, 9 Transall tactical-lift aircraft, 1 Airbus (chartered) strategic-lift aircraft, 1 Boeing 747 (chartered) strategic-lift aircraft, and 2 Antonov An-124. The total mission airlifted cargo weighed 9,000 tons (Kuperman 2004: 46); all for an area of some 4,000 square miles, less than a quarter of Rwanda's area.

Logically, the new French military intervention makes it difficult to reconcile the humanitarian benefits it intended to achieve and the unspoken strategic motives behind its disproportional volume at the time when the war had almost ended. It only becomes clear that it was already too late to truly save lives when *Opération Turquoise* deployed on June 23, 1994. And considering the overt loathing with which French authorities regarded the RPF before, during and after the war, there is even more doubt to cast on whether the mission objectively carried a "humanitarian" characteristic in any fundamental sense.[12] The bewildering fact about this French military redeployment on June 23, 1994, is that the Habyarimana army had already been defeated. The genocide had already claimed 95 percent of the victims. And the so-called "safe zone" had now become the safe haven for the assassin regime and its militiamen. It was in the French patrolled "safe zone" that the remnants of the ailing regime, including government officials, the military, the *Interahamwe* militias, the national radio, the treasury, and any other nabbed public assets, had established their last fort and enjoyed full French protection as they slowly awaited to cross the border into Zaire, now the Democratic Republic of Congo.[13] This overly zealous support by France to the Rwandan government until its final ailing moments was a testimony that the French national interests in this war superseded by far all else and that they had to be defended no matter the cost and no matter the human cost.

It is also difficult to isolate the number of victims incurred by the civil war—exactly because the murderous regime did not stop but rather increased when the plane carrying President Habyarimana (with his Burundian counterpart) was missile downed on April 6, 1994, marking the official start of the genocide of Tutsi—but we know that Rwanda had an approximate population of 7.2 million before the war began. When the genocide had just ended in July 1994, between 800,000 and 1,074,017 (UN and Republic of Rwanda 2002) had been murdered. That month, USAID estimated that 2,576,000 people were displaced inside Rwanda, including 1.3 million in the French-army-controlled *Zone Turquoise*. An additional 2,223,000 people were refugees outside of Rwanda, including 1,542,000 in Zaire, 21,000 in Burundi, 406,500 in Tanzania, and 10,500 in Uganda. That alone represented 5,299,000 people, or 73 percent of the national population, who had been either killed or uprooted.[14] At that time, The RPF did not have presence yet in the French-controlled *Zone Turquoise*. When the French left on August 22, 1994, the militias, the military, the now nomadic government officials, as well as regular fleeing citizens had crossed the Zairian border (now the Democratic Republic of the Congo) and found a safe haven on the other side of Rwanda. The number of Rwandan refugees who had resettled across the border, into Zaire, had risen to over 3 million.

The Ugandan Hand and Invisibility of Great Britain in the War

On the RPF side, Uganda did not send its troops to battle the government of Habyarimana. But it provided the RPF with an array of small arms and other weapons systems, including recoilless cannons and Soviet-made Katyusha multiple rocket launchers. Uganda always denied arming and supporting the RPF, but it is hardly conceivable that the latter would run a vast logistical operation consisting in large quantities of weapons and fuel across the tightly run country across the Rwandan border without the awareness of the Ugandan high-ranking officials (Hammer and de Hoyos 1994: 30). "We are committed to the RPF," one Ugandan military officer once confided in Smyth (1994: 587) in Kampala, "if they didn't have our support, they wouldn't be as successful as they are." In addition, many in Uganda knew that the Rwandan exiles who had helped Yoweri Museveni defeat Milton Obote and accede to power several years ago had done so with the precise calculations that he, in return, would help them remove the government that had oppressed and refused to repatriate them. An invasion against the Habyarimana government had been churning for a while. People knew that nothing else was left for that process to begin. It was a matter of the RPF military commanders' own timing. At one point, the RPF soldiers who had served in the Ugandan army bid farewell to their families and friends even openly (Smyth 1994: 587) or what else would have motivated them to eagerly retire at such a premature juncture of their military experiences.

Right before the invasion time, the RPF soldiers traveled with their weapons in plain view of Ugandan authorities, over two days, and even gathered in a soccer stadium in Kabale, about 200 miles southwest of Kampala and just north of the Rwandan border. Their weaponry included land mines, rocket-propelled grenades, 60 millimeter mortars, recoilless cannons, and Katyusha rocket launchers. Many diplomats, as well as international observers knew and spoke about it that Uganda had willingly provided more arms, food, gasoline, batteries, and ammunition to the RPF throughout the war (idem).

Although France considered the Rwandan civil war a threat posed by the Anglo-Saxons—and therefore made effusive material investments to quell such threat—the supposed rivals (Britain and the United States) were absolutely *materially* uninvolved. And there is no evidence that the battle equipment used by the RPF was manufactured or furnished by the British or the Americans. Furthermore, the material support provided to the Habyarimana government by the French government far outweighed that of what Uganda gave to the RPF. In every material sense about wars that made France the ultimate dominant hand in the Rwandan conflict.

The War, a Skewed International System, More External Actors, and an Arm Race in Rwanda

When the Cold War ended, in the early 1990s, the international community worried more about nuclear arms proliferation, and subsequently ignored trade in light conventional arms. This priority in international security had a direct implication on the Rwandan war. Peacekeeping efforts in conflict-dominated zones became difficult to regulate. Just as in any other small states during that time, Rwanda exploited the systemic legal loopholes in arms trade and embargo to add more weapons in circulation and in the conflict. Opportunities of easy access to arms alone did not lead to wars *per se,* but they made it difficult for enemies to consider ending the conflict. As Goose and Smyth (1994: 88) have described it in the Rwandan case, "arms suppliers rushed to both sides like vultures to a carcass." As the war went on, the government of Rwanda even distributed more arms into the population. At one point, Kalashnikovs in Rwanda became "more common than bicycles" (Smyth 1994: 585).

Russians, Romanians, Bulgarians, Czechs, Slovaks, and others were aggressively promoting arms sales (Goose and Smyth 1994: 89). The collapse of Moscow's central control had given governments and the officials left in charge of existing stockpiles a free hand. Eastern European nations were no longer constrained by the bounds of superpower loyalties; "the only thing that then mattered to them was cash" (Smyth 1994: 586). James Gasana, Rwanda's Defense Minister, said in 1993 that most countries and independent dealers from whom they had acquired arms "were less interested in who won the war than in taking money on it" (idem). By that year, the Habyarimana government had already bought enough arms from Russia, especially Kalashnikov AKMs. But the key suppliers for the government forces were France, Egypt (also sponsored by France), and South Africa. A $6 million contract between Egypt and Rwanda in March 1992, with Rwanda's payment guaranteed by a French Bank, included 60-mm and 82-mm mortars, 16,000 mortar shells, 122-mm D-30 howitzers, 3,000 artillery shells, rocket-propelled grenades, plastic explosives, antipersonnel land mines, and more than 3 million rounds of small arms ammunition.

South Africa also supplied small arms, including R-4 automatic rifles, 7.62 mm machine guns, and 12.7 mm Browning machine guns. The government-owned Armscor had for years manufactured high-quality weapons for its security and defense forces, which could not buy guns abroad because of a U.S. embargo. While this resolution was binding, another one, against buying arms from South Africa, was not. The Rwandan government ignored it. In October 1992, on the heels of the Egyptian deal, Rwanda made a $5.9 million purchase from South Africa: hundred 60-mm mortars, seventy 40-mm grenade launchers with 10,000 grenades, 20,000 rifle grenades, 10,000 hand grenades, spare parts and 1.5 million rounds of ammunition for R-4 rifles, and 1 million rounds of machine gun ammunition. By late 1993, within a year of its initial $5.9 million purchase, Rwanda had decided to standardize its infantry forces with South African arms, especially the R-4 assault rifle, which is superior to the Kalashnikov. These purchases from South Africa were in contravention with the UN Security Council Resolution 558 that opposed importation of weapons from South Africa.[15]

An arms race was underway in Rwanda. More than dozen nations rushed into both make money and help fuel the Rwandan war. And both sides purchased weaponry through private sources on the open market. By its own admission, the Rwanda government bankrupted its economy to pay for those weapons. Former Warsaw Pact countries appear to have supplied both sides, seeing opportunity in Rwanda less than one year after the Berlin Wall fell (Smyth 1994: 586). On the RPF side, combatants carried Kalashnikov AKM automatic rifles, many manufactured in Romania. Not all of the RPF fighters wore military uniforms, but most of those who did had distinctive East German rain-pattern camouflage.

A mass-scale proliferation of arms inside the country was underway. The Rwandan authorities had already distributed large numbers of firearms to militia members and other supporters long before the genocide began.

The proliferation of arms understandably crystalized the conflict even more deeply, violated the international law, increased human rights abuses, and gave strength to the unprecedented pace at which the subsequent genocide would happen in the following months. In the year preceding the Genocide alone, at the height of the civil war, one out of eight Rwandans—one million—had already been internally displaced refugees as a result of the crescendo of the war. It is also to note that while other states—especially Eastern European and South Africa—contributed to the material buildup for the war, their role remained only peripheral. That did not shape the course of the conflict beyond a marginal level. Instead, the decisions that influenced the two sides in a deterministic way and shaped both the balance of power and the outcome of the conflict were made by the French authorities.

THE GEOPOLITICAL CHARACTER OF THE WAR: MANIFESTATIONS OF ANGLO-FRENCH RIVALRY

At glance, Rwanda is not geopolitically germane to great power competition. That is the argument often made to explain the refusal of Western powers to intervene during the 1994 Genocide (Silver 2015: 22; 40–41). Right before the civil war, Rwanda's population counted just 7.2 million, with a GDP per capita of $381 in 1990. Its active duty military force totaled some 5,000 troops (IISS 1993: 215) even though it shot up to 40,000 during the war. Geographically, Rwanda is landlocked, which maintains it perpetually dependent on the Tanzanian and Kenyan port entries for virtually all essential commodities. That means there are not much—outside minerals, coffee, tea, and recently tourism—that Rwanda sells to the world. There was no other special feature to Rwanda's geopolitical predisposition that would eminently cause global powers to go after each other since colonialism.

Yet, geo-locatedly and on substance, Rwanda is far more appealing than simple interpretations have suggested. This is not a perspective based on mere assumptions because, although the two powers (France and Britain) never openly disparaged or exposed each other over their ambitions on Rwanda, their strategies could hardly conceal what was at play behind sight. The two former colonial powers were secretly fighting to control Rwanda in two sharply different ways. The French adopted a more hands-on, militarist approach (Charbonneau 2014: 620; 2016: 121–148; 2008: 282; de Saint-Exupéry 2004; Dumoulin 1997: 123–125; Kroslak 2007), while the British used a subterranean and decentralized hand (Hammer & de Hoyos 1994). These two powers used the same colonization techniques of a century earlier. In Rwanda, France deployed its troops, supported, armed, trained those of the regime fighting the insurgent RPF troops (Gregory 2000: 440–441; McNulty

2000). Conversely, the British officials worked through Uganda to support RPF in its war against the French-backed Habyarimana regime (Hammer and de Hoyos 1994: 24–25).

France's Geopolitical Obduracy and Rwanda's Misfortunes

As early as two days after the war had begun, François Mitterrand, the French President himself designated the Rwanda matter a priority of high order. He immediately ordered a special force of 680 French paratroopers to help the Habyarimana government push the RPF troops back into Uganda. He also commissioned a team of seasoned military advisers who, daily, planned and gathered intelligence on the behalf of the government of Rwanda. Jean Christophe Mitterrand, his son and the head of African policy unit at the *Elysée*, intensified the support to the government of Rwanda over the next years while also providing the oversight of the war on the behalf of the French and the Rwandan presidents.

But even long before they lost hegemonic influence on Rwanda in late 1994 and on the Congo in 1996, French officials and their intelligence had always expressed overt concerns that Rwanda and Burundi were geostrategically ill-perched and worried they would fall to the Anglo-Saxon influence someday, which would displace France's power in the region (Charbonneau 2006; Gregory 2000: 440–443). And the civil war in Rwanda in the 1990s exposed the depth of that concern as well as the extent to which the French authorities were willing to go to prevent it. The Rwandan war was nothing but a new site upon which the customary France–Britain hegemonic feuds took place (Gibson 2011; Horne 2005; Johnson et al. 1980; Tombs et al. 2007), except that this time it was in the Great Lakes Region of Africa (Cummings 2011: 549–555).[16] The opposing sides in the war—one established postcolonial regime, on the one hand, and a denigrated postcolonial insurgency, on the other—were proxy actors in a geopolitical warfare that had brought French and British postcolonial ambitions into collision.

On their side, France wanted to maintain Rwanda (along with Burundi) in its central African sphere of influence as a buffer against the British ambitions to expand westward.[17] President Mitterrand personally worried that the fall of Rwanda (from a Hutu-controlled regime into the hands of the Tutsi-led RPF) would spur a chain reaction that would subsequently disrupt the French established geopolitical order, and hence France would no longer be apt to safeguard its interests and maintain its guarantees in the region (Wallis 2006). But in an effort to quell those fears, the French president was confronted with his own contradictions. On the one hand, there had been a crescendo in the killings of *Tutsi* civilians by the government forces that he had armed and supported during the previous years, and therefore he needed to appear as a patron who cared about human rights and who could coerce President Habyarimana into ending the violence. On the other, President Mitterrand wanted to save his ally, Habyarimana (the regional steward of French interests), from falling. His conversations about the Rwandan crisis with cabinet members during that time juxtaposed both the eminence of France's strategic domination and ethical paradoxes. "The rule is that a French military action should be only when there is a foreign attack and not a tribal conflict. Here, it's a mix, because there is the *tutsi* problem" (quoted in Smolar 2011).

As massacres went on, France found itself in embarrassing and vulnerable, yet pretentious positions. Various speeches by the French officials displayed the desire to defend the French geopolitical interests in the region, but also to settle between ambitions and pretentions, and in between were overt contradictions. On February 15, 1993, for example, Bruno Delaye, a diplomat on African affairs wrote a memo to President Mitterrand ringing a bell to the fact that the members of the RPF were "ready to capture Kigali," but also lamented that "the cunny complicity of the Anglo-Saxon world" along with an "excellent propaganda system that is capitalizing on the unfortunate massacres by Hutu extremists" (quoted in Smolar 2011) had enabled the RPF success.

At some point, everything that happened on the battlefield appeared to be a direct result of decisions made in Paris, by the French officials. Not only did they decide the size, quantity, and type of weapons to provide, the *Elysée* officials indeed designed what the war would look like in both short and long terms. From January 1991, two months after the war had begun, President Mitterrand met regularly with several members of the French security community to build a strategy for Rwanda. He wrote a letter to President Habyarimana on January 30, 1991, clarifying which terms he would have to consider before accepting any political settlement with the adversary. President Mitterand's list of conditions to President Habyarimana was paired with "a massive military support" (idem). On February 3, 1991, Admiral Jacques Lanxade, French Army Chief of Staff, submitted a blueprint for what would happen, including deployment of an onsite military assistance and instruction unit (DAMI).[18] The DAMI had as mandate to "strengthen cooperation" and "toughen up the Rwandan military capability" (idem). Although the goal was apparently to help a French ally win a war against his enemies, the French officials behaved as though winning it was intricately connected to France's geopolitical fate in Africa. Otherwise, their behavior would not justify anything other than the idea that they co-owned (if not over-owned) the fate of this war than the people it affected directly.

Even in the midst of a rain of unambiguous reports stemming from the field on the massacres targeting Tutsi civilians, the French authorities clang

to their ultimate goal of preserving regional influence. Recently declassified files show that on February 18, 1994, the French Bureau of Foreign
Intelligence (DGSE) wrote a warning memo on the "true ethnic cleansing"
and on the 300 deaths identified during the weeks before, clarifying that
"there may be a vast campaign of "ethnic cleansing" directed against Tutsi"
by the higher echelons of the state (quoted in Smolar 2011). Yet, General
Christian Quesnot, the French Army Chief of Staff and special adviser to
President Mitterrand on Africa, moved the attention from the killing of civilians to the threat that France was facing instead. On May 24, 1994, General
Quesnot cautioned the president that "the ascendance to power by a minority
[Tutsi in Rwanda] whose goals and organization are not without analogy
to the system of the 'Khmers rouges' is a warranty to regional instability"
(Smolar 2011). A month before that, April 2, 1994, President Mitterrand had
just ordered an additional 1,000 French troops to take control and to patrol
the surroundings of Kigali and to vet identity cards of those entering Kigali,
which only implied that those entering the city were "the enemies" of the
regime that French troops had come to help get rid of.

Along the way, Paul Kagame, then the leader of the RPF, became both the
target and a pawn in the French strategy to maintain control over Rwanda.
French authorities arrested him while he attended a peace talk in Paris in
January 1992. In his memoire, Kagame described the threat that French
officials made to him if he did not back off from fighting the Habyarimana
government. "Paul Dijoud," the head of African Affairs within the French
Foreign Ministry then—also heading the French delegation at that meeting—
"told us [the RPF] that we were good fighters, but that if we didn't stop, even
if we managed to take Kigali, we wouldn't find our people there because they
would all have been massacred!" (Soudan 2015: 44). Before that, President
Kagame described a squad of armed individuals storming his hotel room and
those of his security guards at 4 a.m., handcuffing and driving them off to an
unknown venue where they were questioned for a day (idem).

Detaining the RPF leader and threatening him with the message of mass
"massacres" of his "people" by the French officials is a testimony to the
great length they were willing to go to win a geopolitical warfare that was
essential to France's foreign interests. For the French officials, Paul Kagame
was a proxy for their power rival (Anglo-Saxon powers) and incarnated well
their interests in the region. Therefore, to wage and win a geopolitical war
against the Anglos included arresting Paul Kagame and threatening him with
a credible message about the demise of Tutsi population that he represented
domestically. It also makes it difficult to imagine that the then French officials
were oblivious to the consequences of their military interventions in Rwanda
and to how the civil war was going to end, "this man must have had some
knowledge that the genocide was about to happen" (idem), Kagame inferred.

The British Indirect Hand: Objectives, Success, and the Cost

For the Anglo-Saxon bloc—connoting a union of the United Kingdom and the United States for the French officials—Rwanda represented the possibility to shore its strategic interests up to the mineral-rich eastern, then, Zaire (Cumming 2011: 449–452). And through the RPF insurgency, Britain had an opportunity to attain that objective. The British intelligence considered Yoweri Museveni, the Ugandan President, "the key regional linchpin" (Hammer and de Hoyos 1994: 24) for realizing the British geopolitical goals in the region. It is unclear whether the British government supplied direct military equipment to the RPF troops—see the section above on brands and origins of their armory—but its intelligence had "full knowledge and approved" (idem) the RPF invasion before the night of October 1, 1991. Unlike the French, however, fighting for Rwanda and for the strategic interests it meant in the region had to be accomplished in such a way that the British hand would not be seen.

It also appears that all the British government, intelligence, and corporate community had a coherent set of objectives around the world, and Rwanda was one of their priority sites (Hammer and de Hoyos 1994). Thoughts had it that the world population was getting out of control and that the problem was costing the British public, and that was even more challenging for Britain in Africa. As a result, aid was set to become insufficient if the population's ability to feed themselves worsened. Or it would require more tax increases in order to provide massive aid to the developing world for several years to come; otherwise, perpetual ethnic wars would become inevitable. Consequently, it would become difficult for the corporations to acquire resources as cheaply as possible without being hampered by military governments, "or any government for that matter" (ibid. 26). This thinking, therefore, called for a new plan that would decelerate overpopulation, use the region as a raw material base, and then recolonized it differently. In its April 15, 1994, issue, the *New York Times* noted "the United States and its allies have decided it would difficult to maintain it [Rwanda] without transforming the country into a United Nations trusteeship or a colonial-style administration" (Sciolino 1994). Three months later, the British Lady Lynda Chalker, then minister of Overseas Development (formerly, the British Colonial Office), told the London Royal Society, "the density of population in Rwanda is one reason why the scale of that tragedy is so enormous," a statement which was published next day in *The Daily Telegraph* with the title "Chalker's Rwanda Warning to Church" (Hammer and de Hoyos 1994: 25). The call echoed the wider sense (among the British elites) of duty for an international legislation of procreation in the developing world (idem).

Implementing these British officials' ideas required recruits who possessed geostrategic aptitudes and adequate levels of regional clout. And Yoweri Museveni, the president of Uganda was the able man to *hire*. Museveni and

Lady Chalker relations were then known as "very luvvie-duvvie" (ibid., p. 26). They had known each other for quite some time; Chalker was indeed the first foreign official to ever meet Museveni in Kampala after he took power in 1986. Therefore, Uganda—a traditional British financial and political outpost in East Africa—served as the "springboard" for expanding the geopolitical ambitions of its neocolonial patron in the region. For the British, Museveni was such an invaluable asset—one can even argue, the implementing mind—to execute that plan. That is why he was seldom criticized on virtually any internationalist governance metrics. Quite the contrary, Museveni's services to the British—economically and geopolitically—earned him exceptional treatment by Western powers.[19] But Rwanda became the site upon which the Anglo-French geopolitical objectives were fought and realized. The Rwandan civil war also exposed the vulnerability and limitations of both rivals' calculations.

For the British (and their American allies), Museveni was the immediate neighbor to Rwanda. He knew well the members of the RPF. They had worked for him. He groomed them and they too knew and had brought him to power a few years before the Rwandan civil war. Fred Rwigema, the initial RPF commander—mysteriously killed in the first few hours of the attack—had been the Army Chief of Staff of the Ugandan NRA. Major-General Paul Kagame, the commander who ultimately propelled the RPF to victory in the summer of 1994, had been the head of Intelligence and Counterintelligence in the NRA. Uganda would, understandably, be the lead face in implementing the British geopolitical plan. Specifically, the Ugandan NRA would be the immediate source of supplies and financing to seize Rwanda (and join it to the British East Africa territory of influence and alliances). Museveni has always denied being behind the plans to attack Rwanda from Uganda. In their regular interactions, he would even give assurances to President Habyarimana of Rwanda that no such attacks to topple him were churning in Uganda; but in private, he would do the opposite (Guichaoua 2020: 82; 87).

But out in conjunction with the task assigned to him by his geopolitical employer, Museveni saw a different opportunity and quickly seized it to a personal end. He used his thumb-on-scale power and privileges to pursue his personal—but quite perilous—ambitions in the region. He sought to turn neighboring countries, namely Rwanda and Burundi, into his own satellite states with Ugandan domination.[20] But his plans have failed and even resulted in open fissure with the RPF over the next years.[21]

CONCLUSION

This chapter has examined whether the patterns of security dynamics that led to the Rwandan civil war had been independently shaped by local actors and whether the analysis should limit to just the region. But contrary to Buzan and Waever's (1999, 2003, 2009) security analysis in Africa contending that the regional security logics in Africa defy the rules of patterns of peace and security formation, the evidence has shown that African regional actors alone have no ability to determine the course of security outcomes. We have also seen that these patterns became grounded at the inception of Rwanda as a republic by colonial powers and that the colonial effects on them were not an inconsequential "overlay" as Buzan and Waever's RSCT suggests. While local and regional actors have ambitions for power and territorial control and may design different strategies to achieve it, they lack comprehensive autonomy in requisite ingredients that produce such dominance through war.

As this chapter has attempted to demonstrate, the dynamics that led to civil war in Rwanda in the 1990s have roots in a political order that was designed during the colonial governance by an external power. Similarly, to the extent that postcolonial Rwanda was not immune to neocolonial influence, both the recipes and the material conditions that shaped the war and produced its consequences were as much a byproduct of geopolitical competition. One geopolitical patron—France—provided infantry, lethal capabilities, intelligence, strategies and advise, and even self-favoring diplomacy, all from both onsite and afar. The other—Britain—while indirectly pursuing its own strategic objectives, became the guarantor of opinion mobilization, and international legitimacy. And the local antagonists in the war aligned to those geopolitical dynamics.

From this case, it can be inferred that African domestic actors' ability to hold onto the state, lose, or seize it is located in and conditioned by the decisions directly made by external powers with geopolitical ties to that territorial boundary. Rwanda's civil war has exemplified that. The security dynamics that led to and defined the outcome of the civil war were a result of externally located hegemonic configurations. Such dynamics had a regional character in display but they were determined by decisions made far away from domestic borders. France actively played the role of material and strategic steward for the security of Rwanda during the war. Britain's role remained materially uninvolved but was not an inconsequential actor in the conflict either. With such configuration of security patterns, domestic actors—the Rwandan government and the RPF—were indeed the ultimate benefactors, but without the French government's military overreach and coercion, the war would not have lasted longer than it did or led to the magnitude of human catastrophe it did.

Great Britain's hand in this conflict was not clean either. But its subterranean approach and its physical absence on the battlefield reinforce the argument that most war damages were attributable to France. France's aggressive and obdurate involvement in Rwanda's civil war radicalized the dynamics of

enmity between both sides. Its military interventions to defend the government of Habyarimana against the RPF at all costs, throughout the conflict,
only "worsened the crisis" (Hammer and de Hoyos 1994: 24). It made it difficult for domestic actors (the Regime and the RPF) to quickly realize that the
war they were waging for the control of Rwanda was not winnable without
generational obliteration and that the ideology that had animated their enmity
and led to denigration and vilification of the "other" was a discursive construct that both of them could fundamentally challenge that they could evaluate gains against losses over, and ultimately end shooting at each other. That
did not happen. Each side changed their calculations as a result of France's
direct and enduring involvement in the war. And insofar as that involvement
was not propitious to peace, enmity deepened, making it difficult for both
sides to hear each other.

Under France's military wings, the government was convinced that it had
secured international guarantees for long-term protection and that the cause it
fought for was winnable and within the reach. The appeal to the public held
that the country was under attack by an ethnic group (Tutsi) that existentially
threatened the order of the majority (Hutu), and France provided protective
guarantees for that not to happen. For the RPF, however, the geo-marriage
that tied the government of Rwanda and its indefectible ally, France, signified
that there were only two possibilities about this war: victory or obliteration.
RPF also always saw the war from the lenses of external French-speaking
powers harking to colonial times. Addressing a large youth crowd in Kigali
recently, General James Kabarebe, who has been a member of the RPF command officers since the war, described the challenges they faced rivaling the
regime to appeal to the public. As he attempted to educate the people of a
small village in northeastern Rwanda on why RPF had come to "liberate" the
country, a *muzungu* (white) priest from a nearby Catholic parish promptly
learned about the gathering and came to ensure the population did not con-
vert to the RPF teachings, before directly warning General Kabarebe and his
men (Ishimwe 2019). "Off to where you, a bunch of scumbags?" Kabarebe
quoted the priest who he said spoke in a *Kinyarwanda* grammar that was
better than that of natives.[22] "For thousands of thrones a *Mututsi* will not step
in Rwanda! If you are real men, stay still! I will go to Ngarama [his Parish]
to report you. They [the government forces] will come and make you feed
off 'the breasts of your mothers' [i.e., humiliate you]," General Kabarebe
recounted. He went on to describe that a swath of military tanks and pickup
trucks began shelling his troops in the hours following the exchange with the
priest, causing him to retreat and to lose the entire territory of Kagitumba
that they previously had under their control. "That is when I understood that
our war would be fought by the courageous ones only. That a *muzungu* was
giving orders to the population to pick up machetes and chase us.. and to the

soldiers of Rwanda and of Zaire. [. . .]. That, to anyone with knowledge on war, was foolish. But we had no other alternative than to continue the fight, dead or alive," he added.[23] For the RPF, the regime had oppressed Tutsi inside and outside Rwanda and that had to change, but France's presence was making it impossible for change to come about. And because France had not been the most objective critic of the RPF ever, it made it baseless for the latter to trust the intentions of French officials—especially following the threat and the temporary incarceration of the RPF leader in France. As a result, defeating the regime along with its corrosive ideology appeared as the only redemptive possibility for the RPF's concerns. Hence, the Arusha Peace Accords signed between the parties in August 1993 quickly declined into a disastrous fiasco.

At the same time, it was almost as if the two sides were oblivious to the international forces that were activating them separately, in two different strategies, with two different foreseeable outcomes. The two great powers also had to find a language to support their respective strategies for achieving the objectives they had set separately. They used a language that was ethnically coded to justify their action and their siding with either of the Rwandan opponents. The discourse differed in both content and strategy. The British officials considered the RPF as "a force for good" (Cumming 2011: 552), while the French leaders and Generals referred to the same as the "Khmers noirs" (Smolar 2011) and "a 'terrorist' bunch of foreigners from Uganda" (Wallis 2006: 1–2).

Therefore, to account for the recipes and the causes of a civil war requires a systematic examination of these three components: ideology, logistics, and geopolitics. This chapter has demonstrated that the *ideology*, out of which the war rhetoric formed, was a construct that an international institution, colonialism, imposed upon Rwandans who, surprisingly, willingly, and unquestionably harbored and nurtured it over the following decades. The dynamics of amity and enmity that plunged local actors into the war had been imposed on them by the same European actors that would divisively pick sides in the subsequent war a century later. And quite remarkably, the domestic actors then in power had no compunction nor the courage to revisit the fundamentals of that state power foundation.

Logistically, the firepower edge provided to the regime by France had an immense psychological impact on RPF troops. It gave them pull back and regroup, but most impactfully, it strengthened their convictions, and ultimately translated them into a blitzkrieg force that swiftly overthrew a regime determined to massacre "your people" as Paul Dijoud in the French Foreign Ministry had accurately warned. But France's material might in this war also gave the RPF even more ground to mobilize logistical support and a diplomatic campaign across the international system, including within France itself. When the war ended, France had spent more than $25 million worth of arms on Rwanda between 1990 and 1993, in addition to army trainers, diplomacy, and advising the Habyarimana system on the war (Smolar 2011).

Geopolitically, France lost Rwanda out of its African sphere of influence despite all of the intelligence, diplomatic, and material support it had invested in Rwanda. But most damning was the human cost that went unaccounted for and has not been part of the assessment of Franco-English geopolitical battles. At the height of Rwanda's tragedy, the French officials were still disowning both the failures and the human catastrophe produced by their geopolitical pursuit in the region. General Christian Quesnot, the Army Chief of Staff and special adviser to President Mitterrand on Africa, stated on May 6, 1994: "the (Ugandan) president and his allies have established a *'Tutsiland'* with the Anglo-Saxon help, aided by the objective complicity of our pseudo-intellectuals. What a remarkable network of Tutsi lobbying, to which a part of our State apparatus is equally sensitive" (quoted in Smolar 2011). This kind of public abjuration confirms further that the structure of the French officials' calculations at the time was that the geopolitical fate was absolutely more important than human cost. Four days after General Quesnot's statement, President Mitterrand finally came out of that denial, taking a rather subdued and conceding tone when he stated: "we are not meant to wage war everywhere, even when it's horror that has hit us hard in the face" (idem). By evoking "war" and "horror" about Rwanda in May 1994, President Mitterrand was not referring to the hundreds of thousands of Tutsi Rwandans massacred by the regime he had buttressed and favored. Rather, he was alluding to the national shame that the RPF (and its Anglo-Saxon allies) had inflicted upon the French prestige despite every bit of power he had invested into it, and that was unthinkable.

Paul Kagame, whom French officials once despised and jailed in Paris in 1992, is now Rwanda's head of state. He grew up in Uganda, a former British colony, and did not speak French. His eventual advent to power was always viewed by French officials as the beginning of the collapse of France's influence or the expansion of Anglo-Saxon influence in the Great Lakes region of Africa. It does not appear that their assessment was wrong. Kagame has since introduced English as the new education and business language, rapidly taking over French. At his behest, Rwanda has joined the Commonwealth community. Rwanda does far more business with a wide and diverse set of English-speaking countries than with France, which is a stark reversal of pre-1990 geopolitical order. But equally unfortunate are the nefarious residues of that geopolitical war in Rwanda. Internally, for example, there is an apocryphally held view that English came to Rwanda because it was the language of the winner, Tutsi being the implication, which too suggests that French, the dominant language and therefore of the majority under the previous regime, is set to disappear at some point. Internal dynamics can indeed develop the propensity along the language of a geopolitical actor. These ideas are rooted in a chain of historical events—as it was in French yesterday, today it is English—and that has direct impact on subsequent imaginings of life. It is therefore incorrect to dismiss the significance of geopolitical forces in the formation of domestic conflict. They do indeed have practical implications on the nation's social and political dynamics before and after a war. Hammer and de Hoyos (1994: 26) summed it all up well: "Rwanda's devastation could never have occurred without outside intervention."

NOTES

1. The second perspective in the RSCT takes a "globalist" approach, which analyzes the globalization-defined set of forces to make sense of how this works. It contends that the globalist perspective—antithetical to realism—consists in deterritorialization of the world. In the globalist theorizing of security, territory is the unit of analysis as well as the ordering principle. Globalization, on the other hand, is the system structure in which the state is seen as a subdued player within the global circuit of transnational entities made up of intergovernmental organizations and regimes. In this realm of logic, the sovereign state and its unassailable capabilities are diminished. Its principal role declines as it becomes a mere means of communication and transportation of ideas, information, and goods. The RSCT holds that the way Western powers have imposed much of, and shaped, security of states in the global south is through aid and its influential clubs such as EU, WTO, NATO, and other forms of pressures. It also claims to extrapolate from the Waltzian (1979) terms by describing further the principles of arrangement of the parts in the system and how the parts are differentiated from each other (Buzan and Waever 2003: 6).

2. My argument is not grounded in the constructivist perspective that Buzan and Waever (2003) consider an alternative approach to studying security dynamics. They contend that, unlike the RSCT, constructivists focus on the "securitization theory," which is always constructed by or in political processes by which security issues get constituted; that is, how those shape the distribution of power and patterns of amity and enmity.

3. Here I delineate that Rwanda's civil war began on October 1, 1990, and ended on April 6, 1994, or the eve of the beginning of the Genocide. The latter date is purposely chosen to clarify and to avoid conflating the war and what was otherwise the carefully orchestrated Genocide of Tutsi.

4. Germany colonized Rwanda first in 1882 but lost all their colonies following the end of World War I. Like Burundi, Rwanda was put under the protectorate of the Society of Nations, and later were added Belgium, then occupying the neighboring Congo.

5. Intriguingly, the Belgian colonial rule used the label "race" rather than "ethnicity" to describe the Hutu and Tutsi categories. Anthropology, the discipline that produced knowledge on cultural studies at the time, relied on techniques and methods that were based on anthropometric measurements. It was the era dominated by *scientific race,* which established a correspondence between certain phenotypical characteristics and intelligence, creativity, rulership, and industriousness, while "others" signified low intellectual predisposition. That experiment in Rwanda produced a racial/ethnic classification in which Tutsi's (albeit the minority) superiority and pastoral acumen was juxtaposed with Hutu's (the majority) autochthony and land-tilling qualities. For more on this topic, see De Lacger, Louis [Roman Catholic missionary] (1939a: 42; 44; 49); see also Sasserath (1948: 27–28).

6. The prefix *Aba-* (as in *Abanyiginya, Abahutu, also varies into Abanya-* as in *Abanyarwanda*) means people of/from.

7. Jean-Pierre Chrétien considers the article '*Appel à la conscience des Bahutu*' (December 1990 edition of *Kangura*) to be the "best expression of *Kangura*'s ideology" and the central role that 1959 played in that ideology. The article argued that the "Hutu regime had been founded [on] the 'pure democracy' of the 'majority people' against the 'feudal Tutsi minority'" (Chrétien 1991: 113; see also Eltringham 2004: 45–46). The article ends with the "Hutu Ten Commandments," of which the commandment ten reads: "The Social Revolution of 1959, the Referendum of 1961, and the Hutu ideology must be taught to all Hutu at all the levels" (see Guichaoua 1995: 605).

8. The key issues in the negotiations of the Arusha Agreement of 1993 were the usual issue of political power-sharing and military integration, and also the return of the Tutsi exiles who had left the country since 1959 as a result of massacres and discrimination. Following a great deal of negotiation, the parties agreed that refugees could return and settle anywhere, as long as they did not impinge on the land rights of others. See, Protocol of Agreement between the Government of the Republic of Rwanda and the Rwandan Patriotic Front on Repatriation of Rwandan Refugees and the Resettlement of Displaced Persons, June 9, 1993, Article 2.

9. There were even accusations from the Habyarimana government side that Belgium was supporting the RPF during the war. But such accusations were untrue; if anything, they reflected the Habyarimana's resentments of Belgian's neutrality in this war (see Smyth 1994: 586).

10. Goose and Smyth (1994: 88–96) and Smyth (1994: 585–588) have extensively documented the arms flow in this conflict. Most of my description of arms proliferation during this conflict is based on that prolific documentation.

11. The French military support went on until end of 1993, but French military intervention in Rwanda resumed a few months later under the humanitarian banner of *Opération Turquoise.*

12. Many testimonies have pointed to the inaction and the enabling attitude of the French troops during *Opération Turquoise* that even led to additional killings of the victims by *Interahamwe* in the West of Rwanda (see Republique du Rwanda 2007: 184–281). For example, in Bisesero, a Western community in Rwanda, the victims rushed out of their hiding places toward the French vehicles in June 1994

for protection—because they had heard on radio that French soldiers were there "to protect" them. However, the same report indicates that French solders saw and spoke to the victims but abandoned them in the plain sight of militias who promptly stormed and "finished" (idem.). The report also points to the involvement of French troops directly engaging in and or supervising sexual violence and rape of women and in torture and assassination of the RPF prisoners of war during the period of 1990–1993 (idem 84–112).

13. I witnessed it with my own eyes from my hometown.

14. Taken from Hammer and de Hoyos (1994: 26).

15. Unlike the UN ban on arms exports to South Africa, which was strictly binding, the import prohibition was voluntary but was soon lifted, in May 1994. The Habyarimana government was able to smuggle more arms out of South Africa even during the prohibition period, which alone was a violation of the law but, legally, was less constraining than the arms deal with Egypt. For more on these two deals, see Smyth (1994: 585–588).

16. The Anglo-French rivalry in the Great Lakes region was not new. It, indeed, had been commonplace dating as back as the Berlin Conference time in 1882. On this topic, see Cumming (2011: 449–555); Anstey (1962: 10–56); Trefon (1989: 13–14); Janes (2000: 162–163); EIU (1993: 37); IRIN (1996); Agir Ici-Survie (1997: 138).

17. In reality, France did not colonize Rwanda, Burundi, and Democratic Republic of Congo (formerly Zaire). Belgium colonized the Congo; Rwanda and Burundi were colonized by Germany. Following its defeat in World War I, the League of Nations ordered Germany to transfer its colonies over to Belgium. Then, following Belgium's long-standing ineffective decolonization that started the 1960s, France seized and integrated those three former colonial territories into its African *pré carré* (sphere of influence) in the 1970s. Britain, however, had had long-standing interests for the Congo and had repeatedly collided with France over it (see Cumming 2011: 449–451). Rwanda's civil war reignited the Anglo-French rivalry, a geopolitical strife that went on until the two powers agreed to "bury the hatchet" and converge mutual interests (see Cumming 2011).

18. DAMI stood for *Détachement d'Assistance Militaire et d'Instruction,* a French military unit created to provide military advising and training assistance.

19. At the height of Rwanda's civil war, his Uganda was described in the *Atlantic Monthly* as an "African success story" (Berkeley 1994). In the wide wave of structural adjustment policies by world governing bodies that systematically redesigned the power of African states in the 1980s, Museveni was hailed as a "true IMF disciple" (Adhola 2020). He has now been in power for nearly 35 years and seldom has he been under pressure to democratize as his fellow African strongmen have. If anything, Museveni has used his international status to question the very internalist standards he, himself, has served. "My version of democracy has the full backing of the British and U.S. governments," he once told the press (Hammer and de Hoyos 1994: 27). British officials treated him and his choices for domestic vision as such. One of the officials was echoed on that UK's government position over Uganda's Museveni "The British are very much behind this government. You

know there is no condition at all on democratization, no multi-party democracy. The President doesn't even pretend [to be] for this, and he is still a darling of the West" (idem.).

20. There is no way to corroborate it, but some accounts have it that Museveni, himself a member of the Hima tribe (or Ugandan tribe likened to *Tutsi*), made a pact with members of the RPF in Uganda (Rwandan Tutsi) that he would put them in power in Kigali. However, Museveni's ultimate motive for extending military and political generosity to the Rwandan exiles was that it would accomplish his personal hegemonic goal of instituting Tutsi rulership and dominance in the region under his own/Ugandan tutelage (Hammer and de Hoyos 1994: 26; see also Guichaoua 2020: 83–84). Internally in his own country, though, a lot of people have not supported him. For many Ugandans, Museveni as a suspicious "Rwandan" who happened to be born in the Ugandan territory of Ankole, a territory that was once part of the Rwanda kingdom before the drawing of African borders at the Berlin Conference in 1882. Ankole is also home to most Hima people.

21. Museveni and the RPF (Kagame) had relatively coherent objectives when they sent troops in the Congo, first in 1996, and again in 1999–2000. But this alliance quickly dissolved and even led to a brutal *fratricide* war that Uganda ultimately lost to Rwanda and registered considerable casualties. Ever since, Museveni has never truly recovered from the humiliation inflicted upon him by the people he groomed and pro-pelled to power and from whom he expected full subordination, which he's unlikely to get. Different reports (UN and others) also placed blame on Uganda's army for instigating the fight in Kisangani that cost up to 3,000 lives. For more on the origins and evolution this Museveni vs Kagame duel, see (Mugahe 2019; The Associate Press 2000; Belof 2019; Ndirima 2019; Katumanga 2000; Turner 2007; Clark 2001).

22. *Kinyarwanda* is the one and only language spoken in Rwanda. The prefix Kinya- means a language of/from.

23. The Catholic Church, both in cities and rural locations, was still very much an organ of the state by then. Parishes across the country were still heavily led by French or Belgian missionaries/Fathers. They, usually, had lived in Rwanda long enough to understand the internal political dynamics and spoke very well the native Kinyarwanda.

REFERENCES

Adhola, Y. 2020. "How Museveni Became a Disciple of IMF, World Bank." *Daily Monitor*, March 15. https://www.monitor.co.ug/OpEd/Commentary/How -Museveni-became-disciple-IMF-World-Bank/689364-5491462-12ohsqm/index .html. Accessed June 4, 2020.

Africa Watch. 1993. "Beyond the Rhetoric: Continuing Human Rights Abuses in Rwanda." *News From Africa*, 5(7, June).

Agir Ici-Survie. 1997. *France-Zaire-Congo*. Paris: L'Harmattan.

Anstey, R. 1962. *Britain and the Congo*. Oxford: Clarendon Press.

Beloff, J. 2019. "The Roots of the Mounting Crisis Between Rwanda's Kagame and Uganda's Museveni." *Quartz Africa*, March 23. https://qz.com/africa/1579313/

the-mounting-crisis-between-rwandas-kagame-and-ugandas-museveni/. Accessed June 5, 2020.

Berkeley, B. 1994. "An African Success Story?" *Atlantic Monthly*, 274(September): 22–30.

Buzan, B., and O. Waever. 2003. *Regions and Powers: The Structure of International Security*. Cambridge, UK: Cambridge University Press

Buzan, B., and O. Waever. 2009. "Macrosecuritization and Security Constellations: Reconsidering Scale in Securitization Theory." *Review of International Studies*, 35(2): 253–276.

Buzan, B., O. Wæver, and J. De Wilde. 1998. *Security: A New Framework for Analysis*. Boulder, CO: Lynne Rienner Publishers.

Calhoun, C. 2013. 'For the Social History of the Present: Pierre Bourdieu as Historical Sociologist." In *Bourdieu and Historical Analysis. Politics, History, and Culture*, edited by P. S. Gorski, 36–67. Durham, NC: Duke University Press.

Charbonneau, B. 2006. "Mastering "Irrational" Violence: The Relegitimization of French Security Policy in Sub-Saharan Africa." *Alternatives*, 31(2): 215–241.

Charbonneau, B. 2008. "Dreams of Empire: France, Europe, and the New Interventionism in Africa." *Modern & Contemporary France*, 16(3): 279–295.

Charbonneau, B. 2014. "The Imperial Legacy of International Peace-Building: The Case of Francophone Africa." *Review of International Studies*, 40(3): 607–630.

Charbonneau, B. 2016. *"France and the New Imperialism: Security Policy in Sub-Saharan Africa*. London/New York: Routledge.

Chrétien, J. P. 1991 "'Presse libre" et propaganda raciste au Rwanda." *Politique Africaine*, 42: 109.

Chrétien, J. P., J. F. Dupaquier, M. Kabanda, and J. Ngarambe, eds. 1995. *Rwanda: Les Médias du génocide*. Paris: Éditions Karthala with Reporters sans frontières.

Clark, J. F. 2001. "Explaining Ugandan Intervention in Congo: Evidence and Interpretations." *The Journal of Modern African Studies*, 39(2): 261–287.

Cumming, G. D. 2011. "Burying the Hatchet? Britain and France in the Democratic Republic of Congo." *The Journal of Modern African Studies*, 49(4): 547–573.

De Lacger, Louis. 1939a. *Ruanda. Vol.1, Le Ruanda ancient*. Namur: Grand Lacs.

Forges, A. D. 1995. "The Ideology of Genocide." *Issue: A Journal of Opinion*, 23(2): 44–47.

Forges, A. D. 1999. *Leave None to Tell the Story: Genocide in Rwanda*. New York: Human Rights Watch.

De Saint-Exupéry, P. 2004. *L'inavouable: La France au Rwanda*. Paris: Arènes.

Dumoulin, A. 1997. *La France militaire et L'Afrique*. Bruxelles: Editions GRIP.

Economist Intelligence Unit (EIU). 1993. *Zaire, Rwanda, Burundi 1992–3*. London: EIU.

Eltringham, N. 2004. *Accounting for Horror: Post-Genocide Debates in Rwanda*. London: Pluto Press.

Gaud, M. 1995. "Rwanda: le genocide de 1994." *Afrique Contemporaine Trimestriel*, No 174 avril-juin.

Gibson, R. 2011. *The Best of Enemies: Anglo-French Relations Since the Norman Conquest*. 2nd ed. Exeter, UK: Impresso Books.

Gourevitch, P. 1995. "After the Genocide: When a People Murders up to a Million Fellow-Countrymen, What Does it Mean to Survive?" *The New Yorker*, December 18.

Gregory, S. 2000. "The French Military in Africa: Past and Present." *African Affairs*, 99(396): 435–448.

Guichaoua, A., ed. 1995. *Les crises politiques au Burundi et au Rwanda (1993–1994): Analyses, faits, et documents*. Paris: Éditions Karthala.

Guichaoua, A. 2020. *Kuva ku Ntambara Kugera kuri Jenoside – Politiki z'ubugizi bwa nabi mu Rwanda (1990–1994)*. La Découverte.

Hammer, D., and L. de Hoyos. 1994. "The British Hand Behind the Horror in Rwanda." *Executive Intelligence Review*, 21(33): 24–31.

Horne, A. 2005. *Friend or Foe: An Anglo-Saxon History of France*. London, UK: Weidenfeld & Nicolson.

Huggins, C. 2009. 'Peacekeeping and HLP Rights in Great Lakes Region of Africa." In *Housing, Land, and Property Rights in Post-Conflict United Nations and Other Peace Operations: A Comparative Survey and Proposal for Reform*, edited by S. Leckie, 179–219. Cambridge, UK: Cambridge University Press.

Human Rights Watch. 1994. "Arming Rwanda – The Arms Trade and Human Rights Abuse in the Rwandan War." *Human Rights Watch Arms Project*, 6(1, January): 1–38.

IISS. 1993. *1993 – The Military Balance 1994*. London: Brassey's.

IRIN. 1996. *Emergency Update 23 on Eastern Zaire*. Nairobi: IRIN. November 14.

Ishimwe, Israel. 2019. "Kabarebe yavuze ku mupadiri w'umuzungu watutse ingabo za RPA ku babyeyi (Video)." *Igihe*. Kuya 19 Kamena 2019 saa.https://igihe.com /amakuru/u-rwanda/article/kabarebe-yavuze-ku-mupadiri-w-umuzungu-watutse -ingabo-za-rpa-ku-babyeyi. Accessed October 24, 2020.

James, A. 2000. "Britain, the Cold War and the Congo Crisis." *The Journal of Imperial and Commonwealth History*, 28(3): 162–163.

Jones, A. 2014. "The Great Lakes Genocides: Hidden Histories, Hidden Precedents." In *Hidden Genocides: Power, Knowledge. Memory*, edited By A.L Hinton, T. La Pointe, & D. Irvin-Erickson, 129–148. New Brunswick, NJ: Rutgers University Press.

Johnson, Douglas, Francois Crouze and Francois Bédarida. 1980. *Britain and France: Ten Centuries*. Norwich, UK: Dawson.

Katumanga, M. 2000. "Uganda and Rwanda's Involvement in DRC: The Pursuit of National Interests." *L'Afrique politique*, 89–103.

Kayihura, E., and K. Zukus. 2014. *Inside the Hotel Rwanda: The Surprising True Story... and Why it Matters Today*. Dallas, TX: BenBella Books

Kroslak, D. 2007. *The Role of France in the Rwandan Genocide*. London: Hurst.

Kuperman, A. J. 2004. *The Limits of Humanitarian Intervention: Genocide in Rwanda*. Washington, DC: Brookings Institution Press.

Lemarchand, Rene. 1970. *Rwanda and Burundi*. New York: Praeger.

Malloy, James M. 1977. "Authoritarianism and Corporation in Latin America: The Modal Pattern." In *Authoritarianism and Corporatism in Latin America*, edited By James M. Malloy, 3–22. Pittsburgh, PA: University of Pittsburgh Press.

McNulty, M. 2000. "French Arms, War and Genocide in Rwanda." *Crime, Law & Social Change*, 33(1&2): 105–129.

Migdal, J. S. 2001. *State in Society: Studying How States and Societies Transform and Constitute One Another*. Cambridge, UK: Cambridge University Press.

Modelski, George. 1978. "The Long Cycle of Global Politics and the Nation-State." *Comparative Studies in Society and History*, 20: 214–235.

Modelski, George. 1979. *Transnational Corporations and World Order: Readings in International Political Economy*. San Francisco: W. H. Freeman.

Mugahe, D. 2019. "The RootCcause of the Tension and Conflict Between Uganda and Rwanda: A Deeper Analysis." *The New Times*, May 20. https://www.newtimes .co.rw/news/root-cause-tension-and-conflict-between-uganda-and-rwanda-deeper -analysis. Accessed June 5, 2020.

Ndahiro, A., and J. Rwagatare, eds. 2015. *Rwanda: Rebuilding of a Nation*. Kampala, Uganda: Fountain Publishers

Randal, J. C. 1994. "Hutus Fear Revenge, Flee Rwanda Rebels. 250,000 Crowd Into Five Squalid Camps." *The Washington Post*, June 28.

Republic of Rwanda. 2002. *Minister of Local Administration Report*.

République du Rwanda. 2007. "Rapport." *Commission Nationale Indépendante Chargée de Rassembler les Preuves Montrant l'Implication de l'Etat Francais dans le Génocide Perpetré au Rwanda en 1994*. 15 Novembre.

Reyntjens, F. 1985. *Pouvoir et Droit au Rwanda. Droit public et évolution politique 1916–1973*. Brussels: Musée Royal de l'Afrique Centrale

Sasserath, J. S. 1948. *Le Ruanda – Urundi : un étrange royaume féodal au cœur de l'Afrique*. Bruxelles, Germinal.

Schimmel, N. 2011. "An Invisible Genocide: How the Western Media Failed to Report the 1994 Rwandan Genocide of the Tutsi and Why." *The International Journal of Human Rights*, 15(7): 1125–1135.

Sciolino, E. 1994. "For West, Rwanda Is Not Worth the Political Candle." *The New York Times*, published on April 15. https://www.nytimes.com/1994/04/15/world /for-west-rwanda-is-not-worth-the-political-candle.html. Accessed June 4, 2020.

Silver, C. 2015. "The US Response to Genocide in Rwanda: A Reassessment." *Graduate Theses and Dissertations*. University of South Florida (USF). http:// scholarcommons.usf.edu/etd/5773

Smolar, P. 2008 "Génocide Rwandais : Ce que savait l'Elysée." *Le Monde – Afrique,* first published on March 12. Updated on September 12, 2011. https://www .lemonde.fr/afrique/article/2008/03/12/genocide-rwandais-ce-que-savait-l-elysee _930489_3212.html. Accessed June 3, 2020.

Smyth, F. 1994. "Arms for Rwanda – Blood Money and Geopolitics." *The Nation*, 258(17): 585–588.

Soudan, F. 2015. *Kagame: Conversations with the President of Rwanda*. Paris: Enigma Books and Nouveau Monde Editions.

The Associated Press. 2000. "The Forces of Rwanda and Uganda Fight in Congo." *The New York Times*, June 11. https://www.nytimes.com/2000/06/11/world/the -forces-of-wanda-and-uganda-fight-in-congo.html. Accessed June 5, 2020.

Thomann, J. C. 1998. "Enquête sur la tragédie rwandaise (1990–1994)." [présentée devant l'Assemblée Nationale], Paris. T. II: Annexes.

Thompson, A. 2016. *An Introduction to African Politics*. London: Routledge.

Tombs, R. and I. Tombs. 2007. *That Sweet Enemy: Britain and France: The History of a Love-Hate Relationship*. New York: Vintage.

Trefon, T. 1989. *French Policy Towards Zaire*. Paris: Center d'Étude et de Documentation Africaine.

Turner, T. 2007. *The Congo Wars: Conflict, Myth and Reality*. Zed Books.

Vansina, J. 2004. *Antecedents to Modern Rwanda: The Nyiginya Kingdom*. Madison, WI: University of Wisconsin Press.

Wallis, A. 2006. "Rwandan Rifts in La Francafrique." *Open Democracy*, December 14. https://www.opendemocracy.net/en/rwanda_france_4183jsp/, Accessed June 3, 2020.

Waltz, K. N. 1979. *Theory of International Politics*. New York: Random House.

Watson, C. 1993. "Exile from Rwanda: Background to an Invasion." *U.S. Committee for Refugees Issue Paper*, February.

Chapter 8

The Sierra Leonean Civil War

An Examination of Internal, Regional, and External Causes

Earl Conteh-Morgan

It is at times argued that no civil war is entirely internal in terms of its causes. Internal, regional, and external factors play a big role in the outbreak and unfolding, as well as scope, intensity, and even duration, of civil or internal conflicts. The Sierra Leonean civil conflict was a national tragedy of far-reaching consequences which also resulted in a security nightmare at the local, national, and regional levels in West Africa. According to the International Crisis Group (ICG) Report (2001), the decade-long civil war internally displaced about two-thirds of the population and generated another 600,000 refugees to neighboring countries. The immediate post–Cold War civil wars in West Africa (Liberia, Sierra Leone, and Ivory Coast) were all shaped by the confluence and effects of internal, regional, and external factors. At the external level, the demise of the Cold War rivalry between the United States and the Soviet Union, the emergence and effects of globalization processes (Ibrahim 2013; Koffi et al. 2018; Ouattara 1977) as a phenomenon, and its reorganization of political and economic space had a jolting experience on civil society, individuals, group insecurities, and the legitimacy of the fragile African state. At the national or domestic level was the consequence of decades of misrule and corrupt practices by incumbent regimes that eventually spawned rebellion triggered by governmental neglect of the masses. The civil wars in West Africa and in particular Serra Leone were unfolding in a context of simultaneous regional/global integration, and internal or national fragmentation exacerbated by existential insecurities in the areas of food, healthcare, income, and overall lack of basic human needs. The nexus of internal, regional, and external globalization pressures in the early 1990s (Gelinas 2003; Mullard 2004; Stiglitz 2002) had a seismic negative impact on African states that had already been weakened by poor governance, predatory state behavior, deepening relative economic depriva- tion, and accelerating loss of regime legitimacy linked to severe existential insecurities.

The objective of this chapter is to examine the factors that contributed to or were associated with the outbreak of Sierra Leone's civil war (1991 to 2002) in terms of (1) internal or domestic factors related to governance or misrule; (2) the contributions of regional factors in particular the spillage of the Liberian civil war into the country; and (3) the impact of political- economic external impositions by the IMF and World Bank and their effect on state collapse.

This analysis of Sierra Leone's civil war is predicated on the impact of the nexus of structural violence (Farmer 2004; Salvage et al. 2012; Schepler- Hughes 2005) and relative deprivation (Davis 1962; Gurr 2011) on the onset of collective political violence in the country. By the 1980s, Sierra Leone had been plagued by profound structural violence which in turn generated severe relative deprivation that eventually triggered widespread rebellion and political violence in the entire country. However, a deeper and more nuanced examination of the Sierra Leone conflict could also be conceptual- ized in terms of historical/long-term, intermediate/short-term, and immediate/ precipitating factors.

LONG-TERM HISTORICAL ANTECEDENTS OF THE CIVIL WAR

The state of Sierra Leone's postcolonial economy leading up to the civil war was in essence the combined effects of precolonial structures, the legacy of colonial rule, and impositions and expectations, as well as the pressures of modern external political-economic and social forces within Sierra Leone, and, in particular, the responses at each epoch and internal political-economic dynamics of incumbent regimes within the country. The impact of precolo- nial, colonial, and neocolonial legacies on Sierra Leone is in contradistinction to Western conceptions of good governance.

Sierra Leone as an African state at independence was far short of an ideal state as conceived by the state in international relations theory. For example, dichotomies of internal/external, and juridical/ empirical sovereignty (Jackson and Rosberg 1982) are largely appropriate when applied to the colonial and neocolonial experiences of African states (Buzan et al. 1993). Especially for a microstate like Sierra Leone, state-building and development issues have been disproportionately influenced by external factors. Many domestic devel- opments in Africa are shaped by external expectations and even impositions, particularly since all African states operate within an international structure foisted on them by advanced industrial nations. In other words, Sierra Leone, like all developing states was incorporated into the world capitalist system as part of the periphery, and in particular relegated into the status of a producer of raw materials (Chilcote 1974; Smith 1979; Wallerstein 1979). This marginal incorporation of Sierra Leone into capitalism has often been reflected in its dependent development.

As a nation-state, it was therefore the outcome of a shift in global conception of reality from colonial rule to anticolonialism and the right to sovereign independence of all territories. Its historical partition and subjection to colonial rule meant that it was not the natural outgrowth of an indigenous political community (Chabal 1994). The ethnoregional and linguistic cleavages, especially between the north and south and eastern regions of the country had not evolved to the point of substantive national integration to facilitate the smooth transfer of power from one regime or political party to another. Accordingly, in postcolonial Sierra Leone, the problems of leadership, ethnoregionalism, distributional equity, and legitimacy would plague the young nation and would consume a great deal of its political energy and even spawn other negative developments that would have tragic consequences for the state and society in exactly three decades after independence.

Sierra Leone as a microstate, though rich in natural resources, has been heavily shaped by the global structural-institutional rules and regulations that pose governance dilemmas and at times limit autonomous decision-making. The consequences of the incompatibilities between precolonial, colonial, and neocolonial, and globalization structures were accordingly manifested in patronage, systemic political-economic corruption, and external constraints (Conteh-Morgan and Dixon-Fyle 1999). Sierra Leone was a weak African state from its inception, and therefore artificial and heavily infiltrated by external pressures and actors which in turn produced weak and ineffective leaders since independence. From independence in 1961, the Sierra Leone state has been plagued by inept leadership, a poor performance of functions and an increasing loss of legitimacy. Sierra Leone falls into the category of developing states described by Caporaso (2000: 2) in this way:

> While heavily influenced and penetrated by "foreign" capital, which rears its head internally as part of the comprador domestic bourgeoisie, peripheral countries are presumed to be frustrated political, economic, and cultural communities struggling to realize their distinctive potential.

Caporaso (2000: 13) further stresses that: "A state that is penetrated from outside, that is subject to every push and pull of the global political economy, may not even be able to form its own goals." This condition of the African state plagued Sierra Leone and was a significant contributory factor in state collapse just after thirty years of independence. In other words, the political-economic behavior and misrule of Sierra Leone's leaders following independence have their antecedents in colonial rule and the incorporation of the territory into the modern capitalist world economy. This process resulted in a psychocultural change and dependent development that generated dilemmas for the postindependence political leadership, as well as stress and strains for Africans in the modernizing world.

STRUCTURAL VIOLENCE AND NATIONAL DEVELOPMENTS AS SHORT-TERM CAUSES OF WAR

In Sierra Leone, the process of development did not combine the expansion of relevant skills fast enough with the realization of personal and group well-being. Changes in sociocultural and economic development are supposed to occur simultaneously. But in Sierra Leone society, there was no synchronization between the two thereby resulting in deprivations, tensions, and strains. The "revolution of rising expectations" in Africa brought about by independence resulted in a change in attitudes, views, and general cultural orientation toward the acquisition of things Western (Mazrui 1996). The failure to achieve this new expectation produced frustration which was aggravated by blatant misrule that eventually produced intolerable inequality and intense deprivation.

Stated differently, before the war, one of Sierra Leone's predicament lay in the fact that the society was culturally westernizing without economically modernizing. The rising expectations for capitalist materialism far outpaced the process of economic development to satisfy economic wants, and after a while, even basic human needs became scarce. It is within this sociocultural and economic context that first Albert Margai and shortly thereafter Siaka Stevens consolidated power and worsened the political economic situation that eventually culminated in the eruption of the civil conflict which produced terrible bloodletting that shocked the rest of the world.

National Sources of Sierra Leone's Civil War

It was the nationalist fervor of the immediate postcolonial period under Sir Milton Margai, the country's first head of state, that helped integrate and contain the different ethnolinguistic groups and potential divisive power struggles. Any potential civil strife or challenges to his rule was also diluted by the euphoria of independence which stifled any challenges against his rule. As a result of this integrative aspect of nationalism and euphoria of independence,

Sir Milton Margai was relatively able to manage the ever-present north–south divide along with the potential for civil strife among the diverse groups and factions that were a part of Sierra Leone politics and society. However, with the passing of Sir Milton Margai, political rivalries sharpened along regional and ethnic lines thereby plunging the young nation into a crisis of legitimacy (Opala 1998; Roberts 1982). This crisis of legitimacy can be considered a key antecedent to the country's destructive civil war three decades later. The crisis began when Albert Margai who succeeded his brother made efforts at power consolidation in order to cement Mende hegemony in Sierra Leone politics and society.

There were deep underlying precursors to Sierra Leone's conflict. The first of these was the persistent misrule that would permeate the entire country following the 1967 general elections that would introduce to the country its first military intervention in politics by the national army to the outbreak of war in 1991. With the exception of Sir Milton Margai's regime, subsequent regimes never gained nationwide legitimacy because of the deep-seated corruption in government perpetuated by patronage and authoritarianism at the local and national levels of government. Over time corruption and lack of account-ability and the politicization of ethnicity and the military wiped out even the modicum of democratic tradition that was present during the immediate independence era of Sir Milton Margai. Beginning with the mid-1960s, the feeling/sense of legitimacy that bound people to rulers was beginning to dis-appear. Albert Margai who succeeded his brother as prime minister in 1964 openly played the tribal card by deliberately favoring his Mende folks, and in the process, alienated the Temnes, Krios, and other non-Mende-speaking groups (FRIS Report 1998). He, in other words, was responsible for injecting ethnic favoritism into Sierra Leone politics. He also in the process politicized and tribalized the Sierra Leone army (Kandeh 1992). Apart from politicizing the army, he also deliberately intervened in and corrupted the Sierra Leone Electoral commission. During his reign, there was a significant increase in the proportion of Mende officers in the army from 26 percent of the African offi-cers in mid-1964 to 52 percent by mid-1967 (Fisher 1969; Horowitz 1985). At the same time, officers from the northern province were marginalized and even arrested and detained as the 1967 elections approached. This further deepened the north–south or Mende versus northern groups' cleavage. The Albert Margai regime made sure that the Electoral Commission was Mende-dominated so that election victories would be called in favor of the Margai Sierra Leone Peoples Party (SLPP) regime. Even before the 1967 general elections, both electoral malpractice and military intervention in politics had become part of Sierra Leone politics. Albert Margai never even pretended to foster unity and build consensus with other groups. He was openly biased in favor of his Mende ethnic group and deliberately hostile and indifferent to the Temnes and Krios. This was in stark contrast to the time of his brother, Sir Milton Margai, when the SLPP was the "catch-all" independence party of national unity. But under Sir Albert Margai, the party became synonymous with the Mende people. It was also during his rule that government corruption began and would later reach shocking levels. He would lay the foundation for the devastating misrule of Siaka Stevens several years later. Albert Margai was also the one who introduced legislation to transform the country into a one-party state that would be centered on his Mende-dominated SLPP. His efforts to solidify Mende hegemony in Sierra Leone politics galvanized the Temnes, Limbas, Krios, and other groups to form the opposition All Peoples Congress (APC) party led by Siaka Stevens.

Sierra Leone inherited political, economic, educational, military, and other institutions based on the British model of government with political independence. However, in order to consolidate his rule and ensure APC regime longevity, he undermined or sabotaged many of them to serve his political objectives. When he eventually assumed power in April 1968 after being denied power for a year after his 1967 electoral victory, the only positive steps he put in place was to incorporate leading SLPP politicians into his APC regime. This he did as part of political expediency and a deliberate strategy of power consolidation and entrenchment in power (Conteh-Morgan and Dixon-Fyle 1999). In the end, this strategy will enable him to ignore democratic requirements, rule of law, and safeguard his rule. Again, he had been denied legitimate rule in 1967 when he won the general elections. The 1967 coups just after the elections deprived him of assuming power until 1968 (Dalby 1967). With each attempted coup to overthrow him such as the one in 1971, Siaka Stevens developed paranoia about the Sierra Leone army (SLA), and its propensity for coups, impelled him to further stifle all opposition and centralize the power of the state (Cox 1978). The specific actions he took were to establish a one-party state in 1978, develop a far-reaching network of patron–client relationships, and ensure that all groups and individuals are submissive to him, especially if they hold key political positions (Koroma 1996). In the end, he increased the repressive power of the state and made the Sierra Leone state more predatory and rapacious and neopatrimonial in nature. Patronage pervaded most sectors of society and government. In particular, the politics of patronage ended up solidifying around the single party, the APC, more than around any other political or bureaucratic entity.

First since the most vocal opposition to his rule and calls for good governance and distributional equity came from college students, and the educated elite, Siaka Stevens therefore decided to include in his cabinet many of these educated elites but at the same time was very successful at corrupting them to engage in personal use of state resources and property without any accountability in order to gain their support.

Perhaps his most important preoccupation was to render his regime coup proof, especially since his bitter experience of having been deprived of legitimate rule by the army for roughly one year after his victory during the 1967 general elections. In order to ensure the longevity and survival of the APC regime, he destroyed the efficiency and professionalism of the army by populating it with northern ethnic groups (including his own ethnic group, the Limba) that were loyal to him, depriving it of very educated officers and disarming it by stripping it of sophisticated weapons (Fashole-Luke 1988; Lancaster 2007). During his rule, personal enrichment by cabinet ministers, top government officials, and the destruction of the SLA as a professional, efficient institution was effected and even reached its highest point.

The misrule by the Stevens regime did not just affect the level of corruption, or politicization of the army, but it was far-reaching and aimed at destroying any modicum of substantive or procedural democracy in the country. In order to accomplish the death of democracy in Sierra Leone, Siaka Stevens transformed the country into a one-party state (Cartwright 1978). Thus, the APC was the only political party allowed and any aspiring politician had to secure the party symbol to be considered a candidate for election to parliament. The APC regime under Siaka Stevens' one-party rule made politicians into sycophants who would do anything from bribing him to violent attacks against rivals in order to secure the party symbol to run for a seat in parliament. In order for cabinet ministers to hold onto their ministries, they were expected to share spoils or loot their respective ministries with the president himself. His determination to destroy democracy and consolidate his authoritarian rule went as far as undermining local/rural politics. This he did by abolishing the twelve district councils in the country. These councils were the training ground for future local and grassroots leaders. They fostered self-government, civic responsibility, and groomed future leaders for engagement with national level of politics. They performed essential functions like tax collection, road construction and repairs, and other public functions. Instead, Stevens replaced these councils with handpicked party loyalists whose interests were far removed from those of these local citizens and with no support base within the districts.

Apart from the problem of ethnolinguistic and regional rivalries, the deliberate destruction of multiparty politics and democratic values, and the lack of accountability displayed by government officials, a great deal of corruption would especially revolve around diamonds, the country's most lucrative revenue source. Accordingly, politicians, the economic elite, top military personnel, and powerful civil servants constituted a kleptocratic elite that monopolized the mining, sales, and profits from diamonds thereby depriving the rest of the people, and especially sectors such as education, health, and agriculture of much-needed revenue for national development (Pham 2005).

Later on, diamonds would play a big role in the brutality of the war as rival warring factions fought for control of the mines in the eastern part of the country.

FROM STRUCTURAL VIOLENCE TO
IMMISERATION AND CIVIL STRIFE

The severe misrule and corrupt practices of postcolonial SLPP and APC regimes, especially beginning with the late 1960s, perpetuated structural violence and psychological harm on Sierra Leone society (Conteh-Morgan 2018). Economic deprivation plagued Sierra Leone society due to corrupt and insensitive policies which robbed people of basic human needs and even a modicum of social welfare benefits. Accordingly, as is the consequence in many countries, it aggravated individual and group frustration associated with institutional policies and governmental actions that triggered the Revolutionary United Front (RUF) rebellion and the widespread anarchy and national bloodletting that ensued. The structural violence that prevailed in Sierra Leone society between 1981 and 1991 comprised of both physical violence and psychological harmful acts by the APC regime. For instance, food insecurity was one of those harmful developments because Sierra Leoneans had limited or no access to adequate food. The combined policies of the APC regime and external impositions by the IMF resulted in healthcare insecurity, lack of inadequate housing, and a dramatic decrease in the quality of education in a country once renowned all over Africa for its first-rate educational standards and its university even known as "the Athens of West Africa" (Paracka 2003).

The intensity of structural violence (Farme 2004; Schepler-Hughes 2005) and its attendant relative deprivation (Gurr 1970) spawned many types of secondary violence in the form of increased crime rates, interpersonal violence, domestic violence, and in particular a steady rise in banditry as precursors to the total breakdown of law and order in 1991 and thereafter, The widespread and intense structural violence in Sierra Leone was conducive to the ease with which the Liberian civil war spilled over into the country and even affected the entire Mano River Union (MRU)—Liberia, Guinea, Sierra Leone—region. In a way, it could be argued that during the 1980s known as the "lost decade" in Africa, the level of structural violence in the MRU was so intense and pervasive that individuals, groups, and communities, and the sub-region experienced destabilization and a "contagion" of collective political violence.

In terms of the modernization dilemma, it is often inevitable that in developing countries with weak state institutions, a low/weak democratic political culture, exclusion and marginalization of individuals and groups occur.

The group and individual competition involved in trying to acquire modern amenities results in marginalization and political-economic exclusion, and even group oppression. The competition to acquire modern amenities has accordingly produced two mutually exclusive outcomes: higher standards of living for some and less than desirable lifestyles for many. The reason for this is distributional inequity associated with governmental corruption, embezzlement of state funds, and a lack of accountability for those holding positions of responsibility. Policies or the lack thereof in the 1980s in Sierra Leone increased insecurity for a few at the expense of most Sierra Leoneans. By the end of the decade (1980s), intolerable inequalities were pervasive and became unbearable because basic human needs were out of reach for most members of Sierra Leone society. The outcome was open rebellion in March 1991. Beginning with the early 1980s, conditions became increasingly worse as the deprivation extended to accessing transportation, health care, educational quality, provision of electricity, garbage collection, and water supply.

The Sierra Leone civil war was a result of severe structural violence which aggravated the level of relative derivation thereby triggering the civil war which lasted for eleven years from March 1991 to 2002. The level of, and detrimental effects of misrule, corrupt government practices focused on self-enrichment by the power elite progressed steadily and with intensity and culminated with intolerable misery and open rebellion triggered by the RUF. In particular, corrupt practices such as co-optation of the opposition, a symbiotic relationship between the ruling one-party and the army, an informal economy heavy on smuggling, and a deliberate embezzlement of state resources, among other things, became institutionalized from the 1970s. This meant that formal state institutions (tasked with functions of national development) became marginalized in favor of an informal market economy. The smuggling of natural resources especially affected the diamond sector, the largest source of national revenue. Diamond smuggling translated into worsening economic conditions because revenues from diamonds benefited only a few citizens who had strong political connections to the APC regime. Starved of funds, the budgets of the public sector could not deliver services to society at large (Magbaily-Fyle 1993). By the early 1980s, Sierra Leoneans had become disenchanted as state institutions like the judiciary, civil service, education, and health care had deteriorated into severe corruption or a lack of sufficient resources to run efficiently and effectively. This condition of severe/intense relative deprivation in resources and institutional values, it could be argued, constituted an intermediate cause of civil war.

While self-enrichment in the form of financial peculation was taking place among the political elite, the state was at the same time engaged in extensive expenditure of national resources. One example of this was the 1980 hosting of the OAU Summit (Roberts 1982). The hosting was motivated by the need for self-aggrandizement by Sake Stevens because it did not contribute in any way to national development but instead robbed the country of badly needed resources for investment in national development. The projects constructed to host the summit did not contribute to GDP growth nor did they contribute to ongoing overall development. In fact the enormous expenditure to host the OAU Summit had a serious and harmful impact only two years later on Sierra Leone society. The APC regime again experienced a significant lack of revenue two years later in 1982. The lack of revenue by the government resulted in dilapidated roads, power blackouts because of short supply of electricity, a halt in garbage collection, reduced and irregular water supply, a deterioration in educational facilities, neglect of healthcare facilities, and worst of all salaries of public workers and officials went unpaid for several months on end.

The political and socioeconomic situation in the country by the late 1980s was a far cry from the situation in the 1960s and 1970s when it was much easier to secure a civil service or teaching position and expect to be paid a regular salary every month. With the drastic change in the country's political economy, existential insecurity in food, and healthcare, and other basic needs worsened. In terms of societal/community security, in particular, the crime rate increased and was manifested in banditries and robberies at night. In other words, the negative effects of pervasive and deep systemic corruption, and governmental overstretch in terms of expenditure in relation to national budget or available resources, were having an inimical effect on communities and society at large and manifested in gradual and steady state collapse that would culminate in full-blown anarchy in the 1990s.

IMMEDIATE AND PRECIPITATING
EXTERNAL CAUSES OF WAR

By the time (1985) Joseph Momoh was handed power, Sierra Leone as a nation-state was ripe for implosion. This implosion came in the form of two catalysts or accelerators that triggered the civil war: IMF austerity policies and the spillage of the Liberian civil war into the country. In Sierra Leone in the early 1990s, there was definitely an inherent tension between the Structural Adjustment Policies (SAPs) of the IMF and neoliberal internationalism, in general, and their impact on African society. With the emphasis on economic efficiency, on trade and open markets, end of subsidies in education, health, transportation, and food, among others, the modicum of distributional equity that was in existence was drastically reduced thereby generating severe relative deprivation. Sierra Leone's economic crisis and in turn its descent into violent conflict was triggered or accelerated by the severe absence of distributional equity and increased immiseration inherent in IMF and World Bank austerity measures (Weeks 1992). The implementation of these external policies worsened economic insecurity manifested in a lack of access by many to basic human needs, especially sufficient food, housing, and health care. In society at large, there was an interruption and in some cases even end to the distribution of services.

By the late 1970s, the euphoria of independence and revolution of rising expectations had slipped into a state of disenchantment and fear of gloomy times to come that would produce increasing relative deprivation and loss of legitimacy for incumbent regimes. In order for the longest serving APC regime to preserve itself, it resorted to a strategy of utilizing both neopatrimonialism and coercion. In Sierra Leone, the intermediate or short-term factors to the tragic civil war were pervasive misrule, nepotism, ethnicity, and endemic government corruption. Besides the dependent character of the Sierra Leone state which translated into weak incumbent regimes also translated into the country being subjected to the external impositions of powerful nations that supplied the resources needed to maintain the neopatrimonial ties between the incumbent APC regime and its key supporters.

The impact on society of maintaining a neopatrimonial system was reflected in the ever-present balance of payments problems, and therefore austerity measures imposed by the IMF since 1979. Specific demands for cuts in public expenditure, end of subsidies in key areas of the economy, and currency devaluation were some of the austerity measures required by external donors. These externally imposed measures widened and intensified the level of relative deprivation experienced by people. These policies coupled with the absence of an industrial base, an ever-present widening urban-rural discrepancy in the level of development, weak state institutions and unproductive education elite worsened state-society relations and served as precursors to civil war.

The one factor that particularly constituted a precipitating or immediate factor that resulted in intolerable misery and violent conflict was the APC regime's decision to request help from the IMF immediately after President Momoh took over the presidency from Siaka Stevens. It was impelled to do so because it was confronted with a serious lack of revenue. During his presidency, Siaka Stevens did not fully implement the austerity measures inherent in IMF loans because he was aware of the negative effects they would have on the population. It was when President Joseph Momoh assumed the presidency in 1985 that he mustered the political will to implement IMF austerity measures. Apart from the privatization of government-controlled industries and investments, a willingness to collect taxes from citizens and small businesses, the IMF prescriptions translated into the end of subsidies on essentials such as rice (the major staple food crop of Serra Leone), petroleum products, health care, and education, among other things.

With the end of subsidies, the price of gasoline increased by 300 percent and that of rice by 180 percent (For Di People 1990). These developments were coupled with the inability of the government to pay wages and salaries of public sector workers in a country where many people are employed by the state. The IMF loans were just enough for President Momoh to continue running the state but not enough for neopatrimonial rewards, and payment of salaries for government workers on a regular basis. Monetary rewards to political supporters and timely payment of salaries were the means employed by incumbent regimes to check or discourage dissent or rebellion against the political system, in general.

In fact, many scholars of the Sierra Leone civil war have implicated, in varying ways, the inimical effects of the IMF SAPs as immediate causes of the Sierra Leone civil war (Mustapha 2019; Weeks 1992; Zack-Williams 1999). They were austere, painful, and deleterious in their impact on Sierra Leone society. The combined effects of blatant misrule by the APC regime coupled with the negative impact of IMF austerity policies deepened existential insecurity such that about 75 percent of the population subsisted on less than $2 a day according to UNDP estimates (2005). The pervasive economic dislocation, structural violence, and rapid descent from state failure to state collapse were reflected in massive youth unemployment and alienation, a lack of delivery of even basic services, as well as a pervasive culture of corruption at all levels of society and politics.

Probably the most traumatic experience Sierra Leoneans experienced before the eruption of violence and during the war itself was the dismantling of the "social welfare contract" between state and citizens. Since independence, Sierra Leoneans had been accustomed to government subsidies which ensured more access to education, health care, food, transportation, and other services. This access lessened the economic gap between the haves and have-nots. The neoliberal globalization impositions had a dislocative effect on society by weakening traditional social identities and relationships, as well as perceptions of legitimacy of government. Government delivery of services was stifled by privatization resulting in a drastic reduction in the access to social needs which resulted in more widespread and severe personal and societal insecurity. The pervasive socioeconomic insecurity was experienced by most segments of the population including marginalized youth whose resentment was easily exploited by the RUF which was fighting to take over power from the incumbent APC regime of Joseph Momoh. The backbone of the RUF insurgents in fact comprised of frustrated and disaffected intellectuals and alienated youth of Sierra Leone with no access to the neopatrimonial spoils of the successive governments. Their frustration was further deepened by the existential shocks brought on by the IMF austerity measures of the late 1980s and 1990s.

Moreover, the manner in which IMF SAPs were implemented in Sierra Leone contributed in speeding up the collapse of the Sierra Leone state. Their implementation took the form of a "shock" that did not in any way alleviate the economic malaise and pervasive existential insecurity in the country. The policies were implemented in a sudden and unexpected manner instead of in a more gradual and tolerable manner (Weeks 1993). In fact the IMF imposed tougher conditions for further loans on the country. These tougher demands resulted in the total elimination of the "informal economy" that revolved around diamond mining and was the source of livelihood for many Sierra Leoneans. President Momoh yielded to private investor demands and IMF requirements by instituting "Operation Clear All" which removed approximately 30,000 illicit miners and traders from mining areas (Foreign Systems Center 1998). The elimination of this informal diamond economy served as one of the key catalysts for the war.

The young miners who were displaced from their source of livelihood interpreted this action as directed against them to benefit outsiders and the corrupt power elite in Freetown, the capital. Many of those uprooted from the mines would later join the RUF in its war against the APC government. Their removal caused greater relative deprivation, made them susceptible to politicization, and galvanized them into action against the government and the SLA.

In particular, Serra Leone already being a weak political economy was especially jolted into economic existential shock by the negative effects of SAPs. The sudden implementation of the austere measures on an already weakened and collapsing state had the effect of a "shock therapy" resulting in unbearable misery and widespread anger (and alienation) at the regime. Many Sierra Leoneans lost access to basic human needs and entitlements in the form of subsidies for health care, access to food items, transportation, and education, and at the same time they lost all means of ever acquiring new "wants." This double condition of decremental and aspirational relative deprivation (Gurr 2011) galvanized Sierra Leone society into violent action when a core of frustrated RUF members became politicized and organized and trained to launch a rebellion against the APC regime in March 1991.

It is not an exaggeration to say that the dismantling of the underground economy in diamond smuggling had a far-reaching effect by further perpetuating misery on a very large segment of society. It was therefore not surprising that some of the displaced 30,000 miners who had been dependent on illegal mining swelled the ranks of the RUF in 1991 and beyond as the civil war unfolded (Opala 1998; SAIS 1998). The termination of this underground economy further resulted in more Sierra Leoneans being deprived of economic sustenance since the displaced miners had many dependents as part of their extended family members.

Furthermore, by this time, the level of frustration, anger, and deprivation was very high among college graduates. This was so because their higher academic attainment of a college degree which had not benefited them produced in them a feeling and even reality of intense deprivation especially in comparison to the ordinary noncollege graduate. In fact they experienced greater anger and frustration because of the discrepancy between their educational capabilities and their value expectations (their wants). Their anger and frustration were made more severe by the fact that those with far fewer qualifications did far better economically because of their stronger political connections to the corrupt APC regime and its neopatrimonial system (Roberts 1982). Sierra Leone in the late 1980s was plagued by frequent student protests, widespread hostility directed at the incumbent regime, and pervasive economic hardship, among a wide cross-section of society encompassing teachers, students, laborers, civil servants, and the like.

Employment opportunities in the country were not just very scarce in the years immediately preceding the outbreak of the war, but securing a public sector position meant working for months on end without remuneration. The combined impact of a very weakened economy due to widespread misrule, and the shock of IMF austerity measures that stripped citizens of even a modicum of social and economic welfare, intensified the misery within the country. However, it could be argued that the severe deprivation which increased anger and hostility against the incumbent regime did not trigger the violence. What actually constituted the immediate catalyst/trigger/accelerator for the war was the politicization of discontent in society by RUF leaders, Foday Sankoh, Abu Kanu, and Rashid Mansaray (Abdullah 1998; Rashid 2016). They also galvanized a portion of Sierra Leone society into open rebellion when they attacked eastern Sierra Leone in March 1991. All three individuals received training in Libya in the late 1980s. They then engaged in recruiting and politicizing others who formed the nucleus of the RUF. Blatant aspects of misrule, and the painful effects of neoliberal internationalism, in particular IMF austerity measures, escalated in 1991 to collective political violence by disaffected members of Sierra Leone society long excluded from the neopatrimonial system, or beneficial connections to government, openly rebelled against the government. The RUF attack in southeastern Sierra Leone was not a spontaneous, unorganized attack but was well-thought-out and planned between Charles Taylor of Liberia and Foday Sankoh as head of the RUF. The RUF itself was formed by Sierra Leoneans in Libya in the late 1980s and spearheaded by Foday Sankoh. It launched its armed campaign in March 1991. It was notorious for its use of terror tactics of mutilation and amputation in the countryside. The barbarity and level of carnage and bloodletting that took place in Sierra Leone during the eleven-year civil war was one of the most destructive in the 1990s following the end of the Cold War.

It is estimated that 30,000 Sierra Leoneans died during the conflict between 1991 and 1996.

The RUF was more of an emotional response to the blatant misrule and gaping inequalities, and also misery that existed in the country. As a result, it did not have a well-thought-out, coherent, political and economic strategy, or manifesto on how to rule the country or win over the hearts of Sierra Leoneans. Its agenda was, in other words, very sketchy and vague and solely focused on the overthrow of the APC government in Freetown. It was not surprising that it resorted to terrorizing the rural population, a tactic devoid of any substantive ideological philosophy to win the hearts of Sierra Leoneans and invest its cause with legitimacy.

This attack by the RUF with the blessing of Charles Taylor as the dominant Warlord in Liberia's Civil War also constituted the spillover of the Liberian civil war into the country. This inevitably impelled the Momoh regime to try and defend the country from the invading RUF rebels, supported by Charles Taylor and his National Patriotic Front of Liberia (NPFL) and Burkinabe soldiers. These were rebels who in 1991 had also participated in Liberia's civil war and were now headed for the southern and eastern regions of Sierra Leone where they unleashed their senseless destruction in rural villages. Led by Foday Sankoh and sponsored by Charles Taylor, who at this time was leader of the NPFL faction in the Liberian conflict. Again, both Charles Taylor and Foday Sankoh along with other Sierra Leoneans had trained in rebel training camps in Libya and Burkina Faso in the 1980s. Their goal was to overthrow the APC government of President Momoh with the greater objective of bringing about a pan-African revolution. Taylor's support for the RUF was also in retaliation for President Momoh's support for the ECOWAS Ceasefire Monitoring Group (ECOMOG) intervention in Liberia in 1990 which had delayed his outright conquest of Liberia's capital, Monrovia. Taylor offered both material and moral support for the RUF because in doing so he saw an opportunity to acquire not just diamonds but other natural resources from Sierra Leone to enrich himself and ensure a regular supply of resources to continue his war effort.

By the time of the RUF attack, the SLA was already a pathetic example of incompetence and top-heavy with senior officers appointed through patronage rather on merit. Besides it had been gutted by Siaka Stevens and therefore lacked effective weapons or war-fighting technology like helicopters, radios, and intelligence gathering material. By this time also the divisions between the APC regime of Momoh and the rural people had widened because they had not benefited from the neopatrimonial system that pervaded the country. In order to confront the RUF rebellion, Momoh was forced to increase the size of the army from 3,000 to 14,000 soldiers. Much of this army included new recruits from the urban unemployed youth and from the Mende ethnic group whose people in the south and east where victims of the worst attacks by the RUF. Neither group had any loyalty to the APC regime because they had largely been marginalized in terms of economic access to government largesse.

This demoralized and largely disgruntled army confronted the RUF with outdated and insufficient weapons. In addition to their lack of new and effective small arms and light weapons, they also lacked radios, boots, and uniforms, among other basic equipment. Frustration grew among the young recruits and especially the young military officers who bore the challenge of going to the war front. Accordingly in 1992, roughly a year after the outbreak of RUF attacks, soldiers returning from fighting the RUF insurgency staged a coup in response to the APC government's ineffective material response to the war and their deprivation and the overall ill-equipped condition as fighting soldiers. Following the coup, Momoh fled to neighboring Guinea and the National Provisional Ruling Council (NPRC) assumed power under Valentine Strasser, who was appointed chairman and head of state. The fact that the Sierra Leone state and society had already degenerated into an utter state of corruption, illegality, and state failure, the emergence of the NPRC did not change peoples' perception of government. Besides, rule by the NPRC did not stop the momentum of the RUF or its determination to take over the country. Sankoh and his RUF in fact targeted the NPRC for over-throw, especially since the latter did not show any intention to include them in its government. NPRC rule did not in any way change the nature and behavior of the Sierra Leone political system. It was still plagued by unprofessional-ism, widespread societal deprivation, and a lack of effective weapons for soldiers to contain the RUF rebel forces. In fact the extensive economic deprivation drove the soldiers fighting the RUF to resort to banditry in rural areas and even cooperated with the RUF for their own personal enrichment. In addition to depriving rural folks of their property, they eventually occupied and gained control of the diamond fields in the Kono District in the eastern province thereby depriving the NPRC government of their main sources of funding and wealth.

To a large extent, Sierra Leone is well known for its diamonds which dur-ing the war became somewhat of a resource curse. Diamonds played a dual role during the war: (1) they were the means of acquiring a steady supply of weapons to continue the war effort both for government and the rebel RUF and (2) they were the means of self-enrichment for individuals either within rebel groups, or within government. However, while the struggle to control the diamond fields was fierce, the war was not centered or focused largely on control of diamonds as a resource curse. The problem in Sierra Leone was much more encompassing than the struggle for diamonds but was one of pervasive misrule that brought about severe structural violence and widespread immiseration. The inequity in distributing national revenue and resources reflected in neopatrimonial politics resulted over the years in the destruction and neglect of government institutions. Diamond smuggling was no doubt a key aspect of the loss of revenue to the Sierra Leone state. In particular, this led to neglect of education, a degraded healthcare system, a less productive agricultural sector, and an expanded kleptocratic state. The explosive, dangerous, and volatile situation that developed hat led a large cohort of young, unemployed, largely illiterate, and very frustrated youth that were later recruited either as government soldiers or rebel fighters. They were responsible for unleashing the most heinous crimes on Sierra Leone society during the conflict. To a large extent, the blatant inequality was a result of the collapse of state institutions because they had been starved of resources which in turn resulted in wiping out the delivery of services which had been the bedrock of the country's modest social welfare system. The Sierra Leone state had become so degraded that graft, nepotism, injustice, and the overall violation of the rule of law had become normalized.

This action by some of the NPRC soldiers fighting alongside RUF rebel allies forced Valentine Strasser and the NPRC leadership to employ the services of Executive Outcomes (EO), a private security firm from South Africa, considered highly professional and effective. It was comprised of ex-members of the South African Special Forces and was employed by the NPRC between 1995 and 1996. They were able to restore the military balance between the government and the RUF. It quickly took control of the Kono District, the main location of the diamonds after only a few weeks of fighting against the combined force of rebels and rogue soldiers (Fanthorpe 2010; ICG 2001). It seemed the mandate of EO was simply to flush out rebels and preda- tory soldiers from the diamond fields. The NPRC, like preceding regimes, turned out to be just as corrupt and focused on self-enrichment. This real- ization by Sierra Leoneans was very disturbing and even shocking because the public had not grasped the true nature and behavior of the NPRC and its soldiers until several years later. Initially, they had experienced a great deal of euphoria and great expectations when the NPRC finally toppled the seem- ingly ever-present and utterly corrupt APC regime in 1992. In fact, the public would eventually learn about the marauding behavior of NPRC soldiers who played the dual role of soldiers during the day and rebels at night. This is why they became known as "Sobels" or soldier-rebels.

By this time (the mid-1990s), the public was tired of the war and was hoping for a responsible government to assume power and stem the tide of anarchy within the country. So when elections were held in early 1996, Sierra Leoneans were very optimistic once more. President Ahmad Tejan-Kabbah, a civilian president, was welcomed into office with a popular mandate. Because he assumed power did not mean he would be able to satisfy the demands of the masses or would be able to calm the fears of all segments of society. Besides, the RUF was still a force to reckon with, along with the army which was still armed and just as deprived and now more aggrieved because of their loss of power. In other words, while the postelection government under President Kabbah instilled some moral authority, Sierra Leone was still a collapsed state and an insecure society. In fact it was during the time of President Kabbah that another very heinous dimension of the civil war was introduced into society— the mutilation of limbs by the RUF of many Sierra Leoneans who voted in the elections for a civilian government. The RUF chopped off the arms and hands of men, women, and children as a deterrent to future voting. Women were especially sexually brutalized and experienced permanent genital damage. Many soldiers in the rogue SLA were still loose in the rest of the country, and especially in rural areas preying largely on the rural civilian population.

It was barely two years into the civilian regime of President Kabbah when in May 1997 disgruntled elements of the army staged a coup which ousted him from power. The new junta called itself the Armed Forces Revolutionary Council (AFRC) and was led by Major Johnny Paul Koroma. In league with the RUF, it embarked on a fresh round of terror on society, looting, and pillaging, and also perpetrating other criminal behavior all over the country. It was during this time that the RUF decided to invade Freetown which up till this time had been spared the horrors of extreme violence experienced by people in the rural areas of the country. The RUF invasion in January 1999 killed over 1,000 more Sierra Leoneans in Freetown. As many as 1.7 million Sierra Leoneans were internally displaced and over 100,000 fled Sierra Leone, after the overthrow of the Kabbah regime by the AFRC and the invitation of the RUF by the new junta.

The AFRC was eventually driven from power by Nigerian forces operating under the umbrella of the ECOMOG in February 1998. ECOMOG was organized in 1990 to intervene in the Liberian civil war. The AFRC responded to its overthrow by retreating to the rural areas, joined forces with the RUF to pillage, and exploit rural people. The number of rogue actors involved in the Sierra Leone civil war was responsible for the high level of bloodletting and carnage that took place not just in the rural areas but in Freetown as well. It is estimated that some 35,000 combatants were involved in the war spread out among three groups—some 14,000 soldiers of the SLA, 3,500 RUF insurgents, and between 15,000 and 20,000 Civilian Defense Forces (CDFs). It is estimated that about 5,000 of the combatants in the Sierra Leone civil war were child soldiers (Abdallah, and Muana 1999). The CDFs and the RUF insurgents had little or no formal military training. The SLA for its part was demoralized, politicized, ill-equipped, and poorly trained. Approximately 30,000 Sierra Leoneans lost their lives during the insurgency between 1991 and 1996. In 1997, as a result of the overthrow of the AFRC, another roughly over 1,000 people also perished. By April 1998, some 462,000 of the country's 4.5 million people became refugees in neighboring countries. In particular, because of the very turbulent events of 1997 and 1998, over 100,000 fled the country, especially after January 1998. Acording to the U.S. State Department, it is estimated that about 1.7 million Sierra Leoneans became internally displaced as a result of all the anarchy (Foreign Systems Research Center 1998; ICG 2001).

The bloodletting within the country during the eleven-year civil war involved many groups as already stated. First was the SLA combatants still poorly armed and unprofessional and politicized which numbered roughly 14,000, then there were the roughly 35,000 insurgents of the main rebel group the RUF. There were also various Civil Defense Forces known by names specific to their geographic locations, such as the Kamajors of the south and east, Kapras of the north, as well as the Donsos of the far north, and so on. In all, they numbered some 15,000 to 40,000. These were civilians who never underwent any conventional military training but simply banded together to protect their subregions in the absence of effective rule and internal sovereignty. The CDFs were government supported, and aligned, although they were not under the operational control of government. They were fiercely anti-RUF and rogue soldiers. It is estimated that about 5,000 of these combatants were child soldiers. It was war that involved combatants who were civilians, soldiers who had never been exposed to any rigorous military training and were poorly equipped, and unprofessional because they played the dual role as soldiers mostly during the day and rebels at night looting and raping just like the RUF. It is estimated that about half the SLA fighters played the dual role of "sobels"—soldiers by day and rebels at night.

During the Sierra Leone civil war, all the internal actors—government soldiers, the RUF, the CDF—were complicit in perpetuation of the heinous crimes and gross human rights violations. The war captured the attention of the international community because of its barbarity, extreme brutality, and its specific signature—the mutilation and amputation of limbs by the RUF. To a very large extent, most of the heinous crimes and extreme brutality were carried out by the combined campaign of the RUF and the AFRC after its overthrow in February 1998. This is not to say that government forces and their allies, the CDFs did not commit serious crimes, but they did so on a far smaller scale of a different nature than those by rebel groups. During the conflict, tens of thousands of civilians were killed and up to one-fourth of the population was displaced. Most other time during the war, which lasted from 1991 to 2002, rebels, and to lesser extent government forces, consistently failed to distinguish between civilians and combatants. Apart from amputations and mutilations, women and girls were subjected to the worst sexual violence imaginable. Besides, many of the combatants were children which meant that all sides coerced and recruited children to fight. In particular, the Sierra Leone civil war was characterized by the widespread use of child combatants. When ECOMOG ousted the AFRC/RUF from power and drove them to the rural areas in February 1998, the level of atrocities intensified and became more widespread and directed almost exclusively at civilians. The reason for the AFRC/RUF commission of such egregious atrocities against unarmed civilians was an attempt by them to regain power. Their combined campaign of terror resulted in killings, mutilations, amputations, rapes, especially between February and June 1998. Both rebel groups lacked legitimacy in the entire country. This forced them to employ tactics of coercion, abduction, forced labor, and overall terror. According to Amnesty International (2000) and Human Rights Watch (2012) all actors—government and non-government—committed numerous violations, abuses, even to the point of extrajudicial killings.

CHILD SOLDIERS AND IRREGULAR
WARFARE ELEMENT OF THE WAR

Another key factor in Sierra Leone's civil war was the nexus of child soldiers and irregular warfare. The participation of children in civil wars during the early 1990s was a common phenomenon in Africa's wars during the 1990s. This is because with the end of the Cold War in the early 1990s a new category of violent civil conflicts erupted in developing countries that defied conventional rules and regulations of warfare in which heinous crimes were directed purposely at civilians (White 1996). In Sierra Leone, many child soldiers fought alongside either the SLA against the RUF or with the RUF against the SLA. Even the CDFs which were comprised of the Kamajors, Donsos, Tamaboros, Gbethis, and Kapras, according to their subregional origins, had in their midst a good number of child soldiers. The number of child soldiers was estimated to be as high as 5,000 or 12 percent of the combatants during the war (Gbla 2003). The entire duration of the war was characterized by unconventional or irregular warfare defined largely as a blatant disregard for rules of warfare reflected in looting, extrajudicial killings, and a widespread disregard for human rights. Incentives (positive and negative) became a key factor in recruiting children to participate in the war. In other words, children between the ages of 8 and 17 were either enticed by promises of reward, or threatened by punishment, or even death, if they did not participate. They are described as child soldiers because according to Human rights Watch and Amnesty International, they are under the age of 18. This fact is also in line with the 2002 Optional Protocol to the Convention on the

Rights of the Child which raised the minimum age from 15 to 18 (Cohn and Goodwin-Gill 1994).

The participation of children in civil wars during the early 1990s was a common phenomenon in Africa during the wars of the 1990s. They were largely coerced into fighting. Those who volunteered saw it as a means to escape abject poverty or give their lives some meaning. In irregular warfare, because rules of war are ignored, the strategies and tactics employed are scorched earth and manifested in raiding villages and towns, attacking civilians and looting their property. Houses are set on fire and children are coerced into participating in the indiscriminate violence. While many of the girls were used as sex slaves and the boys were trained to be young killers. In Sierra Leone's irregular warfare, child soldiers comprised a large portion of the fighters who terrorized civilians in the villages and small towns.

The large size of child soldiers in Sierra Leone's civil war was due to the twin factors of them being coerced to fight and the pressure on many of them for self-actualization, and a sense of self-worth impelled them to participate in order to overthrow a corrupt system. By the mid-1980s, youth in Sierra Leone faced a very bleak future and little or no prospect for success in life. A lack of industrialization or robust private sector to employ high school and college graduates translated into mass poverty and severe economic deprivation for them and for many a willingness to participate in the war in order to overthrow a corrupt APC regime seen as the cause of all their problems.

By the mid-1980s, massive amounts of graduates without employment believed that pursuing education was not a worthwhile endeavor because it is those who are corrupt and embezzled state funds who are successful in life regardless of their educational levels. This mindset was pervasive among the youth of Sierra Leone by the time the civil war erupted. It was therefore no surprise that with the spillage of the Liberian civil war into Sierra Leone participation by the youth spread like the eruption of gasoline and fire in dry grassland.

The plight of teachers who were considered the agents of education was particularly difficult, especially since they became the most impoverished of the educated class. Their economic conditions led the children or the young to develop negative attitudes and even hostility toward schooling. Accordingly, since many students saw their teachers struggling to make ends meet, they concluded that education was not a worthwhile pursuit. The children who volunteered to participate in the war viewed their participation as a way out of poverty and existential insecurity. Their struggle to survive forced many of them to commit some of the most atrocious activities such as shooting captives at close range, looting and torching houses, mutilating civilians and even decapitating captives (BBC 2013). It was due to the effect of hard drugs and the threats of adult group leaders that they were able to carry out such heinous crimes.

The participation of child soldiers was high in Sierra Leone's civil war because with the spillover of the Liberian war, child participation included child soldiers from both countries. The positive incentives of promise of cash and mineral resources galvanized child participation. A great deal of the violence during the war was perpetrated against the eastern and southeastern regions of Sierra Leone where the diamond fields are located. It is therefore not surprising that the conflict was also described as one of a resource war. The RUF utilized large numbers of children as miners and protectors of the mines to ensure that they did not fall into the hands of government soldiers or CDFs (Fanthorpe 2010; Richards 2010).

Child soldiers saw fighting as a way to increase their morale and status in a society that offered little or no opportunities for them to pursue their ambitions. It was therefore easy for both the RUF and rogue elements of the SLA to influence child soldiers into committing atrocities of great magnitude. Many of them were not old enough to remember a Sierra Leone society as a place which was once very peaceful and where even one homicide would be a shocking occurrence. As children they had not yet internalized the traditional values and aspects of society which would consider widespread violence as an aberration. What the RUF did was to ensure that child soldiers used as much violence as possible so that it would win a quick victory. While some children were perpetrating violence, others went through villages and towns in search of loot. Along the way, they were able to recruit more child soldiers. The child soldier phenomenon was an integral aspect of the irrationality of the Sierra Leone civil war, in the sense that the bloodletting, looting, and overall internecine nature of the war was not based on political ideology or national strategy aimed at ensuring the welfare or human security of the entire population. Instead RUF behavior was focused on merely terrorizing the population (Abdallah 2000; Human Rights Watch 2012). The terror perpetrated on ordinary people who had suffered long years of economic deprivation was baffling to many. As a result, the RUF and its widespread use of child soldiers alienated most of the nation, the region, and the international community. Its violation of human rights and the sheer magnitude of its brutality shocked the conscience and the world community. During normal times, the miniscule size and geopolitical insignificance of Sierra Leone mean it would not even make the world news. But the shocking atrocities of the mid-1990s to late 1990s put Sierra Leone in the limelight for heinous crimes of limb amputations, decapitations, extrajudicial killings, and mutilations of civilians, especially women and the like. The scope and intensity of crimes associated with the war, in general, and child soldiers, in particular, galvanized the regional and international community to intervene and stop the war.

CONCLUSION

The Sierra Leone civil war, which erupted in March 1991 and lasted until 2002, was first a result of self-reinforcing negative factors at the national, regional, and international levels which had inimical effects on the country. Second, the war was also caused by the interacting and combined cultural incompatibilities between precolonial and colonial institutional factors, as well as postindependence, short-term, and precipitating developments directly related to severe misrule during the almost twenty-five years of the APC regimes of Siaka Stevens and Joseph Momoh. During APC rule, structural violence deepened and relative economic deprivation intensified and produced severe existential insecurity that was largely responsible for the anarchic struggle for power control of the country's political economy.

The war was an internal and external structural problem which intensified political grievances, deprivations, and widespread misery and eventually led to the implosion of Sierra Leone into full-scale civil strife. All segments of society experienced existential insecurity in the areas of food, health, transportation, and income. Both educated youth and the marginalized ones were affected. Many civil service workers lost their jobs as a result of the implementation of IMF austerity measures. With the widespread misery among people, it was easy for the RUF to recruit Sierra Leoneans to fight against the APC government. Both the RUF and the SLA perpetrated a great deal of violence against rural populations. Both looted, engaged in extrajudicial killings, and terrorized society. Soldiers became so unprofessional that they were labeled "sobels"—soldiers by day and rebels at night who equally looted, raped, and carried out the worst atrocities.

The war was a complex one, in the sense that it comprised of many actors: the RUF as the rebel army which sparked the war by attacking the country from southeastern Sierra Leone, the SLA which in the end turned out to be a rogue and unprofessional army, the EO a mercenary army, whose mission was solely to fight as soldiers of fortune, and was employed by the NPRC for roughly one year to restore the military balance and take control of diamond mines for the government, ECOMOG which played the critical role of stopping the advance of the combined forces of the RUF and the AFRC from taking over the whole of Freetown, the presence of a small force of British soldiers that also played a deterrent role against rebel soldiers and the RUF in Freetown, the eventual deployment of the United Nations Peacekeeping

Mission in Sierra Leone (UNAMSIL), the participation of CDFs representing and protecting their varied regions in the south, east, and northern regions of the country. To a large extent, the conflict itself was based on irregular warfare, child soldiers, and the most heinous of societal bloodletting in the form of extrajudicial killings, looting, and indiscriminate violence, along with coups and countercoups carried out by the NPRC and AFRC.

In sum, the Sierra Leone civil war was a classic example of the combined effect of a national/regional/and external nexus. At the national level was the inimical effects of gross misrule by the APC regime for over twenty years which produced serious existential insecurities; at the regional level was the "contagion effect" of the Liberian civil war, the role Burkina Faso, and the destabilizing effects of the post–Cold War environment on microstates within Africa served as key factors that produced a tragic and bloody war in the country. At the external level, the weak and dependent Sierra Leone state impelled the Momoh regime to agree to IMF austerity measures which had the effect of an economic shock therapy on Sierra Leone society and further aggravated the misery and economic insecurity that provoked full-blown violence within the country. The Sierra Leone civil war despite all of its notoriety should more properly be called the Sierra Leone conflict or civil strife because it was not a war based on ethnopolitics, or religion, and not even solely based on resource struggle but a societal conflict provoked by misrule which caused severe structural violence and aspirational and decremental deprivation that became so intolerable that the RUF decided to overthrow the APC regime. In 1999, with the intervention and pressures from regional and external actors like ECOMOG, the United Nations, and Britain the intensity of the war wound down. The deployment of more effective and better armed fighter like the EO, and the British troops guarding Freetown, may have been a motivating factor for the RUF's decision to sign agreements like the Lome Peace Accord, the Conakry Accord, and the Abidjan Accord and eventually produce effective control of Sierra Leone by the civilian government of President Ahmad Tejan-Kabbah's regime and the final demise of the RUF and its allies.

REFERENCES

Abdallah, Ibrahim. 2000. "Bush Path to Destruction: The Origins and Character of the RUF." In *Between Democracy and Terror: The Sierra Leone Civil War*, edited by Ibrahim Abdullah, 41–65. Dakar: CODESRIA.

Abdallah, Ibrahim, and Patrick Muana. 1999. "The Revolutionary United Front of Sierra Leone." In *African Guerrillas*, edited by Christopher Clapham, 172–194. Oxford, UK and Bloomington: James Currey, Fountain Publishers and Indiana University Press.

Amnesty International. 2000. *Sierra Leone: Childhood – A Casualty of Conflict.* London: Amnesty International. August.

Buzan, Barry, Charles Jones, and Richard Little. 1993. *The Logic of Anarchy: Neorealism to Structural Realism.* New York: Columbia University Press.

Cartwright, John. 1978. *Political Leadership in Sierra Leone.* Toronto: University of Toronto Press.

Chabal, Patrick. 1994. *Power in Africa: An Essay in Political Interpretation.* New York: St. Martin's.

Cohn, Ilene, and Guy S. Goodwin-Gill. 1994. *Child Soldiers: The Role of Children in Armed Conflict.* Oxford: Clarendon Press.

Conteh-Morgan, Earl. 2018. *Structural Violence and Relative Deprivation: Precursors to Collective Political Violence in Sierra Leone.* Joint Special Operations University, Center for Strategic Studies.

Conteh-Morgan, Earl, and Mac Dixon-Fyle. 1999. *Sierra Leone at the End of the Twentieth Century – History, Politics, and Society.* New York: Peter Lang,

Cox, Thomas S. 1976. *Civil Military Relations in Sierra Leone: A Case Study of African Soldiers in Politics.* Cambridge, MA: Harvard University Press.

Dalby, David. 1967. "The Military Take-Over in Sierra Leone." *The World Today,* 23 January–December.

Davis, J. C. 1962. "Towards a Theory of Revolution." *American Sociological Review,* 27: 5–19.

Fanthorpe, Richard. 2010. "Beyond the Crisis of Youth? Mining, Farming, and Civil Society in Post-War Sierra Leone." *African Affairs,* 109(435): 251–272.

Farmer, Paul. 2004. "An Anthropology of Structural Violence." *Current Anthropology,* 45(3): 305–325.

Fashole-Luke, David. 1988. "Continuity in Sierra Leone: From Stevens to Momoh." *Third World Quarterly,* 10(1): 67–78.

Fashole-Luke, David, and S. P. Riley. 1989. "The Politics of Economic Decline in Sierra Leone." *Journal of Modern African Studies,* 27(1): 133–141.

Fisher, H. J. 1969. "Elections and Coups in Sierra Leone." *Journal of Modern African Studies,* 7(4): 611–636.

For Di People (Freetown Weekly), 1990. November 5, 1.

Foreign Systems Research Center. 1988. *Analytical Study of Irregular Warfare in Sierra Leone and Liberia.* Englewood, CO.

Fyle, Magbaily C. 1993. *The State and the Provision of Social Services in Sierra Leone Since Independence, 1961–91.* Senegal: CODESRIA.

Gbla, Osman. 2003. "Conflict and Post-War Trauma Among Child Soldiers in Liberia and Sierra Leone." In *Civil Wars, Child Soldiers and Post-Conflict Peacebuilding in West Africa,* edited by A. Sesay, 167–194. Ile-Ife: College Press.

Gelinas, Jacques B. 2003. *Juggernaut Politics: Understanding Predatory Globalization.* London: Zed Books.

Gurr, Ted Robert. 2011. *Why Men Rebel.* New York: Paradigm Publisher.

Human Rights Watch. 1999. *Shocking War Crimes in Sierra Leone – New Testimonies on Mutilation, Rape of Civilians,* June 24. https://www.hrw.org/news/1999/06/24/shocking

International Crisis Group (ICG). 2001. Sierra Leone Time for a New Military and Political Strategy. *ICG African Report.* No. 28, Freetown/London/Brussels.

Jackson, Bruce, and Jeffrey A. Larsen. 1998. *Analytical Study of Irregular Warfare in Sierra Leone and Liberia.* Denver, CO: Foreign Systems Research Center.

Jackson, Robert H., and Carl Rosberg. 1982. "Why Africa's Weak States Persist. The Empirical and Juridical in Statehood." *World Politics,* 35(1): 1–24.

Kandeh, Jimmy D. 1992. "Politicization of Ethnic Identities in Sierra Leone." *African Studies Review,* 35(1): 81–99.

Koffi, Stephane Landry Yao, Zimmy Samuel Yannick Gehe, and Zhou Xian Ping. 2018. "Globalization Effects on Sub-Saharan Africa: The Impact of International Trade on Poverty and Inequality." *International Journal of Innovation and Economic Development,* 4(3): 41–48.

Koroma, Abdul, K. 1996. *Sierra Leone: Agony of a Nation.* Freetown, Sierra Leone: Andromeda Press.

Koroma, Rashid. n.d. "Siaka Stevens: The Good, the Bad and the Ugly: How Much Did He Destroy Sierra Leone Politically and Economically?" www.thisissierraleone.com/.

Lancaster, Carol. 2007. "We Fall Down and Get Up." Sate Failure, Democracy and Development in Sierra Leone." Center for Global Development Essay, http://www.cgdev.org

Mazrui, Ali. 1996. "Perspective: The Muse of Modernity and the Quest for Development." In *The Muse of Modernity: Essays on Culture as Development in Africa,* edited by Phillip G. Altbach and Sala M. Hassan, 1–18. Trenton, NJ and Asmara, Eritrea: Africa World Press.

Medard, Jean-Francois. 1982. "The Underdeveloped State in Tropical Africa: Political Clientelism or Neo-Patrimonialism." In *Private Patronage and Public Power,* edited by Christopher Clapham, 162–192. London: Frances Pinter.

Muana, Patrick K. 1997. "The Kamajor Militia: Civil War, Internal Displacement and the Politics of Counter-Insurgency." *Africa Development,* 22(3&4): 77–100.

Mullard, Maurice. 2004. *The Politics of Globalization and Polarization.* Cheltenham, UK: Edward Elgar.

Mustapha, Marda. 2010. "Global Inequalities and Peace in Postwar Sierra Leone." In *Sierra Leone Beyond the Lome Accord,* edited by Marda Mustapha and Joseph J, Bangura, 145–160. New York: Palgrave Macmillan.

Opala, Joe. 1998. "Sierra Leone: The Politics of State Collapse." Paper Presented at the Conference on "Irregular Warfare in Liberia and Sierra Leone." Denver, CO: Foreign Systems SAIS.

Ouattara, Alassane D. 1997. *The Challenges of Globalization for Africa.* Address Delivered at the Southern Africa Economic Summit. Harare, Zimbabwe, May 21.

Pham, J. Peter. 2005. "Democracy By Force?: Lessons from the Restoration of the State in Sierra Leone." *The Whitehead Journal of Diplomacy and International Relations,* 6(1): 129–147.

Rashid, Ismail. 2016, May 24. "Sierra Leone: The Revolutionary United Front." *The Journal of Complex Operations,* 6(4): 80–91.

Reno, William. 1995. *Corruption and State Politics in Sierra Leone*. New York: Cambridge University Press.

Richards, Paul. 1996. *Fighting for the Rain Forest: War, Youth, and Resources in Sierra Leone*. London and Portsmouth, NH: James Currey and Heinemann.

Roberts, George O. 1982. *The Anguish of Third World Independence: The Sierra Leone Experience*. New York: University Press of America.

Salvage, J., K. Melf, and I. Sandy, eds. 2012. *Structural Violence and the Underlying Causes of Violent Conflict*. London: Medact.

Schepler-Hughes, Nancy. 2005. "Dangerous and Endangered Youth: Social Structures and Determinants of Violence." *Annals of the New York Academy of Sciences*, 1036: 13–46.

Stiglitz, Joseph E. 2002. *Globalization and Its Discontents*. New York: W.W. Norton & Co.

United Nations Development Program. 2005. *Human Development Report*. New York: UNDP.

Weeks, John. 1993. *Development Strategy of the Economy of Sierra Leone*. London: Macmillan.

White, Jeffrey B. 1996. "Irregular Warfare: A Different Kind of Threat." *American Intelligence Journal*, 17(1): 57–63.

Zack-Williams, A. B. 1990. "Sierra Leone: Crisis and Despair." *Review of African Political Economy*, 17(49): 22–33.

Chapter 9

The South Sudanese Civil War

Francis Onditi

The lack of peace and stability in South Sudan has been attributed to deep-rooted culture of insurgency, leading to intractable internal military intervention and interethnic tensions that has provided magnet for "complex mixed wars." Furthermore, mechanisms and institutions for managing civil conflict and bringing about durable peace remain weaker (Beza 2015). These factors have been fueling civil conflict among Sudanese people as early as the 1950s through the 1970s (Rolandsen 2011a; Sambanis 2004; Sharkey 2007). Lessons from history of this country show that all these bouts of conflicts, civil wars, and the various attempts of conflict resolution have been derailed by political machinations, territorial maneuvers, and militarization of institutions (Kon 2015). Lack of an effective political architecture is sustained by the absence of a culture of political discourse as a means of achieving consesus in addressing political violence (Straus 2012). Some scholars argue that the secession of southern Sudanese in 2011 was merely an extension of the previously northerly conceived kleptocracy—a militarized, corrupt neopatrimonial system of governance that only serves those capable of accessing the economic, political, and military power (Radon and Logan 2014). Undoubtedly, these are conditions reinforcing civil wars and conflicts in the country. Elsewhere, I have observed that the complex nature of conflict in fragile and conflict-affected states in Africa will, undoubtedly, require new methods of analyses and interventions (Onditi 2020).

South Sudan has had a long history of persistent civil wars emanating from several structural and systematic factors. The SPLM's (Sudan's People's Liberation Movement) dominance, embedded in the history of the liberation struggle, has made South Sudan a *de facto* one-party state. This arrangement has left top political elites with little choice but to struggle from within the SPLM for power. Even though there exists an institutional framework within the East African Community (EAC) for a collective response, translating the peace and security principles into action remains a challenge (Kisiangani 2018). Although the SPLM has always been regarded as "Dinka-dominated," in reality, it has been a forum for a variety of competing individuals or groups interested in controlling the resources and clientelist structures that come with state power (Lacher 2012). When confronted with growing contestation of his leadership and calls for reform, in July 2013, President Salva Kiir made the decision to dissolve the SPLM's party structures and dismiss his entire cabinet. This move contributed to the tensions at the National Liberation Council (NLC) meetings that produced the December 2013 political violence.

The power contest within the SPLM is among three distinct factions. A combination of military, economic, political, boundary, and sociocultural forces have reconfigured South Sudanese conflict into a "new wars." New wars entail riskier forms of military intervention than the conventionally envisaged classic state security doctrine. Hence, in this chapter, I have coined this type of war as "complex mixed wars"—a mixture of wars (political struggle among organized groups, economic deterioration, and organized crime). Since new forms of violence dominate the contemporary peace and security landscape in the country, this chapter's central concern is an examination of how the complex mixed wars, economic forces, and institutional failure converge and sustain civil wars and conflicts in the country. However, these forces have origin in the country's colonial condominium policy as well as hyped ethnic divisions.

The role of colonialism in impoverishing the African Continent cannot be denied, alteration of existing boundaries which forced groups that had no historical links to live together and the dismantling of precolonial social order are some of the colonial legacies that left the continent both socially and politically amorphous (Cohen and Middleton 1970). On the economic front, colonialism, which lasted for hundreds of years, deprived Africa of its natural and human resources (Genoud 1969). But several decades after political independence, exploitation is continuing although in a different and more sophisticated way whose corollary is palpable: from slow economic growth to overdependence on foreign aid, political violence, and ethnic exclusion. Therefore, colonialism alone can be used as an explanation of Africa's misfortunes. The sociopolitical and economic situation in South Sudan indicates that these challenges are self-inflicted and ethnicity—by extension "ethnicization of politics"—plays a significant role in calcifying the already worsening conflict situation.

There seems to be a compelling argument that underscores the damaging effects of ethnicity in South Sudan even though the same ethnic groups were united against the Arab north. Some scholars aptly posit that ethnically divided countries like South Sudan face enormous unification challenges and more often ethnic identity becomes more instrumental than national identity (Holmquist and Githinji 2009; Horowitz 2000). This leads to competition for relative advantage in the political sphere, a phenomenon that has been attributed to the exclusion of ethnic groups in ordinary times and in extraordinary times. When ethnically biased state reneges on the social contract and fails to secure its citizens, there is a likelihood of political violence, civil war, and even genocide (Horowitz 2000: 25–34). So, what are the causes of the country's complex civil conflicts?

This chapter begins by providing the contextual and historical landscape of the country. The second section details the three forces sustaining the civil wars and conflicts in South Sudan. As mentioned earlier, the three forces are (1) complex mixed wars, (2) political economy and vandalism, and (3) institutional failure and inequalities. The conclusion proffers policy options for addressing the contemporary new wars and conflicts in the country.

THE CONTEXT

The Republic of South Sudan is the world's newest nation, born on July 9, 2011. South Sudan has a population estimated at 12 million people spread over an area of 640 000 square kilometers in ten states with a life expectancy of forty-two years (International Federation of Red Cross and Red and Red Crescent Societies 2014). The country has some of the worst development indicators on the African Continent and therefore in the world. Nationally, 51 percent of the population lives below the poverty line (55% in rural areas and 24% in urban areas). Eighty percent of the poor households depend on agriculture for their livelihood. Education and health indicators are among the lowest in the world, reflecting the impact of protracted conflict and limited provision of social services. Only 6.3 percent of children under 2 years are fully immunized (UNOCHA 2013), and only 27 percent of the adult population is literate, compared with 87 percent in Kenya, and less than half of all primary school-age children are in school (51% of boys and 37% of girls). The infant mortality rate in South Sudan in 2006 was 102 per 1,000 live births, while the maternal mortality rate was 2,054 per 100,000 live births, the highest in the world (South Sudan Development Plan 2011).

The country is emerging from the longest and most destructive war in African history, which left over 2 million people dead and more than 4 million displaced. South Sudan may be defined both as a postconflict state, which is recovering from 50 years of war, and also as a state that continues to suffer from conflict in the form of militia activity, military interventions, and intercommunal violence. These conflicts, fought between the Sudanese government and movements arising within Sudan, are commonly rooted in the exploitative leadership of the Government of Sudan and the unequal distribution of power and wealth among the Sudanese population (Enough Project 2015). Currently, the country is at war with itself, hence civil conflict, a conflict that erupted in December 2013 following disagreements between the various military factions. Despite various agreements and mediations by IGAD, the conflict is yet to come to an end. However, on August 26, 2015, South Sudan president Salva Kiir signed a peace agreement with the *Sudan People's Liberation Movement In Opposition* (SPLM-IO) that brought with it high hopes for peace and stability in the country. However, this seems to have been the end of peace and the beginning of fierce civil conflict.

South Sudan is an extremely diverse nation with a multitude of languages and customs (Schomerus and Allen 2010). The country contains more than sixty cultural and linguistic groups, each of which has a stronger sense of citizenship/belonging in their ethnic groups than in the nation. The main glue that bonded the country's multiple ethnicities together was the history of their struggle for freedom and collective opposition to the Arab north. However, with independence of South Sudan and the relative peace between the two countries that followed, divisions emerged along ethnic and clan lines. South Sudan is highly patriarchal with women occupying a very low status in society. Violence against women and lack of recognition of women rights as human rights is a key feature in South Sudan. If peace meant the separation of southern Sudanese from the larger Sudan, the Republic of South Sudan would be peaceful, secure, stable, and probably richer than many other countries on the continent. However, "secession" does not necessarily denote peace. As aforementioned in this chapter, the secession of the south from the larger Sudan did not necessarily deliver sustainable peace (Onditi et al. 2018). Instead, the power-sharing arrangement has drifted away any effort that would allow the population safe spaces to access humanitarian assistance. As a result of this skewed approach to conflict resolution, less attention is put on "real" issues which include the emergence of new wars, economic deterioration, institutional failure, and interethnic animosity. Unfortunately, the state and other stakeholders in this conflict have put too much emphasis on national security and power sharing as opposed to human and individual forms of security.

These contextual issues have far-reaching implications on whether the country could extricate itself from this cyclic civil conflict. It would be inaccurate to paint a rosy picture of the conflict resolution situation of the country since any new political arrangement does not necessarily guarantee sustainable peace. In the end, federalism is only a structure. The informal practices of patrimonialism, presidentialism, and "Big Man" politics, so deeply embedded in the country's political system, make it difficult for even the most carefully calibrated mechanism to succeed. Efforts to decentralize power, a position traditionally held by the SPLM-IO's leader Dr. Machar, is a fundamental element of the process of state formation. Yet, President Salva Kiir remains impervious to new ideas capable of breeding inclusivity. Thus, it is imperative to strike a balance between the strength of both the central and state governments, something neither of the warring parties appears capable or willing to establish and implement. The most significant challenge can be identified as the increasing competition by the ruling elites to access wealth and power. President Kiir's decision to remove Riek Machar from his post as vice president in 2013 meant not only that he was alienated politically but also that he was cut off from access to the economic levers necessary to fuel his patronage network. Since then, the crisis has been defined by the mobilization of ethnic grievances on the basis of the rent-seeking behavior of political elites. Negotiations have been conducted among these elites on the assumption that they legitimately represent certain ethnic or regional constituencies. The rationale behind the intractable conflict is the (re)distribution of power among these elites (De Waal 2014). In an oligarchic form of government, wealth sharing is done at two levels: formal (government budgetary allocation) and informal through patronages and primitive accumulation. The cracks brought about by applying the latter method of resource allocation has sustained interethnic and group fighting in various counties.

In this chapter, this pattern of conflict, in which human security facets are ravaged through acts of nonstate actors, superficial military intervention, and a "rogue state," coupled with human security short-comings, is what I have coined here as "complex mixed wars." It is important we understand this emerging trend in the country because it is a combination of these structural and systemic forces that offer a magnet for the cyclic conflict and civil wars in the country.

SOURCES OF "COMPLEX MIXED WARS"

Wars and conflicts in both Sudan and South Sudan have evolved since the beginning of liberation movement in early 1950s, basically from the type confined to struggle of identity and secession, to a more complex engagement form of "new wars." While conventional wars were fought by regular armed forces, these wars are fought through networks of organized groups, nonstate actors, breakaway units of security forces, paramilitary groups, warlords, and criminal gangs. The second issue this chapter will tackle is the political economy of war and vandalism. The colossal spending on military hardware and other informal allocation of economic resources to those perceived "powerful" in the country is a clear manifestation of economic vandalism. The final force this chapter discusses is the institutional failure and inequalities in form of violence against women in South Sudan including factors sustaining civil war in the country: domestic violence, forced marriage, child marriages, dowry-related violence, marital rape, sexual harassment, intimidation at work and in educational institutions, forced pregnancy, forced abortion, forced sterilization, girl compensation, and forced prostitution.

The New Wars and Conflicts

The lived realities in South Sudan have constructed the concept of "security" beyond state. The "soft" attributes such as poverty, inequality, deprivation, ethnic animosity, and environmental deprivation as encapsulated in the notion of human security seem to have taken central role in redefining (in)security in this country. Furthermore, the country's state machinery is mainly concerned with regime survival and oligarchical rule. Thus, the notion of "peace" is represented, among other factors, as a military-dominated regime's quest for legitimacy in the face of domestic socioeconomic fragility and political power struggle. Unlike the "cold war" of the twentieth century, which shaped the predominant post-conflict security thinking and focused on neutralizing "belligerents" through military action, "new wars" tend to be wars of nation-building. They are characterized by ethnic animosity, economic degradation, and normalization of violence as means of expressing alternative opinion. Yet these emerging waves of wars and conflicts cannot be prevented merely through the trigger of a gun. Rather, "new wars" need to be addressed through a commitment to tackling the root causes of conflict.

Over the years, the notion of (in)security has evolved remarkably, especially in the past three decades, with significant conceptual and policy implications for scholars and policy-makers alike. As with many other key terms in the social sciences, security, a largely subjective, complex, and multidimensional concept, remains difficult to strictly define. This is more so in complex conflict environment such as South Sudan where the challenge of defining (in)security, arguably, revolves around three interrelated philosophies of the mind: (1) What you see depends on how you look at it (2) Who counts defines who is counted (3) What is counted depends on who counts, how, and why. In other words, who benefits? Whereas in conventional intraconflict situations the struggles between the state and nonstate actors dominate the scene, "new wars" are saturated with networks of security forces who pay allegiance to different leaders, paramilitary groups, warlords, criminal gangs, and mercenaries. In much of the intraconflict situations in Africa, the basic point of departure is either geopolitics or ideological inclination. However, for the "new wars" in South Sudan, exclusion, ethnic identities, and bigotries are key drivers sustaining civil wars and conflicts. In this type of civil war, humanitarian catastrophes are central tactics of warfare leading to internal displacement and denied access to basic human needs. It is therefore difficult to end "new wars," because warring parties are sustained by continuing violence and humanitarian catastrophes. All these culminate into the dilemma that surrounds the concept of "security." No matter how one would want to wish away the relativist perspective on different concepts, various complex factors matter in understanding the link between the notion of "new wars" and the concept of "'security." This distinction is a necessary step in stipulating its meaning in a scholarly endeavor such as this.

In a Eurocentric type of thinking, security was parochially constructed as presence of the military and police, either providing physical protection or thwarting any dissenting voices against the incumbent regime. It denotes mainly military defense of state territory and interest (Baldwin 1997). No wonder the notion of "security" was consigned to the domain of *Strategic Studies* or *Security Studies*. However, as Smith (1999: 79) observes, the preoccupation of security studies with "military statecraft limits its ability to address the many foreign and domestic problems that are not amenable to military security." In this view subsists the idea of the growing *insecurity of security* (Madut 2013): a situation wherein the continued prioritization of military concerns at the state level in traditional discourses and practices of security have served to further individual insecurity and failed to respond adequately to the most pressing threats to individuals throughout the world (Busumtwi-Sam 2002).

Intrastate, rather than interstate, conflict has been predominant in the (in) security discourse ever since the conclusion of the Cold War. This is arguably due, among other possible explanations, to the growing recognition of the "Janus-faced nature of the state" (Smith 1999: 74). That is, the state as source of both security and insecurity for the citizens. The implication of this dynamic for accessing economic and political opportunities in South Sudan is not far-fetched. The widely acknowledged failure of the leadership of the country in quelling of civil wars and conflict through its military-centric approach with its characteristic inadequate attention to the structural ambience fueling the crises is a case in point. Indeed, security, as a concept, has increasingly assumed a more encompassing connotation (Buzan and Waever 2009). Beyond its initial centeredness on the state's military might, security has been deepened and widened to include economic, political, social, and environmental considerations (Buzan 1991). Akin to this, Choucri (2002: 99) summarized the widening scope of security under three broad domains namely, (1) military capacity and defense, dubbed Military Security (MS); (2) modes of governance and regime performance, dubbed as Regime Security (RS); and (3) Structural conditions and environmental viability, dubbed as Structural Security (SS). As far as Choucri (2002: 100) is concerned, "A state is secure to the extent that all three dimensions or conditions for security are in place; and it is insecure to the extent that one or more conditions (or dimensions) of security are threatened or eroded." Herein lies the association between national and human security.

Based on the foregoing discourse, the notion of national security is increasingly being subsumed under the idea of human security, with emphasis on the security of individual rather than merely that of the state (McDonald 2002; Menkhaus 2004; Thomas 2001). As Shamieh (2016: 1856) observed, central to HS is the valuation of individual's interest in terms of the "vulnerabilities faced and capacities gained," thereby, addressing the policy question of security "for whom," " by whom," and "how should it be realized." Unsurprisingly, in his address to the United Nations Security Council (UNSC) meeting on AIDS/HIV in Africa, on January 10, 2000, the erstwhile World Bank President, James Wolfensohn, submits: "When we think about security, we need to think beyond battalions and borders. Rather, we need to think about HS, about winning a different war, the fight against poverty" (cited in Thomas 2001: 161). The idea of HS underscores a strong sense of universality and comprehensiveness of security. Thus, consistent with the UNDP's seven subcategories of human security according to its 1994 Report, Shamiel highlights these categories with their main corresponding threats thus: Economic security: main threat poverty; Food security: main threat hunger; Health security: main threat diseases and injuries; Environmental security: main threats pollution and environmental degradation; Personal security: main threat all forms of violence; Community security: main threat discrimination, and political security: main threat political repression (Shamieh 2016: 1856).

Human security is understood as both "freedom from fear" and "freedom from want" which are two inseparable sides of the coin. It accents "security against economic privation, an acceptable quality of life, and a guarantee of fundamental human rights" (Axworthy 1997: 184). The lack of such freedoms, in the case of South Sudan, has been directly and indirectly linked to the acts of "new wars." Fundamentally, HS "describes a condition of existence in which basic material needs are met, and in which human dignity, including meaningful participation in the life of the community, can be realized" (Thomas 2001: 161). However, in South Sudan, security is "largely characterized by the forceful repression of public discontent, the co-optation of local government officials" who are "in power and a system of top-down financial allocation." Hence, a paradigm shift by the various stakeholders in the South Sudan conflict with regard to its security focus from an authoritarian state-centric perspective that views descending voices as "enemy of the state" is needed in order to address the woes of new wars. In the meantime, lack of this understanding has promoted the heavy-handed approach of the state, which prefers to regard the agitators as "criminals," "insurgency," "dissidents," or "rebels."

The relatively low success rate of this approach is perhaps explained in terms of its negligence of the HS dimension of the crises engendered by various structural anomalies in terms of the outcomes of power relation, vis-à-vis, economic distribution. As Thomas (2001: 160) rightly observed, human (in) security is a direct outcome of structures of power at several levels (global, regional, state, and local) "that determine who enjoys the entitlement to security and who does not." Unsurprisingly, insurgencies are often directed at existing power structure at these several levels, and especially the state. Thus, concepts that broadly describe "complex mixed wars/conflict" include, among others, poverty, inequality, as well as terrorism/insurgency.

Meanwhile, in construing these concepts as forms of insecurity, it is worth bearing Chroucri's three truisms in mind; (1) "One's security may be another's insecurity; (2) strategies designed to create security may enhance insecurity; and (3) security may be "objective" but in the last analysis it is in the eye of the beholder, that is, "subjective." These considerations are critical especially, their implications for the *"Revitalized Agreement on the Resolution of the Conflict in the Republic of South Sudan (R-ARCSS)"* noticeable politicization or militarization of the development process, making it difficult for the citizens to access both economic, political and social opportunities.

However, the difficulty begins from the very lack of structures to regulate the allocation of economic opportunities. The political economy of war is mainly driven by economic vandalism as demonstrated in the following subsection.

The Political Economy of War and Vandalism

In fragile societies such as South Sudan, sprouts of political discourses (ingredients for a democratic political architecture) are usually subdued by the power of the gun before they mature. The power of the gun in the country has been perfected leading to socioeconomic and political woes (De Waal 2014; O'Donnel 2008). Some of the contributing factors to the continued militarization of development in the country may seem old, but still exert pressure on possibilities of attaining sustainable peace: (1) the rapid unraveling of regional codes of warfare ethics since 1991 and (2) absence of political will to transform previous patterns of interethnic competition over scarce economic resources into rule of law and administration of justice (Adeba 2015; Ibekwe 2012; Madut and Hutchinson 2014). This subsection discusses some of the key factors that explain the political economy of war in the country.

The larger Sudan is known for having experienced two civil wars after independence in 1956, but it actually has a long-lasting history of repeated conflict events starting well before independence. Like many African conflicts, Sudan's conflict took its roots in the colonization period, even though they had experienced brutality of external forces from the Arabs before the nineteenth century (Johnson 2014a). South Sudan seem to have suffered double tragedy; on the one hand, the colonial brutality of the British administration, and, on the other, the Arab domination and "hate-phobia" against the black southerners. The unfortunate situation is that even after secession, the southerners continue to experience internal civil conflict. Much of the existing literature on the politics of South Sudan emphasizes the South-North repulsive relationship and paucity of resources (Maystadt 2014). Yet, the Anglo-Egyptian Condominium (1899–1956) policy seems to have generated most of the political tensions even after secession of the southerners. British administration applied this policy selectively, resulting in further marginalization of the black south Sudanese, leading to the formation of rebel movements against both the British and the Arab (Collins 1983; Johnson 2014b; Kon 2015).

The latency of conflict in South Sudan is undebatable (Astill-Brown 2014). In what most analysts describe as the "Red Christmas," South Sudanese civil war resumed on December 15, 2013, this time round, internal ethnic clashes paying homage to their respective ethnic kings (Natsios 2015). Although the exact figures are subject to debate, it is estimated that the consequences of the renewed conflict have been tense with 2 million displaced, with at least 400,000 South Sudanese having fled to neighboring countries by July 2014, and as many as 715,000 refugees anticipated in subsequent years (UN High Commissioner for Refugees 2014). The threats of famine and of sexual violence have sharply increased and ethnic tensions and violence have returned to the forefront of intra-South Sudanese relations (Deng 2010; Johnson 2014). In many parts of the country, persistence of active or latent conflict can be attributed to several factors, mainly lack of cohesive and coherent national agenda and policies for a political architecture. Even though the Dinka and Nuer ethnic groups are the main protagonists in the South Sudanese conflict, they are perceived to have relatively easier access to economic and political opportunities and public resources through their patrons in the government or within the SPLM (Menocal 2011; Pinaud 2014). In most societies, ethnic identities are socially and politically constructed to achieve either societal or individual ends (Edwards 2007). Some scholars observe that the decentralized form of government in South Sudan seem to have exacerbated ethnic and regional tensions. For instance, the concept of *Equatorians* as an identity is based on a cluster of thirty-six ethnic groups that managed to construct a region of inhabitant as a common identity rather than ethnic affiliations (Markakis 1987). Bahr el Ghazal and Upper Nile regions have failed to recognize and adopt such regionalized identity over ethnic and tribal identity.

Overdependence on oil revenue is a consequence of weak institutional oversight by poorly structured governance architecture that is conducive for conflict (Radon and Logan 2014). The country heavily relies on oil revenue to fund about 80 percent of its budget (Perlo-Freeman et al. 2016). However, output has reduced significantly since the country's slide into conflict in 2013 and the rapid decline in oil prices. In 2014, total income from oil stood at $3.38 billion. But after deducting $884 million in payments due to its neighbor Sudan, and $781 million as loan repayments to donors as well as international financiers, South Sudan remained with just $1.715 billion from oil revenue. During the same financial period, South Sudan's military spending rose to $1.08 billion in 2014, up from $982 million in 2013. This means that Juba spent more than 60 percent of its net oil revenue on the military (Kelley 2015). The high military spending trend in the youngest African nation continues to elicit questions about governance and political leadership in Juba, especially now that the African military expenditure fell by 5.3 percent in 2015, reaching an estimated $37.0 billion, following eleven continuous years of rising spending. Total spending in 2015 remained 68 percent higher than in 2006 (Perlo-Freeman et al. 2016).

Militarization seems to diverge efforts toward democratization of the South Sudanese society. However, the absence of full democracy is not unique to South Sudan. Studies across the globe reveal correlation between levels of development and archetype of democratization. There is, however, general consensus that globally democratization outlook has been impressive since the fall of Berlin Wall in 1989 (Besley and Robinson 2010), but this is not always the case, especially in fragile societies where the weak forms of democracies reinforce both political and developmental problems. For instance, the trend spanning over thirty years (1970–2007) indicate that still 36.5 percent of countries are still under the yoke of authoritarian regimes, 37.2 percent are silently persevering flawed democracies, and 14.0 percent are surviving hybrid regimes (Besley and Persson 2008). The same study shows that only 12.3 percent of people live in full democracies. Although the archetype of "democracy" dominating the literature has been contestedx as being overly Westphalian, most scholars have agreed that the civilian government needs the army to avoid internal violence, but a larger army reduces the opportunity cost for the military to run a coup d'état and seize power (Costa et al. 2012).

In other words, lower levels of income per capita increase the probability of militarization of security agencies. Consequently, militaristic behavior among those in power is most likely to "breath" high levels of income inequalities and ethnic fractionalization. In the same vein, some scholars have argued that contrary to the popular view that dangers posed by military rule relates to its intrinsic authoritarian regime (Ikpe 2000). It is the patrimonial tendency in military rule that creates the most transcendent and pernicious effect on democracy. South Sudan's bouts of civil wars and the successive peacemaking attempts divulge vicious interethnic acrimony and rivalry, particularly between the Dinka and Nuer. In 2013, Riek Machar exploited this tone and managed to delegitimize the government of President Salva Kiir, thereby creating hostile environment and eliminating prospects for the growth of a political architecture based on principles of democracy.

The cartographical formulation and geopolitics are also key forces facilitating complex mixed wars in South Sudan. Calls for federalism or self-determination have a long history in South Sudan and are rooted in the fear that a political and ethnicized entity will come to dominate (Adeba 2015a). From 1956 to 2005, successive civil wars were fought over issues related to the centralization of power and resources by a minority of northern mixed-Arab tribes. During the rather short-lived time of peace under the Addis Ababa Agreement from 1972 to 1983, the government in Khartoum provided a certain degree of regional autonomy for the south. President Jafaar al-Nimeiri used this agreement to take advantage of divisions in the south, periodically reshuffling the power structure and dissolving the regional governments. These moves eventually led to a resumption of conflict in 1983. When the CPA was signed in 2005, the SPLM was granted almost complete autonomy within a Sudanese federation, an arrangement the population ultimately rejected when they voted for independence in 2011 (Johnson 2014a, b). South Sudan emerged as a nation inheriting a system of ten states with Juba replacing Khartoum as the central power. Since signing the CPA, the SPLM government has been accused of diverting resources away from the Nuer lands where the country's oil fields are located to develop Juba, Bahr el Ghazal, and other mainly Dinka areas. The opposition claims that Juba has become the "new north," removing resources from Greater Upper Nile and Greater Equatoria to the benefit of a small elite while providing little in the form of development to these resource-rich areas (Adeba 2015b). Despite the fact that the constitution invokes the principle of decentralization, South Sudan has in fact become a unitary state in which political power is almost entirely vested in the central government (Chol 2015), a factor that is deeply contested by the various organized groups, and especially the Riek Machar led faction-SPLA-IO.

It is clear that South Sudan has undergone a period of emancipation from 1950s, demanding equitable access to political power, social provision, and cultural recognition. Amid these interwoven realities, four issues have been particularly intractable: ethnic politics, violence, community relations, and inequality. Resolving such conflicts can be a complex process. State-building and conflict management literature allude to the fact that there are "limits of institutional engineering alone" in achieving sustainable peace (Wolff

2011). As aforementioned in this chapter, institutional arrangements that promote consociational governance have importance in promoting inclusive governance in divided societies (Wolff 2011). In South Sudan, particularly, inclusivity can be instrumental in contributing to evolution of "institutional maturity," but still, domestic violence and gender inequalities remain deeply rooted in the society.

Institutional Failure and Inequalities

Some scholars have argued that weak oversight institutions and lack of general civil education among the populace contributes immensely to intractability of conflict in South Sudan (Gerenge 2015). Owing to several factors including inadequate civic education among communities, somehow, South Sudanese embraced ethnic rule, supported by the military, thereby weakening the establishment of the rule of law and order, as well as peace and security (Kon 2015). Institutional weakness has been attributed to the absence of favorable climate for political discourse—a prerequisite for a sustainable, long-lasting peace. As a result of this vacuum, the military systems of governance in the country have undermined the role of civil society, multiparty democracy, and freedom of speech and movement. Nonetheless, the unresolved post-separation issues with Sudan have pushed the country between a rock and a hard place, (mis)leading the political leadership to adopt profligate military spending. As a result of this overly focus on the military arm, human security facets, such as, gender equality are underbudgeted; hence, affecting women and children disproportionately. This continues to perpetuate civil wars in the country.

The prevalence of SGBV in South Sudan remains unknown. A study by CARE International estimates that 57 percent of women who experienced SGBV do not report it or share it with others (Martin 2014). However, while the exact figures are not reliable due to underreporting and difficulties with data collection (related to the deteriorating security situation), it is clear that violence against women and girls is an endemic problem in South Sudan. Domestic violence is widely accepted by both women and men in South Sudan: 82 percent of women and 81 percent of men agree that "women should tolerate violence in order to keep her family together" (Republic of South Sudan 2014). There is no specific domestic violence law in South Sudan. Early marriage is very common: 45 percent of girls are married before they reach 18 years old and 7 percent of girls are married when they are younger than 15 years old. Bride price paid by the husband to the girl's family is the norm. To obtain cattle for the bride price, cattle raids have increasingly targeted women and children in the attacks. Polygamy is also very common with 41 percent of unions involving more than one wife.

Divorce is extremely difficult for women to obtain: traditionally, only men can ask for a divorce and the wife's family has to pay back the bride price. SGBV in South Sudan is driven by a culture of silence and stigma, masculine identity tied to cattle raiding, the bride price, a lack of access to legal recourse, and customary practices that favor compensation for crimes like rape.

Services for survivors of SGBV are severely lacking; women and girls have few ways of reporting violence, and even fewer options for care. This stems from the lack of empowerment and economic independence of women and is deeply embedded in cultural and customary practices. In South Sudan, the SGBV survivor has the freedom and right to report an incident to anyone (Republic of South Sudan 2014). She or he may seek help from: leaders in the community (i.e., Boma leaders, chiefs, headmen, religious leaders, women's group leaders, etc.); SGBV activists in the community or working groups; health, community workers, or NGO staff; and anyone whom the survivor believes can be of assistance to her/him (friend, relative, neighbor, etc.). The person receiving the initial report should attend to the survivor and make a timely and appropriate referral, according to the nature of the case, to the local authorities, police, attorney general, or a health practitioner. In May 2014, the South Sudan National Police established a new Directorate of Gender Affairs at police headquarters to promote gender issues (Martin 2014). The directorate's mission is to combat and investigates crime, with particular attention to vulnerable groups, especially women and children, and to create and maintain a safe, stable, and peaceful environment.

South Sudan's governance structure has changed tremendously and is still changing since the signing of the peace deal in August 2015. Before the peace deal, there were deliberate efforts to involve women in various governance positions. For instance, on August 5, 2013, and in accordance with the constitutional gender threshold of 25 percent, South Sudan president, Salva Kiir, appointed five female ministers and an equal number of deputies in his government (Sudan Tribune 2013). The signing of Comprehensive Peace Agreement (CPA) gave an opportunity for women in South Sudan to enter into politics. The affirmative action clause was included in an effort to address historic injustices and imbalances in women's representation in politics. The CPA increased the number of women in decision-making positions. However, despite the operationalization of the CPA, most women remained marginalized and insecure (Tambwari and Edema 2014). Further efforts to address the gender balance in politics were evidenced by the launch of the Transitional Constitution of South Sudan in 2011. Section 16 (3 and 4[a]) of the constitution states that women have the right to participate equally with men in public life. It further promotes women's participation in all levels of government and stipulates that their representation in the legislative and executive organs should be at least 25 percent, as an affirmative action measure to redress imbalances created by history, customs, and traditions.

A year after independence, South Sudan launched the National Elections Act (2012), which emphasized the allocation of 15 percent of the proportional party list to women. It included provisions ensuring that women are likely to be elected from the list and stipulating that placement must be done in consultation with women's groups. Seats for women in parliament are reserved, with rotations of each constituency in each election. A National Women Parliamentary Caucus was established to enhance women's impact on political decision-making within the national assembly. Since it began, the caucus has advocated for greater inclusion of women in leadership positions in the national assembly. Women still face challenges in public life, some of which are sociocultural, while others relate to the different status of women. Such challenges hinder women's full participation.

Although South Sudan has adopted some legislation that ensures and protects the rights of women and girls (including the parliamentary quota system and the criminalization of forced and early marriage), South Sudan lacks specific laws regarding violence against women. In addition, the Penal Code Act excludes coerced marital sex from the definition of rape, and the law enforcement and justice systems are ill-equipped to effectively address domestic violence. One of the concerns around the reporting of SGBV to the police is that, in many parts of South Sudan, violence against women in certain contexts is not considered to be a police matter—this is particularly the case when it comes to domestic violence. South Sudan also faces the challenging task of reconciling customary law with the guarantees of human rights that are enshrined in the constitution. Furthermore, the current armed conflict presents a challenge to the implementation of the laws and policies. Judges and other government personnel were also affected by the conflict and moved with the populations, resulting in a shortage of personnel. Several private and governmental institutions were torched while ethnic consciousness overtook formal legal processes with judgments reflecting tribal perspectives in line with customary laws. Despite the laws, women and girls are still subjected to degrading practices such as forced and early marriage, wife inheritance, and the payment of girls for outstanding debts. This is mostly due to deeply rooted, harmful traditions and practices.

Before the conflict erupted in 2013, some studies showed that the South Sudanese Police Force was made up of former rebels who fought the Sudanese regime. According to the North-South Institute, unconfirmed official estimates say that around 25 percent of the police force is female (Martin 2014). However, women's roles are often limited to administrative tasks, as such, their contribution to improving the police service is often overlooked. Women also face gender discrimination within the police force.

Men have traditionally dominated the legal profession, as well as the key institutions of the rule of law, including the judiciary and the Ministry of Justice. Their dominance has created an environment that is uncomfortable for women. There has been no change in the participation of women in the judiciary in the past years, due to the lack of new appointments. However, in recent appointments, 38 percent of legal assistants for the judiciary, 21 percent Second Grade County Court judges, 10 percent First Grade County Courts judges, and 10 percent High Court judges were women (Martin 2014). This presents some hope that the understanding of the impact of the law on women and girls will improve. South Sudan has not been involved in peacekeeping missions due to the precarious nature of their nation-state. However, the country is a beneficiary of the United Nations Mission in the Republic of South Sudan (UNMISS) peacekeeping mission.

South Sudan is still saturated with weapons following the long civil war that resulted in its independence in 2011 (Rolandsen 2011b). The weapons that were once in the hands of the rebel forces now officially belong to the newly established state defense and security forces (Small Arms Survey 2014). However, South Sudan has formally committed itself to removing surplus small arms and light weapons (SALW) from its state holdings. Since gaining independence, state-building has been severely hampered by the legacy of the five decades of conflict, which has included the militarization of society and armed violence in almost all its expressions. The ongoing internal conflict that erupted in December 2013 further exacerbated latent tensions, undermining the fragile national cohesion and dragging the country into large-scale armed confrontations, with spreading armed violence.

Between 2005 and 2013, there were efforts to control SALW in South Sudan. They included:

- Disarmament and demobilization programs: Several exercises were conducted in this respect since the CPA was signed in 2005 (Republic of South Sudan 2015). In practice, however, the results in terms of weapons reduction proved to be modest and did not reverse the trend, as the number of illicit weapons circulating in the country was not considerably reduced. This is because most of the reasons behind the demand for weapons remain unchallenged as a result of cattle rustling and clan and ethnic fighting.
- Institutional and capacity building: A National Focal Point on SALW was established in 2008 under the name of Bureau for Community Safety and Small Arms Control (BCSSAC), a state institution within the Ministry of the Interior. Although the BCSSAC was mandated to coordinate the action and initiatives of the state's ministries and domestic civil society, it has not fully succeeded in establishing a regular working framework with

institutional partners, because, among others, it suffers from severe budget shortages to conduct its activities.

- A Small Arms and Light Weapons Control Bill was drafted in 2012, with the support of Saferworld, with the objective of lining up the national normative architecture with regional and international standards contained in the UN Program of Action and the Nairobi Protocol. The bill could not be signed into law before the eruption of the December 2013 crisis, and it is impossible, at the time of drafting, to predict when the process will be brought to an end.
- Marking of state-owned weapons: The Regional Center on Small Arms provided the BCSSAC with two marking machines that were used, in 2011, to mark newly imported weapons by the Ministry of Interior (between 40,500 and 47,000 weapons according to available data). Since then, and despite the fact that the exercise was initially planned to last over a period of three years, no subsequent marking exercises were conducted, mainly as a result of the lack of adequate funding and operational capacities. Such an initiative produced limited results and appears to be a missed opportunity, as it failed to mark weapons in conformity with the Nairobi Protocol's Best Practice Guidelines, and it did not produce any usable records.
- Sensitization campaigns: Several public awareness-raising programs were conducted in South Sudan focusing on promoting peaceful coexistence and reducing the appeal of owning arms. The perception of security among the population, deeply affected by the traumatizing experience of the liberation wars, and influenced by both cultural and social traditions and longstanding tensions are factors that inextricably drive demand for firearms.
- Improvement of stockpile management practices. Several workshops and training sessions addressed to security officers have been organized by the BCSSAC in order to sensitize the institution about international standards and best practices.

Hundreds of millions of dollars in donor funding from a multitude of actors have flowed into South Sudan since the signing of the CPA. And it is not possible to assess the gender component of each and every program. However, some broader lessons can be learned. A 2009 study on funding provided for gender equality in southern Sudan noted that of the larger pooled funds, "None of these funds were established with the help of gender experts, none have a gender policy or gender markers to ascertain whether they address women's rights and equality" (UNDP 2010). However, there have been some notable programs of support for women, including the World Bank's Grant for Adolescent Girls Initiative, which provided US$ 500,000 for capacity-building in livelihood skills. According to the World Bank's Gender Specialist, the Multi-Donor Trust Fund (MDTF) earmarked approximately

US\$ 10 million out of a total of US\$ 535 million for projects focused on gender. Although almost all of the other MDTF projects mainstreamed gender in their design, the World Bank's South Sudan Gender Specialist was unable to say exactly what proportion of each project had been dedicated to gender.

Individual donors have tendered support to women and girls in South Sudan a priority, particularly with regard to education. Following on from a USAID program of support, which targeted 5,000 girls, the UK's Department for International Development, through the multidonor Capacity-Building Trust Fund, is planning a five-year program that intends to support access to education for 250,000 girls, one-quarter of all girls in school-going age. By providing services such as cash transfers to families, the program hopes to tackle the financial and societal barriers that prevent girls from attending school, such as the tendency to keep girls in the home to perform household tasks.

During the various conflicts that the people of Sudan and South Sudan experienced over decades, women played various active roles: from protecting their lands, to fighting alongside their male comrades, to important nonmilitary roles such as porters, cooks, field nurses, and in some cases, the informal intelligence officers (the "eyes and ears" of the army) (Republic of South Sudan 2015). The South Sudan National Commission on Disarmament, Demobilization, and Reintegration states that "Once SPLA has selected women for demobilization, female fighters and Women Associated with Armed Forces are entitled to the same DDR benefits and provisions as men. These women have sacrificed their educational, family and career opportunities in precisely the same way as their male colleagues. They deserve all the support DDR can provide as they move back into civilian life." The first person to be formally demobilized in southern Sudan, during the launch of DDR on June 10, 2009, was a woman.

At the start of the DDR program, a needs assessment was done of the women who would access the program (Stone 2011). There were female staff at each site, a separate space for women to gather in, separate toilets and facilities for women, and female-appropriate reintegration packages. At the reintegration training centers, childcare facilities were provided so that women with children could participate. In the early stages of the program, 49 percent of those in the DDR program were women. Stone (2011) sees the encouragement of women to demobilize, and the subsequent good representation, as a way of excluding women from the formal military formed after the civil war. She shows that women were reluctant to leave the military and often did not demobilize voluntarily. Nevertheless, and despite a slow start to the process, the female DDR recipients interviewed by Stone were grateful for the material support provided by the program and the opportunity to develop their literacy and livelihood skills.

CONCLUSION

From the discussion, it is clear that certain issues can be rightly deemed as security problems yet falling outside the military domain. These issues form the core of the "new wars" landscape in the Republic of South Sudan. Indeed, security in complex situations is not limited to militarism and policing. Rather, failure to embrace human security pillars, economic deterioration, patriarchy, and institutional failure and deep ethnic division throw much weight on the conflict puzzle. In some instances, the country's economic recession is significantly degrading possibilities of finding sustainable peace. In other words, plans to resolve "new wars" should incorporate thinking about the relationship between access to economic opportunities, on one hand, and the capacity to address institutional failure and societal inequalities, on the other.

The South Sudan's pseudopolitical arrangement was crafted on military realignment between the SPLM and SPLM-IO, which means that the military arsenal of each of the leaders will play a significant role in governing the fragile state over the transition period. Disheartening lessons from the previous agreements anchored on ethnic dividends in South Sudan, particularly the hegemonic tendencies of Dinka and Nuer, have (re)produced a generally volatile social space for the country by defining the mode of political settlement of the state and undermining the generation of social capital for conflict management in the country.

Colonialism has had a fair share of blame for the continued manifestation of ethnic polarization in the political, social, and economic spheres of the country. Indeed, within the European strategy of "divide and rule," the use of one's ethnic identity to discriminate against others or the ever-growing animosity among ethnic groups in South Sudan can be explained by looking at how colonial administrators marginalized some regions than others in the same country. This argument has been reinforced in this chapter using many existing kinds of literature on colonialism among African states.

This chapter has clearly demonstrated how the vulnerability of women ex-combatants or women associated with armed actors was compounded by a lack of participation in decision-making and low literacy levels which left them unqualified to participate in building peace. Their lack of access to economic and political opportunities directly translated into a continued struggle—a phenomenon that continues to sustain civil wars in the country. However, reinforcement of the domestic legislative and regulatory framework has the potential of mitigating the effects of inequalities, hence, increasing possibilities for sustainable peace in South Sudan.

REFERENCES

Adeba, Brian. 2015a. "South Sudan: Where Does Durable Peace Lie?" *AllAfrica*, April. Available at: http://allafrica.com/stories/201504031594.html. Accessed February 8, 2020.

Adeba, Brian. 2015b. "Splitting South Sudan into 28 States: Right Move, Wrong Time?" *African Arguments*, October. Available at: http://africanarguments.org /2015/10/07/splitting-south-sudan-into-28-states-right-move-wrong-time/. Accessed February 8, 2020.

Astill-Brown, Jeremy. 2014. "South Sudan's Slide into Conflict: Revisiting the Past and Reassessing Partnership. Africa Program." *The Royal Institute of International Affairs*. Chatham House. London, United Kingdom. Available at: http://reliefweb .int/sites/reliefweb.int/files/resources/MAASS001_14DOP.pdf. Accessed February 8, 2020.

Axworthy, Lloyd. 1997. "Canada and Human Security: The Need for Leadership." *International Journal*, 52: 183–196.

Baldwin, A. David. 1997. "The Concept of Security." *Review of International Studies*, 23: 5–26.

Besley, Timothy and Torsten Persson. 2008. "Wars and State Capacity." *Journal of the European Economic Association*, 6(2&3): 522–530.

Besley, Timothy and James Robinson. 2010. "Quis Custodiet Ipsos Custodes? Civilian Control Over the Military." *Journal of the European Economic Association,* 8: 655–663.

Beza, T. Yohannes. 2015. "Challenges for Peace in South Sudan: Problems and Opportunities of Solving the Current Civil War." *International Research Journal,* 4(2): 49–55.

Busumtwi-Sam, James. 2002. "Development and Human Security: Whose Security, and from What?" *International Journal: Canadian Journal of Global Policy Analysis,* 57(2): 253–272.

Buzan, Barry. 1991. *People, State, and Fear: An Agenda for International Security Studies in the Post-Cold War Era,* Boulder, CO: Lynne Rienner.

Buzan, Barry and Ole Wæver. 2009. "Macro-Securitization and Security Constellations: Reconsidering Scale in Securitization Theory." *Review of International Studies*, 35(2): 253–76.

Chol, T. Tot. 2015. "Why the SPLM/A-IO Calls for Federalism in South Sudan." *Nyamilepedia*, April 8. Available at: http://nyamile.com/2015/04/08/why-the -splma-io-calls-for-federalism-in-south-sudan/. Accessed April 23, 2020.

Choucri, Nazli. 2002. "Migration and Security: Some Key Linkages." *Journal of International Affairs*, 56(1): 97–122.

Cohen, Ronald and John Middleton, eds. 1970. *From Tribe to Nation in Africa: Studies in Incorporation Processes:* Scranton, PA: Chandler Publishing.

Collinson, Sarah and Mark Duffield. 2013. "Paradoxes of Presence: Risk Management Consociationalism in Resolving South Sudan's Ethnopolitical Conflict in the post-Comprehensive Peace Agreement Era." *African Journal on Conflict Resolution*, 18(1): 37–64.

Costa, Jacopo, Raul Caruso and Roberto Riciuti. 2012. *The Probability of Military Rule in Africa 1970–2007*. Working Paper No. 17. Department of Economics, University of Verona, Italy.

De Waal, Alex. 2014. "When Kleptocracy Becomes Insolvent: Brute Causes of the Civil War in South Sudan." *African Affairs,* 113(452): 347–369.

Deng, B. Luka. 2010. "Social Capital and Civil War: The Dinka Communities in Sudan's Civil War." *Journal of African Affairs,* 109(435): 231–250.

Edwards, Aaron. 2008. "Interpreting New Labor's Political Discourse on the Northern Ireland Peace Process." *Peace and Conflict Studies,* 15(1): 60–76.

Enough Project. 2015. "Sudan and South Sudan." *Center for American Progress,* December. Available at: https://www.americanprogress.org/issues/ext/2015/12/22/128012/enough-project-founding-director-john-prendergast-testifies-in-south-sudan-hearing/. Accessed April 23, 2020.

Genoud, Roger. 1969. *Nationalism and Economic Development in Ghana:* New York: Praeger.

Gerenge, Robert. 2015. "South Sudan's December 2013 Conflict: Bolting State-Building Fault Lines with Social Capital." *African Journal of Conflict Resolution,* 15(3): 85–109.

Holmquist, Frank Mwangi wa Githinji. 2009. "The Default Politics of Ethnicity in Kenya." *The Brown Journal of World Affairs,* 16(1): 101–117.

Horowitz, L. Donald. 2000. *Ethnic Groups in Conflict. Updated Edition with a New Preface.* University of California Press.

Ibekwe, Chux. 2012. "Natural Resource Conflict: The Bakassi Lesson for Sudan and the Republic of South Sudan over Abyei." *Journal of Global Initiatives: Policy, Pedagogy, Perspective,* 7(1): 66–77.

Ikpe, B. Ukama. 2000. "Patrimonialism and Military Regimes in Nigeria." *African Journal of Political Science,* 5(1): 146–162.

International Federation of Red Cross and Red and Red Crescent Societies. 2014. "Development Operational Plan South Sudan." Available at: http://southsudanhumanitarianproject.com/wp-content/uploads/sites/21/formidable/GBV-SOPs-South-Sudan.pdf. Accessed February 7, 2020.

Johnson, Douglas. 2014a. "Briefing: The Crisis in South Sudan." *African Affairs,* 113(451): 300–309.

Johnson, Douglas. 2014b. "Federalism in the History of South Sudanese Political Thought." *Rift Valley Institute,* 1–37. Available at: https://riftvalley.net/publication/federalism-history-south-sudanese-political-thought. Accessed April 23, 2020.

Kelley, Kevin. 2015. "Khartoum Accused of Arming South Sudan Rebels." *The East African,* June 6. Available at: http://www.theeastafrican.co.ke/news/Khartoum-accused-of-arming-South-Sudan rebels--/-/2558/2742520/-/34mdtrz/-/index.html. Accessed February 8, 2020.

Kisiangani, Emmanuel. 2018. "The East African Community and Threats to Peace: Tensions Between Common Purpose and Collective Responses." *The Horn,* 1(4, December). Available at: https://horninstitute.org/wp-content/uploads/2019/02/eHORN-Bulletin-Vol-I-Issue-IV-November-December-2018-i.pdf. Accessed April 23, 2020.

Kon, Madut. 2015. "Institutional Development, Governance, and Ethnic Politics in South Sudan." *Journal of Global Economics*, 3(147): 1–6.

Lacher, Wolfram. 2012. "South Sudan International State-Building and Its Limits." *SWP. Research Paper*: 1–33. Berlin. Available at: https://www.swp-berlin.org/fileadmin /contents/products/research_papers/2012_RP04_lac.pdf. Accessed April 23, 2020.

Madut, J. Jok. 2013. "State, Law and Insecurity in South Sudan." *Fletcher Forum of World Affairs*, 37(2): 69–81.

Madut, J. Jok, and Sharon. H. Hutchinson. 2014. "Sudan's Prolonged Second Civil War and the Militarization of Nuer and Dinka Ethnic Identities." *African Studies Review*, 42(2): 125–145.

Markakis, John.1987. *National and Class Conflict in the Horn of Africa*. Cambridge, UK: Cambridge University Press.

Martin, Rita. 2014. "Security Council Resolution 1325, Civil Society Monitoring Report 2014, Women Count, A Project of the Global Network of Women Peace Builders, EVE Organization." Available at: http://www.gnwp.org/sites/ default/files/resource-field_media/ICR_2014_SouthSudan%20%207.27.15_0.pdf. Accessed February 7, 2020.

Maystadt, Jean-Francois, Margerita Caldevone and Liangzhi You. 2014. "Local Warnings and Vviolent Conflict in North and South Sudan." *Journal of Economic Geography*. DOI: 10.1093/jeg/lbu033. http://joeg.oxfordjournals.org/content/early /2014/09/08/jeg.lbu033.full. Accessed February 8, 2020.

McDonald, Matt. 2002. "Human Security and the Construction of Security." *Global Society*, 16: 277–295.

Menkhaus, Ken. 2004. "Vicious Circles and the Security Development Nexus in Somalia." *Conflict, Security and Development*, 4(2): 149–165.

Menocal, Alina Rocha. 2011. "State Building for Peace: A New Paradigm for International Engagement in Post-Conflict Fragile States?" *Third World Quarterly*, 32(10): 1715–1736.

Natsios, Andrews. 2015. "Lords of the Tribes: The Real Roots of the Conflict in South Sudan." *Foreign Affairs*. Available at: https://www.foreignaffairs.com/ articles/sudan/2015-07-09/lords-tribes. Accessed February 8, 2020.

O'Donnell, Catherine. 2008. "Political Discourse in the Republic of Ireland and its Function in the Troubles and Peace Process in Northern Ireland." *Peace and Conflict Studies*, 15(1): 43–59.

Onditi, Francis. 2020. *Conflictology: Systems, Institutions and Mechanisms in Africa*. New York and London: Lexington Books.

Onditi, Francis, Kizito Sabala and Samson Wassara. 2018. "Power-Sharing Consociationalism in Resolving South Sudan's Ethno-Political Conflict in the Post-Comprehensive Peace Agreement Era." *African Journal on Conflict Resolution*, 18(1): 37–64.

Perlo-Freeman, Sam Aude Fleurant, Pieter Wezeman and Siemon Wezeman. 2016. *Trends in World Military Expenditure, 2015*. Stockholm, Sweden: Stockholm International Peace Research Institute (SIPRI).

Pinaud, Clemence. 2014. "South Sudan: Civil War, Predation and the Making of a Military Aristocracy." *African Affairs*, 113(451): 192–211.

Radon, Jenik and Sara Logan. 2014. "South Sudan: Governance Arrangements, Wars and Peace." *Journal of International Affairs*, 68(1): 147–167.

Republic of South Sudan. 2011. "South Sudan Development Plan, 2011–2013." August, Juba. Available at: http://mofep-grss.org/wp-content/uploads/2013/08/RSS_SSDP.pdf. Accessed April 23, 2020.

Republic of South Sudan. 2014. "Standard Operating Procedures (Sop) for Prevention, Protection and Response to Gender Based Violence (GBV) in South Sudan, Ministry of Gender, Child and Social Welfare." Available at: http://nyamile.co/2015/08/20/gender-and-politics-the-case-of-south-sudan/. Accessed February 7, 2020.

Republic of South Sudan. 2015. "National Disarmament, Demobilization and Reintegration Commission." Available at: http://www.ssddrc.org/ddr-in-south-sudan/women-in-ddr.html. Accessed February 8, 2020.

Rolandsen, H. Oystein. 2011a. "The Making of the Anya-Nya Insurgency in the Southern Sudan, 1961–64." *Journal of Eastern African Studies*, 5(2): 211–232.

Rolandsen, H. Oystein. 2011b. "A False Start: Between War and Peace in the Southern Sudan, 1956–62." *Journal of African History,* 52(1): 105–123.

Sambanis, Nicholas. 2004. "What is Civil War?" *Journal of Conflict Resolution,* 48(6): 814–858.

Schomerus, Mareike and Tim Allen. 2010. "Southern Sudan at Odds with Itself: Dynamics of Conflict and Predicaments of Peace." *LSE Research Online* Available at: http://www.lse.ac.uk/collections/DESTIN/Default.ht... Accessed February 7, 2020.

Shamieh, Luna. 2016. "Human Security Providers in Fragile State under Asymmetric War Conditions." *World Academy of Science, Engineering and Technology, International Journal of Social, Behavioral, Educational, Economic, Business and Industrial Engineering*, 10(6): 1689–1695.

Sharkey, J. Heather. 2007. "Arab Identity and Ideology in Sudan: The Politics of Language, Ethnicity and Race." *African Affairs*, 107(426): 21–43.

Small Arms Survey. 2014. "Excess Arms in South Sudan." Available at: http://reliefweb.int/sites/reliefweb.int/files/resources/MAASS001_14DOP.pdf. Accessed February 7, 2020.

Smith, Steve. 1999. "The Increasing Insecurity of Security Studies: Conceptualizing South Sudan Development Plan. 2011." Available at: https://landportal.org/library/resources/lex-faoc149673/south-sudan-development-plan-2011-2013. Accessed February 8, 2020.

Stone, Lydia. 2011. "We Were All Soldiers": Female Combatants in South Sudan's Civil War." In *Hope, Pain and Patience: The Lives of Women in South Sudan*, edited by F Bubenzer and O Stern, 25–52. South Africa: Fanele.

Straus, Scott 2012. "Wars Do End! Changing Patterns of Political Violence in Sub-Saharan Africa." *Journal of African Affairs*, 111(443): 179–201.

Sudan Tribune. 2013. "South Sudan's Kiir Makes New Changes: Appoints More Women Ministers." Available at: https://sudantribune.com/spip.php?article47554. Accessed April 23, 2020.

Tambwari, Limbani and Darius Edema. 2014. "Gender and Politics: The Case of South Sudan." Brandeis University, Nyamilepedia News, Media and Analyses

Limited. Available: http://sudantribune.com/spip.php?article47554. Accessed February 7, 2020.

Thomas, Caroline. 2001. "Global Governance, Development and Human Security: Exploring the lLnks." *Third World Quarterly*, 22: 159–175.

United Nations Development Program. 2010. "Price of Peace: Financing Gender Equality in Post-Conflict Reconstruction." *Synthesis Report*. New York. Available at: https://reliefweb.int/sites/reliefweb.int/files/resources/43F20AAC1DDC03A D492577C8000C2640-Full_Report.pdf. Accessed February 8, 2020.

UN High Commissioner for Refugees. 2014. "UNHCR Seeks Massive Boost in Funding for South Sudan Refugees." July 11. http://www.unhcr.org/53bfdc1a6 .html. Accessed February 8, 2020.

UNOCHA. 2013. "South Sudan: Humanitarian Bulletin." July 29–August 4. Available at: http://reliefweb.int/sites/reliefweb.int/files/resources/OCHA %20South%20Sudan%20Weekly%20Humanitarian%20Bulletin%2029%20July-4%20August%202013_0.pdf. Accessed February 22, 2020.

Wolff, Stefan. 2011. "Post-Conflict State-Building: The Debate on Institutional Choice." *Third World Quarterly*, 32(10): 1777–1802.

Chapter 10

The Colonial Roots of the Lord's Resistance Army War in Postcolonial Northern Uganda

Sabastiano Rwengabo and Julius Niringiyimana

Beyond the myriad postcolonial causes and triggers of armed violence in many African societies during the 1980s and 1990s, many of the civil wars on the continent can be traced to deeper historical processes of structural change in these countries. Thus, Foday Sankoh and Charles Taylor catalyzed deep-seated processes that gave rise to destructive wars in Sierra Leone and Liberia, respectively (Sessay et al. 2009), as did Jonas Savimbi in Angola, the Katanga wars in Kongo-Zaire, and ravaging conflicts in Rwanda-Burundi since the 1950s. This chapter explains war onset (commencement), not continuity or metamorphosis of the Lord's Resistance Movement/Army (LRM/A) war in northern Uganda. It focuses on the relationship between colonial security policies and civil war outbreak, not general civil and political violence. It traces the processes which sowed seeds of this armed rebellion, not the changing dynamics of the war after outbreak.

Joseph Laor Kony's LRM/A rebellion inherited several pre-Lord's Resistance Army (LRA) armed groups in Acholiland but began and also concentrated in Acholiland, indicating an ethnoregional dimension. This is so, despite the LRA attempts, during the early 2000s, to cross to Teso subregion, and later transnational aspects seen in the extrusion of the LRA into South Sudan, Democratic Republic of Congo (DRC), and Central African Republic (CAR). While scholars have examined this armed conflict (Atkinson 2009; Doom and Vlassenroot 1999; Finnstrom 2006; van Acker 2004), a mechanism tracing onset from colonial security policy eludes many possibly because of the war's delayed outbreak compared to say Burma, Nigeria, India, or Sudan, where civil war erupted soon after independence (Atofarati 2013; LeRiche and Arnold 2012). Without process-tracing the origins of war onset, scholarly attention is focused on immediate triggers, leaving glaring gaps in understanding the origins and metamorphosis of one of Africa's longest and most devastating conflicts.

This chapter develops a causal argument that also caters for the LRA's delayed onset. The conflicts attracted analysts that stress postcolonial causes, like institutional failures and post-Amin turmoil (Gertzel 1980), with less emphasis on structural change during colonialism. No doubt there has been scholarly silence about the war since the early 2010s, not because the war ended but because it has become transnational and had significant reductions in battle-related incidents and deaths and its international media and political attractions started waning (Bailey 2016; Finnegan 2013; cf Finnstrom 2012). While the LRA war has waned since 2005, having been extruded from Uganda, through South Sudan and DRC to CAR, with support from the United States Africa Command (AFRICOM) (Demmers and Gould 2018), important insights for understanding its onset remain crucial. Explanations for the conflict range from structural causes, like ethnic antagonism and fear of domination (Horowitz 1985), to institutional weaknesses (Huntington 1968), proxy warfare, weak neighbors, or transnational ethnicity (Gleditsch 2007; Prunier 2004; Salehyan 2007). Structural analysts believe ethnic (religious, ethnoracial) and regional differences create incentives for intergroup opposition owing to fear of, or in opposition to actual, domination and ethnoregionally biased governance. The LRA conflict, then, appears as a north-south conflict between northern Luo and southern Bantu in an ethnoregional struggle for postcolonial state power (Rwengabo 2009).

Institutional analyses posit Uganda lacked strong institutions for managing ethnopolitical and security conflicts in a sociopolitically mobilized postindependence polity; hence, political violence (Fearon 2011; Huntington 1968) involving coups, countercoups, purges, and armed conflicts (Rwengabo 2013). Why did purges target the Acholi under the governments of Amin, Obote II, and later Yoweri Museveni's National Resistance Movement/Army (NRM/A)? The institutional viewpoint, like structural arguments, hardly explains *why particularly the Acholi* suffered ethnicised conflicts unlike other communities under the same sociopolitical environment. Yet it is known that former Abote II soldiers metamorphosed into the LRA after crossing into Sudan following the NRM/A's capture of power in January 1986. They regrouped and counter-attacked using their newfound base in southern Sudan (Gersony 1997). But this does not explain why the war concentrated in Acholiland upon onset and why Sudan, not Zaire (now the Democratic Republic of the Congo) or Rwanda or Kenya, was the chosen operational base.

Using a process-tracing approach, we decipher how the British colonial security policy sowed seeds of armed violence in Acholiland through over-representation of the Acholi in security services relative to their number and other groups, making the Acholi apparent threats to groups which controlled postcolonial political power. In an attempt to ethnically balance the Acholi, ruling groups threatened the latter, forcing the Acholi into conflict due to threat and counterthreat perceptions. Militarized group cohesion and threat perceptions are key mechanisms through which the LRA war broke out. Military dominance: (a) turned the militarily skilled and experienced Acholi into threats to militarily underrepresented groups and (b) ethnomilitarism created Acholi cohesion and unity, making the Acholi capable of organized, united, cohesive armed action, as shown during the 1979–80 (post-Amin) attacks against West Nile groups, the 1985 coup, and post-1986 wars.

The chapter reviews literature on the LRA to explain conflict onset, not continuity since 1987. Supplement to analyses that correlate precolonial decentralization to postcolonial violence we develop a historically rooted causal argument for this violence. Our process-tracing technique connects important historical junctures to underscore the causal link between the theorized cause, colonial security policy; and the effect, civil war onset. A theory-building case, our study differs from theory-testing case studies, which derive from quantitative generalizations, and examines a selected case to show correlations between variables, through "nested analysis" (George and Bennett 2005; Liberman 2005). We also supplement quantitative analyses that link precolonial decentralization with postcolonial violence given the absence of authority structures with which postindependence leaderships would negotiate concessions (Wig 2013) and those that adduce quantitative evidence of the martial doctrine in colonial security policy (Ray 2013). We demonstrate that colonial military service reduced precolonial disunities within Acholiland, created strong bonds among coethnics in security services, concentrated coercive capabilities in the newly created Acholi martial race, thus engendering audacity to negotiate through violence. When threatened nonmartial groups sought to reverse this trend, violent conflicts erupted. This approach explains the assumption that precolonial decentralized societies are more prone to armed violence than centralized societies, by offering qualitative links among precolonial decentralization, colonial security policy, and postcolonial violence. This explains why armed violence occurs among some hitherto decentralized groups not others—say among the Acholi and not the Bakiga or Bagishu.

The next section critically examines explanations for armed insecurity in postcolonial societies, in relation to the LRA conflict. A framework for understanding the relationship between colonial security policy and postcolonial armed conflict follows. The empirical section demonstrates that: (a) the Acholi were a decentralized society, which made them preferable for British recruitment in security services, (b) relative dominant position in colonial security services gave the Acholi politico-military unity that nearly erased precolonial decentralization; hence, solving collective-action problems, (c) the Acholi threatened postcolonial regimes, which, relying on their coethnics for power, created a boomerang, and (d) the Acholi formed the core of various pre-LRA and LRA rebellions. The conclusion outlines implications of the evidence and argument for grasping different armed conflicts in postcolonial societies.

EXPLAINING POSTCOLONIAL ARMED VIOLENCE

We sidestep conceptual categorizations and simply call the LRA a postcolonial "armed conflict." Civil wars are not unique to Africa (Sarkees and Wyman 2010). But, they "continue to dominate the headlines in our generation and now play as important a role in the international community as traditional interstate war" (Rasler 1983: 452). The LRA defies mainstream characterizations on two grounds. First, definitions which dichotomize "modern" from "primitive" wars may wrongly conceptualize the LRA as a "primitive" war. According to Turney-High (1971: 254), "tactical warfare is the external force arm of the political state," while "subpolitical systems of social control," such as rebel groups "practice primitive war." Holding that "No guerrilla force, no matter how able, has ever won against the conventional troops of a civil state" (Turney-High 1971: 258), the victories of guerrilla armies (in Uganda, Ethiopia, Rwanda, Zaire) against states, and guerrilla forces' ability to secure concessions from states, all negate Turney-High's conceptualization. The LRA has resisted organized state militaries for decades and defied support from regional states and a superpower (Demmers and Gould 2018). The LRA's methods—guerrilla, terrorist, appeal to supernatural powers—are approaches to war intended to ensure effective command and loyalty, not features of "primitive warfare."

Second, the LRA is more than "intrastate conflict" according to Wiberg and Scherrer (1999: 3–7) because of blurred boundaries between its internal and transnational dimensions, difficulties of distinguishing "intrastate" from "extra-state" and "non-state" wars, based on who is affected, how to define state authority, and the distinction between initial objectives and outcomes (as the Sudanese People's Liberation Movement/Army's experience reveals (LeRiche and Arnold 2012). When the SPLA and LRA fought in the DRC or Sudan it was a "non-state war." When Uganda's military pursued the LRA in Sudan, DRC, and CAR, it participated in "extra-state war," which "involves fighting by a state system member outside its borders against the armed forces of an entity that is not a member of the interstate system" (Sarkees and Wayman 2010: 193). Thus, the LRA is all of *"extra-state"* and *"non-state"* and *intrastate* war. Clearly, the LRA is not an "inter-state" armed conflict but a Ugandan one, studies of which stress identity causes; institutional-structural factors; rebel greed (as opposed to objective grievance); transnational ethnicity; and states' weaknesses.

Other studies consider proxy warfare. Building on the authority-structure thesis, explanations for the LRA's outbreak stress precolonial decentralization, namely that the LRA war gathered force "in the absence of a credible Acholi political leadership" (van Acker 2004: 335). Structural theorists may stress Amin's persecution of Acholi (and Langi) soldiers (ethnicity); and atrocities committed by Acholi soldiers in Luwero Triangle during the 1981–1986 civil war (state weakness), which created fear of southern revenge. Thus, the LRA conflict is made to appear rooted in several factors: post-Amin turmoil, deinstitutionalization of politics, colonial legacy, external/Sudan factor, structural causes (Gersony 1997; Ward 2001). This makes parsimonious explanation elusive. Another key variable in structural theorizing is identity.

Identity theories argue that ethnicity, in form of ethnolinguistic, ethnoracial, and religious differences, causes conflicts. Horowitz's (1985) study of "ethnic groups in conflict" reveals the relationship between ethnic affiliation, on one hand, and identity prejudices and collective fears of domination in a polity, on the other. Groups fear domination from "others," leading to see-saw and attrition coups, purges, electoral polarization that heightens fears of electoral-based ethnic dominance. Groups may resort to armed conflict, to "retrieve a lost position of ethnic pre-eminence" or end ethnic domination, creating difficult-to-reverse ethnic antagonisms (Horowitz's 1985: 473–525). Brass (2006), Varshney (2003), and Wilkinson (2006) underscore the identity dimension of persistent intergroup violence between Hindus and Muslims in India, though they differ on causal factors and mechanisms of violence. These studies underscore "significant ethnonational components" in intergroup conflicts' composition, objectives, and causes (Wiberg and Scherrer 1999: 3–7).

Structural analysts may view the LRA war as representing conflict between northern Luo and southern Bantu, given the colonial north-south divide of the country. Horowitz indicates that Uganda's ethnic politics of the 1960s involved conflicts over Buganda's dominant position and Obote's attempt to isolate the Baganda. While the Acholi consisted of less than 5 percent of the Ugandan population, they occupied at least one-third of the army at independence. Obote tried to reverse this domination not just by retaining the Acholi but also recruiting his Langi coethnics, expanding military budget and strengthening the General Services Unit (GSU). The GSU, an intelligence outfit filled with Langi officers and men, combined with the military and together were increasingly hostile to Baganda. Security agencies got drawn into ethnopolitical conflicts. After suppressing southern opposition, northern ethnic coalitions crumbled, hence the 1971 coup, thereafter Amin's brutality. Gersony and Kasozi (1994), Lindermann (2011), Rwengabo (2013), and

Tripp (2010) reproduce this thesis while also highlighting northern Uganda's intraregional heterogeneity. They cannot explain why the war erupted in Acholiland and not Langoland, yet both societies were extruded from power in 1971 and 1986. This inadequacy is rooted in limited attention to the colonial origins of these ethnopolitical dynamics.

According to Ronnquist (1999: 46), analyzing regional institutionalization helps us understand conflicts' territoriality. Institutions, he argues, "reflect and reproduce a collective history of the area," and that institutionalization "is of decisive importance in the emergence of a common regional identity," which survives for generations. Such institutions regulate, regularize, and moderate political behavior, producing "a civil peace through nonviolent civil bargaining" (Wig 2013: 1). Institutions like constitutional provisions for conducting public affairs; inter- and intra-party dialogues; regular, free and fair elections; and judicial and quasijudicial conflict-resolution mechanisms, resolve intergroup disputes and ensure predictable political behavior and outcomes. Institutional rules assign different roles to different actors, and also delink military from political roles to prevent military intervention in politics (Huntington 1968; Rwengabo 2013). Absent strong institutions, ethnic antagonism bred conflicts between Lango and Buganda; Lango and Acholiland; Amin's Kakwa-Nubians and Acholi in the army; between Kakwa and Madi, Alur, and Lugbara (Horowitz 1985: 490; Kasozi 1994); and Langi and Acholi in post-Amin Uganda wherein the northern conflict metamorphosed.

The institutional thesis has a double-pronged weakness: First, institutions have not explanatory but intervening influence. Conflict-affected states always have some administrative, judicial, and constitutional arrangements for regulating and regularizing political behavior. Institutional provision and personal conduct sometimes contradict. Some institutional arrangements, such as electoral politics, may create ethnoelectoral dominance as Horowitz indicates. Second, it stresses the extent to which postcolonial societies have mimicked Western institutional forms, to test the "strength" and "effectiveness" of institutions, not institutions' origins. Judging precolonial governance as being "not institutionalized" breeds West-centrism, thus biasing our understanding of political violence. Sociopolitical institutions are not a Western innovation, hardly an innovation of any particular regional-racial spaces but part of the universal process of sociopolitical development. There cannot be orderly, organized societies, as precolonial societies like Buganda or Ghana were, without institutions. The dividing line between formal and nonformal institutions is thin. If we admit that organized societies with formal political structures have "strong," "effective" institutions, then *institutional disruptions* caused by exogenous factors, herein colonialism, become important. Western-imported institutions are most times bereft of their regulatory and regulative promise because the postcolonial state constructed along these institutional technologies lacks local legitimacy and ownership (Englebert 2000).

The foreign intervention thesis links armed conflicts with external subversion intended to affect domestic politics, like regime change as occurred during the Cold War. Whatever the intent, the intervener should ideally identify, train, encourage, and arm domestic actors, who then resort to armed conflict. For Meredith, Cold War proxy wars prevailed in Africa as superpower struggles between the United States and USSR supported some rebel groups (Jonas Savimbi in Angola) and governments (Mobutu's Zaire, Somalia), leading to persistent conflicts. Prunier views the LRA as proxy warfare between Sudan and Uganda: Sudan supported the LRA until 1993, when Uganda started supporting the SPLA in retaliation. From a proxy warfare viewpoint, the LRA war is viewed as Sudan's intervention against Uganda (Prunier 2004; Vinci 2009).

In as much as foreign intervention may be demonstrable, it remains unclear whether foreign states originate conflicts or support ongoing ones. Consider the rationality of proxy warfare: sponsoring states must calculate civil war's effectiveness as a foreign policy tool. Conflict-conducive conditions are necessary because rebels, whether or not they have foreign support, need minimum domestic support. Thus, rebel groups' prior existence, relative strength of rebel groups, vis-à-vis target states, group leadership and organizational features, rebel group ideology vis-à-vis the sponsor's, and rebel groups' potential to implement sponsors' foreign policy objectives are important but not easy considerations. Rebel groups may weigh foreign support against group autonomy. The resulting dilemma of foreign support versus rebel-group autonomy and of foreign policy coherence, effectiveness, and costs, for sponsor states may complicate choices (Salehyan et al. 2010). Such calculations, in an unpredictable environment of changing military capabilities of the target state and the rebel group, may complicate the instrumentalization of rebel movements. Thus, even if former Acholi soldiers were available for Sudan to support or instrumentalize, *why them* and not others?

The famed greed-grievance thesis holds that dependence on primary commodity exports, together with a large diaspora, substantially increase the risk of civil conflict (Collier and Hoeffler 2002), because resources incentivize *greedy* war entrepreneurs to scramble for resource exports and diasporic funds. Falling under the resource-conflicts theory (Auty 2004), the thesis presents warlordism as violent entrepreneurship. Collier and Hoeffler find no evidence that inequality and political oppression increase the risk of conflict, writing off the repression suffered by the Acholi during Amin and Obote's regimes and Uganda's north-south development inequality, with, perhaps emphasis on financing from the Acholi Diaspora Community because diasporic communities tend to be more able to release large financial resources and publicity to keep local combatants active in native countries. Why the Acholi, and not the Banya-Kigezi diasporic community?

This thesis reduces war to simple rationality. As Keen (2012: 757) argues, it ignores the influence of inequalities between groups. Attempts to salvage the greed-grievance thesis with the *feasibility argument*, which stresses financial (natural resource and diasporic funding) and military (wrestling, controlling, territory from state forces) feasibility of rebellion, as opposed to opposition parties (Collier et al. 2009) became unhelpful. Collier et al. (2009: 1) state that "Financial and military viability are evidently interdependent: conditional upon the efficacy of government security there is some minimum military scale of rebellion which is capable of survival, and this determines *the height of the financial hurdle that must be surmounted by an organization that aspires to rebellion.* Viability is likely to be assisted by some combination of a *geography* that provides safe havens and an *ineffective state.*" Here, diasporic support and state failure are entwined with geography. There must be something about Acholi soldiers, which made them central to the war, which hindered their integration into the NRA despite the NRA's overtures.

The above analyses hardly explain why some ethnoregional groups are more prone to armed violence than others. Beyond greed, resource endowments, ethnic differences, we need an approach which addresses "formal and informal institutional factors that create the synergy between private and public spaces for overcoming collective action problems of maintaining peace" or causing violence (Soysa 2002: 395). Tracing the colonial origins of postcolonial political behavior may offer such an approach. The extant precolonial authority thesis writes off the colonial period, arguing that colonialism was too short-lived to have significantly changed pre-existing control structures (Herbst 2000). For Wig (2013: 2), "strong traditional political institutions facilitate credible nonviolent bargaining between excluded ethnic groups and the State," thereby reducing conflict propensity. Politically excluded groups which had centralized traditional institutions are less likely to engage in political violence than their decentralized counterparts, because institutions, being path-dependent, involve historical continuities, which facilitate nonviolent engagement between societies and the state. Apparently, then, Bunyoro does not engage in armed conflict because the Banyoro (implying the people of Bunyoro), relying on their centuries-old institutional history, can peacefully engage the central state for concessions, unlike the Acholi's decentralized structure lacking legitimate authority to represent it in negotiations.

Contrarily, Englebert indicates that state legitimacy crises are higher in states with precolonial centralized societies, whose precolonial authority structures did not inform state structures at independence: "The more state-like were a country's precolonial institutions, the weaker the allegiance of these populations to the post-colonial state," for this state is "less acceptable, less legitimate, more arbitrary" than precolonial bases of authority (Englebert 2000: 20). This viewpoint approximates Buganda, not Acholiland. Structural changes colonialism wrought upon precolonial decentralized societies remain unexplained. Understanding these structural changes will help us explain why some precolonial decentralized societies have engaged in armed violence.

COLONIAL SECURITY POLICY AND POSTCOLONIAL ARMED VIOLENCE

"Colonial Security Policy" implies the choices and preferences for recruitment into the colonial state's security services. The policy structurally changed precolonial societies, sowing seeds of postcolonial violence. Narrowly, recruitment into colonial military and police forces favored decentralized groups, thus creating lasting structural changes that impact postcolonial politics. The colonist's challenge was deciding which among the different ethnolinguistic communities security personnel would come from and the implications for such groups' access to instruments of violence for colonial survival (Stokes 2009: 508). The British, for instance, did not recruit from centralized Buganda and Bunyoro but preferred Northern Luo communities, mainly the Acholi for the uniformed services: army, police, and security guards (Omara-Otunnu 1987). This gave the Acholi experience, military skills, militarized unity, and new capabilities—advantages which later ignited anti-Acholi resentment from Amin's West Nile groups (Ward 2001: 191). Preference for decentralized societies and minority groups spanned the British Empire (Ray 2013).

It remains unclear why the British preferred such societies. Mazrui (1976) hypothesizes that avoidance of certain communities in recruitment for armed forces may have been informed by considerations such as the calculation by colonial officials that equipping some communities with arms might create problems for the colonial state. Mazrui's hypothesis indicates justifiable fears that in case colonial and indigenous authorities clashed the British might not rely upon armed subjects from the contending centralized authority to suppress such resistance. Yet, by preferring the Acholi, colonial security policy created "an artificial Acholi military identity," giving the Acholi a dominant role in Uganda's postcolonial security crises. Clearly, then, the LRA conflict is rooted in ethnic overrepresentation in colonial military service that replaced precolonial decentralization with military unity in two ways: militarized unity and collective threat perceptions (figure 10.1).

From figure 10.1, military service builds bonds of military unity. These bonds facilitate collective identity among formerly different clans. Military unity eases collective action as military culture encourages combined efforts

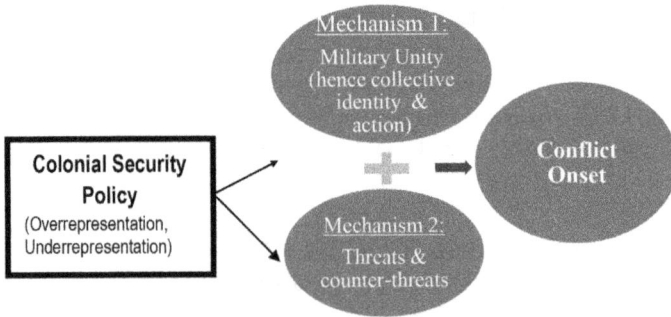

Figure 10.1 Colonial Security Policy and Postcolonial Armed Conflict. Authors' Conceptualization

(Soeters et al. 2006). It evokes threat perceptions for politically dominant but militarily underrepresented groups, since the "martial" group has preponderance of coercive capabilities. If militarily underrepresented groups hold political power, they feel threatened by the "martial" group. Attempts to reduce this preponderance, including changing the composition of security forces, may generate threat perceptions in the martial group. Threats engender counterthreats, hence collective response from the martial group to safeguard its military power. These tensions may translate into armed hostility. Both militarized unity and threats/counterthreats perceptions may occur independent of each other; they can also be concurrent and self-reinforcing. In the latter case, military unity creates threats, real or perceived, that create incentives for generating collective identity consciousness and military action or new counterthreats, giving rise to armed conflicts.

Military Service and Unity

Overrepresentation of a particular ethnoracial group in colonial armed forces, hence underrepresentation of other ethnoregional groups, created a martial race in which warrior mentalities were colonially constructed. Groups which were politico-military centralized before colonialism were underrepresented. Those which had minimal levels of precolonial politico-military centralization were overrepresented. This process unified hitherto decentralized societies. Ultimately, "any differences in the propensity of military service across ethnic groups had been erased by the time the colonies got independence" (Ray 2013: 3). Overrepresented groups acquired coercive leverage over underrepresented groups: "groups that had developed fighting skills in the precolonial period," such as Bunyoro-Kitara, "experienced gradual erosion of their fighting capabilities." They "bore the brunt of colonial 'pacification' campaigns" (ibid). Coercive power generates political unity, in that when political struggles intensify the martial groups can exploit their coercive advantage over rival groups. Unity results from participation in military service because the military institution is inherently totalizing and unifying. It erases differences, creates a common identity out of military service.

Military service creates unity through its occupational culture acquired from training, lived experiences, interdependence among comrades, shared threats related to the nature and environment of work, and regular interactions. Military personnel and institutions tend to shun discrimination in preference for comradeship. As a result, the overall military culture generates a common identity—comrades in arms—identities more articulated in colonial militaries that quell anticolonial dissent. Other groups see militarily dominant groups as different, if monstrous, social groups in cohort with colonizers. British colonialists justified this bias through stereotypical claims as height, skeletal, and muscular structure, courage, masculinity and the "warrior tradition." This constructed tradition "intrudes and conditions attitudes, especially in situations where soldiers attempt to monopolize the central institutions of power," supplemented by an "ambition to foster collective prosperity," and leads inevitably to "militarized economic acquisitiveness as an aspect of the warrior ethos" (Mazrui 1976: 26). Hitherto less powerful groups become powerful and collectively self-conscious overnight.

This self-consciousness politicizes militaries. "Under the form of an hegemonic domination of the political and administrative system by elements of armed forces and with the latter's support," there occurs "politicization of military institutions . . . because, in Africa, the professionalization or the confinement of the military to its institutional functions has not prevented attempts at political interferences and organizational restlessness" (Martin 2006: 188). Military intrusion in politics, under conditions of praetorianism and patrimonialism, becomes inevitable because these institutions neither represent nor reflect the societies they purport to defend. Thus, the politico-militarily powerful group conflicts with other groups, leading to the second mechanism in which overrepresentation in militaries breeds armed violence: threat perceptions.

Threat Perceptions

Threat perceptions arise from (a) new groups seeking to secure a presence/influence within the security and political landscape and (b) militarily dominant groups whose position is challenged. In this dual context, three-pronged threat perceptions emerge: first, political authorities, not controlled by militarily dominant ethnolinguistic groups, feel threatened by a military that is not "Ours." Second, the ethnicized military itself feels threatened by political authority from "Others." Third, within the Martinian politicized

military, self-identifications—based on ethnoregional, sociolinguistic, communities from which different officers and armed personnel hail—compro-
mise military unity. The foregoing conditions strain civil-military relations
in two ways: first, military demands upon the political leadership, whether
or not they are genuine and rooted in military corporate interests, are perceived to imply opposition from the "Others" dominating the military.
Second, attempts at reorganizing the military to reflect its mother society—to
become a Janowitzian military—by including other groups may be viewed
as intended to erode the dominant group's military preponderance (Janowitz
1960/1971). The military's resistance to reforms may be couched in the language of military autonomy, control over internal military affairs. But this
strains civil-military relations.

Politicians may desire representative militaries, attempt to rhetorically justify military inclusiveness, even when their motive is to enlist coethnics. Even
if it were supposed that politicians' motives may be genuine, the ethnomilitary institution may not perceive it thus. Where politicians face resistance,
they may create rival groups to the military, like elite presidential guards
dominated by politicians' coethnics or mercenaries. Mainstream militaries
perceive these groups as functional rivals, further straining civil-military relations. These "Coup-Proofing" strategies reflect Huntington's (1957) notion
of "Subjective Control" (Quinlivan 1999; Rwengabo 2013). To reflect its
mother society, the military needs encouragement, so to speak, from relevant
sociopolitical forces. When these forces suffer ethnoregional conflicts, the
military may intervene in politics—not as a unified entity but as a fractious
institution in which ethnomilitary factions jostle for political-militarily influence in a highly contentious politico-military space. Coups threats, countercoups, and coupproofing measures become the norm (Nordinger 1977). One
recalls how Idi Amin, worried about the Acholi and Langi dominance in
the military and other security services, targeted Acholi-Langi-Madi-Alur-
Lugbara soldiers and political opponents; the Langi were Obote's coethnics;
the Lugbara and Baganda attempted assassinations and coups against him
(Horowitz 1985: 490). Under such conditions of ethnoregional and ethnopolitical consciousness, threat perceptions and fears, civil conflicts inevitably
concentrate in specific ethnic regions.

ARMED CONFLICT IN ACHOLILAND: MILITARIZED
UNITY, THREAT PERCEPTIONS, AND WAR ONSET

The Acholi, being dominant in the armed forces, suffered during the 1981–
1986 counterinsurgency, as mainly frontline soldiers. This partly explains
the 1985 coup. By 1985, the Acholi were an organized, politico-military

unified, entity. Precolonial decentralization had ceased with military unity and group cohesion. But the Acholi were equally collectively threatened as a group. Group unity, concurrent with perceived threats, is key to understanding the LRA war onset. Tore Wig's analysis would appeal to Acholiland's decentralized authority structures to explain their violent methods of political negotiation, augmenting van Acker's (2004: 335) view that the absence of a credible Acholi political leadership, which would negotiate with Kampala, provided momentum for LRA war. But this presupposes that colonialism had not structurally changed Acholiland. This view misses the influence of Acholi dominance in colonial armed forces, sidestepping the influence of colonial security policy on postcolonial Uganda's political and security landscape. Precolonial decentralization is not unimportant; its explanatory value derives from its influence on decisions regarding colonial recruitment and the subsequent unity forged among Acholi servicemen from different clans. This section outlines the nature of precolonial decentralization in Acholiland; demonstrates Acholi overrepresentation in British armed services; and examines threat perceptions between the Acholi and postcolonial regimes which forced the Acholi to dominate pre-LRA and LRA wars.

Precolonial Decentralization in Acholiland

Precolonial Acholiland had different clan-based chiefdoms inhabiting different territories. Each clan was headed by a *Rwot* (Chief). No centralized structure brought all Rwots under a higher authority. The Rwots themselves had no major powers over families within their clans. For Heike, some Acholi clans were not under a central structure but "constituted around thirty chiefdoms in what is now Acholi." The chiefdoms "were extremely changeable with constant splintering and new foundings," each running its own affairs (Heike 1999: 15). It is unclear whether the Rwot had real political power. Even if *he* had, Rwot power was limited to small clans encompassing few families. Possibly the Rwot depended on consensus among clan elders, who would either overthrow or abandon him for another Rwot. This "consensus democracy" limited Rwots' power to their subjects' unanimous approval, with vital ramifications for possible group action.

From table 10.1, the Acholi were a free people not under the totalizing autocracy of central-state structures prevalent in Bunyoro, Rwanda, and Buganda (Mazrui 1977). Disputes between Rwots, lineage heads and elders, if unresolved consensually, might lead to armed clashes. The Acholi organized armed expeditions under Rwots, clan or lineage heads, or local strongmen where necessary. Some analysts believe the Acholi lived under dual authority: (i) the Rwot's administrative, politico-military, consensus-based leadership and (ii) priests who performed periodic rituals and spiritual

Table 10.1   Precolonial Decentralization and Implications for Collective Action

Nature of Decentralization	Extent of Decentralization	Implications for Collective Action
Politico-Military and Administrative	Different clans, headed by consensus-based *Rwots elected because of success in military expeditions* Lineages, headed by Lineage chiefs Military expeditions organized on clan basis, composed of males 15+ years. War songs Clan-based "International" relations and war	Small, consensus-dependent authority structures. Limited powers for *Rwots* and Chiefs. No structure unifying different clans under a single authority. Fragmented mobilization, limited coordination, and costly to ensure collective action. Small-sized expeditions, and decentred command arrangements. Ad hoc, sometimes conflictual, relations among clans and chiefs. Limited diplomatic unity against non-Acholi and other "small-scale segmentary societies." Men "not accustomed to hierarchical political or military structure."
Sociocultural	Various priests in each clan Similar cultural practices and language	Competition for allegiances between *Rwots* and priests. Influence over social relations limited to small group. Language unifying institution
Economic	Animal and crop wealth controlled at family level State-like extraction limited	No central largesse, claim, or control over resources. Limited ability to small community. Land-owned communally, limiting "big-man" or statist land appropriation

Sources: Constructed by the Authors from Omara-Otunnu (1987); Heike (1999)

services, including initiating Rwots (Heike 1999). The Rwot's House stood in the middle of his subjects' huts. His influence never extended beyond few villages. This authority-structural arrangement precluded large, central, politico-military authorities, which typified areas like Buganda, Bunyoro, Rwanda, and Mandika. In this semi-Republican geo-social space control was limited to elder-mediated, consensus-based, interclan relations that aided conflict resolution and peace.

Colonial and missionary discourses represent precolonial Acholi as having "a warrior tradition." Ironically, "the colonized subjects, rather than the oppressive colonialists, were labelled as warlike" (Finnstrom 2006: 204) despite the fact that colonial rule in Uganda had been violently imposed. This was not a "tradition" but a security necessity for armed operations against neighboring Karamojong to the east, Langi to the south, West-Nile groups to the west. Conflicts among different Acholi clans did arise (Gersony 1997: 6), absent centralized regulation of interclan relations. This was unlike the dynamic Bunyoro-Kitara empire whose standing army, *Abarusuura*, influenced Rwanda's military, the *Ingabo* (consisting of the *abatabaazi* or defense forces and the *abacengeri* or invasion forces), under King Kigeli Mukobanya and Mibambwe Mutabaazi (sixteen century) and subsequent kings (Weinstein 1977). Acholi had no monarchy. Colonialists preferred and enlisted the Acholi, possibly calling them "warrior-like" to disguise colonial inclinations.

Acholi Overrepresentation in Colonial Armed Forces

Colonial authorities enlisted the Acholi and other northern ethnoracial communities "for the uniformed Services," which enabled the Acholi to participate "with the British in World War II in combat theatres throughout the world" (Gersony 1997: 8). The resulting Acholi martial race produced a disproportionate number of soldiers, gave the Acholi coercive advantage, changed their self-perceptions, and altered pre-existing structures and institutions. Mazrui (1976: 262) writes: "Since recruitment into the Ugandan armed forces gave preference to candidates who were 5'8" or over, the northern communities had the advantage because of their physical attributes. Among the northerners, the Acholi later expanded this edge through actual recruitment into the armed forces." Ironically, this ethnoracial bias in security policy was not supplemented with formal education until 1959, keeping surging numbers of Acholi soldiers in the rank and file. By 1971, writes Omara-Otunnu (1987: 10–11) "the Acholi constituted the largest single group in the armed forces of Uganda, although in relation to the rest of the population they were clearly one of the smaller groups of Uganda. Between one-third and one-half of the Ugandan army consisted of Acholi." This exclusionary security policy bequeathed, to postcolonial Uganda, an Acholi-dominated security landscape (Mazrui 1976) wherein the Acholi had acquired preponderant experience and military capabilities that evoked resentment from Amin's West Nile communities during the 1970s (Ward 2001: 191). The so-called "warrior tradition," martial prowess, resulted from colonialists' concentration of recruitment for armed services in Acholiland.

These findings alter the suggested link between precolonial decentralization and postcolonial violence by demonstrating that colonially constructed martialness of the Acholi was bequeathed to independent Uganda. Overrepresentation in colonial military created and perpetuated the Acholi martial race. The exclusion of groups like the Banyoro and Baganda meant that coercive capabilities tilted the balance of politico-military power. This approach straddled the British Empire: in Kenya, by 1942, the Akamba made up 30 percent of the KAR Kenya component; 32 percent of the East African Army Education Corps; 43 percent of the Military Police; 46 percent the East African Artillery force; 46 percent of all signalers; and only 13 percent of non-combatant labor services. Hence, one-third of all employed Kamba males served the military from 1943 to 1946—one of every five Kamba men aged 15–45 years served in the army. Compare with the Kikuyu's 18 percent and Luo's 6 percent, and Nandi and Kipsigis' combined 10 percent (Parsons 1999: 683).

A colonial officer determined the soldierly qualities of Kenya's different ethnoracial communities in 1932. He looked for "adaptability, reaction to discipline, steadiness under bombing, stamina and staying power, powers of leadership, intelligence, spirit de corps, cleanliness and turnout, capacity for hard living, general health, ability to fraternize, and fighting qualities" (Kabwegyere 1974: 115–117; Mazrui 1977: 259). What peculiarity inherent in particular ethnoracial groups, absent in others, engendered ethnomonopoly over these qualities? Throughout British colonies, only decentralized groups had these qualities. In India, following the 1857 Sepoy mutiny, the British spread a stereotype that certain eastern India subraces could actually bear arms; other communities lacked soldierly qualities. They crafted a reliable army for internal policing and gave coercive power to hitherto less-dominant groups (Ray 2013; Parsons 1999). Ironically, and this bias is reproduced by some postmodern scholars, "centralized societies" were modern states with governance structures and fighting capabilities similar to Europe (Mazrui 1976). Marginalization of centralized groups impacted the martial groups' self-identification and group relations, sowing seeds of ethnic confrontations. "An ethnic basis for the recruitment of soldiers," into the armed forces and the persistence of ethnic stereotypes" (Mazrui 1976: 260) implied that "the composition of the military by the time of independence in many African countries carried all the potentialities for ethnic resurgence."

In Uganda, militarized unity replaced precolonial decentralization by creating group cohesion. "Groups that never before considered themselves as a cohesive political community were converted into one by colonial methods of administration" (ibid). Acholiland became martialed and unified. In a 1932 Ordinance, east Acholi's Chua County and west Acholi's Gulu county were merged. Previously, people in these territories followed clan identities. Each clan occupied its territory but similar cultural-linguistic practices existed. A colonial officer, Barrell, named the amalgamated territory "Acholi District" because at the time there was "no native name for the country [of the Acholi peoples] as a whole" (ibid.) Acholi land had been created. This amalgamation "created ethnic-wide political consciousness" (ibid): people began to see themselves as a unified, politically self-conscious, Acholi community, and persistent east-west tensions notwithstanding. "The simple fact that a broad new Acholi political consciousness became superimposed over narrower parochialisms of the subunits of the Acholi" (ibid: 261) meant that centralization had taken root. In the military, a "largely Acholi military identity developed. . . [and] after independence the Acholi presence in the army gave them a disproportionately significant role in the bloody and damaging fluctuations of Ugandan history" (Sturges 2008: 204). This alteration of precolonial sociopolitical structures, via colonial militarization and centralization of Acholi land, had serious ramifications for postcolonial relations between the Acholi and other communities.

Throughout the political power shifts, from Obote (Lango) to Amin (West Nile) in 1971, back to Obote in 1980, and to Museveni (Nkore) in 1986, the Acholi still dominated the military. Throughout these phases, the martial race seemed to threaten the different political races. Group unity and consciousness had, in the perception of the different ruling groups, positioned the Acholi against contending groups. With the Acholi now politico-administratively "centralized" and militarily dominant, three developments occurred (table 10.2). First, they militarily domineered over other groups. Military preponderance potentially threatened postcolonial non-Acholi leaders. Second, the Acholi had been unified. Their new interests transcended precolonial interclan relations. They became a powerful force in a country whose northern region had been socioeconomically marginalized during and after colonialism. Third, the ethnomilitary consciousness, which had developed, necessitated careful dealings if non-Acholi leaders were to control the military. Ironically, most times Acholi soldiers behaved professionally but became victims of leaders' threat perceptions in subsequent years until they could bear it no more. As leaders undertook ethnic balancing measures to overcome perceived Acholi threats to their power, political leaders threatened the Acholi.

Ethnicized Threats and Counterthreats

Three experiences illustrate threat perceptions between the Acholi and other northern Uganda ethnic groups, on the one hand, and between southern and northern Ugandans, on the other: Obote's civil-military relations and measures until 1971; the Amin–Acholi/Langi relations, 1972–1979; and Obote II's counterinsurgency operations, 1981–1985 (table 10.2). During the Amin–Obote phases, the Acholi were victims of ethnic balancing; the post-1986 period put them on the defensive. The Acholi did not immediately erupt into civil war mainly because the north-south divide informed the immediate postindependence politics of the 1960s and created a short-lived sense of northern unity against the south, when the two Luo subgroups—Acholi and Langi—dominated the military and politics, respectively. It was only Amin,

Table 10.2 **Phases and Implications of Colonial Militarization of Acholi Society**

Phase of Militarization	Implication for Military Unity	Implication for Threat Perceptions
1890s–World War II	Recruitment for colonial security services: Northern Ugandans (colonial military), Sudanese mercenaries & Baganda fighters Vs others (e.g., Kabalega's Bunyoro): *Beginning of military unity among recruits from different clans*	Locus of power (Colonialists) not threatened. Acholi co-opted in colonial control. Acholi instrumentalized by the British to *domineer over southern Uganda*
1945–1962	Continuation of previous Acholi dominance: *Unity continues with near uni-ethnic military*	Acholi-dominated security forces Vs anticolonial resistances. Acholi servicemen *threatening pro-independence groups*
1962–1971	Bequeathal of Acholi-dominated military to UPC/KY independence government: *northern alliance develops cracks after 1966*	Langi/Acholi/Kakwa – Northern alliance. Obote tries to increase Langi influence in military, reduce Baganda's influence. *Limited threats of Langi increasing influence*
1971–1979	Amin's rule: purges against Langi & Acholi; dominance of minority Kakwa-Nubian alliance: *unity with non-Acholi anti-Amin groups; participation in anti-Amin UNLA fores*	Perceived threat to Amin. Real threat from Amin forces many of Acholi into exile. *Maximum threats from Amin's Kakwa-Nubians; Collective threat, collective persecution*
1979–1985	Obote's return, with Acholi dominant in UNLA: *Acholi unity continues, with their dominance in anti-insurgency operations in Luwero Triangle.*	Acholi dominance persists. Obote favors Langi causes discontent from Acholi officers. NRA threat against both Langi & Acholi in Power: *Perceived threat to Obote's Langi, and civilian supporters of NRA.*
1985	Acholi generals (Okellos) overthrow Obote: *from military unity to political unity/power*	NRA Vs Acholi: *Real threat from the NRA; Acholi threat to NRA and its Baganda supporters*
1986-8	NRA takeover, pacification campaigns	*NRA threat to Acholi; memory of Amin's purges, Obote's ethnic balancing. Acholi flee into Sudan, start UPDA, later HSM and finally LRA*

Sources: Constructed by the Authors from Morrison et al, pp. 670–675; Horowitz, pp. 486–525; Omara-Otunnu

neither a Langi nor an Acholi, who disrupted this unity and purged both these groups during the 1970s.

At independence on October 9, 1962, power was handed over to executive Prime Minister Apollo Milton Obote, a northern Langi, and Buganda's *Kabaka* Edward Mutesa II as president. But the 1962 constitution—providing for an executive prime minister (Obote) as head of government, and president (Mutesa II) as head of state—faced challenges of implementation. First, the president and commander-in-chief had limited control over the northern-dominated military in the context of north-south animosity. Second, while Obote's Langi were not militarily dominant, the military was more likely to listen to Obote than to Mutesa because of Obote's northern origins. Meanwhile, Obote also increased the Langi influence in security services to counterbalance the Acholi. Third, Mutesa's and Obote's respective ethnolinguistic communities did not have common strategic governance principles. Disagreements between them would lead to serious confrontations between central government and Buganda kingdom, vindicating Englebert's argument that precolonial centralized societies tend to see the postcolonial state as alien and illegitimate. Fourth, though the Acholi dominated the armed forces, Obote favored non-Acholi officers like Idi Amin, who, as it later surfaced, also disliked Acholi military preponderance. When Amin, on Obote's orders, attacked the Kabaka in 1966, this heightened the military's politicization. The civil-military situation favored Obote because of his northern origins, not ethnic unity between northern communities. Obote used this advantage against the Baganda whose cordial relations with colonialists had created some anti-Buganda sentiment (Bwengye 1985).

Amin overthrew Obote in 1971. His greatest threats were Langi, Obote's coethnics, and the militarily dominant Acholi. Amin initially received support from Baganda who had hated Obote following his overthrow and exile of the Kabaka, abrogation of the 1962 constitution, abolition of Kingdoms, and enactment of the 1967 Republican constitution: "The Baganda rejoiced and applauded the change not because they liked Amin but because they hated Obote . . . Violence was the only way left to change government" (Kasozi 1994: 103). Now Amin had to contain the Langi and Acholi—relying on West Nile's Kakwa and Nubian subethnic groups. For Kasozi, northern power hitherto held by a combination of Luo subethnic groups—Langi, Acholi, West Nilers—began to disintegrate when it became individualized under Obote, later Amin. This created threats and counterthreats among these northern groups. "Power never belongs to an individual but to an organized group. The weakening of the Acholi-Langi alliance meant that Obote could not hold onto power. The [Luo] group was no longer united," and ethnoregional antagonisms in northern Uganda erupted (ibid: 173; Mazrui 1976; Morrison *et al* 1984: 670–675). Northern-originated leaders considered Acholi influence in the military as a threat but had allied with them between 1962 and 1980s to contain them in what appeared as a struggle between northern and southern communities. Now consider Amin's treatment of the Acholi.

Amin quickly established the State Research Bureau (SRB) and Public Safety Unit (PSU)—intelligence units famed for extrajudicial killings—and surrounded himself with West-Nilers in the SRB, PSU, and Military Police. He quickly purged the Acholi and Langi.

> By the time Amin captured power from Obote, Amin was all too aware of the preponderance of the Acholi within the armed forces . . . Amin asserted that the Acholi, in alliance with Obote's own ['tribe'], the Langi, had plotted to disarm all other soldiers, and to assert a complete ethnic monopoly of military power in Uganda. Thus, tensions against these two communities started from the early days of Amin's assumption of power. Since then, thousands of Langi and Acholi have perished in the wake of Amin's political and military insecurity. (Mazrui 1976: 261)

Amin suspected Acholi soldiers to have allied with Ugandan exiles to invade Uganda. This accusation forced more influential Acholi into exile. Amin's murderousness allowed no space for political or military opposition nor survival of soldiers suspected of anti-Amin plots (Agaba 2009: 670–675; Horowitz 1985; Rwengabo 2013: 10). By the time Amin was overthrown in a Tanzania-supported war, the Acholi had had enough suffering at the hands of the Langi and West Nile groups to cement their ethnopolitical conscious- ness because of threats from other groups. They formed the core of anti-Amin fighters in 1978–1979. By the time Obote returned to power, the Acholi dom- inated the military as incoming liberators and surviving low-ranking Amin soldiers. Amidst post-Amin mayhem, the Acholi quickly attacked pro-Amin West Nile groups in their first wave of retaliation (Ogenga-Latigo 2008).

The Obote II government (1980–1985) depended on an Acholi-dominated military. Obote's stint in power, 1962–1971, had seen an increasing enlist- ment and influence of the Langi. This perhaps explains why Amin persecuted both Acholi and Langi soldiers. After Amin's ouster, Obote returned in 1980 following a disputed election that was followed by Museveni's NRA rebel- lion. Although Amin had purged Acholi and Langi, "the Uganda National Liberation Army (UNLA) which had a high proportion of Acholi soldiers, was the chief military force that liberated Uganda" and "helped ensure the return of president Obote" (Morrison et al. 1984: 674). The role Acholi sol- diers played during counterinsurgency operations against the NRA in Luwero Triangle, 1981–1985, further illustrates threat perceptions. Two key Obote loyalist commanders of UNLA during the 1978–1979 war were Lt.-Col. David Oyite-Ojok (a Langi) and Col. Tito Okello (an Acholi) (ibid).

Soon Acholi soldiers "provided the mainstay of the anti-insurgency operations in the Luwero Triangle of Buganda," in what "was an increasingly bitter war in which the demoralization and desperation of the UNLA contrasted with the cohesion, discipline, and fighting spirit of their opponents," the NRA (Ward 2001: 192). Obote did not treat Acholi soldiers better. He privileged Langi officer commanders. For example, when Brig. General David Oyite-Ojok died in a plane crash during an anti-NRA operation in 1983, Obote promoted Captain Smith Opon-Acak, a fellow Langi, to brigadier, crossing the ranks of Major, Lt. Colonel, and Colonel, in a parachuted promotion. Obote also appointed the now Brig. General Opon-Acak to replace Oyite-Ojok as chief of general staff. This violated the military chain of command, displeasing senior Acholi commanders who possibly deserved such promotion and appointment (Kiribedda 2010). Interference in militaries' internal affairs tends to create civil-military tensions. The resulting discontent increased frustration among senior and frontline Acholi soldiers during the anti-NRA counterinsurgency operations. Acholi soldiers were believed to have committed atrocities against civilians mostly during "Operation Bonanza" of 1983. They later complained that Obote sent them to the frontline to die of NRA gunfire (Ward 2001: 192).

The Acholi, not the ruling Langi, became infamous for atrocities in the Luwero Triangle in an ironical twist of responsivity. By fronting and having Acholi soldiers blamed for government misdeeds under a Langi-headed government, Obote perhaps harbored anti-Acholi sentiments he only concealed because of the Acholi's military dominance. Besides Obote as an individual, whom many Baganda disliked since 1966, people in Buganda knew that it was Acholi soldiers who were killing and brutalizing civilians. This had two costs on the Acholi. First, Acholi commanders resented political interference in counterinsurgency operations in a manner that placed the Acholi at risk both as soldiers and as a people now defined as civilian tormenters in the Luwero Triangle. Similarly, Obote's violation of the military chain of command in the aforesaid Ojok-Acak appointment violated military autonomy and displeased Acholi officer commanders. Second, Acholi officers realized that they were fighting a subethnic conflict between themselves and the Langi even when both Luo subgroups held political and military power together. Ward mentions that these mounting frustrations forced two Acholi generals—Tito Okello and Bazilio Okello—to oust Obote in 1985.

The 1985 "Okellos' coup" gave the martial Acholi short-lived political power. They tried peace talks with the NRA, mediated by Kenya's President Daniel Arap Moi. But the NRA's achievements, by December 1985 when peace talks were held, and civilians' dislike for the Acholi as a result of atrocious record in the Luwero Triangle, were irreversible. The NRA violated the Nairobi Agreement and overthrew the Okellos on January 25–26, 1986.

This ended Acholi and northern military and political power in Uganda. A new anti-Acholi threat had emerged: they considered the NRA's violation of the peace deal an act of betrayal. Having tested the reigns of political power, albeit briefly, they were now politically and militarily excluded, endangered.

The Acholi, a unified martial race, brutalized under Amin, having suffered under Obote, accused of atrocities in Luwero Triangle—now felt politically betrayed, militarily defeated, collectively threatened. There was no credible commitment, by the new regime, to ensure their professional and societal survival under Museveni's NRA. Threat perceptions intensified: "Museveni is a southern president who overthrew an Acholi-dominated regime. Acholi soldiers retreated north to their homeland, or across the border into Sudan, *fearing massacre at the hands of troops loyal to the [new] government*" (Sturges 2008: 204). Museveni's government asked retreating soldiers to disarm, join the NRA, and build a unified national military. Few UNLA soldiers, such as General Edward Katumba-Wamala, Uganda's former Inspector-General of Police and second Chief of Defense Forces after late General Aronda-Nyakairima, was an UNLA officer who was absorbed into the NRA, now UPDF. He now serves as minister of Works and Transport. But most Acholi soldiers remained skeptical. They recalled what Amin had done to them in 1971–1972. They continued fighting hoping to reorganize and counter-oust the NRA. The NRA pursued them northward. Reaching Acholiland, some hid their guns and joined civilian populations. Others told civilians that the pursuing NRA would inflict revenge attacks and fled across into Sudan. By April 1986, the NRA controlled Acholiland itself. A predominantly Acholi group which fled to Sudan attacked Uganda in August 1986. These soldiers, plus civilians that joined them, made the future mainstay of the LRA (Gersony 1997).

THE ACHOLI AND NORTHERN UGANDA CONFLICTS

Former Acholi soldiers formed the core of various pre-LRA armed groups. They still dominate the LRA leadership and fighters (rebels)—and as victims. This in no way implies that the Acholi are inherently pugnacious as colonial stereotypes had presented them. Any ethnoracial group threatened by neighboring groups or competing with others for resources and/or power develops some degree of pugnacity and appropriate approach to the conflict. Similarly, the Acholi's precolonial decentralization in no way implies that centralized societies were more effective fighters than decentralized ones. Mazrui's analysis of the warrior tradition shows that many societies were warlike, with Buganda and Bunyoro having organized fighting forces over different historical epochs. It means states with monarchical authority structures had hegemonized over groups and could easily ensure broad mobilization for war and centralize command over armed services; decentralized societies, on the other hand, involved limited hegemonic control over people.

Other armed groups existed prior to 1986–1990, but the LRA galvanized around Acholi leaderships, officers, and rank-and-file. Most groups are rooted in colonial, pre-Amin, and former UNLA militaries. Former UNLA soldiers who had crossed into Sudan formed the Uganda Peoples Democratic Army (UPDA) in Juba, March 1986. In May 1986, Acholi military leaders among them identified key areas in Acholiland that they would attack first. In August 1986, they overran the NRA "at Ukuti, northeast of Namu-Okora, a few kilometers from the Sudan border" (Gersony 1997: 202). Though the NRA later regained control, this initial success might have motivated the UPDA officers and men. Military unity and collective threat perception had generated war as these soldiers had refused to join the NRA. Doom and Vlassenroot examine the "stages and content of Acholi nationhood, from vague notions in precolonial days, through the building of an ethnomilitary identity during the colonial period, until the Acholi heyday after Obote II." They argue that Uganda's post-Obote II period indicates an "Acholi-hood on the defensive," whereby the UPDA was conceived as a form of "political resistance" against potential southern domination (Doom and Vlassenroot 1999: 5).

The UPDA was composed of former UNLA soldiers. Within four months, it had not had the time to recruit and train more fighters when the NRA was pacifying Acholiland. Its fighters included mostly Acholi officers like Brig. Odong-Latek. These officers and men, now based in Sudan, "were determined from the outset" to fight the NRA. They co-opted former UNLA soldiers "who had returned to their villages and buried their weapons and ammunition," awaiting developments and young men who had never served in the army but were potential recruits (Gersony 1997: 22). Other UPDA fighters followed Alice Auma, 28, who claimed guidance from the Holy Spirit, to purify, clean, and redeem Acholiland. She had become a *Lakwena* ("prophetess" by which title she is famously known in intelligence, scholarly, and journalistic works). Following the UPDA's demoralizing defeat, August–November 1986, Auma, now *Lakwena*, seized the opportunity. She acquired 150 combatants and their weapons from one of the UPDA commanders and led the struggle (ibid) under the Holy Spirit's Mobile Forces (HSMF). Auma's 150 strong soldiers assisted her to recruit more for a group she later called the Holy Spirit's Salvation Army (HSSA), a military wing of her Holy Spirit's Movement (HSM). Mysticism, rituals, spiritualized practices informed *Lakwena's* new approach to war (Rwengabo 2009). Initial successes against the NRA motivated some young Acholi and former UNLA soldiers who had returned to their villages. They joined the *Lakwena*. Some remaining UPDA units also joined Auma's group or suffered her attacks

(Gersony 1997: 25). Many Acholi may have believed Auma's spiritual power claims. Her promise to "remove the blood stain upon Acholi from the reputation of former UNLA soldiers resonated positively" (ibid: 26). Auma's HSM suffered reversals between June and November 1987.

Meanwhile, the NRA negotiated peace talks with Odong-Latek's UPDA section, and offered them amnesty. About 2,000 UPDA soldiers were absorbed into the NRA. However, some UPDA soldiers returned to their villages. Others joined Auma. Odong-Latek himself returned to Sudan, and later agreed with Kony to continue fighting. Thus, the UPDA, HSMF, HSSA, HSM, and finally LRA, were easy to be found because the structural conditions had, over the years, become conducive for recruiting and training fighters or justify war given the collective threat the Acholi perceived by 1986 and the initial atrocities caused by NRA soldiers in the region. Most fighters were already trained. A long history of military experience engendered militarized unity, which overcame collective action problems. The Acholi frustrations at the time—loss of pride, military humiliation, sense of betrayal following NRA atrocities, Karamojong cattle raids, and the impact of losing government power—were exacerbated by general political turmoil by 1986. These conditions were further given impetus by former soldiers' readiness to fight. Thus, the region's development marginality is unimportant: Acholi was not Uganda's only region lagging behind in socioeconomic transformation or facing institutional and structural deficiencies: Bunyoro, Busoga, Lango, and Karamoja suffered the same. But reinterpretations of these frustrations may have resonated meaningfully. Grievances were instrumentalized to justify the war but were misrepresented as expressions of ethnicity, decentralized authority, or weak institutions, as some argue.

After Auma's defeat, some of her soldiers returned to Acholiland. Her father, Severino Lukoya, took over from her, to save the Acholi from "Museveni's plan to destroy them" (Gersony 1997: 29), even when the NRA's initial disciplined conduct in Acholiland naysaid expectations of brutal revenge. Meanwhile, Joseph Laor Kony, 26, believed to be Auma's cousin, had joined the UPDA's Black Battalion in Atanga, southwest of Kitgum town in early 1987. Having acquired leadership over the group, Kony possibly appreciated the UPDA's disintegration, and the role Auma, and her father, Lukoya, had played in the Acholi struggle. After the NRA–UPDA agreement, some UPDA remnants, Auma's followers who had lacked effective leadership under Lukoya, and other young men, joined Kony's Atanga-based UPDA wing. Kony's movement "is reported to have always been almost exclusively Acholi" (ibid: 30). Kony, like Auma, offered mystical leadership guided by a Spirit General Staff composed of several spirits (ibid; Rwengabo 2009: 150). Under Kony, the Acholi-based HSM II—renamed the Lord's Salvation Army (LSA) from around 1987, and then LRA in early

1990s—continued (Ward 2001: 192). Kony relied on trained former military officers like Kenneth Banya, Vincent Oti, and perhaps Odong-Latek himself, to train abductees. The rest of the LRA war, which has since become transnational and global in terms of its reach and actors involved (Atkinson 2009; Demmers and Gould 2018), is now a question of *continuity and post-onset metamorphosis*, which is beyond the scope of this study.

CONCLUSION

Colonial security policy impacts the security future of postcolonial societies. The structural changes colonial machinations wrought in colonized society have had lasting influence on postcolonial ethnopolitical relations. The tendency to underrepresent some ethnic groups, in preference for minority groups which characterized British colonial-security-recruitment practices, explains the preponderance of hitherto decentralized groups in British colonial armed forces. The privileging of decentralized societies engineered the necessary social forces that sowed seeds of postcolonial violence. The Acholi's military preponderance over underrepresented groups created an Acholi-dominated security architecture, which generated threats and counterthreats with dire consequences. The LRA rebellion, and armed rebellions before it, originated as an Acholi self-defense measure against seemingly anti-Acholi political maneuverings of the time, which responded to suspicions and fears that the Acholi threatened political actors who acquired power at various historical junctures. As these groups sought to counterbalance the Acholi, the martial race felt threatened. By unifying hitherto different, sometimes conflicting, Acholi clans, colonialism reduced collective action problems in Acholiland. The resulting militarized group cohesion and threat perceptions became important mechanisms by which the northern Uganda conflict would evolve. Military-coercive power, under conditions of underdeveloped civil-military relations, threatens political power. Reducing a group's coercive power, through political means, boomerangs via politicization of the military and/or militarization of politics.

These findings improve the authority-structure thesis by demonstrating the mechanisms by which colonial military and other security policies impacted postcolonial security. This analysis shows that colonialists had incentives to rely on precolonial decentralized societies. This preference bred postcolonial violence through an intricate process of structural change and historical continuities of those changes. This supplements quantitative correlations between precolonial authority structures and postcolonial ethnopolitical behavior, particularly armed violence. The approach can also explain the relative prevalence of armed violence among and/or involving different ethnoregional groups. In Acholiland, it was easy to start a rebellion, given the history and experience of military services: a readily available pool of highly trained and experienced military personnel reduces costs of recruitment and training. This was less so in other societies and subregions. This study also reveals the trajectory of change in authority structures across time and space.

Structurally, by independence the Acholi were no longer as "decentralized" as they were before colonial rule. Having developed unity among the soldiery since world wars, the Acholi were no longer a militarily and politically unimportant minority group. The relative numerical and socioeconomic prowess of other ethnic groups, such as the Baganda, might give them electoral advantages but their limited control over means of violence meant that they either negotiated with northern groups as equals or plunged the country into turmoil. Indeed, acts of ethnic balancing bred more suspicions and fears, which by 1986 had reached climax levels. Van Ecker (2004: 335) believes "the social disorder" that Museveni "inherited in 1986 after the downfall of the Acholi-led Okello regime, contained the root causes for continued insurgency." This social disorder is not reducible to postcolonial institutional weaknesses or precolonial decentralization in Acholiland. It reflects the impact of colonial security policy. Threatened from experience, by 1986, the Acholi soldiers' recourse to violence seemed as inevitable as it became. In Ogenga-Latigo's words, "The Acholi were provoked."

REFERENCES

Agaba, Andrew. 2009. "Intelligence Sector Reform in Uganda: Dynamics, Aspects and Prospects." In *Changing Intelligence Dynamics in Africa*, edited by S. Africa and J. Kwadjo, 41–60. Birmingham: GFN-SSR and ASSN.

Atkinson, Ronald R. 2009. *From Uganda to the Congo and Beyond: Pursuing the Lord's Resistance Army*. New York: International Peace Institute.

Atofarati, Abubakar A. 1992. *The Nigerian Civil War: Causes, Strategies and Lessons Learnt*. US Marine Command and Staff College. http://www.africamasterweb.com/BiafranWarCauses.html, Accessed June 24, 2020.

Auty, Richard. 2004. "Natural Resources and Civil Strife: A Two-Stage Process." *Geopolitics*, 9(1): 29–49.

Brass, Paul. 2006. *The Production of Hindu-Muslim Violence in Contemporary India*. Seattle and London: University of Washington Press.

Bwengye, Francis W. 1985. *The Agony of Uganda: An Analysis of the 1980 Controversial General Election and its Aftermath*. London: Regency Press.

Callahan, Mary P. 2003. *Making Enemies: War and State Building in Burma*. Ithaca: Cornell University Press.

Clayton, Anthony. 2004. "The 1964 Army Mutinies and the Making of Modern East Africa." *The Journal of Military History*, 68(4): 1313–1314.

Collier, Paul and Anke Hoeffler. 2002. *Greed and Grievance in Civil War*. Oxford: Center for the Study of African Economies.

Collier, Paul, Anke Hoeffler, and Dominic Rohner. 2009. "Beyond Greed and Grievance: Feasibility and Civil War." *Oxford Economic Papers*, 61: 1–27.

De Soysa, Indra. 2002. "Paradise is a Bazaar? Greed, Creed, and Governance in Civil War, 1989–99." *Journal of Peace Research*, 39(4): 395–416.

Doom, Ruddy and Koen Vlassenroot. 1999. "Kony's Message: A New *Koine*? The Lord's Resistance Army in Northern Uganda. *African Affairs*, 98(390): 5–36.

Englebert, Pierre. 2000. "Precolonial Institutions, Post-Colonial States and Economic Development in Tropical Africa." *Political Research Quarterly*, 53(1): 7–36.

Englebert, Piere. 2002. *State Legitimacy and Development in Africa*. London: Lynne Rienner Publishers.

Fearon, James D. 2011. *Governance and Civil War Onset*. World Bank Background Paper. Washington D,C.: World Bank.

Fearon, James D., and David D. Laitin. 2003. "Ethnicity, Insurgency, and Civil War." *The American Political Science Review*, 97(1): 75–90.

Finnstrom, Sverker. 2006. "Wars of the Past and War in the Present: The Lord's Resistance Movement/Army in Uganda." *Africa: The Journal of the International African Institute*, 76(2): 200–220.

Finnström, Sverker. 2008. *Living with Bad Surroundings: War, History, and Everyday Moments in Northern Uganda*. Durham: Duke University Press.

George, Alexander L., and Andrew Bennett. 2005. *Case Studies and Theory Development in the Social Sciences*. Cambridge, MA: MIT Press.

Gerring, John. 2007. *Case Study Research: Principles and Practices*, Cambridge, MA: Cambridge University Press.

Gersony, Robert. 1997. *The Anguish of Northern Uganda: Results of a Field-Based Assessment of the Conflicts in Northern Uganda*. Kampala: US Embassy.

Gertzel, Cherry. 1980. "Uganda after Amin: The Continuing Search for Leadership and Control." *African Affairs*, 79(317): 461–489.

Gleditsch, Kristian Skrede. 2007. "Transnational Dimensions of Civil War." *Journal of Peace Research*, 44(3): 293–309.

Heike, Behrend. 1999. *Alice and the Spirits: War in Northern Uganda 1986–98*. Oxford: James Curry.

Herbst, Jeffrey. 2000. *States and Power in Africa: Comparative Lessons in Authority and Control*. Princeton, NJ: Princeton University Press

Horowitz, Donald D. 1985. *Ethnic Groups in Conflict*. London: University of California Press.

Huntington, Samuel P. 1957. *The Soldier and the State: The Theory and Politics of Civil-Military Relations*. Belknap: Harvard University Press.

Huntington, Samuel P. 1968. *Political Order in Changing Societies*. New Haven: Yale University Press.

Janowitz, Morris. 1960. *The Professional Soldier: A Social and Political Portrait*. New York: Free Press.

Joseph L. Soeters, Donna J. Winslow and Alise Weibull. 2006. "Military Culture." In *Handbook of the Sociology of the Military*, edited by Giuseppe Caforio, 237–254. Springer: New York.

Kabwegyere, Tarsis B. 1974. *The Politics of State Formation: The Nature and Effects of Colonialism in Uganda*. Nairobi: East African Literature Bureau.

Kasozi, Abdul B. K. 1994. *The Social Origins of Violence in Uganda*. Kampala: Fountain.

Keen, David. 2012. "Greed and Grievance in Civil War." *International Affairs*, 88(4): 757–777.

Kiribedda, Mica. 2010. *Uganda's Political Turmoil Post-Idi Amin: Who Killed Brig Oyite Ojok?*. Broomington, IN: Author House.

LeRiche, Matthew and Matthew Arnold. 2012. *South Sudan: From Revolution to Independence*. New York: Cambridge University Press.

Lieberman, Evan S. 2005. "Nested Analysis as a Mixed-Method Strategy for Comparative Research." *The American Political Science Review*, 99(3): 435–445.

Lindemann, Stefan. 2011. "Just Another Change of Guard? Broad-based Politics and Civil War in Museveni's Uganda." *African Affairs*, 110(440): 387–416.

Low, Donald Anthony. 2009. *Fabrication of Empire: The British and the Uganda Kingdoms, 1890–1902*. New York: Cambridge University Press.

Martin, Michel Louis. 2006. "Soldiers and Governments in Postpraetorian Africa: Cases in the Francophone Area." In *Handbook of the Sociology of the Military*, edited by Guisseppe Caforio, 221–250. Cham: Springer International Publishing AG.

Mazrui, Ali A. 1975. *Soldiers and Kinsmen in Uganda: The Making of a Military Ethnocracy*. London: Sage Publications.

Mazrui, Ali A. 1976. "Soldiers as Traditionalizers: Military Rule and the Re-Africanization of Africa." *World Politics*, 28(2): 246–272.

Mazrui, Ali A., ed. 1977. *The Warrior Tradition in Modern Africa*. Leiden: E.J. Brill.

Morrison, Donald George, Robert Cameroon Mitchel, and John Naber Paden. 1984. *Black Africa: A Comparative Handbook*. New York: Irving Publishers,

Nordlinger, Eric. 1977. *Soldiers in Politics: Military Coups and Governments*. Englewood Cliffs, NJ: Prentice-Hall.

Ogenga-Latigo, Moris. 2008. "The Acholi Were Provoked." Ri-Kwangba. Interview with IRIN. From http://www.irinnews.org/Report/72475/SUDAN-UGANDA-The-Acholi-were-provoked-Prof-Morris-Ogenga-Latigo. Accessed April 23, 2020.

Omara-Otunnu, Amii 1987., *Politics and the Military in Uganda, 1890–1985*. London: Macmillan Press.

Parsons, Timothy H. 1999. "'Wakamba Warriors Are Soldiers of the Queen': The Evolution of the Kamba as a Martial Race, 1890–1970." *Ethnohistory*, 46(4): 671–701.

Prunier, Gerard. 2004. "Rebel Movements and Proxy Warfare: Uganda, Sudan and the Congo (1986—99)." *African Affairs*, 103(412): 359–383.

Quinlivan, James T. 1999. "Coup-Proofing: Its Practice and Consequences in the Middle East." *International Security*, 24(2): 131–165.

Rasler, Karen. 1983. "Internationalized Civil War: A Dynamic Analysis of the Syrian Intervention in Lebanon." *The Journal of Conflict Resolution*, 27(3): 421–456.

Ray, Subhasish. 2013. "The Non-Martial Origins of the "Martial Races": Ethnicity and Military Service in Ex-British Colonies." *Armed Forces and Society*, 39(3): 560–575.

Ronnquist, Ralf. 1999. 'Identity and Intra-State Ethnonational Mobilization." In *Ethnicity and Intra-State Conflict: Types, Causes and Peace Strategies*, edited by Håkan Wiberg and Christian P. Scherrer, 45–65. Aldershot: Ashgate.

Rwengabo, Sabastiano. 2009. "Contesting the Ugandan State: Religionizing Ethno-political and Ethnoregional Power Contestations." *Ibadan Journal of Religious Studies*, 41(2): 137–157.

Rwengabo, Sabastiano. 2013. "Regime Stability in Post-1986 Uganda: Counting the Benefits of Coup-Proofing." *Armed Forces and Society*, 39(3): 531–559.

Salehyan, Idean. 2007. "Transnational Rebels: Neighbouring States as Sanctuary for Rebel Groups." *World Politics*, 59(2): 217–242.

Salehyan, Idean, David Cunningham and Kristian Skrede Gleditsch. 2010. "Explaining External Support for Insurgent Groups." *International Organization*, 65(4): 709–744.

Sarkees, Meredith Reid and Frank Whelon Wyman. 2010. *Resort to War: A Data Guide to Inter-State, Extra-State, Intra-State, and Non-State Wars, 1816–2007.* Washington DC: CQ Press.

Sessay, Amadou, Charles Ukeje, Osman Gbla and Olawale Ismail. 2009. *Post-War Regimes and State Reconstruction in Liberia and Sierra-Leone.* Dakar: CODESRIA.

Soeters, Joseph L., Donna J. Winslow and Alise Weibull. 2006. "Military Culture." In *Handbook of the Sociology of the Military*, edited by Giuseppe Caforio, 237–254. Boston, MA: Springer.

Stokes, Jamie, ed.. 2009. *Encyclopedia of the Peoples of Africa and the Middle East.* New York: Infobase Publishing.

Sturges, Paul. 2008. "Information and Communication in Bandit Country: An Exploratory Study of Civil Conflict in Northern Uganda, 1986–2007." *Information Development*, 24(3): 204–212.

Tripp, Aili Mari. 2020. *Museveni's Uganda: Paradoxes of Power in Hybrid Regime.* London: Lynne Rienner Publishers.

Turney-High, Harry Holbert. 1971. *Primitive War: Its Practice and Concepts.* Columbia, SC: University of South Carolina Press.

Van Acker, Frank. 2004. "Uganda and the Lord's Resistance Army: The New Order No One Ordered." *African Affairs*, 103(412): 35–357.

Varshney, Ashutosh. 2003. *Ethnic Conflict and Civic Life: Hindus and Muslims in India.* New Haven and London: Yale University Press.

Vinci, Anthony. 2009. *Armed Groups and the Balance of Power: The International Relations of Terrorists, Warlords and Insurgents.* London and New York: Routledge.

Ward, Kevin. 2001. "The Armies of the Lord: Christianity, Rebels, and the State in Northern Uganda, 1986–1999." *Journal of Religion in Africa*, 31(2): 187–221.

Weinstein, Warren.1977. "Military Continuities in the Rwandan State." In *The Warrior Tradition in Modern Africa,* edited by Ali Mazrui, 48–68. Leiden: E.J. Brill.

Wiberg, Hackan and Christian P. Scherrer, eds. 1999. *Ethnicity and Intra-State Conflicts: Types, Causes and Peace Strategies.* Aldershot: Ashgate Publishing.

Wig, Tore. 2013. *Peace from the Past: Precolonial Political Institutions and Contemporary Civil Wars in Africa.* Oslo: Peace Research Institute.

Wilkinson, Steven I. 2006. *Electoral Competition and Ethnic Riots in India.* Cambridge: Cambridge University Press.

Part III

LESSONS AND INSIGHTS

Conclusion

Beyond Civil Wars in Africa

Kelechi A. Kalu and George Klay Kieh Jr.

The post–"Cold War" era has witnessed increased intervention by the United Nations (UN), regional and subregional organizations in civil wars in Africa. And these interventions have assumed several forms, including peacemaking, peacekeeping, and postconflict peace-building. For example, the UN deployed peacekeeping forces in Angola (1991, 1995, and 1997), Burundi (2004), Central African Republic (1998 and 2007), Chad (2007), Cote d' Ivoire (2004), the Democratic Republic of the Congo (1999 and 2010), Liberia (1993 and 2003), Mali (2013), Mozambique (1992), Rwanda (1993), Sierra Leone (1998 and 1999), Somalia (1992 and 1993), South Sudan (2011), and Sudan (2005 jointly with the African Union). Similarly, the African Union was involved in peacemaking and peacekeeping in Burundi (2003), Sudan's Darfur region (2004), Mali (2013), and Somalia (2007). In the case of the Economic Community of West African States (ECOWAS), for example, it has been involved in peacemaking and peacekeeping activities in Cote d'Ivoire (2003), Guinea-Bissau (1998), Liberia (1990 and 2003), and Sierra Leone (1997). In the same vein, the Southern African Development Community (SADC) was involved in peacemaking and peacekeeping activities in Lesotho (1998 and 2014). Khadiagala (2018: 3) captures the thrust of African regional and subregional organizations' robust conflict management activities thus:

> African regional institutions are playing major roles in . . . conflict management. This reflects in part, efforts since the early 2000s to transform the African Union (AU) into a strong, collective security and norm-building mechanism. It also stems from the growing role of Africa's regional economic organizations, notably the East African Community (EAC), the Economic Community of West African States (ECOWAS), the Inter-governmental Authority on Development

(IGAD)), and the Southern African Development Community (SADC). They have contributed to . . . conflict management initiatives, including peacemaking and peacekeeping, in numerous countries.

Importantly, the central question is what follows conflict termination, including civil wars? How can these postconflict states avoid the relapse into conflict and civil war? These two questions constitute the foci of this chapter. To address these two major questions, the chapter begins with a discussion of the lessons learned from the civil wars in Burundi, Cameroon, Ghana, Liberia, Nigeria, Rwanda, Sierra Leone, South Sudan, and Uganda. Then drawing from the lessons, some insights are provided on concrete measures that need to be implemented to help minimize and avoid both the relapse into war by the postconflict states, as well as war avoidance by African states that have not experienced civil wars.

THE LESSONS

Some lessons that apply to all the cases include the following: By its design, postcolonial African states have limited autonomy in economic and political decisions. States in Africa are sites for high stake struggles for power between economic, religious, and political elites with the masses as mere pawns in the elite struggles for control of the state. Those that succeed in taking power in African states become entrenched in their control of all aspects of state functions, especially in their use of force to oppose contenders for political and economic powers. The centralization of power and political control and governing by force rather than legitimacy becomes the norm. The consequence is a retreat by politically excluded individuals and groups into ethnic, regional, and religious communities that sometimes become a base for challenging state legitimacy and power. Except for the case study on Ghana, lack of access to state power by merit, the hijacking and over-centralization of power leaves African states in a persistent condition of conflict involving the central government against a regional, religious, ethnic group, criminal and terrorist gangs. As Nathan (2001: 22) notes, it is the responsibility of government and its associated institutions to carry out their core functions of "conflict management" and the "business of governance." "Where a state lacks the resources and expertise to resolve disputes and grievances, manage competition and protect the rights of citizens, individuals and groups may resort to violence. If the state is too weak to maintain law and order, then criminal activity and private security arrangements may flourish" (p. 4) as evident in the cases of the DRC, Nigeria, Somalia, Libya, and Liberia; a "large-scale violence in the national sphere . . . [is] a manifestation of intra-state crises that arise from four structural conditions: authoritarian rule; the marginalization of minorities; relative socio-economic deprivation; and weak states" (p. 22). Therefore, the nature of the state and the larger external contexts in which contemporary African states were created and have learned to exist within the structure of the international system partly explain the incessant intrastate conflicts in the continent. The impacts of external interests within existing international political and economic structures that continue to be sources of support for, and legitimacy crises for African *governments* are present in all the case studies, except Ghana.

Specifically, if low-intensity wars of small-scale massacres are permitted to fester, then the scale of genocide will increase as was evident in 1965, 1972, 1988, and 1993 and become normalized. Also, as Nagar (chapter 2) argues in the case of Burundi, normalizing the culture of violence and killings will eventually hunt those who orchestrated the conflict in the first place. For example, the contemporary landscape of violence has changed from Tutsis or Hutus to include opposition political parties, government military forces, and self-inflicted "political genocide" by the government's *Imbonerakure* youth wing. Another lesson that applies across cases is that while elections and the involvement of international election observers, peacekeepers, and peacemakers are important, they are not helpful if the outcome of the elections are manipulated against the will of the masses, while a state's militarized, autocratic, and repressive system remains intact. Such outcomes merely recycle the culture of violence and groups that lack civic nationalism devoid of ethnic, regional, or class fragmentations. Instead, such manipulated electoral outcomes fail to expand economic opportunities and political access necessary to terminate future challenges to state legitimacy through civil wars.

To answer such troubling questions as Agbor poses: "What has happened to my husband since his abduction? When will the youths in the vicinity be released from detention? Who ordered the execution of my comrades? What was the underlying motive behind these atrocities?" in postconflict African states require some form of "a national mechanism" like "a truth commission," "fact-finding commission," or a "commission of inquiry." The lessons are that; in cases such as Nigeria, Cameroon, Burundi, Liberia, and Sierra Leone, civil conflicts are never fully resolved in the minds and hearts of the larger community without some form of cathartic release through public confessions/discussions and narratives for moving forward. In a sense, persistent civil wars in Africa are more likely to be terminated by reforming the states and their institutions and by establishing mechanisms that hold people accountable where justice is seen to be done to victims of state and group violations of political and human rights of citizens. As Agbor notes (chapter 3), a form of truth and reconciliation platform "affords the country the opportunity to . . . examine its history and identify its fault lines," to permit the "pursuit of justice . . . in dismantling . . . failed and unsustainable system of Cameroonian politics that has been cancerous to the entire national psyche." It is the pursuit of justice against atrocities that will signal the end of an era of impunity and replace it with accountability as a precondition to ending intrastate wars and civil violence.

The issue of psychological counseling is important, especially in a context in which traditional chieftaincy institutions exist under the aegis of a state that bifurcates traditional and formal state responsibilities, sometimes without accountability by the custodians of traditional stools. The Ghanaian case study reveals the need for African states to think about the psychological long-term effect of conflict on the combatants, but especially on the larger community. Thus, while psychological counseling is in short supply in most of the conflict zones across the continent, incorporating psychological counseling as strategies for postconflict healing and conflict management process is likely to impact positively on the health of the community and help survivors become productive citizens. As Appiah-Boateng, Kendie, and Aikins (chapter 4) notes, "The deep-seated emotions, pains, irritability, fright, among other symptoms when not psychologically handled, can in themselves revive the conflict."

As Kieh Jr. notes (chapter 5), in addition to the external dimensions of the Liberian civil wars, in situations where a peripheral state remains unreformed, ethnic scapegoating, political human rights violations, blatant corruption, and support from external actors shape the onset and durability of civil wars. These findings are consistent with some of the explanations on intrastate conflicts in African states such as Sierra Leone and Nigeria. Another lesson is that external mediation does not always lead to the end of civil conflicts; instead, they often lead to a recurrence of civil wars as the case of Liberia demonstrates. And, while peacemaking and peacekeeping are important for the temporary cessation of conflicts, the politics of external interventions, for example, Liberia, sometimes undermine the search for peace and stability. In the end, policies that improve human security in countries like Liberia and Sierra Leone are more likely to facilitate civil war termination.

Personality conflicts as the case study on Nigeria demonstrate are a recurring issue, from colonial to postcolonial African states. Politicized ethnicity, ethnic nationalism, ethnic entrepreneurship, and religion can exist in the same state and political process without leading to civil wars. However, personality conflicts, as the case of Nigeria demonstrates rode on the back of nationalist agitations for independence and resorted to politicized ethnicity to compete for power and control of the Nigerian state after political independence. The lesson that Ediagbonya hopes we learn is that the Nigerian civil war was not inevitable. The personality could have compromised to spare everyone the trauma of the thirty months of civil war, which although ended in a "no victor, no vanquished" declaration but remains a challenge to the Nigerian state, forty years later. Again, without reforming the state to forge a civic nationalism that overcomes entrenched divisions, Nigeria, similar states, and their people remain vulnerable to manipulation by personalities jockeying for political power and control of state apparatus.

A consistent theme in the case studies is that without external intervention, many African states and regional actors do not have the capacity and the ability to sustain long-lasting conflicts or implement postconflict durable security. As Bienvenu (chapter 7) opines, "While local and regional actors have ambitions for power and territorial control and may design different strategies to achieve it, they lack comprehensive autonomy in requisite ingredients that produce such dominance through war." This is an important lesson and as Kalu (chapter 1) notes, in many of the intrastate conflicts in African states, external actors have been consistently present as either supporters of the central governments or the rebels. And, in many instances, mercenaries are deployed by external actors and by central governments in intrastate wars across the continent. Regarding the geopolitical dimensions of the Rwandan genocide and civil war, for example, Bienvenu (chapter 7) argues that "One geopolitical patron—France—provided infantry, lethal capabilities, intelligence, strategies and advice, and even self-favoring diplomacy, all from both onsite and afar. The other—Britain—while indirectly pursuing its strategic objectives, became the guarantor of opinion mobilization, and international legitimacy. And the local antagonists in the war aligned to those geopolitical dynamics."

To be sure, the Sierra Leone civil war was shaped by national, regional, and international factors with a strong precolonial and colonial institutional trigger. And, the same issues of external intervention, unreformed state institutions, corruption, poor economic policies, and political exclusion and marginalization of political oppositions converge to produce civil war in Sierra Leone that lasted for eleven years. Similar to Liberia, the use of child soldiers, looting, rape, and amputations are legacies of the civil war whose lessons remain the need for an inclusive political process, policy autonomy that promotes human security, and educational institutions that produce civic nationalism devoid of ethnic, religious, and regional essentialisms. Another lesson from the Sierra Leone case is that the use of mercenaries, like the Executive Outcome, has consequences beyond war termination as "efficiencies" in carrying out their duties can and do leave scars that last for generations, and vacuum national resources into the pockets of warlords. As Conteh-Morgan (chapter 8) argues, "the Sierra Leone civil war was a classic example of the combined effect of a national/regional/and external nexus. At the national level was the inimical effects of gross misrule by the APC regime for over 20 years which produced serious existential insecurities; at the regional level was the 'contagion effect' of the Liberian Civil War, the role of Burkina Faso, and the destabilizing effects of the post-Cold War environment on micro-states within Africa." All combined, intrastate wars in African states, like Sierra Leone, remain a probability because the Sierra Leonean state is economically dependent on external support, lacks policy autonomy, engages in political exclusion, and responds to legitimate demands from citizens with force and violence.

The lesson from the case study on South Sudan is that most postindependent African state leaders rarely learn the right lessons from history. On assumption of power, the leaders in this new state have replicated the same old colonial strategies of using ethnic groups to divide and conquer the people and leaving them only legacies of insecurity and human rights violations. One of the newest states in the continent, South Sudan elites united to fight for and demand separation from Arab-dominated Sudan, only to fall back to the conflict fault lines of what Onditi (chapter 9) characterizes as the "failure to embrace human security pillars, economic deterioration, patriarchy, and institutional failure, and deep ethnic division" that threw South Sudan into a civil war, barely two years after independence. And, civil war in South Sudan is an example of how inadequate attention to human security—providing educational, economic, political, social services, and access to participatory politics—in the planning and implementation of development policies in African states degrade possibilities of civil war termination and sustainable peace.

Political exclusion, marginalization, politicized ethnicity, religion, and regionalism are embedded in the colonial and postcolonial African state infrastructure. The externally imposed states continue in their autocratic governance style, which exposes them to challenges by non-state actors with the support and sometimes forced support of state-marginalized groups or regions. In the case of Uganda, the colonial legacy of decentralization for purposes of controlling the territory, the privileging of one region over others, and the militarization of politics are legacies that continue to fester in postcolonial African states, as the case of Uganda demonstrates. As Rwengabo and Niringiyimana (chapter 10) note, "The Acholi's military preponderance over" other ethnic groups "created an Acholi-dominated security architecture, which generated threats and counter-threats" and laid the foundation for armed rebellion and civil wars in Uganda. And, without reconstituting the postcolonial states and their institutions to reflect the values and aspirations of the citizens, the legacies of equipping one region or ethnic groups with military training and access to weapons like the case with the Acholiland in Uganda and Hausa-Fulani in Nigeria, leaves African states vulnerable to continuing manipulations by external state forces and mercenaries. Thus, elections—external forces preferred options for ending civil wars in Africa—become merely a camouflage for continuing interventions in the internal affairs of African states without durable resolution of the core issues of state capacity, inclusive politics, and human security-based economic decisions. In the end, African states' weaknesses and lack of autonomy that make them vulnerable to intrastate civil wars must be understood as a structural reality in the architecture of colonial security policy that remains in the core crevices of African states. Without remaking African states and their institutions to reflect what various African communities want, civil war and its human casualties will continue into the foreseeable future in the continent.

INSIGHTS: TOWARD WAR AVOIDANCE IN AFRICA

Background

Undoubtedly, war termination is quite important, because it provides a modicum of stability for the engagement in the critical multidimensional process of peace-building. In other words, while war termination is a necessary condition, it is not sufficient for avoiding a postconflict state's relapse into civil war. Instead, the stability that is occasioned by war termination must be used to engage in addressing the major roots of a civil conflict and the resulting war.

Against this backdrop, this section of the chapter is intended to proffer some suggestions for war avoidance both by postwar states, as well as others in Africa. Specifically, the suggestions revolve around some of the major issues that are common root causes of civil wars on the African Continent, such as the pedigree of the postcolonial state, undemocratic governance, ethno-communal conflicts, and human insecurity. While the suggestions do not constitute an exhaustive list of the root causes of civil conflicts and wars on the African Continent, they, as we have discussed, were prominent causal factors in the various civil wars that plagued the region, including the cases in this volume.

The Drivers: Citizens and Leaders

Citizens and leaders must be the key drivers of societal transformation in Africa. In terms of the citizens, they must develop certain major characteristics. A key one is a civic nationalism that appreciates and adapts to ethnic, religious, and regional differences across communities. This entails a commitment to the country above all other loyalties, especially ethnic, regional, and religious. In this vein, the nationalist orientation would enable citizens to transcend the boundaries of social identities and build a partnership that is hoisted on service to their countries. Another major characteristic is civic education (Mirra et al 2013). Nationalistic citizens would need to learn and acquire civil knowledge that will enable them to participate in the affairs of their respective polities in an informed manner. As well, citizens must be consistently engaged in the affairs of their respective countries. This will help, among others, to ensure that the leaders are held accountable.

In the case of the leaders at both the national and local levels, they must have two major orientations: service and transformation. In the case of the former, servant leadership, as Greenleaf(1970: 1) asserts, would require that the leaders be "servant(s) first . . . care is taken by the servant-leader(s) to make sure that other people's highest priority are being served" Similarly, in the latter case, transformational leadership requires "leaders who seek new ideas and perspectives to create a new path of growth and prosperity . . . . [T] hey mobilize [citizens] to make fundamental change in [society]" (Korejan and Shahbazi (2016: 454).

State Reconstitution

As we have argued elsewhere, the democratic reconstitution of the postcolonial state in Africa is indispensable to the minimization and avoidance of civil wars in Africa (Kalu and Kieh 2021). This is because the state sets the parameters within which societal activities spanning the broad spectrum of spheres—from cultural to social—take place. In this vein, the postcolonial state in Africa (with few exceptions) has performed the aforementioned role in two major contradictory ways. On the one hand, it has created propitious conditions for the ruling elites and their relations to enjoy the full battery of the material comfort of life. But, on the other hand, it had visited abject poverty, social malaise, and deprivation on the majority of Africans. As Ihonvbere (1995: 148–149) argues,

> The post-colonial state [is] a continuation of the colonial state with very minimal changes, mostly in terms of personnel rather than structures, functions and relations to civil society. Thus, it remained an interventionist, exploitative, and repressive as its predecessor. It is therefore inappropriate to expect good governance, transparency, social harmony, respect for human rights, adherence to the rule of law, and political stability in social formations presided over by weak and non-hegemonic elites.

The poor performance of African states led Samatar and Samatar (2002: 5) to observe that the state in Africa is the "wrong type." Thus, Africa needs a new state type. In this vein, several major issues are germane to the state reconstitution project. A key one is the centrality of a vision. This is because as Mutua (2002: 11) observes, "The state itself is . . . a receptacle or empty vessel" Using Mutua's metaphors, the state is receptive to the dominant vision that is plucked into it or deposited in it. And the emergent vision shapes and guides the nature, character, mission, and political economy of the state.

Against this backdrop, the new state in Africa must have certain major attributes. A major one is the imperative of the autonomy of the state (Edigheji 2005; Mkandawire 2001). This means the states in Africa must be independent of the control of all social forces, including classes, and external actors so that they can make policies in the interest of the broader citizenry. Another dimension is embeddedness (Edigheji 2005; Evans 1995). This requires the "maintenance of strategic relations with the wider society" (Seddon and Belton-Jones 1995). In addition, the state must be protective (Ansell 2019; Mbaku 1999). At the core is the protection of citizens from what Galtung (1969: 173–180) calls "structural violence," physical violence, and exploitation by both internal and external forces. Similarly, the state must be productive (Mbaku 1999; Mkandawire 2001). This includes the formulation and implementation of policies that would, among others, help generate employment, promote viable and rewarding economic activities, and ensure agricultural productivity and the resulting impact on food security. Furthermore, the state must empower citizens so that they can play pivotal roles in the formulation and implementation of public policies. As Eyben (2011: 2) asserts, "Empowerment happens when [citizens] imagine their world differently, and to realize that vision by changing the relations of power that have kept them in poverty, restricted their voice(s) and deprived them of their autonomy."

Governance

The issue of governance is discussed at two major levels: the genre and the organizational cum policy. In the case of the genre or type of governance, democratic governance is proffered (Bevir 2006; Haque 2016). The rationale is that democratic governance transcends the technicist-centric "good governance" model that is championed by the developed liberal democracies and their Bretton Woods—International Monetary Fund and World Bank. That is, democratic governance is about the empowerment of citizens. As Bevir (2006: 426) argues, "citizens play an active role in making and implementing public policy," within the framework of the rule of laws.

At the organizational-cum-policy level, there are several major dimensions, and these include respect for political rights and civil liberties, accountability, transparency, the rule of law, "checks and balances," peaceful coexistence and tolerance, and inclusion and equity in power relations. In terms of political rights and civil liberties, all citizens, irrespective of their social identities, must have the freedom to participate in the political process through running for office (if eligible), voting, and peacefully protesting repugnant government policies and actions. Similarly, among others, all citizens must enjoy the freedoms of assembly, association, religion, thought, movement, and of the press.

And, the essence of accountability without exceptions is the extent to which public officials and citizens are held responsible for their actions within the established rule of laws. In the case of public officials, this can be done in three major ways: vertical accountability, horizontal accountability, and diagonal accountability. Horizontal accountability entails public officials and public institutions holding one another accountable (Luhrmann et al. 2020). Vertical accountability revolves around citizens holding public officials accountable through various means, including elections (Luhrmann et al. 2020). Similarly, diagonal accountability focuses on nongovernmental actors such as civil society organizations and the media holding government officials responsible for their actions (Luhrmann et al. 2020).

Transparency is another major area, especially against the backdrop of the perennial lack of openness in the operations of the governments of states in Africa. Citizens' knowledge about the operations of their governments is important for several reasons (Hollyer et al. 2011). A key one is that it positions citizens to exercise "vertical accountability" over the government more effectively. Another reason is that transparency serves as a deterrent against engagement in corrupt activities by public officials, who fearful, that their actions will become public knowledge in a matter of time, will moderate their rent-seeking behaviors. Furthermore, openness helps build the trust of citizens in their governments.

And, the "rule of law," ensures that everyone, irrespective of their socioeconomic status or role in the society, is answerable to the law and legal process for their official behavior (Waldron 2021). In other words, the "rule of the law" ensures that all citizens, including the head of state and head of government, as well as top government officials, are not above the law. The effective enforcement of this foundational plank of democratic governance is important for several major reasons. For example, the "rule of law" militates against the "culture of impunity," which is a major cornerstone of authoritarian and hybrid states in Africa. This is done by ensuring, among others, that no one is given preferential treatment in the application and enforcement of the laws, irrespective of political and socioeconomic status and connections in society. Also, a rule of the law-based public policy increases the citizens' confidence and trust in the legal system as a fair and impartial arbiter of disputes. As well, the "rule of law" minimizes the resort to extra-legal means in the settlement of disputes, especially the use of violence. And as discussed previously, the rule of law enables citizens to have faith in the legal system as a platform to address their grievances fairly and in conformity with a verifiable law.

A system of "checks and balances" is also indispensable to ensuring democratic governance (Holcombe 2018). Essentially, this would require the distribution of authority among the three major branches of government—legislative, executive, and judicial—in ways that enable each of them to have both sufficient and necessary authority to checkmate the excesses of the other branches. The effective and efficient operation of a system of checks and balances makes it difficult for a public official or a branch of government to subordinate other branches and usurp their authority. In sum, the system of "checks and balances" curtails authoritarian tendencies, especially in a democratic system of governance.

Another important element is the imperative of peaceful coexistence and tolerance. Since the overwhelming majority of African states are, inter alia, multiethnic and multireligious, it will be critical for these divergent groups to coexist peacefully. Among others, this will require respect for one another and a commitment to resolve differences peacefully. In addition, effective, enabling, and empowering states in Africa are those that create and enable access to their citizens without privileging any group in the allocation of resources, like jobs in the public sector and project locations for socioeconomic development. In essence, as Mengisteab (2007: 111) cautions, an "ethnic state" is an anathema to democratic governance. Equally, tolerance of divergent views and ways of life is a major pillar of democratic governance. This means that at the broader societal levels, enshrined civic education is necessary for citizens to learn and practice tolerance of divergent cultures, religions, social, and political views. Cumulatively, peaceful coexistence and tolerance are indispensable to the maintenance of peace and stability.

As well, power relations must be restructured at various levels, both within the broader society and the government. In terms of the larger society, for example, restructuring the framework that provides access to power, without gender discrimination, is necessary to ensure that women are active and effective contributors to economic growth and maintenance of peace and security in Africa. The historical privileging of men has not led African states and peoples out of the malaise of economic dependency on commodity exports, foreign aids, and incessant debt crises. To be sure, privileging men over women has not resulted in a feeling of sustainable peace and security in many postcolonial states across the continent. Although there has been an appreciable level of improvement in the quest to dismantle the vestiges of patriarchy, for example, in Rwanda and Ghana, much work needs to be done in many other states. Essentially, equity in power relations between men and women must be anchored on the foundational principle that patriarchy is an unjust and undemocratic system of subjugation that is an anathema to democratic governance. Alternatively, women and men must have equal opportunities, and be equally rewarded for doing the same work, and this must start with enforceable legislation for the education of boys and girls. In addition, women should have an equal role in policy-making and implementation in all spheres of society. At the governmental level, constitutional design, and the resulting constitutionalism must ensure that no official of government, branch, or agency has the preponderance of power that would lead to suzerainty.

Nationhood

Undoubtedly, nation-building has been an elusive quest in Africa (Udogu 1999). This is because the state and its custodians, by and large, have privileged one ethnic group over the others in, *inter alia,* the allocation of resources. In addition, some dominant ethnic groups tend to demonstrate hubris toward the other ethnic groups by, among others, disparaging their humanity and their cultures. And these attitudes have and continue to contribute to conflicts, including civil wars as has been the case in Nigeria, Rwanda, South Sudan, and Ethiopia.

Hence, since various multiethnic states in Africa have failed to anchor their nation-building projects on inclusion, peaceful coexistence, and democratic pluralism, citizens have tended to shift their loyalties to various ethnic groups (Osaghae 2005). This is because they believe that their ethnic groups accord them greater citizen rights and privileges than the state. Thus, poor and ineffective nation-building strategies result in the problem of competing loyalties to the state and ethnic groups. Importantly, the absence of nationhood as embodied in the nation-state has engendered citizens' treatment of the state as an irritant that is irrelevant to their lives.

Given the importance of civic nationalism to the establishment and maintenance of long-term peace and stability, multiethnic African states need to rethink their nation-building projects— starting with reforms and restructuring of the state as a framework for collective efforts in political and economic governance. The emergent post-rethinking nation-building projects should include several major elements. As has been discussed, the key one is a shared vision that represents the interest of all the groups, while making the interests of the state (the collective) paramount. Another is the centrality of inclusion. All the ethno-communal groups should be treated equally by the state and its custodians. In addition, the members of these groups should have equal rights and privileges of citizenship in all spheres. As well, an enabling environment of mutual respect for differences in society is critical. Linked to this is mutual respect for each group's culture. An effective state provides for the physical security for all its citizens and groups to contribute their best in securing sustainable security, peace, and economic wealth and influence of the state.

Human Material Well-being

Background

The human material well-being deficit has been a major contributing factor in virtually all the civil wars in Africa. At the core is the Janus-faced nature of the African state: on the one hand, the state in Africa provides propitious conditions for the members of the various local ruling classes and their relations to live fulfilled lives (Kieh 2017). However, on the other hand, the state visits mass deprivation, including abject poverty and social malaise on the vast majority of Africans (Kieh 2017). The major resultant effect is that the majority of the citizens become alienated from the state and disaffected with the custodians of state power at various historical junctures. Ultimately, this contributes to the erosion of the legitimacy of the state and its governments. Insurgent groups then use the disaffection and alienation of citizens from the state and its regimes as the motor force (either real or pretentious) for undertaking armed violence against incumbent regimes.

The material well-being of citizens as a core element of human security must be at the apex of the agenda for managing and resolving civil conflicts, including civil wars. Similarly, in those African states in which civil wars have ended, the postconflict peace-building agenda must give priority to the advancement of human material well-being as the foundation for building durable peace (Kalu and Kieh 2021). While liberal democracy is important, for example, it should not be delinked from human material well-being. This is because freedom transcends the political realm and includes the economic, social, and other spheres (Marshall 1950; Sen 1999).

Poverty

Economic deprivation, political exclusion, and the constant survival mode that is the condition of many Africans, especially young people, leave them vulnerable for recruitment into conflict projects that often incubate intrastate violence and wars. Therefore, the prevalence of poverty in Africa is one of the major paradoxes of a region that is well endowed with natural resources, including agricultural resources, minerals of varying types, and oil. In 2020, for example, about 40 percent of the population in Africa subsisted at below the US $1.90 a day (Donnonfeld 2020). In the region's two largest economies, Nigeria and South Africa, the poverty rate was 46 percent and 26 percent of the population, respectively (Hendrik 2021).

How can Africans exit the "poverty trap?" Several major strategies are noteworthy in both the short and long terms. In the short-term, given the severity of poverty on the African Continent, governments should consider conditional cash transfers; for example, parents ensuring that their children are enrolled and stay in school. As Millan et al (2019: 119) posit, "[Conditional cash transfers are] short-term poverty reduction [strategies] via cash transfers, and long-term enhanced poverty reduction through investment in human capital."

In the long-term, at the core is the consideration of a new development paradigm that is "people-centered and community-oriented" (Torjman 1998: 1). Based on this framework, specific policies can be formulated and implemented. For example, a policy that transparently enforces political inclusion, equitable distribution of wealth and income, and fair access to justice to win the hearts and minds of the citizens and communities will advance the cause for national peace and security. This is quite important because, as will be discussed later, small groups own disproportionate shares of the wealth and income, which is a source of visible feelings of deprivation and unfairness among the citizens. Another policy option is public investment in quality education, from the elementary to the tertiary level. The thrust should be on the development of the knowledge base and skills sets of students in various subject areas. Then, at the tertiary level, the focus should be on preparing students to specialize in various fields spanning the broad gamut of disciplines—from the arts and humanities to the natural sciences. The rationale is that poverty and the broader crises of development that plague the African Continent require the expertise of trained personnel from multiple disciplines. In addition, vocational education should also be prioritized. This will enable students, who are desirous of learning trades such as carpentry and plumbing, to do so. The acquired vocational skills will position the students to seek employment or to establish small businesses that will provide sources of livelihood for them, as well as for those who they will employ.

Job creation should also be pursued as a major plank in the efforts to address the scourge of poverty. In terms of the role of the state, it should formulate and implement various policies that will create favorable conditions for the creation of jobs, for example, the use of policy incentives to encourage local entrepreneurship. This can be done by, among others, providing low-interest loans, a duty-free privilege for some time, tax holiday for a while, preferential treatment over foreign businesses in the awarding of public contracts and training.

Also, the development of the physical infrastructure such as roads, bridges, communications, water, the electrical grid, and storage facilities will contribute to socioeconomic development in two major ways. First, it will help facilitate commerce between and among the various parts of a country, thereby making goods accessible, reducing the difficulties of doing business, and enabling entrepreneurs to generate revenues and employment opportunities. Second, infrastructural policies, competently implemented, to provide amenities like pipe-borne water and electricity, will help improve the quality of life for all citizens in the country.

With enhanced educational learning in the arts, humanities, science, and technology in a framework of a stable political system, African states should invest in the development of a technological base for smart industrialization that preserves the built communities for future generations. This will enable businesses to manufacture value-added products that can be competitive and generate employment opportunities for the well-being of the citizens while ensuring a greater amount of revenues for business than the perennial reliance on the export of primary products such as coffee, cocoa, oil, and minerals.

Furthermore, strategic industrial and trade policies should be developed by the state that will entail the identification of industries and products that are critical to economic security. In turn, the state can use its various levers, for example, duty-free and tax breaks, to support these industries and products, while simultaneously supporting all nonstrategic businesses and products.

Quality health care is also an important area that is indispensable to addressing poverty. The state should invest in the development of a first-rate public healthcare system as a "public good" that is available to all citizens, irrespective of their class or positions. In other words, quality health care should be a universal right for all citizens. Quality health care starts with establishing and maintaining quality medical schools and training centers to produce qualified medical personal, like doctors, nurses, pharmacists, and hospital administrators to staff state-of-the-art medical facilities— hospitals and health centers, supplies, equipment, and other medical logistics. And, such medical services and facilities must be accessible to people, irrespective of their locations—rural and urban—and at an affordable cost.

Lastly, to end the plague of corruption—the basis for primitive accumulation of capital by most public officials who deploy the agency of their respective offices for rent-seeking—sustained efforts should be made to address corruption and its impacts on the fabric of governance in various African states. These state managers employ various means such as the stealing of public funds, bribery, extortion, fraudulent contracts, and procurement schemes to amass personnel wealth. In turn, these illicit acts deprive the citizenry of the financial resources that should be invested in addressing their material deprivation. A major anticorruption mechanism is the establishment of an anticorruption body—fully independent of the executive and the legislative branches of government—that is clothed with investigative and prosecutorial authority outside of the sphere of the Ministry of Justice. Such an approach would help to give the anticorruption body the independence that is imperative for its effectiveness.

Wealth and Income

The distribution of wealth and income in Africa is skewed in favor of the members of the ruling class. In terms of wealth, Nigeria and South Africa, the African Continent's two largest economies provide good examples of the gross disparities in the distribution of wealth and income (Squazzin 2021). In Nigeria, in 2017, "five of Nigeria's wealthiest people, including Africa's richest man, Aliko Dangote [had] a combined wealth of $29.9 billion—more than the country's entire 2017 budget" (Oxfam International 2021). As for South Africa, in 2020, "the richest 10% of the population own[ed] more than 85% of household wealth" (Squazzin 2020: 1).

In terms of the distribution of income in Africa, in 2019, the top 10 percent cornered about 50 percent (Robilliard 2020) of the total income, leaving the bottom 90 percent with the remaining 50 percent. The distribution of income is inequitable, and it is a major reason for the prevalence of poverty on the African Continent that is often used as an excuse by ethnic entrepreneurs and terrorists to violently challenge government authorities and legitimacy.

Contrary to the claim by some, the skewed distribution of wealth and income in Africa is not the result of differences in work ethics and skills. Instead, inequities in wealth and income are by-products of structural factors such as disparities in political and socioeconomic power between the ruling class and the masses that are embedded in Africa's political economy. Accordingly, the solution to inequities in wealth and income lies in "altering the social, political and economic structures that create and maintain income [and wealth] inequality" (Carter 2020).

Employment

According to the World Bank, in 2019, the unemployment rate in Africa stood at about 6.6 percent. In a continent where census figures lack legitimacy, especially in the larger states, where educational facilities are mostly under-performing, and with the population explosion in a context without adequate education and employment opportunities, we think the figures from the international institutions, like the World Bank, grossly under-report the depth of the region's unemployment problem. Thus, the data on unemployment in Africa that is provided by the various international organizations, especially the International Labor Organization (ILO), fails to adequately and fully capture the severity of the unemployment crisis in Africa. Even anecdotal evidence suggests that a large swath of the eligible labor force in Africa is unemployed or underemployed. Similarly, youth unemployment is underestimated at about 10.7 percent (International Labor Organization 2020). In terms of the African Continent's two largest economies—Nigeria and South Africa—the data does not capture the severity of the unemployment crisis.

For example, in the case of Nigeria, in 2020, the unemployment rate was about 33.3 percent (Oluwole 2021). For South Africa, the unemployment rate stood at about 34.4 percent (Oluwole 2021). In terms of youth unemployment, the rate was about 53.4 percent in Nigeria and about 64.4 percent in South Africa (Trending Economics 2021).

What are some of the solutions to the unemployment crisis in Africa? One major solution is public investment in education so that people can develop the requisite skills sets in various fields that will help make them marketable and potentially spark their entrepreneurial spirits and aspirations. This should include vocational education that will enable people to develop various technical skills. In this vein, the state should provide an enabling environment for job creation and the associated "adequate wages" and good working conditions that are likely to generate more employment opportunities.

Food Security

Food insecurity in Africa is one of the major challenges confronting the continent. For example, in 2020, an estimated 100 million people faced what the African Center for Strategic Studies (2021: 4) referred to as "catastrophic levels of food insecurity." Among the African states that face the highest increases in food insecurity were the Democratic Republic of Congo, Mali, Chad, Ethiopia, Sudan, Cameroon, and Zimbabwe (African Center for Strategic Studies 2021); and, except for Zimbabwe, these countries are also suffering from intrastate wars. Importantly, food insecurity is linked to various diseases that are consequences of hunger and malnutrition, including high blood pressure, heart disease, and diabetes.

Food insecurity in Africa is a multidimensional phenomenon that includes violent conflicts, inadequate food production, availability and access challenges, and climate change. In the case of violent conflicts, existing cultivated farms, farmlands, and food supplies are destroyed; and in time, it becomes difficult to continue agricultural activities, which consequently results in food insecurity. Investment in an agricultural food chain is another major solution that will encourage sustainable food production, food safety, and reduction in food insecurity. As Pawlak and Kalodziejczak (2020: 2) observe, "The agricultural sector plays a strategic role in improving the availability of food and achieving food security." Thus, increased food production and effective and efficient distribution will help address the availability problem. In addition, efforts should be made to ensure that food products are reasonably priced, by taking into account the objective economic conditions in the various African states. Furthermore, internal and continental efforts should be made to address the root causes of climate change and its resulting adverse effects on agricultural productivity. This requires governments across the African continent to work together to reduce the emission of harmful gases into the atmosphere that continues to negatively impact food production, availability of clean drinking water, and the health of the citizens. For example, climate change has, among others, contributed to drought in various African states, especially those in the continent's Sahel region.

Housing

Poor economic growth and income inequality are evident in the housing crisis and its adverse effects, like homelessness and slums housing, for example, in Nairobi, Lagos, and Accra. The shortage of affordable housing on the African Continent is quite pervasive. For example, in Kenya, there is a gap of about 2 million homes. Similarly, in Egypt, the shortage of affordable housing has, for example, resulted in about 12 million people "liv[ing] in informal buildings" (Oxford Business Group 2021). As has been raised, one of the adverse consequences of the housing crisis in Africa is the emergence of slum communities, especially in major cities like Lagos, Nigeria, Nairobi, Kenya, and Johannesburg, South Africa. In this vein, in 2020, about 59 percent of the people residing in urban centers live in slums (Habitat for Humanity 2021).

Addressing the daunting challenges of the housing crisis in Africa will require a multidimensional and integrated approach that seeks to weave together the major factors. As the Africa Report (2021: 1) argues, "[Housing] development must be linked to a broader system of financial inclusion, a strong regulatory and institutional framework to govern service delivery and construction, resilient economic demand for service, long-term low-cost capital, and technology and innovation." Addressing housing shortage as an aspect of peace and security requires enforceable land tenure reform laws, planned communities, and focused efforts in creating employment opportunities at all levels that enable citizens to earn an income they can survive and thrive on. The derivatives have to include the construction of affordable housing, providing credit to purchase homes, addressing the lacuna of slum communities, and providing quality housing for economically poor segments of the urban populations.

Water and Sanitation

The twin problems of access to clean drinking water and acceptable sanitation are quite pervasive on the African Continent. For example, about 400 million people in Sub-Saharan Africa do not have access to basic drinking water (Holtz and Golubski 2021: 1). The problem is made worse in several cases by the privatization of water. This means that drinking water that communities are used to fetching from streams is now commoditized and sold at prices that are sometimes unaffordable to the poor. Policies that commoditized a basic gift of nature, like water is antithetical to Goal 6 of the United Nations

Sustainable Development Goals (Holtz and Golubski 2021), especially in situations where many families do not have an income earner. An overarching solution is for African states to make investments in the provision of safe drinking water so that it can be available to citizens, irrespective of socioeconomic status and location. In short, as a "fundamental human right recognized by the United Nations," safe drinking water should be a "public good" that is available and accessible to all the residents of a country (Holtz and Golubski 2021).

Similarly, acceptable sanitation is a major challenge in Africa. For example, in 2020, only about 12 percent of the population in Sub-Saharan Africa had access to basic sanitation facilities (Our World Data 2021). The problem is exacerbated by the fact that about 18 percent of the population engaged in open defecation (One World Data 2021), with consequences for the health and well-being of the citizens in that community. The remedies must link sanitation with access to clean drinking water and hygiene (United Nations 2021), both of which assume formal and informal educational opportunities for members of the community on the necessity of good sanitation practices to their health. That is, the major requirement for an effective sanitation system is the availability of water and the practicing of good hygiene by the residents of specific communities and urban centers across states in the continent of Africa. City, municipal, and urban public services that construct public lavatory facilities to militate against open defecation, a functioning garbage collection, and disposal system will significantly contribute to sustainable solutions to the current challenges with water and sanitation infrastructures in many countries in the continent.

CONCLUSION

This book has attempted to address two major questions: What are the major causes of civil conflicts, including civil wars, in Africa? What steps need to be taken to address the root causes of these conflicts, so that the resort to civil wars can be prevented? First, civil conflicts, including civil wars in Africa, are caused by several factors. Among them are undemocratic governance, socioeconomic malaise, including inequalities in income and wealth, and the instrumentalization of ethnicity and other primordial affinities. In terms of undemocratic governance, since the postcolonial era, African states (with few exceptions) have retained the authoritarian governance system that was bequeathed to them by the colonial powers. This has been reflected in, among others, vitriolic human rights abuses, economic and political exclusions, and the holding of fraudulent elections. As for human material well-being, the postcolonial state in Africa and its various regimes have performed two contradictory functions: On the one hand, the custodians of state power have created propitious conditions for the members of the ruling classes and their relations to enjoy the material comfort of life and, on the other hand, the ruling elites visit abject poverty and deprivation on the majority of the citizens. Similarly, the custodians of state power have instrumentalized ethnic and other primordial identities as the core of their "divide and rule" strategy. That is, state managers in various African states have privileged one ethnic group over the others and allotted to the privileged primordial groups disproportionate amount of the national resources. This visible practice of political and economic exclusions is directly tied to several instances of intrastate violence and wars across the continent of Africa.

Against the backdrop of the major causes of civil conflicts in Africa, including civil wars, the remedial measures must be tailored to the specific circumstances of the various countries, as well as taking cognizance of shared factors among African states. The overarching shared causal factor that is the root cause of civil conflicts, including wars, in Africa is the pedigree of the postcolonial state. Thus, the democratic reconstitution of the postcolonial state in Africa should be the centerpiece of the efforts to minimize and prevent the occurrence and recurrence of civil wars. Undoubtedly, a democratic state that is anchored on human security will provide the best framework for addressing the maladies of authoritarianism, the human material well-being deficit, and ethnic privileging and exclusion.

Finally, the transformation of African states will require the commitment and involvement of two major actors: citizens and leaders. In the case of the former, citizens need to be informed about the affairs of their countries and governments and to provide oversight. This will help check the regime in power. Leaders at various levels constitute the other major actor. Essentially, leaders must subordinate their interests to the general interests of the state. For example, public funds must be used for the general good of the citizenry and not serve as a source for the private accumulation of wealth by state managers. Furthermore, leaders must be visionary and transformative in their orientation. This would mean, inter alia, the development of the requisite political will to jettison customs, traditions, rules, processes, and policies that do not serve the general good. And the imperative of demonstrating the willingness to formulate and implement policies will ensure that Africans enjoy what Marshall (1950: 3) called "social citizenship."

REFERENCES

African Center for Strategic Studies. 2021. *Food Insecurity Crisis Mounting in Africa*. February 16.

Africa Report. 2021. *Africa Housing Revolution Needs More Than Bricks and Morters.* February 19.

Aussell, Christopher. 2019. *The Protective State.* Cambridge: Cambridge University Press.

Bevir, Mark. 2006. "Democratic Governance: Systems and Radical Perspectives." *Public Administration Review*, 66(3): 426–436.

Carter, Valerie. 2020. "Income Inequality." *Encyclopedia Britannica.* www.britannica.com. Accessed July 26, 2021.

Donnefeld, Zachary. 2020. "What is the Future of Poverty in Africa?" *ISS Today.* March 2, 1–2.

Edigheji, Omano. 2005. *A Democratic Developmental State in Africa? A Concept Paper.* Johannesburg, SA: Center for Policy Studies.

Evans, Peter. 1995. *Embedded Autonomy: States and Industrial Transformation.* Princeton, NJ: Princeton University Press.

Eyaben, Rosalind. 2011. *Supporting Pathways of Women's Empowerment: A Brief Guide for International Development Organizations.* Pathway Policy Paper. Brighton: Pathways of Women's Empowerment, RPC.

Greenleaf, Robert. 1970. *The Servant As a Leader.* South Orange, NJ: Robert K. Greenleaf Publishing Center.

Habitat for Humanity. 2021. "What is Affordable Housing?" *Affordable Housing in Developing Countries.* www.habitat.org. Accessed March 2, 2021.

Haque, M. Shamsul. 2016. "Understanding Democratic Governance: Practical Trends and Theoretical Puzzles." *Asian Journal of Political Science*, 24(3): 340–347.

Hendrik, Jurie. 2021. "African Countries Continue to Have the Highest Poverty Rates in the World." *Development Aid.* February 25, 1.

Holcombe, Randall G. 2018. "Checks and Balances: Enforcing Constitutional Constraints." *Economics*, 6(57): 1–12.

Hollyer, James R. et al. 2011. "Democracy and Transparency." *Journal of Politics*, 73(4): 1191–1205.

Hotz, Leo and Christina Golubski. 2021. "Addressing Africa's Extreme Water Insecurity." *Brookings Institution's Africa in Focus Series.* July 23.

International Labor Organization. 2020. *Global Employment Trends for Youth: Africa.* Geneva, Switzerland: ILO

Kalu, Kelechi A. and George Klay Kieh, Jr. 2021. "Conclusion: Building Durable Peace in Africa's Post-Conflict States: Lessons and Insights." In *Peacebuilding in Africa*, edited by Kelechi A. Kalu and George Klay Kieh, Jr., 237–256, Lanham, MD: Lexington Books.

Korejan, M. Moradian and H. Shahbazi. 2016. "An Analysis of the Transformational Leadership Theory." *Journal of Fundamental and Applied Science*, 8(3): 452–461.

Luhrmann, Anna et al. 2020. "Constraining Governments: New Indices of Vertical, Horizontal, and Diagonal Accountability." *American Political Science Review*, 114(3): 811–820.

Mengisteab, Kidane. 2007. "State-Building in Ethiopia." In *Beyond State Failure and Collapse: Making the State Relevant in Africa*, edited by George Klay Kieh, Jr., 99–114. Lanham, MD: Lexington Books.

Millan, Teresa Molina et al. 2019. "Long-Term Impacts of Conditional Cash Transfers: Review of Evidence." *The World Bank Research Observer*, 34(1): 229–159.

Mirra, Nicole et al. 2013. "Educating For a Critical Democracy." *Democracy and Education*, 23(1): 1–10.

Mkandawire, Thandika. 2001. "Thinking About Developmental States in Africa." *Cambridge Journal of Economics*, 25(3): 289–313.

Mutua, Makau. 2002. *Human Rights: A Political and Cultural Critique.* Philadelphia, PA: University of Pennsylvania Press.

Oluwole, Victor. 221. "South Africa, Namibia, Nigeria Have the Highest Unemployment Rates in the World." *Business Insider/Africa.* August 25, 1.

Osaghae, Eghosa. 2005. "State, Constitutionalism and the Management of Ethnicity in Africa." *African and Asian Studies*, 4(1&2): 83–105.

Our World Data. 2021. *Sanitation.* June.

OXFAM International. 2021. *Nigeria: Extreme Inequality in Numbers.* www.oxfam .org. Accessed March 15, 2021.

Oxford Business Group. 2021. *Africa Looks to Solve Housing Shortage Amid Growing Population.* www.oxford.businessgroup.com. Accessed March 2, 2021.

Pawlak, Karolina and Malgazata Kolodziejczak. 2020. "The Role of Agriculture in Ensuring Food Security in Developing Countries: Considerations in the Context of the Problem of Sustainable Food Production." *Sustainability*, 12: 1–20.

Robilliard, Anne-Sophie. 2020. "What's About Income Inequality in Africa?" *World Inequality Lab, Issue Brief 2020-03.*

Seddon, David and Tim Belton-Jones. 1995. "The Political Determinants of Economic Flexibility With Special Reference to the East Asian NICS." In *The Flexible Economy: Causes and Consequences of the Adaptability of National Economics*, edited by Killick Tony, 325–364. London & New York: Routledge.

Squazzin, Anthony. 2021. "South Africa Wealth Gap Unchanged Since Apartheid, Group Says." *Bloomberg Equality.* August 5, 1.

Torjman, S. 1998. *Community-Based Poverty Reduction.* Ottawa, Canada: The Caledon Institute of Social Policy.

Trending Economics. 2021. "Youth Unemployment Rates in Nigeria and South Africa." *Data Set.* www.trendingeconomics.com. Accessed April 2, 2021.

Waldron, Jeremy. 2021. "The Role of Law and the Role of the Courts." *Global Constitutionalism*, 10(1): 91–105.

World Bank. 2020. *DataBank.* Washington, DC: World Bank.

Index

Italicized pages refer to tables.

About the Editors and the Contributors

Kelechi Kalu is professor of political science at The University of California, Riverside. As the founding vice provost of International Affairs at UC Riverside (2015–2020), he was responsible for setting the vision for UCR's internationalization efforts. He is an active member of several international education organizations, including NAFSA, AIEA, and IIE. Kalu currently serves on the Board of Governors for the Congo Basin Institute and previously served as a member of the Challenge of Change Commission for the Association of Public and Land-grant Universities. In 2019, he was appointed a YALI Ghana Regional Center Global Ambassador. He previously served as associate provost for Global Strategies and International Affairs and professor of African American and African Studies at The Ohio State University (2012–2015). Before his associate provost role, he served as the director of the Center for African Studies at The Ohio State University. He was a Korea Foundation visiting scholar at the Graduate School of International Studies and The Institute for Development and Human Security at Ewha Womans University, South Korea (2011–2012), and as faculty affiliate at the Mershon Center for International Security Studies at The Ohio State University. His research and teaching interests are in international politics, African political economy, and U.S.–Africa relations. He is widely published and has served as a consultant to the World Bank on Public Sector Governance and the Asian Development Bank on Managing Sustainable Development in Resource-Rich Countries. He is a recipient of grants from The Ford Foundation, The Mershon Center, and The Korea Foundation. His publications include articles in *International Journal of Politics, Culture and Society, Africa Today, Journal of Nigerian Affairs, Journal of Asian and African Studies, Journal of Third World Studies, Journal of African Policy Studies, West Africa Review, The Constitution: A Journal of Constitutional Development, Medicine and*

Law, International Studies Review (Seoul), *Journal of International Politics and Development, Social Research, African Journal on Conflict Resolution* and several book chapters on African and Third-World issues. He is editor of *Agenda Setting and Public Policy in Africa* (2004), and co-editor of *West Africa and the U.S. War on Terror* (2013), *Territoriality, Citizenship and Peacebuilding: Perspectives on Challenges to Peace in Africa* (2013) and *United States–Africa Security Relations* (2014).

George Klay Kieh Jr. is currently the dean of the Barbara Jordan-Mickey Leland School of Public Affairs and professor of political science at Texas Southern University, and professor in the Graduate Program in International Relations at the African Methodist Episcopal University (AMEU), Liberia. Prior to that, he served as the interim chair of the Department of Criminology and dean of the College of Arts and Sciences at the University of West Georgia, dean of International Affairs at Grand Valley State University, Michigan, USA, and chair of the Department of Political Science at Morehouse College, Georgia, USA. His research interests include peace and conflict studies, and also security studies.

Avitus Agbor is research professor (associate) in the Faculty of Law, North-West University, South Africa. He has held numerous academic and practitioner portfolios prior to this appointment. His research interests are international criminal justice, international human rights law, peace-building in Africa, and criminal law. He is currently interested in research that deals with hate speech and the intellectual architecture that foments the commission of hate crimes.

Kenneth Aikins is senior research fellow, Department of Peace Studies, University of Cape Coast, Ghana.

Sabina Appiah-Boateng is research fellow at the School for Development Studies, University of Cape Coast, Ghana. Her research interests are in the areas of conflict, migration, psychosocial well-being, humanitarianism, human security, and development.

Fiacre Bienvenu is visiting assistant professor of Africana studies and political science at the College of Wooster in Ohio. His research interests include postconflict political order in Africa, international affairs of Africa, power and violence in politics.

Earl Conteh-Morgan is professor of international studies in the School of Interdisciplinary Global Studies (SIGS) at the University of South Florida.

He is also series editor of Politics and Human Security in Africa, and former senior research Fellow at the Norwegian Nobel Institute, Oslo. His research interests are in the areas of American foreign policy, international relations, international conflict. Further he is the author of, among other books, *Democratization in Africa: The Theory and Dynamics of Political Transitions* (1997); *Collective Political Violence: An Introduction to the Theories and Cases of Violent Conflicts* (2004); co-authored *Sierra Leone at the End of the Twentieth Century: History, Politics, and Society* (1999); and co-edited *Peacekeeping in Africa: ECOMOG in Liberia* (1998). His most recent book is *The Sino-African Partnership-A Geopolitical Economy Approach.* In addition, he has published on human security, conflict and peacebuilding, state failure, the impact of globalization on state cohesion, and Sino-American rivalry in Africa, among others, in refereed journals such as the *Journal of Global Security and Intelligence Studies, Air and Space Power Journal, Armed Forces & Society, The Journal of Conflict Studies, Peace and Conflict Studies, The International Journal of Peace Studies, Journal of Social Philosophy, Journal of Military and Political Sociology, and Insight Turkey,* among many others.

Michael Ediabonya is currently lecturer of history at Ekiti State University, Ado-Ekiti. He obtained PhD in political history from the University of Benin, Benin City, Edo State. He has published twenty-five articles in various academic journals.

Stephen Kendie is professor of integrated development studies at the University of Cape Coast, Ghana.

Dawn Nagar is specialist and senior researcher in the deanery of the Faculty of Humanities at the University of Johannesburg (UJ), South Africa.

Julius Niringiyimana is a PhD candidate (political science) and assistant lecturer, School of Social Sciences, Makerere University, Uganda; CODESRIA laureate and mentee under the College of Academic Mentors Institute. He has attended various international conferences and summer schools, including the 2018 conference organized by African Studies and Research Forum (ASRF) at the University of West Georgia, USA. His research interests include conflicts, governance, and political economy of development

Francis Onditi heads the School of International Relations and Diplomacy, Riara University, Nairobi, Kenya. He has led global research teams leading to conferences and publications, including the co-edited book on *Contemporary Africa and the Foreseeable World Order,* 2019. He is also the author of

Conflictology: Systems, Institutions and Mechanisms in Africa. He is the recipient of the 2019 AISA Fellowship at the Human Sciences Research Council (HSRC), Pretoria, South Africa. This prestigious award was given in recognition of his research and scholarly work on *Positioning African States in the Dynamic Global System*

Sabastiano Rwengabo as an independent consultant. He holds a PhD from the National University of Singapore (NUS), where he was a research scholar, president's graduate fellow, and graduate teacher, 2010–2014. His research covers areas of international politics and security, regionalism, civil–military Relations (CMR), postconflict transformation, and democratization. His consultancy work covers areas of fragility and resilience assessments (FRAs), political economy analyses (PEAs), institutional capacity assessment and development, and nation building. He undertook the History Makers Training (HMT) and Oakseed Executive Leadership Course (OELC) with the Institute for National Transformation (INT). He is the author of *Security Cooperation in the East African Community* (2018) and several other publications.